Wrong Sex, Wrong Instrument

First published in 2006 by
Apex Publishing Ltd
PO Box 7086, Clacton on Sea, Essex, CO15 5WN

www.apexpublishing.co.uk

British Library Cataloguing-in-Publication Data
A catalogue record for this book
is available from the British Library

ISBN 1-904444-71-7
978-1-904444-71-8

Typeset in 10pt Times New Roman

Production Manager: Chris Cowlin

Cover Design Andrew Macey

Cover Photos: Mark Walmsley, Yorkshire Evening News

Cartoon: Jeremy Ballard

Printed and bound in Great Britain

Reference books by Maggie Cotton:
* *Percussion Work Book (1993), ISBN 0952209101, www.percussionworkbook.com*
* *Agogo Bells to Xylophone (1996), ISBN 0713643145, Published by A&C Black Ltd*

Wrong Sex, Wrong Instrument

Maggie Cotton

APEX PUBLISHING LTD

Dedicated to the memory of Adrian Smith.

Musician, writer, teacher and dear friend who gave unstinting time and patience, enabling me to climb many learning curves during the writing of this book.

FOREWORD

Maggie Cotton has been a presence in my life for 40 years, ever since as a university undergraduate in Birmingham I attended my first City of Birmingham Symphony Orchestra concert and spotted this redhead with attitude playing in the orchestra's 'kitchen' department.

I hated her for a while when she was brought in as a professional to play the percussion part in a university-promoted performance of Stravinsky's *Soldier's Tale*, something which, as an amateur percussionist, I'd coveted myself.

I hated her even more when several years later she started to make the occasional (but always telling) contribution to *Classical Music* magazine, bringing revealing insights from the player's side of the rostrum. "This woman is not only a fabulous musician, but she can write, too!" I grumped to myself.

But it was a pleasure to get to know her when I was fortunate enough to be invited to spend time touring with the CBSO, and to experience her warmth, her friendliness, her innate commonsense, her inability to suffer fools (a trait we share) and her undimmed idealism.

And when she retired from the orchestra I was quick to invite her to join my hand-picked reviewing team on the *Birmingham Post*. I know it took her a lot of courage to accept, but she worked assiduously at the technical nuts and bolts of the task, writing to length, meeting deadlines, taking on board the quirks of italicisation and punctuation, and learning to swallow hard and shrug her shoulders when her fondly-shaped criticisms were mangled by insensitive subeditors.

Naturally there are restrictions on her reviewing work. She obviously has to steer clear of anything involving the CBSO and its extended family, and it was a while before I thought it fair to ask her to comment upon the work of other British orchestras as well, as she knew so many of their members. There are still certain composers and instruments which make her eyes glaze over, but she is a marvel at gritting her teeth and biting the bullet if I beg her to: that's part of her boundless good nature, and that is a quality which leaps from the page in this fascinating blend of autobiography, social history and musical plain speaking.

I like to think of this as only the first instalment of Maggie's Memoirs. The life she has led since retiring from the CBSO has been full of interest and incident, travel and cookery, gardening and talk-giving - and she has never lost her passion for the young, and for encouraging their talents.

More than enough material for at least another volume! But for the moment, enjoy this one. You will be hooked and enthralled, as I was when she first shyly (unusual quality for her) showed it me.

Christopher Morley
Classical music correspondent, Birmingham Post

CONTENTS

'We are the music makers, we are the dreamers of dreams.'

1
Setting the Scene

Whatever possessed the powers-that-be to go to the girls' grammar school to look for a timpanist for the local youth orchestra, rather than to the lads' school down the road at Huddersfield College, one will never know. Choral rather than instrumental music was the order of the day for the young ladies, albeit seasoned with a good layer of piano rivalry, producing high standards of accompanying and solo performances throughout the school.

As a bemused bunch of fifteen-year-olds, we duly presented ourselves at the empty, old-fashioned school hall used for orchestra rehearsals and watched as an old lady struggled to pull the legs out of a pair of hand-tuned timpani before levelling the instruments ready for playing. Miss Brearley was of doughty Yorkshire stock, from a dynasty of fine musicians. Her father had been the conductor of a respected local amateur orchestra and, with brothers playing professionally in both the Hallé and Liverpool Philharmonic orchestras, it seemed only natural that Alice, the youngest in the family, should be called upon to "tune those drums" – the very pair of timpani now being used by the youngsters in the Youth Orchestra. Eyes sparkling, she always enjoyed a good kettledrum part with plenty of neatly turned tonics and dominants confirming very satisfactory final cadences; her enthusiasm was catching.

The sticks that she had brought along were made of slightly flexible, golden-brown Malacca cane, with small, turned, ebony knobs set with a mother-of-pearl star at one end and firm felt balls at the business end. These were fixed onto the cane through a flattish rosewood disk. I was shown how to turn the taps on the old-fashioned, deep-bowled instruments: clockwise to sharpen the note; anti-clockwise to flatten the note. For the life of me I could not hear a specific note on either instrument, just the ominous creaking of the calfskin heads when tension was being applied. Head down, hum into the skin, and if a sympathetic note came back, then the drum was tuned evenly. It was quite a feat listening for subtle changes of pitch in the hot rehearsal hall whilst counting bars and trying to work out how to play a neat drum roll. But I realised immediately that this was what I wanted to do: play in an orchestra – any orchestra. Fortunately, I must have shown more spark than the other candidates. Perhaps it was the workmanlike manner in which I dusted the calfskin heads, but in any event I was the one subsequently chosen to replace the absent Huddersfield Youth Orchestra timpanist.

With the Blackpool Music Festival looming on the horizon, and Mendelssohn's *Ruy Blas* overture on the music stand, I had been thrown in at the deep end, the only tuition on offer being a detailed explanation of the layout of timpani music. For a pianist to have only two notes to worry about was indeed a novelty and, in spite of also having hordes of rest bars to count, this did not seem too tall an order, but my first experience of orchestral playing was that everything was very loud. I could not hear the strings at all when the brass sections were at full throttle, but then that added to the novelty of an inside-out orchestra sound from my new viewpoint: brass in front, strings at the back. There was no time to worry about being brave enough to come in with personal contributions as the music flew by, as I had enough to do to keep my place on that strange-looking part.

For some time I had flirted with the idea of learning an instrument to give me access to playing orchestral music, after being bowled over by a performance of Sibelius's First Symphony by the now defunct Yorkshire Symphony Orchestra in Huddersfield Town Hall. This was to be a turning point in my young life. Up to then there had been the usual *Peter and the Wolf* experiences, but this was a very different kettle of fish. I had no idea that music could sound like that, and now, in retrospect, I guess that those sweeping phrases, sparse open-air harmonies, urgent rhythms and gutsy, physical music touched my northern soul. It was as simple as that. (Decades later, in the City of Birmingham Symphony Orchestra [CBSO], conductor Simon Rattle casually remarked in rehearsal that Sibelius's music followed the Finnish speech patterns. Suddenly all became obvious and clear – the stuttering, lisping rhythms creating unique music, even more understandable after we visited Helsinki and heard the language for ourselves.) I reeled around for weeks trying to recapture the intoxication of that music, driving my parents mad by searching for more Sibelius on the one and only radio at home. My father, a dedicated Beethoven fan, could not for the life of him understand what all the fuss was about.

This musical 'Road to Damascus' was the catalyst for a year of agonies trying to learn the viola at school, achieving little success in spite of getting into the local Schools' String Orchestra. The tenor clef always eluded me, so I cheated by reading the music interval by interval. When it dawned that the nasty noises emanating from my patch in the orchestra were of my own making, I had the grace and sense to give up the unequal struggle. It must have been obvious from the start that the viola and I were not made for each other. However, I know that my volatile Polish teacher had been initially deceived, as I was an accomplished pianist and obviously musical, so possibly he imagined that I was being deliberately obtuse.

* * *

Born in 1937, I knew only the privations of wartime and post-war Yorkshire, all so very normal to me, secure in the love of two working-class parents who had waited six years for my appearance. Mum was not supposed to have children because of a heart condition. "Our Renie gets puffed; can't run; shouldn't exert herself" were the oft-repeated litanies in our house – not that she seemed to heed any warnings to take it easy or slow down. I longed for a brother or sister but the belief that 'no one should bring children into this wicked world' echoed down the war years. Now I realise that my parents were only too delighted with their single child. Many of my contemporaries are 'only' children: siblings were rare during a World War.

Childhood was a drab, conventional country. Colour was regarded as vulgar and somewhat daring: nothing other than dark brown would do for treacly paintwork; beige and brown lino on the floor, with a daring rust colour possibly being permitted for the overlarge uncut-moquette three-piece suite. No bright plastics in those days; no coloured crayons or cheerful fabrics. My idea of heaven was realised when dad, Arthur, produced handmade wooden toys decorated with burnt-poker work, such as perpetually pecking chickens mounted on a table tennis bat, a little wooden horse to sit on or push along, bricks in a truck, a helter-skelter-style marble run, and a simple doll's house. As a highly skilled craftsman, he fashioned these from offcuts from his work as an engineer's pattern-maker. One Christmas a doll was proudly produced, nestling in a shoebox and dressed in hand-knitted, hand-sewn clothes. I vividly remember asking what to do with it and, after undressing and dressing it, saying something like, "What next?" I had never seen a newborn baby and, until the day my son was born all those years later, I had certainly never held a tiny baby.

We lived in Halifax at the time and, as steep Pennine hills were not conducive to ride-on toys, it was not until I was eleven years old that I became the excited owner of a bicycle. But then, for a young child, life revolved around the seasons more. Anticipated delights throughout the year minimised the need for man-made toys.

Autumn was my very favourite season with piles of leaves to scuffle through on the way to the small local Primary School, glossy conkers to prise from their prickly shells, acorns to throw, the smell of wood smoke, golden sunshine and the promise of glorious winter snows. An apology for Bonfire Night (November the Fifth) was celebrated, but only those with contacts in the local firework factory were able to get proper fireworks to let off. With wartime requisites swelling the ranks of items such as flares, maroons, distress rockets and explosive railway-line fog warnings on the manufacturing agenda, fireworks were few and far between, and anything that illuminated the sky, such as a bonfire, was certainly not allowed in the strict night-time blackout. There were plenty of unwanted explosions to be heard daily throughout the country, so nobody really needed further reminders of the war; it was there for twenty-four hours a day. We did have indoor fireworks though; a poor substitute for the real thing, but, with nothing for comparison, I thought that these were wonderful. Firelight would be the only illumination, as these sad novelties were lit on the hearth in the gloom. I found it difficult to appreciate the ash serpent that was left after a particularly long smouldering white tube had gone through its paces. Real snakes were not within my experience and I doubt if I had ever seen an illustration of one in the largely pictureless children's books of the time. Oh, but sparklers were a joy and delight! They were fairy wands to let the imagination soar, safe and magical.

It was traditional in Yorkshire to have special treats on Bonfire Night in the shape of sticky home-made parkin and cinder toffee. Every housewife seemingly had her own recipe for parkin, which had to be made early so that it could mature to the required moistness. This was called letting it 'come to', something that was impossible in our small house, as the wonderfully fragrant, newly baked smell advertised its presence in every room. Parkin is a ginger cake made in a baking tin and cut into bite-sized squares – seemingly simple to store and therefore easy to hide from the family. Not so. Dad would systematically search all the favourite spots for the parkin tin, and when he found it he just had to try a piece. Mum was crafty though, as she always hid another batch elsewhere. Now I realise that this was an annual game they played, creating much good-natured teasing. Cinder toffee was a different matter. This meant that hard-to-get ingredients had to be found, and this was where granddad came into the picture.

There is a strong entrepreneurial streak in my family, which emanates from Luther Bedford, my mother's father. It was said in the town that Luther could "sell snow to Eskimos" and also that he was so generous that "he would give you the coat off his back". Everyone knew Luther, so finding ingredients on the sly for making toffee was no problem for him. Butter and sugar were at a premium, but, with a bit of judicious trading in cigarettes and eggs from our hens (illegal, I am sure, as eggs were collected regularly for the wartime Ministry of Food 'pools'), he returned home with the necessary items hidden in an innocent-looking brown paper parcel: men never carried shopping bags.

Resplendent in a large apron, he would preside over the toffee making. I was his helper. The silky, dark-gold scalding mix was stirred until what granddad would deem to be the correct moment, and then my favourite bit of alchemy would happen. The pan was huge and the inside surfaces were constantly being wetted with a caterer's brush so that the mixture would not stick. Then came the magic. A small amount of bicarbonate of soda was flung into the lethally hot concoction, whereupon it immediately frothed up to the top of the pan, threatening a lava flow all over the kitchen. Prepared and buttered shallow tins were at the ready, and the airy mixture was poured into them to set hard for the next stage. With great solemnity, a small toffee hammer was produced, and the hardened, bubbly toffee was tapped into smallish chunks. If you hit it too hard, you ended up with a lot of sugary, delicious powder, so this was a delicate operation. This is where I came in as helper, because, of course, it was necessary to test the toffee. Local dentists must have had a lot of new victims after November the Fifth, but I am sure that many thought that the pleasure of champing through teeth-gluing cinder toffee was well worth it.

Blackberrying was another autumn pursuit. Naturally, the best ones were always the most inaccessible, usually found hanging low at the sides of the local canal. Nothing deterred my mum though, and we would return triumphantly with pounds of sweet, dark fruit. I carried a small, round basket, and we always took an old walking stick to help pull the prickly branches aside to reach the largest hidden berries. Granddad was also the chief jam maker, the result of his labours being jars of gleaming, translucent bramble jelly neatly arrayed on the cellar shelves. His skills have been passed down through the family, and whenever I go to my pantry for a jar of home-made bramble jelly, damson jam or chutney I think of him.

Every year there was the glory of snow for what seemed like the whole of winter. Out came sturdy home-made sledges and there were snowmen to fashion, massive creaking snowballs to roll, small igloos to live in and snowball battles to weather. Chapped hands and backs of knees rubbed raw by Wellington boots were normal for me, as girls never wore trousers. Hand-knitted woollen socks, mittens and pixie hoods were forever drying on the clotheshorse in front of a coal fire.

Winter was also rife with childhood ailments. "Your Margaret sounds just like a dog!" This was a frequent observation from neighbours and friends. My bronchitic cough was legendary in the street, never improving in spite of inhalants and Vic chest rubs. Fogs and smogs were frequent in the damp valley, with thousands of domestic coal fires adding to the yellow miasma. Little surprise that children were the first to fall foul of the impossible air quality. Finally, in desperation, my parents were advised to have my tonsils removed. This necessitated a hospital stay, of course, but no one thought to tell me about what was going to happen. In those days it was apparently perfectly acceptable to drop a child off in a hospital, to be picked up a week or so later when the deed had been done. My parents must have been distraught, but no visiting was allowed and the only contact I had with home were letters containing lots of stick-men drawings by my dad. As I was only four years old, reading was hardly a strong point, so I became more and more silent, regressing into puzzled misery. No toys were allowed because of the germs they might bring with them, so the only bright spot in my painful stay was copious amounts of ice cream and jelly served up to the miniature patients – soothing for sore throats.

Christmas brought more familiar rituals and excitement. Mum and I made paper chains from strips of newspaper painted with powder paints and glued with home-made flour paste, and then dad balanced on a small stool to pin them from corner to corner in our small living room. It wasn't until I was considerably older that I realised that real Christmas trees could be brought indoors to be decorated. We had a scratty-looking, small artificial tree which was kept in the airing cupboard. I could hardly contain myself when it was brought out, taken from its long, grimy cardboard box, shaken and dusted. The spindly branches would be pulled away from the trunk and then it was time to decorate it. My grandparents had bought three identical sets of decorations, one for our tree and one each for my cousins' trees in Dewsbury – my mother's two sisters each had two children – and we children always compared trees on the Christmas family pilgrimages. I was fascinated with the tiny baubles and glass novelties. There was the celluloid fairy, which just would not face front, and a pretty glass lantern containing a scrap of tinsel, which had to go on a lower branch. According to my mother, every item had its right and proper place. Fragile glass birds with fine tails of spun glass threads were clipped on near the top, which was resplendent with a glass spike and tiny silver glass bells. One of the Dewsbury trees sported a star, but I thought that ours was far superior. I would trundle home from school breathing cold air (dragon fire) and present my mum with more offerings for the tree: cut-out coloured shapes covered in glitter, star-spangled painted cotton reels, pompoms made from scraps of wool and strings of silvered beech nuts. They all added individuality to the insubstantial, somewhat pathetic fake tree.

To me Father Christmas was very real, and he received many pleas both verbally and on paper, the latter being dropped into the fireplace to float up the chimney to the North Pole. One year I was desperate for a pile of comics, but somehow he did not seem to hear my request. There were no stockings hung up on our mantelpiece. Instead he came in the middle of the night, ate a bit of Christmas cake with his glass of milk and then, after giving a carrot to the reindeer (why only one reindeer? – I never asked), he left my presents in a pillowcase on the end of my bed.

It was a very early start on Christmas Day as my beloved daddy came to get me and the presents, which were to be unwrapped downstairs. There was a great fuss as I heaved onto dad's back for a piggyback, and we then proceeded into the living room where a fitful, newly lit fire tried to make inroads into the cold air: wood smoke and coal, melting Jack Frost patterns on the inside of the windows, hot tea and rustling paper. Oh, it was all so exciting! Everything was wrapped in newspaper as there was no wrapping paper in those straitened times, but the 'oohs' and 'ahhs' came thick and fast as all the surprises were unfurled.

I always had a 'good book' from one particular aunt – in other words a children's classic. These were treasured over the years to be read and re-read. Then there were puzzles, jigsaws, paints, crayons, things to make and, if we were lucky, an orange to share. There was always a new coin and a few sweeties at the very bottom of the pillowcase. Liquorice Allsorts were a firm favourite, as it was possible to extend the pleasure by splitting the sandwich types, nibbling the tiny pimples one by one from the lurid blue and pink cushions, and sucking the black logs until they were a mere shadow of their former selves. The hard, unyielding gum of tiny red Cherry Lips was very scented, but little girls loved them as they used them as lipstick. Adults favoured hard-boiled Yorkshire Mixtures with traditional humbugs, mints and acidic pear drops to choose from. I used to beg to have one of the sugary fishes to suck, holding it by its tail. These sticky delicacies could be made to last for days but one had to be very careful that they did not gather an outer coat of fluff and hairs. Ugh! Then came the pleasure of scrunching up all the paper and having a paper fight with dad. The way round the Father Christmas myth was to tell me that various relatives had asked him to send specific presents, so there was no escaping the ritual of thank you letters on Boxing Day.

When the weather heralded that indefinable first whiff of spring, children were dragged into town for a new outfit of clothes. This was something I hated, even more so when I was old enough to have main items made by a local dressmaker. Cloth could be purchased direct from the woollen mills and nearly every family we knew had at least one contact for this.

Miss Maude was our dressmaker. She lived in a tiny, dingy, overcrowded terraced house with all the trappings of her trade much in evidence. Some very fine work came from that little room. With a treadle sewing machine and a mouthful of pins, Miss Maude could transform any piece of fabric into something indistinguishable from shop made – our highest accolade. She would have made a fortune had she been in business in the twenty-first century. My mother maintained that "every woman should have a *good* classic navy-blue costume in her wardrobe" so that it could be dressed up or dressed down.

I hated my first two-piece suit and only wore it under protest for very special occasions, so it was a great relief to all when I eventually grew out of it. Clothes were always handed down to younger children, but as I was the eldest of the cousins my clothes were always new, or newly home-made.

This was also the time of year when whips and tops, hopscotch and skipping ropes reappeared. Hectic playground games were rediscovered, the more physical of them being counterbalanced by solemn bunches of small children playing life-and-death marbles, 'Jacks', 'five stones', or more intensely the boys swapping cigarette cards, and little girls swapping loose beads kept in sweetie tins. These were serious currency in my childhood.

Every spring mum and I went to a nearby bluebell wood and picked armfuls of flowers. It was such a joy to have sweet-smelling spring indoors, along with branches of pussy willow and nodding catkins. From early childhood I would keep back a tiny portion of my weekly spending money and buy a miniature bunch of violets from the market, or take home delicate snowdrops. I had never seen these flowers growing in my neck of the Yorkshire woods, but I knew only too well the effect they had on lifting the spirits. Mum always pretended to be amazed when I produced them, and then would gently reiterate her simple philosophy for a nice house: "Have clean net curtains, always have clean milk bottles on the doorstep and keep fresh flowers in the house". Just so!

Summer, when it came, always seemed to be far too hot and dusty. White cotton socks became uncomfortable as they were eaten by sandals, disappearing in wrinkled misery under my heels. It was far better to run about barefoot, but then this was not acceptable and "Put something on your feet!" was a regular war cry from my mother; all part of the taming process, one assumes. Sunday afternoons were set aside for the obligatory walk, a time for my small family to get together and see something of the nearby countryside. To me these perambulations were a trial of endurance, as one had to behave: it was Sunday. Best clothes were worn, and a strict sense of decorum had to be observed, with no running or excessive chatter. How I hated Sunday afternoons. Rain was a real bonus, as it was then acceptable to stay indoors and make things or read – what bliss!

"When that church clock strikes seven, I want you in this house. I don't care how dirty you get, but don't tear your clothes!" Mothers would stand at the doors of their little terraced houses in the steep streets and yell for their kids at bedtime. "Margreeeeeeeeet!" With the pitch rising astronomically at the end, the sound of my long drawn-out name would cut through any game and send me scurrying home should I fail to hear that wretched church clock. No excuses were accepted.

Parents never knew where their children were. We played in the big old cemetery on the hillside, in the woods, by the canal, at the farm of a school friend, in the hayfields, pulling turnips to eat raw, or begging for chewing gum scraps at the factory near our little school.

"Your Margaret's such a tomboy" was a familiar accusation, but as there were no girls in the immediate vicinity I did not have much choice of playmates. I longed to be a boy, and it was quiet, persistent dare-devilry that urged me to become the champion tree-climber in our patch, and the inventor of dangerous challenges. No doubt having to keep up with the seemingly superior lads was early training for my future career in a male-dominated profession. One of my most hazardous exploits consisted of running lightly along the top of drystone walls, the top layer of which consisted of vertical stone slabs placed like books on a shelf and, as the name implies, with no mortar used to secure them. One particular wall had a terrifying drop at one side, so of course this was the one we all ran along (one at a time), with the stones constantly shifting slightly. No passing adult seemed in the least bit

9

perturbed that children were doing this; maybe we were only carrying on a local tradition. It was not until a boy fell and died from falling from such a high wall that my mother elicited a promise from me that I would not indulge in such foolishness: "Don't contradict!" had become the password in my 'do as you're told!' upbringing. Now I would interpret this as a rebuke to an enquiring mind, but, in accordance with the strict conventions of those days, one was definitely expected to be seen and not heard. Still, there were always trees to climb. Bits of rope were found and crude swings were made, yawing wider and wider over impossible drops. Dens were constructed in the undergrowth and secret gangs were rife.

I was a skinny, pale, serious little redhead with a 'donkey fringe'. We did not actually starve, but we children were often hungry as food was certainly short and a constant talking point. Every crust was devoured to the last crumb. "Eat up all your crusts, and you'll have curly hair", I was told, but, to my everlasting disappointment, no curls were forthcoming. It was not uncommon for the three of us to have a meal consisting of a shared tin of sardines and one tomato cut into three pieces. Bread with margarine or a scraping of delicious beef dripping was filling and not on ration, so bellies could be full if not entirely satisfied. I had never seen a banana; apples and pears were rare; and oranges were a Christmas treat. Mum dreamed of the day when she could sink her teeth into a grapefruit, trying in vain to describe the taste to me – "A sort of cross between a lemon and an orange" – but it made no sense at all. Neither fruit was familiar to me, so it was a non-starter.

When the news got out that the local shop had received a small consignment of Mars Bars, everyone would be there in the queue. Dad loved these, so there was always a little stash of sweet coupons put on one side for just this eventuality. The chocolate bar was brought home and, with great ceremony, he would fetch the breadboard, carefully unwrap the booty and then, with a sharpened carving knife, he would slice it into thin pieces (divisible by three). I always seemed to get the end bits with the most chocolate – strange, that! Raw carrots and the crunchy inside stalks from cabbages were healthy alternatives to sweets, with rare tastings of mixed cocoa powder and sugar, or sugar and oatmeal, eaten slowly with a wetted finger from the palm of the hand – truly delicious.

My biggest hope was that one day the harassed mother of a cheerful tribe up the street would offer me a hunk of margarine-spread bread dipped in sugar. This delicacy was regarded as very vulgar by my mother, however, and fit only for poor families. The children in question consisted of my best friend

10

Brinton, under-school-age twins, a toddler and a grubby baby constantly trailing a soggy nappy. The older ones always seemed to be munching through these delicious bread doorsteps. I longed for a brother or sister and envied the closeness of this large family, but my imagination was totally incapable of understanding how such a rumbustious crowd could cope in a house as small as ours. Mum would have been appalled if she had realised the extent of my disloyal thoughts.

When Coventry was blitzed, men from there were billeted with families countrywide. Two young fellows arrived on our doorstep and to this day I cannot imagine where they slept in our tiny house. However, they gave us something that was very special: a few lumps of genuine Turkish Delight. I imagined that they were on leave from the Middle East before they found themselves doing war work in a Yorkshire factory. I proudly took my bit of treasure to show to our hens, but the cockerel got the better of me by jumping up and stealing it from my hand. I was terrified and fled home in floods of tears. My squeamish, soft dad did no more than take the axe and chop Mr Rooster's head off. He wasn't having any bird attacking his little sweetheart, and I learnt to treat live poultry with more respect – or was it suspicion? We had chicken stew for a week after that, so some good came from my childish ignorance.

Life was not all drab and drear. For instance, it was a red-letter day when food parcels arrived from America for my parents' best friends. We were always generously included in the sharing out of the goodies – such wonderful things. We children loved the floating white soap, and our craving for sugary food was held at bay for a while with tinned pineapple or apricot jams. There was dried fruit, brown and white sugar, dried eggs, tinned butter, pork, corned beef and sinful chewing gum (denounced as 'common' by my mother). I have no doubt that there would have been a bit of gentle bartering with our regular supply of fresh eggs, too, on these special occasions.

One memorable day my mum arrived home from the mill with half a box of fresh fruit won with a friend in a raffle. There was, of all things, half a fresh pineapple nestling in shredded tissue paper. No one knew quite how to deal with this and so, to extend the pleasure, mum cut it into chunks, which she then put into a glass jar with sugar syrup. Every piece was counted and so, when temptation got too much for me and I pinched one, she knew immediately. Needless to say, I was in deep trouble, not for stealing the irresistible morsel, but for the fact that I denied doing it. Honesty in my family came at the top of all the virtues: trust was everything. This episode ended in a confession, recriminations, tears, and a hard lesson learned.

Cricket was a passion with my father; he was a good player and captain of his works' team. One of his tricks was to throw a cricket ball as high as possible until it seemed to disappear into the sky, then stand around with studied casualness until it came hurtling back to earth, whereupon he would catch it with the greatest of ease, earning himself a round of applause. He was the joker in the pack, making wide wooden cricket bats for the home team and little, narrow, holey ones for the visitors. The first ball connecting with the narrow bat always did a grand demolishing job; then everyone laughed and was in a good mood for the proper start of the match. Wives and sweethearts made thin potted-meat sandwiches, which curled at the corners as they dried out, and we drank fizzy pop. If we were lucky, the sun shone and there were fairy cakes to eat covered in lurid icing sugar. Camaraderie was the name of the game, with everyone pulling together: neighbours, friends, workmates and families. Indeed, most streets were thriving, lively, mini-communities. Doors were left ajar, except in the coldest weather, so that friends and neighbours could pop in. The doorstep call of "Anybody in?" usually answered by "Come in, it's a shop!" was the start of many a chat, bit of advice, query, or heads together with a cup of tea.

Mum worked part-time at a cotton mill, so she was always there when I got home from school. Not for me the uncertainty of being a latchkey kid – there was always a warm welcome waiting. When dad came home from work on Fridays he handed his sealed pay packet to my mother, whereupon it was opened, money was extracted and then the remainder was handed back for him as his own reward. This meant a pint and a game of dominoes or darts at the local pub, and maybe a flutter on the horses on Derby Day. A sectioned tin with slots in the lid lived on the mantelpiece and this was where outgoings such as rent, electricity, rates and insurance were put. A small amount was earmarked weekly for clothes and the Christmas Club at the mill, and the remaining cash went into a housekeeping purse for food, bus fares, piano lessons and other necessities. The insurance man came every few weeks and the rent man was a Friday regular. We also had visits from the 'Hoover man' who disembowelled and inspected the vacuum cleaner for its regular service. A piano tuner came twice a year, when I was allowed to forgo my practice so that the piano could settle after its ordeal. Everything was paid for in cash. In addition, Monday was 'bank day' at school: "Don't forget your penny and your bank book!" It was important to encourage good habits from a very early age.

From time to time there was an added excitement in the street when a handbell announced the arrival of the 'Pot Man'. He was a colourful character resplendent with horse and cart, which jangled with pots and pans, cutlery, cooking utensils, glass and enamelware. A knife-sharpening service was on offer, along with tinkering skills. Housewives would take worn pans out to him, a diagnosis would be made, and a price agreed. He would then perch on a step or the pavement edge and mend the pan with a metal patch on both sides, accompanied by much hammering and tapping. "Good as new, missus!"

Another annual caller was the cheery Indian with a huge battered brown suitcase overflowing with tea towels, floor cloths, dusters, face cloths and cream-coloured fringed towels sporting three thin green stripes across each end. I longed to see something more colourful, so it was quite a thrill when my mother eventually broke with tradition by buying brightly striped towels just after the war. Even then all she could think of was: "What will the neighbours think?"

Gypsies frequently came round to the working-class areas, their opening gambit usually being, "You have a lucky face dear", whereupon one was required to cross a palm with silver or a curse would be forthcoming. Sensible and down-to-earth though she was, my mum believed in all this implicitly, so invariably bought something from them, be it paper flowers, a bunch of wild flowers or crude clothes pegs whittled from hedgerow wood. Tramps always fared well at our door too, even if they only got a cup of tea and slab of bread and margarine. "You never know, you might be in need of that some day," mum used to say darkly.

Finally, we looked forward to the arrival of our milkman every day. He would toil up the steep street with Peggy his horse pulling the heavy wooden milk float. I would be sent out to him for a measure of milk, which was poured into a big white jug kept for that purpose. A large ladle was hooked onto the edge of the churn and the creamy milk poured out with just the correct amount of flourish to eliminate any drips. Peggy would then plod unbidden to the next customer. My biggest thrill was to be allowed to give her a saved apple core. The huge nibbling teeth and soft velvety lips were a great wonder to me, but she was always very gentle as she peered down with her soulful eyes. If the milkman was in a generous mood he would sometimes let small children have a ride on the back step of the cart: an added excitement.

Children as young as five years walked to school through the very large, mature cemetery on the hillside. We knew that dead people were in the graves, but this did not worry us. Mr Dobby, the chief gravedigger, knew all the children by name and let us peer into the holes he created in the heavy soil. He did yell at us, though, when we used the sloping flat gravestones as slides (the mossier, the better), and got mad with us when we tipped the slimy green water out of the old stone urns, but on the whole he was cheerful and I imagine that he liked to see the little flocks of chattering, carefree children passing through the gloomy Victorian burial grounds.

School to me was a treasure trove of sand, water, books, games, nature tables, singing, painting and, best of all, the company of lots of lively children. Every child was required to carry a gas mask, the tinies being given the Mickey Mouse ones with painted faces and appendages of big round ears. I thought that these were wonderful, so was inconsolable when I realised that mine was to be one of the standard kind. This was kept in a beige, canvas-covered, box-shaped container and had to be carried at all times when out-of-doors. We were drilled every day in the use of these monstrous, claustrophobic contraptions and were marched outside to line up and be counted in serried ranks in the playground. Evacuation of the tiny village school was a serious business for the teachers, who timed the operation diligently and were proud to announce when we had clipped a minute or two off our previous efforts.

The only aeroplanes we heard were at night, flying over Halifax to Liverpool, or on their way back to Germany. All the adults paused in what they were doing, turned off the house lights and then went out into the street to look up in the sky and listen intently. Animated discussions followed about whether or not a plane had been 'one of ours'. If the pattern of the droning engines was low and laboured, my dad reckoned that the planes were full of bombs – this theory being confirmed on more than one occasion by an immediate howling of the air-raid sirens. I hated the way they whined their way into a frenzy, especially as I knew that I would be brought downstairs and a safe bed would be made up for me in the bath in the scullery.

Our little house had one living room downstairs, with a narrow side scullery that served as the kitchen. In previous times families would have used the semi-basement as the kitchen, complete with black range and single cold tap. We used the small side-cellars for coal and for keeping food chilled. In those days refrigerators were luxury items. We had no bathroom, and the lavatory was in a whitewashed, chilly, smallest building down a few steps and in front of the little terraced house. We had no loo paper either, just squares of newspaper hanging by a string loop on a nail. The resident woodlice and

14

spiders terrified me, but I wouldn't have admitted this for anything as no one was allowed to be 'soft' in my household. Hot water was forthcoming from the back boiler behind the stoked-up coal fire, but this was a luxury for Friday bath night and Monday washday only. The bath in question was a large cast iron affair with claw feet, which took up far too much room in the scullery, so it had a heavy wooden lid that could be hooked up against the wall when the bath was needed. Otherwise the lid was used as a primitive kitchen worktop. The other use it had was one of protection for me during air raids. My parents went into the small cold cellar, which had been reinforced with brick pillars, but in their wisdom I was put to bed in the bath with the lid down. Corks under the edge of the wood afforded a gap large enough to see through, but it was a very frightening experience, though understandable from the parents' point of view. Miss Lord, a very creaky old lady from next door, would often come in and peer through the gap, whereupon she always said, "Eeeeh … doesn't she look cosy?"!

* * *

At the age of six I was sent, at my request, to dancing class. History reveals that I came home and pronounced that it was boring, so "Can I learn the piano instead?" Learning to play the piano was another foray into the world of imagination. It also offered the satisfaction of conquering finger skills and proved to be the start of a terminal disease, that of an obsessive love of music in its many guises. My parents were not especially musical, although the family boasted a far-flung ancient relative who was an organist of considerable local repute. Dad sang with a light tenor voice and mum blundered through the piano accompaniments of the sentimental ballads he favoured: *'Holy City', 'Nirvana', 'Friend O' Mine'* and such like. She was a great asset at family gatherings and could vamp unselfconsciously through any popular tune, as sing-songs were a normal part of life. Such niceties as correct harmonies or key changes did not bother her, but there were always lots of frilly runs and twiddly bits to delight her audiences.

I was also attracted to the piano for an altogether different reason. Reading had become one of my 'only child' passions at school, so therefore I was intrigued to learn how anyone could interpret those weird dots of musical notation and translate them into magical piano music. Although many working-class households possessed an upright piano, books were another matter. Dad sometimes dipped into a set of hard-backed Dickens' novels, which had been acquired by collecting cigarette cards. Stiff and unyielding, they were rammed into their own tiny oak bookshelves. Other than that, any reading rarely ventured beyond the local paper and mum's *Woman's Weekly* for knitting patterns and hints on how to cope with the restricted food rations. Birthdays and Christmas eventually became a reliable source for books: Father Christmas never let me down. I loved painting and drawing and making things from scraps of cardboard and bits of fabric, but most of all I loved to curl up with a book and escape into another world.

Piano lessons began. Saturday morning was the designated time, when I duly presented myself to 'Phyllis Grundy LRAM, ARCM'. If people had letters after their names it meant that they had their 'cap and gown', which quite rightly earned them deep and unquestioning respect from mill worker mum and pattern-maker dad. Fortunately, old-fashioned Miss Grundy was good with children and, as far as I can remember, I devoured everything she suggested, loving every minute of my lessons.

At a very tender age I trekked alone to her house: down the street, across the main road, over a drystone wall, then through our hen-run, down the cobbled lane, over the canal bridge, between two enormous woollen mills in the little valley, up the steep lane at the other side, peering for and then waving to my mother on the home side of the great divide, continuing through a short, scary, echoey tunnel under the railway line and finally up a narrow street that met the wide main road by the Halifax Royal Infirmary. I then had strict instructions to wait for a lady – any lady – to see me across the road. Apart from that it was absolutely no talking to or taking sweets from strangers (as apparently they were poisoned!) I then continued my way to the semi-detached 1930s house where musical magic materialised for half an hour every week. The two-way journey took twice as long as the lesson itself.

I cannot remember ever having any problem with learning to play the piano or read music. From the age of six it was a glorious adventure to be anticipated week after week. Apparently mum announced that she knew that I would be a pianist as soon as I was born, as I had long fingers even then, every half-moon on every fingernail being clearly visible. History relates that the nurses came to 'ooh and aah'! My mum's fervent ambition from then on was to see me in black velvet and pearls, playing a grand piano.

Daily piano practice was as predictable as teeth cleaning. When dad came home from work he would settle down in his chair with a cup of tea and listen to my daily efforts. He listened every day until I was well into my teens, but never lost his love for Beethoven, his favourite. Eventually he heard many, many Beethoven sonatas, and a huge amount of the solo piano repertoire:

ancient and modern. When we went away for our annual holiday week, it was necessary to find a boarding house with a piano so that I could keep up the good work. Christmas Day was the only day when I did not practise – playing for carol singing didn't count.

I knew from the very beginning that I would always be involved with music, the one true constant throughout my life. My teacher was of the opinion that examinations were the road to take, rather than music festivals or competitions, so I was soon working for my first Royal Schools of Music piano examination. As a little tot I was taught to curtsy to the examiner (boys had to bow) and was given instructions on how to find middle C on a grand piano and not to begin until I was seated as comfortably as possible on the piano stool. This often necessitated the arrangement of thick music books to enhance the height of the stool, and perching on the very edge of the stool so that I could reach the pedals: not a very comfortable set-up. Reflections of my fingers in the highly polished woodwork were mesmerisingly offputting, but on the whole I did not suffer excessively from nerves and enjoyed the performance aspect of the experience.

I was brought up on a mixed, balanced diet of Bach, Beethoven, Chopin, Mozart and Schumann, with plenty of contemporary compositions as contrasts. These were simple, imaginative pieces, often with accompanying words. Scales and arpeggios were carefully rationed, with not too many per term, and the weekly aural tests were fun musical games, although reading at sight was not always my favourite activity. Every pupil had a notebook into which comments were written in Miss Grundy's tiny, illegible handwriting, stating the progress or otherwise at each lesson. Marks out of ten were awarded for work done and at the end of each year the child with the highest marks could choose a volume of music as a prize. This was embellished with a very elaborate bookplate giving the name of the winner and the date of the acquisition. In this way I unwittingly offset the expense of buying a number of piano scores, becoming the proud possessor of numerous prizes, from Beethoven sonatas to Mendelssohn's *Songs Without Words*. All these were beautifully bound expensive copies, still cherished and in use to this day.

Piano examinations were eagerly worked for and, by the time we had all moved on to live in Huddersfield away from the dank valley bottom, I had clocked up Grade VI at the age of ten. Such activities were interspersed with pupils' concerts, which also incorporated the presentation of the annual prizes. After all, musicians are performers and it seemed perfectly logical that we should share our efforts with an audience. I gave my first public performance at the tender age of seven. The piece in question was a little waltz from Tchaikovsky's *Children's Album* and I loved every minute of it: the music and the presentation. And, of course, all the aunties and uncles were eager to hear 'Our Margaret', or I like to think that they were, although it was more than likely that they were expected to be interested in the somewhat precocious brat, come what may. If anyone talked through my efforts, I would always stop playing. This was indulgently interpreted by my mother's over-sentimental younger sister as, "Oh, she's very temperamental, you know!" As far as the family was concerned, I had really reached the pinnacle of achievement when I played anything in which the hands crossed or there were flocks of impressive black semiquavers, and when I accompanied dad in his ballads.

It seemed only natural that I played the piano at school, learning most of the hymns in the school hymnal and wading through marches for morning assembly. These experiences were no doubt a good basis for being sensitive to outside influences: keeping steady time for marching feet and correct tempi for breathing, singing humans. One cannot learn too early the value of good listening skills.

* * *

My mother had many ambitions for her single chick, ranging from nice clean jobs such as working in the Post Office, or even working in a bank (perish the thought!), to being a hairdresser or a florist, as I was, in her words, 'so artistic'. I duly listened to all this, but could not work up any enthusiasm or imagine what life beyond school could possibly bring. Mum was one of the lost generation with regard to a university education. She was intelligent, with a sharp, enquiring mind, but had had no formal education beyond the age of fourteen. Blessed with practical and organisational skills as well as a strong business sense, she could have carved out a professional career in a variety of fields. All she lacked was education and opportunity, so I was forever being reminded to work hard to better myself.

There was fierce competition to get into the first rank of grammar schools in Huddersfield, the Eleven Plus examination results grouping the town's hopefuls into three lists according to brightness. Consequently, there was no one more amazed than myself when I discovered that I had been awarded a place at Greenhead High School for Girls, a traditional all-female establishment two bus rides away from home. Fortunately, the music teacher there, Miss ('Tilly') Townsend, was an imaginative and inspiring teacher, so at least there was one subject in which I could shine. Once more I found myself playing hymns, together with the dubious delight of thrashing through piano duets, delivering marching, indifferent girls into morning assemblies, the top favourite being Schubert's *Marche Militaire*.

I struggled to keep my head above the parapet in a grammar school situation. End-of-term reports were, for the most part, not a happy read, and I dreaded the heart-stopping moment when the envelope was opened and the contents slowly and sadly digested by my parents.

It was so difficult for me to concentrate on any subject that did not immediately fire my interest: for instance Latin ("Margaret seems to make little effort") and Mathematics ("Her grasp of facts is not clear") were beyond my comprehension. (At my final interview with the headmistress at the end of my school career I was told, "You are mentally defective at arithmetic") Science subjects caused me much puzzlement and boredom, as I could not see any point in all that brain cudgelling and it was such a pity that French was taught in a tedious, academic fashion. No one managed to communicate to me that all subjects were brain fodder, training for future applications of intelligence, ways of thinking, opening the mind and so on, and I was too restricted by my narrow upbringing to work it out for myself until much, much later. My interest in Geography earned me high marks in the pecking order, however, and eventually came to life when the oft-repeated phrase, "Join an orchestra and see the world", came to fruition. My position as goalie in the hockey 1st XI earned me some kind of kudos with my peers also, but standing in the goalmouth in freezing weather after school was not my idea of fun. As a loner, I loved reading, but the two subjects in which I shone were music and art.

My eyes were eventually opened in art classes by seemingly strange questions from the Paris-trained teacher, Jean Lloyd. She would fire questions at the poker-faced lumps of Yorkshire girls, such as "How many steps are there to the school main entrance?" or "What colour are the curtains in the hall?" or "How many buttons are there on a policeman's tunic?" All this left us wondering about her sanity, but her constant wearing away at our hard-eyed indifference certainly paid off in my case, as I began to take notice of the world around me. It was far too much to expect any unbidden, spoken response, however, as we had never been encouraged to show any overt emotions. Not for us the delight of verbally shared daily experiences of unusual interest or beauty; nor was lateral thinking on the agenda. Sadly, only limited visual arts were on offer: painting, drawing, some calligraphy and a brief study of heraldry. The restrictions of the set curriculum did not allow for any voyages of discovery into the world of three-dimensional crafts, apart from a little experimentation with papier mâché and simple cardboard modelling.

One unique incident stands out, however, when on a stormy day a rainbow appeared in the school grounds. The end of the bow came to rest in some dark rhododendron bushes, bright and ethereal. I found this totally irresistible and cautiously went towards it, eventually standing inside the weird light and shiny raindrops. To this day I remember the awe and excitement from my friends as the colours, which I was unable to see, shone around. Perhaps this was the beginning of being able to describe exceptional experiences without imagining my father's damning response of "Don't be so soft!" The nearest he could get to expressing his feelings when looking at any of his favourite views of his beloved Yorkshire was a quiet "I'n't it grand!" Eventually, as an adult, I was amazed to discover the fascination of previously hated history, sciences, and the domestic skills so necessary for bringing up a family.

School parties, resplendent in full school uniform, were taken to visit museums and mills, or on day trips to Brontë Country, York and Manchester, and attended occasional choral concerts, recitals and full-blown orchestral concerts to inspire our growing imaginations (or bore us to death, as the case might be). At the ripe old age of fourteen, I was allowed to attend evening performances escorted by my dad, where we usually arrived by motorbike with myself as a willing pillion passenger. If my beloved parent decided that the programme was too 'difficult' or 'modern', he would go to the nearest hostelry for a swift half before collecting me at the end of the evening. Music was as natural as breathing to me, but this is not to say that it came easy, as I had to work very hard at all aspects of my favourite subject. There was always something musical happening, however, from playing for assembly, singing in the choir and accompanying instrumentalists or singers, to out-of-school participation in three amateur orchestras. Piano examinations came and went and I crammed in as much orchestral playing as I possibly could, and most Saturdays saw me in Leeds Town Hall listening to the Yorkshire Symphony Orchestra.

* * *

Little wonder, to return to the event described on the first page, that I took to playing in my very own Youth Orchestra like a duck to water. Initially there

20

was no one to show me how to play the instruments, but Miss Brearley counted bars during rehearsals and kept me on the right track. She always gave me encouragement but not very much guidance as regards the actual playing techniques. Very early on she said something to me that I was to remember all my life, passing it on when appropriate: "Music is a jealous God". One's family ultimately comes first, of course, but not without a struggle on occasions. It was not until I was able to refuse offers of work that I felt that I was truly in charge in terms of how I ran my life, but the pull to perform and endlessly explore music was evidently part of my basic make-up.

Now that I had got the bit between my teeth, I became a regular concert-goer, travelling to Leeds by train every Saturday to hear my heroes in the Yorkshire Symphony Orchestra. The cheapest seats were behind the orchestra, so I became a permanent fixture sitting as near to the timpani and percussion section as I could decently get. My sharp eyesight enabled me to follow the music and eagerly watch every move. At every performance I noted down on my programme the percussion instrumentation and number of players required for each piece. (This subsequently became the basis for my *Percussion Work Book*, which gives percussion details of every piece in the repertoire of a busy professional orchestra, performed over a span of forty or so years: a reference resource saving countless hours for percussionists and others worldwide.)

Eventually I plucked up courage and asked the timpanist if he would give me an occasional lesson. I could not possibly afford to have regular lessons, as my two morning newspaper rounds, added to weekly pocket money, barely covered train fares and concert tickets. So on red-letter Saturdays I arrived at Leeds Town Hall early, clutching a pair of timpani sticks, a tuning fork and a notebook. I suspect that Walter Robertshaw, the timpanist, was less than thrilled with this commitment, as he was a shy, quiet soul and I bombarded him with far too many impatient, eager questions. Should any of the percussionists come in early to set up instruments, I was in an agony of self-conscious embarrassment, playing on their patch as it were. The irony was that, in not too many years from then, I would be working with one of them as my boss in the CBSO.

The conductor of the Huddersfield Youth Orchestra, Wyndham Williams, was a man who jealously guarded his players, short-sightedly discouraging anyone from playing in other local orchestras; such activity being regarded as a disloyal, heinous crime. But, of course, timpanists cannot practise their art

21

in solitude – they need an orchestra, so it was not long before I did the unforgivable thing and joined two other amateur orchestras in the area. My very first venture into percussion rather than timpani was playing cymbals and triangle in Wagner's *Mastersingers* overture. This was truly exhilarating and confirmed what was patently obvious – that it was not for me to be lurking inside a string section or to be buried by countless wind players. Playing timpani or percussion was far more individual: a heart-thumping, one-and-only part in the orchestra; a make-or-break situation. It was worth all the shifting of heavy instruments, getting to rehearsals early, finishing after everyone else, and going home in a grubby state as a result of delving into dusty store cupboards. Sometimes I would be helped, especially if dad took me to the rehearsal or maybe when a cheery brass player lent more muscle power. However, I was very conscious of the fact that I was a girl playing what were then deemed to be boys' instruments, so I attempted to be independent even to the extent of being far too proud to ask for any help with the physical aspects of the job. This is something that all percussionists have to learn to live with from day one.

* * *

I knew little of life beyond the West Riding, so it was a miracle that I chanced to hear that auditions were being held in Leeds for The National Youth Orchestra of Great Britain (NYO). This was 1954, and by this time I was playing as often as possible with my three local amateur orchestras. At that time the age limit for the NYO was nineteen years, so at seventeen I decided to have a go. Needless to say, I kept my decision a deadly secret and for once in my young life behaved in a devious, underhand manner, announcing that I had to visit the dentist and needed the whole morning off school. Having found the audition venue in Leeds, I was dismayed to discover that not only was there no percussionist there to judge my efforts, but also that young composers, pianists and aspiring conductors were hoping to be taken into my specialised section. I had practised the wickedly awkward glockenspiel part from Dukas's *Sorcerer's Apprentice*, which I duly played on my own instrument, and then I was given what were no more than aural tests and asked copious questions about my hopes and aspirations. Afterwards I realised that some time would elapse before any results from my truant day emerged, so I kept very quiet about my adventure. So far, so good.

Tilly Townsend, the initial instigator of my orchestral madness, was determined to find out if she was going down the right road by encouraging me, and so, unbeknown to me, she contacted Sir John Barbirolli for advice. Lady harpists and string players had long graced the orchestral platform, but women rarely appeared in other sections; however, unusually, Sir John actively encouraged women to join his orchestra when the men went to war. For instance, the Salvation Army was the source of his fine principal trombonist Maisie Ringham, whose presence along with that of timpanist Joyce Aldous must have raised many an eyebrow. Many years were still to elapse (half a century in the case of the Berlin and Vienna Philharmonic Orchestras) before everyone accepted the fact that musicians can come in all guises and, indeed, why should the male of the species have all the musical plums? A letter from Sir John's secretary revealed Joyce Aldous's address and a meeting was arranged.

I continue the tale with references to diary-style notes I made at the time:

November 18th 1954.

The appointment was made for today at 11.00am at the Free Trade Hall, Manchester. Miss [Tilly] Townsend went with me on the 9.40am train and we arrived at the hall at 11.05am.

After wandering through a labyrinth of corridors, we found ourselves in a side balcony guided by timpani noises from the stage. Miss Aldous spotted us and told us how to get down, meeting us halfway. She first spoke to me with a laugh about getting lost, then was formal but pleasant with Tilly.

Tilly had given me flowers to give to Miss Aldous - I felt a bit self-conscious about them I must admit. Anyway, I was thanked nicely: "Very sweet, you shouldn't have", etc. I felt very guilty seeing that they weren't really mine to give. We all went onto the platform, Tilly being tactful and sitting at the side, then, "I'll hear you perform first Margaret, and then I can tell how best to advise you."

She tuned to A and E (I couldn't pitch the A at all), then asked if I had ever used pedal timps before. "Yes", thanks to Walter Robertshaw [my YSO teacher]. So I tuned them to G and E with the pedals, which was OK. She then had me play a bit of Dvořák's Fifth Symphony. Not too bad, though I made a bit of a mess of a fortissimo roll. I was then asked to play a diminuendo roll down to nothing, and was shown how to use fingers for it and not just wrists. It was lovely just to watch. The first thing I was asked to do was to hold the heavy sticks differently to the way I was being

23

taught by Mr R., then I was given a mini-lesson on rolls.

Miss A told me that when she was fourteen years old her [musician] brother locked her in a room for a week until she had learnt how to do a snare drum roll, and said that if she couldn't master it he wouldn't have anything more to do with her. Needless to say, she did it!

It was at that point that Tilly asked if I would be capable of achieving what I wanted to do. "Oh yes - she'll do it all right. She's enthusiastic enough and I know that she'll do it!" It was suggested that I carry on with orchestral work and then to my amazement she said that I had a natural flair and a gift for timpani, but was not very good on snare drum. Then to me, "If you want to do a thing badly enough you'll never be satisfied until you've had a damned good shot at it!"

It was then suggested that I should try to get into the Northern School of Music, and that if it was all right by Miss Townsend we could try to see the principal of the college before we went back to Huddersfield. I was then shown the solo timpani piece being worked on - in manuscript and in ordinary blue ink. I thought at first glance it had a lot of cues in it, then realised that that was the actual part. One line looked like a zigzag pattern, and then it dawned on me that the lines were all glissandos. Phew!

There was a piece of paper on the music stand which turned out to be a notice about a school concert that afternoon.

"Would you like to come?"

We were supposed to be going back to school: I looked at Tilly.

"Well, Margaret, I have to go back, but you can stay if you'd like to."

"Oh, yes, if it will be all right."

We were then taken down to the orchestra rooms and saw the huge notice board with the diary of commitments for the whole orchestra. Quite soon they have a stretch of twenty nights of concerts including London and Paris.

"It's all right, but when this happens I never have time to wash my smalls through."

Miss Aldous came with us to the College which is near to the Free Trade Hall, but not easy to find. While we were on our way in the rain, we passed a couple walking slowly by. The woman nudged the man and muttered something. He then turned round and stared at Miss Aldous and nodded. Oh to be famous!

The Northern School of Music is a dingy little building; brown, shabby and squashed looking. It is on the main road and is just a building in a block, somewhat unnoticeable.

We were taken to see the principal, who was very nice, but a bit overpowering. Her room is very old-fashioned - it even smelled old-fashioned, with fusty stiff chairs and bookcases full of books on harmony. There were also two baby grand pianos thrown together at one end of the room. Miss Aldous told her that I would definitely be a good student, but the principal didn't seem too keen to offer me a place. There was some chat between the two teachers about school music, then a final comment from the principal of "Well - I wouldn't do orchestral work if it were the last thing left in music."

So after a few helpless looks between myself and Miss A we all decided to call it a day, said our goodbyes and with myself feeling pretty dazed, left the room.

[Tilly then shot off back to school leaving me to spend the rest of the day in a haze of disbelief and starry-eyed bliss.]

It turned out that Miss Aldous had spoken to some of her students about me, so four girls took me off to the student canteen where we had a pretty poor lunch. I was introduced to lots of students, then we all went along to the afternoon concert. As it was a schools concert we weren't supposed to go in, but at 2.10pm a head popped round the door:

"Hello Joyce, can we come in?"

"Yes, come on, would you like a mint?"

"Yes please" to both.

"You can all go into the side balcony seats - cheerio Margaret!"

We could see the timpani and percussion section perfectly and the girls told me that their nickname for the principal was 'Passion Flower'- the oldest one is Tom. I told them that I always think of the one with a beard as Dracula, and that he always seems to be behind the beat with the cymbals. They all laughed at this.

Joyce had to demonstrate the surging sea sounds in Fingal's Cave overture. The percussion players were very naughty as they kept looking up and winking at us! It was a super programme with lots of percussion. [Dukas's Sorcerer's Apprentice, Bartok's Rumanian Dances, Edward German's Nell Gwyn overture.] After they had finished, Joyce looked up, grinned and waved goodbye. Jolly nice of her.

The girls took me into town and left me when they were sure that I could find the station. 'Home James', lots of thinking. What a day.

Looking back on all this, I am amazed and deeply grateful that Joyce Aldous went to so much trouble for an unknown youngster.

December 4th 1954
This morning I received a letter from London:
'Dear Margaret, this is to inform you that you have been chosen as a member of the National Youth Orchestra for the course December 28th to January 6th. Concert on January 5th in Bradford, orchestral course in Bingley ...'

2
Small Fish: Large Pool

When I was growing up, *Children's Hour* on the BBC Home Service was as alien to me as a continuous stream of spoken Chinese, because, as a northerner, I could not relate in any way to what I thought of as posh accents, fanciful stories and improbable situations portrayed by those oh-so-perfect children every day at teatime. What is more, at that time I had no idea that I too had a distinctive accent, as I spoke in exactly the same way as everyone I knew, old and young.

In the summer holidays of 1954, I had my first taste of concentrated music when, encouraged by Miss Townsend, I attended the Queenswood Summer School in Hertfordshire. Anywhere south of Cheshire was 'down south' to gritty northerners, where the population was alleged to be softer both in speech and temperament. We were made of down-to-earth, sterner stuff, or so we imagined. So it was no bad thing for me to comprehend that musicians come in all shapes, sizes, nationalities and ages and from all social strata: a never-ending diversity of types. It was no longer a case of sitting in an audience admiring unapproachable performers. Instead, I found myself playing as an equal and trotting out jaw-breaking foreign names that belonged to new friends, musicians all. I had to pinch myself to keep a grasp on the reality of the situation, as this was very bemusing for a narrow-minded, conventional and somewhat sheltered youngster. My mother's dictum had always been clear, however: "You have just as much right to be there as the next person - treat everyone as you would wish to be treated yourself". But father was hidebound with outspoken prejudices and bigotry. Nothing escaped his criticisms, with race and religion heading the list of his far-fetched suspicions. And such clumsy compliments that might come from him always ended in a short pause and then the downer of "Aye but ...", as he rounded off his comments with a final denigration. He was then a happy man.

It took years for me to realise that there were many shades of grey between the black and white of my upbringing. Fortunately, the scales began to fall from my eyes as soon as I left the confines and influence of my own family and I began to think for myself. Initially the novelty of being at Queenswood was overlaid with back-against-the-wall defensiveness about my unusual instruments and feelings of self-consciousness over the way I spoke. The flat

27

delivery of my strong Yorkshire accent caused a great deal of teasing, but eventually we all saw beyond dissimilar exteriors and began to appreciate the characters within. I have no doubt that many adolescents embarked on the road to adulthood during that short summer music course.

Arriving in Bradford for my very first National Youth Orchestra course in late December 1954, I was nevertheless on my guard for any repeat of the summer episodes. From the very start, however, everything fell into place with ease. Youngsters from all social classes and from all corners of the British Isles were accepted by their peers. The only decisive factor was whether or not one was a keen, reasonably talented musician who was ready to learn. I have always had a great capacity for observing everything around me without actually joining in, so I stood aside and was duly fascinated by the gathering of all these bright, chattering, thirteen- to nineteen-year-olds.

When I was asked by Michael, a fellow percussionist, "Which school do you go to?", it took me some time to relate to the fact that he was a public schoolboy, as undoubtedly it did for him to meet a grammar school pupil. To him that question had a subtly different slant to the literal way I understood it, and no doubt my chanting of "Greenhead High School, Huddersfield" made him think about hidden class implications too. His fruity upper-crust tones were as curious to me as were my northern utterances to him and, whilst I was intrigued by the fact that he lived in a boarding school, he in turn was deeply envious of my home life. His parents worked abroad in the diplomatic service and therefore his holidays were also spent in school – he had no choice in the matter. I had read many boarding school adventure stories, but it had not occurred to me that these could have had any remote parallel in real life. None of this mattered, of course, as we were all there for the same purpose, but initially it came as a severe culture shock and took some time to get used to. We were soon swapping stories, however, and became good friends into the bargain; equals in our chosen enthusiasms.

Some time prior to my very first course, a large brown envelope had arrived at home bearing the legend **'Music, Do Not Bend'** and the NYO logo. This caused huge excitement, especially when I discovered that I had been sent the tambourine part for Dvořák's *Carneval* overture. At that point in my life there had never been an opportunity to play a tambourine, although I had watched with fascination when the YSO players performed, carefully noting all the varied techniques needed for that clever little instrument: shaking, tapping, flat of hand, flat of knuckles, against the knee for really loud, punchy rhythms, and the smooth purring sound achieved by rubbing a wetted thumb round the edge of the skin. I also took special note of the fact that the professionals were most careful not to let the jingles sound when picking up the instrument or putting it down. This was obviously something I needed to study, so I contacted the local Salvation Army where I was very kindly lent an instrument to practise with. My bedroom then became a tambourine studio, much to the curiosity of our neighbours. They had previously managed to discover that the little bells they had heard came from a glockenspiel, all of these observations leading to intense intrigue about what else might be lurking there in that small end-of-terrace house.

Contrary to common belief, it is perfectly possible for percussionists to practise much of their art quietly. I would kneel on the floor in front of the settee and use the two cushions as timpani heads, learning how to become conversant with the spatial skills required for all percussion instruments, and raising a lot of dust in the process. Special care needs to be taken when moving from one instrument to another, as it is only too easy to knock one stick against the other, losing one or both as a result. This is a total disaster in a concert situation, but fun for the audience to observe any frantic rescue attempts. A thick, black rubber, close-fitting practice pad was brought into play when it came to working out tricky snare drum rhythms. This fitted snugly on top of the playing head, but the 'feel' was not as responsive as that of a skin head. This was all to the good though, as the real thing then came as a pleasant surprise: bouncy and with a crisp sound. In rehearsals, underemployed percussionists are fidgets, often to be found trying out tricky or repetitive technical studies on a folded duster, the knee of a crossed leg, a padded chair seat or, in fact, anything that does not produce a sound. Rubber beaters are used when it comes to practising the tuned percussion instruments, as not only does one not drive everyone else crazy with penetrating sounds, but also one's own ears are protected from the painful vibrations of the instruments at close quarters.

Walter Süsskind was the conductor for this, my very first NYO experience. Just turned forty, he had a lively and genial affinity with such a young orchestra. That first downbeat for the *Carneval* overture was a real shock to the system though, setting off an excitement that continued throughout the course. Goosebumps and big grins were the order of the day for me, as I had no idea that the piece was intended to fly by at such a pace. My personal solo practising at home had been a somewhat sedate affair in comparison. Then there were the never-to-be-forgotten thrills of a true Czech interpretation of Kodály's colourful *Háry János* suite, with doubled-up brass and woodwind, hordes of strings, a comprehensive percussion team and, last but not least, a piano that could cunningly be switched to a cimbalom sound by the pressing of a pedal. When this instrument made its first entry in the music, everyone was stunned by the twanging, hard-edged harp-like sound it made. None of us had ever encountered anything of its kind before. At one point in the music, it sounded to me for all the world as if someone had fallen down a flight of cellar stairs with a disintegrating old pub piano. (Later in life I was to hear a cimbalom for real, played by gypsies in a cellar dive in Budapest - an exotically different experience.)

Ruth Railton, the orchestra's founder, was ever-present, keeping a strict rein on the powder keg of over a hundred adolescents. She had instigated many rules and codes of behaviour, which were very irritating and constantly questioned (and sometimes flouted), but they proved a marvellous foundation for later life – if one had only realised it at the time. Whenever players were on a concert platform, whether playing or not, they had to sit and, as she put it, 'make atmosphere'; in other words, look interested and involved in what was going on. All players were required to sit on stage throughout a concert and all had to listen to everything even if they were not personally occupied. The 'making atmosphere', being aware of watchful, beady eyes: "If you can see any member of an audience, they can see you". I doubt if the words 'body language' were in vogue in the 1950s, but now it is intriguing for me to look at an orchestra from an audience's point of view and observe just that: it speaks volumes.

Individual sectional rehearsals were taken by specific 'Professors'. Our professional teacher was the Philharmonia timpanist, Mr James Bradshaw. We youngsters did not realise at the time that he was one of the most revered and well-known exponents of his instrument both in the UK and abroad, but it soon dawned on us that he ate, dreamed and probably slept timpani playing and music. He was very tall and from a family of musicians (his nephew Howard was to become the CBSO timpanist for a short while some years later), with a lugubrious demeanour something akin to that of a weary bloodhound. He rarely smiled and had a deliberate, quiet, Geordie accent. This was not to say that he was a cold person. On the contrary, we all warmed to him and treated him with deep respect, working very hard to please him. Praise from Mr B was praise indeed, and had to be earned. On the rare occasions when he illustrated a point, we were truly astonished by his skills. Insistent on control at all times, one of his awe-inspiring little demonstrations consisted of playing a fortissimo roll in the air about half an inch away from someone's nose end. The sticks fanned out into an alarming blur and the victim was hard pressed to stay still, but there was never any danger of physical contact. When he wasn't teaching us, we could sometimes hear him as he privately practised technical exercises, putting our teenage indolence to shame.

Dvořák's *New World* symphony presented the opportunity of learning to play the humble triangle, an instrument much maligned in its apparent simplicity. Not for nothing did Berlioz state that "a triangle trill added to a red-hot orchestra turns it white-hot", an effect that can lift the music by adding an indefinable silvery edge with thrilling effect. Mr Bradshaw also warned that the smallest of triangles could sound like a fire alarm if handled badly. We all took this to heart, and each learnt to treat it with the respect it deserved.

* * *

Jim Bradshaw's triangle eventually found its way to the CBSO as it had been willed to Douglas Milne, the CBSO's long-standing principal percussionist. As a young man, Doug had been a regular extra (not on permanent contract) with the Philharmonia Orchestra and as such often found himself landed with triangle parts to play. As a sensitive performer he always enjoyed these, something that was duly noted by Jim, the owner of the aforementioned fine old triangle. It was a large instrument that needed a firm hand and light touch, but if used with discretion it could certainly put an added sparkle into a score – a simple hair-raising trick of the trade (for example, as at the end of Stravinsky's *Firebird Suite* and in numerous Mahler symphonies).

When Doug died, I became the custodian of what has become my favourite triangle. Other players in the CBSO dubbed this particular instrument the 'killer triangle' and eventually few people (apart from myself and one brave extra) would play it, preferring to use a thick, modern, shiny monstrosity (more 'ping' from the beater than 'ting' from the instrument!) suspended from a stand and played with two beaters. To my mind one can phrase the music far better with one beater, with the instrument swinging free from a thin nylon loop. Held high in the hand it is a simple thing for the player to see the instrument, music and conductor and, last but not least, the sound is not obscured. Jim Bradshaw's maxim was that most triangle parts can be played with one beater, the instrument being easily controlled (damped for sound, and prevented from swinging) and, most importantly, the music can be shaped and expressed naturally.

* * *

In the NYO, hard work was the norm, with daily detailed sectional rehearsals interspersed with a constant supply of ginger biscuits and orange juice. We all grumbled at the enforced quiet time every afternoon but, when it came to it, sleep often obliterated all those black music dots for a short while at least, after which we then returned refreshed and ready for the next intense training session.

It was a different world, one populated by famous names and revered conductors such as Hugo Rignold, Jean Martinon, Norman del Mar, Sir Adrian Boult and Sir Malcolm Sargent. And which brass player would ever forget taking part in a fanfare for the arrival of Master of the Queen's Music, Sir Arthur Bliss, at one course? The list of teaching professors reads like a 'Who's Who' of top soloists: Malcolm Arnold, Dennis Brain, Jack Brymer, Archie Camden, Douglas Cameron, Keith Cummings, Leon Goossens, Ernest Hall and Gareth Morris, to name but a few.

Looking back, it is obvious that these illustrious souls also enjoyed the freedom to let their hair down. Social evenings, dances and parties bore witness to that, with everyone joining in from matron to the youngest fiddle player. At New Year there was much dressing up by the teaching staff for topical sketches and singing of amusing words to pieces being currently worked on. Everyone came together for fun and games: all very innocent, of course, but greatly enjoyable for all that.

On the more serious side, there were private performances most evenings when we were privileged to hear our famous teachers doing their own thing, be it solo recitals or together in lovely chamber concerts. Dennis Brain did a school-style presentation complete with hosepipe and horn, and then he played glorious Mozart and R Strauss. (I noted in my diary, "He's very formal – a proper concert manner, excepting for dress – grey flannels, pullover and corduroy lumber jacket.") Douglas Cameron seemingly played Saint-Saëns' 'Swan' from *Carnival of the Animals*, but in fact it was dubbed out of sight by a wonky violin, causing a lot of hilarity. All old chestnuts, but funny nevertheless and an ideal way to wind down, sending us smiling to bed after the late-evening cocoa session.

Living in boarding schools and residential colleges was a novelty for the great majority of the students, and we were a truly mixed bunch, some coming from deepest rural Ireland and others from high-profile public schools. Everyone pitched in with positive enjoyment, many to continue studying their chosen instruments to an elevated professional standard. Looking at the orchestra lists from that period, there are numerous well-known names from musical families, not that any of us were aware of these at the time. Some from my short time with the orchestra made it to become conductors, soloists, composers and musicologists – notably, Iona Brown, Ken Sillito, Christopher Seaman, Simon Standage, Rohan de Saram, Tim Reynish, Guy Woolfenden and Nicholas Braithwaite; added to which, many became respected orchestral players. Not all were destined to be professional musicians, however, as many gained fame and fortune in other professions. For instance, the then leader of the orchestra, Colin Gough, became, and still is, a close family friend as well as the highly respected and renowned Professor of Condensed Matter Physics at Birmingham University. He also continues to play chamber music at a professional level. We were all on a rollercoaster of shared musical experiences, which generated lifetime contacts and a strong bond that is always recognised and acknowledged even now when the question "Were you in the NYO?" comes into a conversation. A unique rapport constantly crosses all generations as experiences from the time spent in this very special orchestra are recalled.

* * *

Diary extracts from my very first NYO course (the orchestra's 21st) in Bradford, January 1955:

All the Yorkshire members had a photo taken at the civic reception with the Lord Mayor, so because of this I only managed to get one meringue with my cup of tea. It was soon over and when we had finished we all went back to the corridor for coats when a door opened and a man came out with two letters in his hand. He turned to me and said, "Could you tell me if Miss Cotton is here please?" I nearly dropped! There was a five-shilling book token for me from an anonymous well-wisher, addressed to St George's Hall.
Concert day:
Early breakfast, then to Bradford in our fleet of coaches. I was in the 'van party' to unload instruments with all percussionists and bass players. The harpist just went to supervise. Miss Railton had objected about the girls

33

helping, or even being in the van party, but she didn't say anything to me. Mr Dalby (Ruth Railton's assistant) wanted a couple of boys to carry some chairs, so I'm a boy now. No one seemed to mind, but the harpist was never included. The platform was too tiny for chairs, so we got everything else on, and then arranged it on the spot. All our careful moves had to be worked out again, and Michael had to play two of my cymbal rolls, as I couldn't reach. The rehearsal went quite well, although a lot of people (strings) couldn't play, as there was no room on stage for everyone.

I needed a chair for **Carneval** overture; this was to help balancing on one leg to play the tambourine against my knee. No room, so I wore socks instead of stockings (which are silky and slippery) and just stood on one leg to play, steadying the one against the other. Phew! Miss Railton didn't notice thank goodness or she'd have kicked up a fuss. At 6.50pm a man came to the back of the hall and blew a whistle – we took the hint and cleared off. Reports came back stage about people "fighting at the booking office" and "crowds can't get in". We didn't believe them.

It's a change to see Süsskind in a decent suit instead of blazer and open-necked navy sports shirt. The orchestra room is awfully hot and dark, everybody wildly tuning and Mr Hirsch (Leonard Hirsch: violin) going mad because no one stayed in tune for two minutes together.

Miss R wished us luck, then Mr Dalby told me that the tambourine was never quite on the beat. We eventually got onto the platform where Rodney (our tall cymbal player) spent ages unnecessarily 'consoling' me for Mr D's tactless remark. The hall was full and I soon spotted people I knew – from school and the Huddersfield Youth Orchestra, family, and even some YSO players. We were all quiet, but shuffling – trying to eke out an extra inch here and there. Süsskind followed leader, Colin Gough, on to a roar of applause and then we started.

After **Carneval**, (no hitches), we all sat down. It was very cold; I was shivering like anything.

The best thing for me was the Malcolm Arnold **(Homage to the Queen)**, it was wonderful! Süsskind surpassed himself and really worked us. It was fantastic to hear the orchestra respond so gladly. In the first movement of the Kodály, Alan's stand (timpanist) partly fell. The top rod holding the music slipped and the music went floating away into the bassoons. Impish grins from them, we didn't move a hair. They passed it back of course; we counted bars and remained immobile. The audience

34

*laughed at **Napoleon's Funeral March**. I was very surprised and pleased.*

We stayed afterwards to clear instruments. I seem to spend half my time tramping round with half a xylophone on my back. Dad came backstage and got in the way, then we went downstairs for farewell speeches. Aunty Ruth (Ruth Railton) shook hands with everyone and said to my mum, "Margaret is shaping up nicely". The boys packed the lorry and van, which went post-haste to London, and then we went back to the college to finish our own packing.

In the morning we were all up bright and early and bought papers on the station platform. Good reports and our names, as 'locals', were mentioned in the Yorkshire Post.

* * *

In due course, during my two years in the orchestra, I was destined to play a great deal for two of the conductors I first encountered as a teenager in the NYO, namely Sir Adrian Boult and Hugo Rignold. My first immature experiences were very much at odds with my eventual professional understanding of the said gentlemen, so it is curious to re-acquaint myself with some of my initial impressions as noted in diaries of the time:

22nd Course, April 1955, Canterbury
This was shared by Hugo Rignold, who took the orchestra to Amsterdam and Brussels, and Sir Malcolm Sargent who did a concert at the Royal Festival Hall prior to the trip abroad.

To a down-to-earth eighteen-year-old from Yorkshire, Hugo Rignold came over as "smarmy and smug - can't stick him!" However, in the fullness of time, as a full-blown pro I respected and liked him as the true professional he was, and suspected that he was probably somewhat at a loss as to know how to treat a bunch of bright and lively musical youngsters.

As usual, all players were required to attend every rehearsal, so the percussion team was there in full force for Sir Malcolm Sargent's first rehearsal with the orchestra: the fourth movement of Dvořák's *New World* symphony:

He's rather jerky to watch. No sports flannels for him though – immaculate morning suit, dark grey with dazzling white shirt and blue satin tie. He also uses a monocle at times. A real stickler for detail.

Sunday April 15th
A recital by students for Sir M. A 16 yr old Ceylonese boy played (Rohan de Saram, cello) – brilliant! And one of our percussionists played three of his own compositions.

Monday April 18th
As the percussion section is free we're to keep an eye on the two piano soloists: Wendy Waterman 10 yrs and Allan Schiller 12 yrs. All Allan wants to do is to get his hands on a drum, so we are going to let him play bass drum in the National Anthem when he's not doing his Mozart concerto.

Tuesday April 19th
Bach all morning so we were free. I discovered later that I have been chosen to go abroad. Oh whoopee! After supper we were all shooed out for an hour in warm coats as mysterious things were happening inside. When we returned we saw a large ice cream van outside and the kitchen was ablaze with light. After waiting in the corridor we were led into a darkened dining room where a set piece had been rigged up with cakes and candles for the orchestra's seventh birthday. All the professors were there and Sir Malcolm had the two youngest members to help him cut the largest of the cakes with a huge knife, then we all sang Sir Arthur Bliss's **Birthday Greetings** *to Sir M. He is 60 this month. He liked the 'rendering'. After that he spoke to all his 'godchildren' and said that he wouldn't abandon us again for another 7 years. We all had a birthday present from Sir M of a postcard-size photo of him. After that we tucked into ice cream, chocolate eclairs, orange crush and birthday cake.*

Sir Adrian Boult came over at the time as a bland teddy bear, not in the least as I was to remember him from the stop-gap year with the CBSO (before Hugo Rignold arrived in 1960). He conducted the NYO at the Royal Albert Hall Proms in August 1955 where I observed that, "We were all down below the platform in two small, stuffy and dingy orchestra rooms … not much room on the platform" (nothing changes!) The press trumpeted the fact that the NYO was the first amateur group to perform at The Henry Wood Proms:

36

a feather in the cap for the orchestra.

Going back to school seemed very tame after such holiday experiences: playing for world-renowned conductors in Amsterdam's famous Concertgebouw, Brussels' Palais des Beaux Artes, London's Royal Albert Hall and Edinburgh's Usher Hall.

All this - together with television performances, broadcasts, interviews for the local as well as the national press and constantly being the centre of attention by being "the only girl playing all those strange instruments at the back of the orchestra" (as one lady put it at a posh reception) - might have had a detrimental effect on my outlook on life. Not so, I hope. We Yorkshire folk are far too down-to earth to believe all that flattery and fuss, and I soon settled back into normal term-time activities.

Life became very busy, what with 'O' Level exams, piano exams, orchestras, attending concerts, and becoming a volunteer steward for the Huddersfield Music Society. This is where I had my first taste of professional chamber music. Bartok Quartets were a bit of a shock, and I well remember getting the giggles at the back of the audience, sniggering into my school beret, unable to come to terms with the extraordinary sounds emanating from four perfectly ordinary stringed instruments. One town hall concert, which my father and I attended, was given in aid of Russian exiles. It seemed to go on for ever, but none of the audience made any move to leave, mesmerised as they were by father and son Oistrakh: David and Igor. We were totally riveted by their contributions in the long-winded ragbag of a programme. Dad had to go to work the following morning and I to school, but we stayed until well after 10.30pm when there was still no sign of the end of the lengthy programme.

I went to anything and everything, eventually finding myself in demand to play for light opera productions by local amateur groups. Dad would load up my few instruments in the motorbike's sidecar, I would hop on the pillion and we would be off to some church hall or other so that I could make a contribution to such entertainments as *Student Prince*, *Goodnight Vienna* and numerous Gilbert and Sullivan gems. This was all good experience, although I cannot imagine how it sounded as I never seemed to have the correct instruments and spent much of my time getting lost in the scrappy-looking orchestral parts. One autumn, Mr Rees, the conductor of the Huddersfield Philharmonic Orchestra asked me if I would like to play in a performance of Gounod's *Faust* in Cheshire. Naturally I responded with an eager "Yes please!", but I then realised that I was not actually a free agent and, of course, was expected to attend school. Mr Rees did no more, but went to see my headmistress and somehow managed to convince her that my school work would not suffer and thus persuaded her to release me from school for a week. This was on condition that I attended Manchester City Library during the day and completed any work set for me from school. My parents were assured that I would be well looked after, as I was to be a house guest of one of the members of the cast. So, it was with great excitement that I was duly delivered to my hosts prior to entering into the world of grand opera for the first time. It was such a shock to see the cast in costume at the dress rehearsal, and I well remember how impressed I was by Mephistopheles, not only by his deep voice, but also by the sight of his glittering eyes – sequins stuck onto his top eyelids. At the end of the week I was solemnly presented with my very first grown-up powder compact and a huge bouquet of flowers.

Other unusual experiences were to be found in the local church 'Sings'. At various times of the year, church choirs and congregations would gather out of doors with a bunch of musicians, usually local brass players, to sing favourite sacred pieces. Familiar hymns and lusty selections from Handel, Bach, Mozart or Haydn would float across the surrounding hills, where we could see people standing at their doorsteps listening and joining in. These excursions would necessitate lugging a pair of kettledrums up rocky pathways, levelling them on rough, tussocky, moorland grasses and getting stuck into playing the great tonic/dominant timpani parts. I loved it, especially if I could also sing along. Dad always accompanied me on these trips; he enjoyed the music and also liked to keep an eye on his daughter. I suspect that he might also have felt a little frisson of pride in my unusual achievements but, of course, would never have shown his feelings to me.

The fateful day eventually came in the National Youth Orchestra when James Bradshaw, my timpani professor, asked me, "Now then, Margaret, when are you going to music college?" This came as a total surprise, so my immediate reply was, "I'm not, because I'm a girl!" The assumption that he was referring to studying timpani and percussion was correct, but at the time the very idea was as bizarre to me as aspiring to become a rocket scientist. "Well then, we'll have to see about that!" came back the matter-of-fact response. This prompted swift action on my part. I applied to two suitable colleges to study piano and timpani/percussion and, as a sensible alternative option, a teacher-training college. Eventually I was invited to attend interviews and auditions in London and Manchester and spent a day at Bretton Hall Training College in Yorkshire.

A letter must have been sent from the NYO to my headmistress, Mrs Doherty, as I was duly summoned to her lair. She had decreed that anyone that was not university material would be given the opportunity of three other choices according to which year they happened to be in. The three-year cycles were for teacher, secretary or nurse. My particular year fell on the secretarial option; any other ideas were of no consequence to her. However, unbeknown to her, I had been offered provisional places by The Royal Northern School of Music, Bretton Hall Training College (music, art and drama) and The Royal Academy of Music (RAM) in London. This cut no ice with Mrs Doherty, however, as in her estimation I was to be a secretary or nothing.

As I was over the age of sixteen and legally allowed to leave school, I did this as quickly as possible. In fact, I never completed my final Upper VI year. However, in spite of the fact that I had three excellent possibilities open to me, I found that it was impossible to get a grant from my Local Authority. Wyndham G Williams, head of the Huddersfield School of Music, was apparently in charge of the 'thumbs up' or 'thumbs down' for this, so, as he put it, "There's no point in giving you a grant as you are the wrong sex and wrong instrument!" I did not realise that I could have asked for other (unprejudiced?) advice or applied elsewhere for help, so the only alternative seemed to be to fund myself, with, of course, massive support from home. Jim Bradshaw had long discussions with my parents, who must have been even more bemused than I, but eventually a plan of action was hatched.

It was decided that I would work during term time as a classroom assistant in one of the big local Secondary Modern schools, put my weekly wage of £4.50 straight into the bank, along with the total of 75p that I earned doing two newspaper rounds every day. I would continue with my advanced piano studies and get as much experience as possible playing in orchestras, and then, during the holidays, I would do any paid temporary work that I could get. I eventually found myself making fireworks during the summer (where I was paid extra danger money for working with gunpowder), delivering Christmas post, sorting mail and being one of Father Christmas's gnomes behind the fake fireplace in the grotto at the local Co-op in Huddersfield. It was hoped that this would yield enough to keep me for one year at the RAM, after which I would be on my own.

Working in a school where some of the boys were bigger than me was traumatic to say the least, but I did as I was bid: playing the piano, taking children to the swimming baths, supervising school dinners, hearing hopeless readers, fetching and carrying and basically growing up.

39

In May 1955, I was offered a definite place by the RAM (which was deferred for a year), and I suspect that this news and the fact that my parents were going away for a fun weekend with friends – I was to stay at home alone for the very first time – contributed to my mother having a massive heart attack whilst I was on one of my early paper rounds. By the time I had been found and brought back home, it was too late: she had died instantly. My father and I faced a bleak future without her and only a sense of total unreality kept us going. Neither of us knew how to mourn; indeed it seemed indecent to weep for such a vibrant person. We imagined that she was always just coming home from work, or out shopping, but not *dead*, not my mum, Renie. She and I had just begun to relate to each other as real pals and it was so cruel that she never knew how everything eventually turned out. She was only forty-six, with everything to look forward to. I was just nineteen. My father received much well-intentioned advice with regard to my future from ancient relatives, ranging from "You want to get her wed!" to "Send her off to t't mill to addle some brass!" (earn some money). It is to his eternal credit that he continued with the optimistic campaign agreed previously with my mum.

3

Square Peg

"Our Margaret's going to London!" None of my family could believe it. To them, London was like the ends of the earth, especially as I was one of the first to fly the nest towards higher education. One cousin was held up to the rest of us as being clever, especially when he got his degree and his cap and gown, so now I also had the responsibility on my shoulders to do as well for the distaff side of the family.

The negative attitudes of those empowered to help young people with advice and finance made me all the more determined to 'show 'em'. I would make something of myself if it killed me. It seemed obvious that I had to prove that I was just as good as the boys going away to college, but at the same time bear in mind that I was a girl and must not fall into the trap of becoming aggressively unfeminine. An early letter home said much about the attitudes prevailing at the time:

I was at the RAM at 9.15am and spent approx. ½hr shifting instruments and little tables while men stood around and watched. 'If you want it, you get it!' If I'd fallen down the stairs with the table there'd have been a helluva stink. Why should the girls have to cart tables when 2 hall porters and a lift are available? I dunno! But I was so wild that I'd have brought them down from the 5th floor - blow 'em!

This was a difficult line to tread, but as long as I was confident with my playing I imagined that everything would be all right. I had had my first heart flutterings of the agonising puppy-love variety, but was still very nervous of boys, who just knew that they were far superior to the female of the species.

After making enquiries about available accommodation near the RAM, I managed to find a YWCA (Young Women's Christian Association) hostel near Euston station and within walking distance of the Academy. There were no halls of residence for aspiring musicians and, as I knew no one and had very little money, this seemed the ideal solution. I was so nervous at the thought of leaving home and living in such an alien city that I never gave a thought as to how my father would be feeling. We had always been close, so my going away must have been a traumatic wrench for him. Not only had he lost his life partner, but also his only child was leaving him to fend for himself in an empty house. My own feelings were those of stepping off into the unknown: part apprehension, part excitement. Not given to showing our emotions, I doubt very much if anything was said at our final parting at Huddersfield railway station, apart from a quiet "Now then, you behave yourself!" accompanied by a bone-crunching hug from my ever-loving parent. But I still remember the sight of that sad little figure waving as the train drew away from the platform. I looked into my closed hand and found that he had given me a pound note as a parting gesture. Feeling very vulnerable and forlorn, it finally dawned on me that I knew no one in London, and I really had left home for good.

Packing for this adventure had been somewhat fraught, as I had few clues about what to include. However, since I was about sixteen my mother had always made sure that every birthday and Christmas would include a sensible present for my future life as a traveller, musician or not. She had also taught me the art of packing a suitcase prior to my first trip abroad as a schoolgirl, a lesson I never forgot and have always valued. I had therefore unwittingly accumulated a core of useful items, such as a lightweight, soft-topped suitcase in which to put the folding travel iron, a small hairdryer, folding coat hangers, a travel washing line (complete with pegs), a smart toilet bag, shoe bags and a small sewing kit. And finally, I was the proud owner of an initialled leather briefcase sturdy enough to hold music and many drumsticks. My grandmother had given me a single electric ring, which was large enough to take a small saucepan. Though potentially dangerous, this was immensely useful for my impoverished future. I would soon discover that a slice of bread filched from breakfast and half a packet of the new-fangled, inexpensive dried onion soup made a very acceptable, if meagre, lunch. There was no money for any fripperies and, anyway, I didn't care. No one would know that I was still wearing navy blue school knickers. There would be time enough for pretties when I was a wage earner. I was far more anxious to have enough music for my split first study of piano/timpani and percussion.

My new abode, Ashley House, consisted of three tall terraced houses knocked through to make one large building. Young women from all over the world were welcomed through its doors and there was a friendly atmosphere in the place. One of the first things I noticed was a somewhat battered but serviceable baby grand piano in the visitors' lounge. Later it transpired that music students were welcome to practise on it all day. That was a real bonus. It was the end of the summer holidays, so I had the shared room to myself to begin with. Without personal things around, it looked very bleak. I sat on the bed nearest the door and surveyed the scene: dark green linoleum on the floor, three beds – each with a small bedside locker and reading light, a mat, a wooden chair, a chest of drawers and a wardrobe. All the paintwork and bedspreads were in dreary greys and maroons, with a simple table by the window to complete the picture. The view was over roofs and backyards, but at least there were some birds flying around, probably pigeons from nearby Euston railway station.

At the end of that first afternoon, as soon as I had unpacked and stowed my belongings, the door burst open and in came two young women. Not having had the experience of living in close proximity with anyone of my own age, I had worried about how I would cope with a shared living space. I need not have feared, though, as Edna, a pretty, garrulous trainee primary school teacher and Sheila, a quiet medical student, were perfect room-mates. They cheered me up and immediately whisked me down to the bowels of the hostel to the cafeteria-style dining room. Supper ('tea' to a northerner) consisted of basic student fodder such as sausages, cold meat and salad, things on toast and, on Fridays, fish and chips. Ice cream, a piece of fruit or a slice of cake would follow, and there was always plenty of bread and margarine to fill empty corners. Tea made with the hard London water came as a nasty shock, however. Not only did it have a scummy film on top, but also it was totally tasteless. I soon changed my plea of "Just a little milk, please" to "No milk, thank you!" Even then, there was no flavour that I recognised. Eventually I splashed out on a precious jar of instant coffee, which became a special treat for us to consume secretly in our room.

Autumn term had begun, and for the very first time I walked from the hostel down the Marylebone Road and found myself in the imposing entrance of The Royal Academy of Music: heart thumping, nerves tingling. That first day was full of confusion, instructions, directions, noise and things to sign, with no time to be homesick. Sounds of instruments being practised were everywhere, and friends were forever greeting each other in loud, confident voices. This all seemed very glamorous to me as I quietly observed and assessed my surroundings. The fact that I was a real *student* seemed totally unreal, so I spent some of my hard-earned cash on the purchase of a college scarf – at least I could attempt to look the part, even if I didn't feel it. As raw newcomers, we were welcomed to college by the Warden and then an introductory meeting was held in one of the lecture halls so that we could ask any questions and clear up any worries we might have. Timetables were discussed and confirmed. Term had begun in earnest.

To my delight, I discovered that I had been allotted the position of timpanist in the First and Third Orchestras and the Opera Orchestra. What I didn't realise was that such instrumentalists were relatively rare, so the powers-that-be were probably relieved to have a keen player in the new student intake.

It soon became apparent that I was the only one not to have received a grant from a local authority. Money seemed to be no object for most of my peers, so I kept quiet and steadfastly refused offers of cups of tea, which I could never hope to repay. My third letter home reflected very real anxieties about my impecunious state:

Sept 21st 1956

Dear pop,

I've been having a big 'reckon up' and taking into account food (12s 6d to 15s per week at least), fees for the Academy (£25 per term), and cost of accommodation (this included breakfast and a very basic supper) I've got just under £30 to last me for the year. That'll be for concerts, clothes, fares, music, books, manuscript paper, stamps, toothpaste, etc. What a carry on!

I decided to walk everywhere, make sandwiches whenever possible and buy any necessary fresh food from nearby street markets. Then it was a case of chin up and get on with it.

My father kept every letter I wrote to him during that RAM year. These had regularly plopped through his letter box and were long and descriptive. I usually had time to write copious amounts during orchestral rehearsals, as the timpanist and percussionists were not exactly stretched by imaginative programming. Reading them now, in the fullness of time, I realise how single-minded I was (blinkered and naive could be another way of putting it).

A shortage of money was not my only problem, as, for instance, I found it embarrassing to admit that I had come to the Academy primarily to study percussion, so I usually said that I was one of Mr Britton's piano students. However, I felt very strongly that as I was funding myself I was fully entitled to decide my own priorities now that I was within the hallowed walls. Frank Britton must have been somewhat startled to have one of his new students strike a bargain with him at the very first lesson. I told him that the only reason I was doing piano was that it looked better on my application form, and that I really wanted to concentrate on playing in the orchestras and learn as much as possible about timpani and percussion. However, I agreed to work hard for him and pass all the necessary piano examinations in college, as long as I did not have to perform at his end-of-term student concerts. He was naturally amazed at this approach, but acquiesced without a murmur, bless him. And I eventually fulfilled my part of the bargain by passing all the required pianistic milestones.

Another major decision was that I would aim to see as much of London as possible: going to the theatre, concerts and museums, walking in the parks, and exploring such places as Windsor, Richmond, the East End and historical sites. It was perfectly possible to savour many unique London experiences for little or no financial outlay, and I intended to take every advantage of being in the capital city.

Life went by in a whirl of lectures, essay writing, practice and, best of all, lessons and orchestra rehearsals. I joined the local public library and explored the possibility of joining amateur orchestras in the evenings. The only problem with the latter was that there was always a subscription to pay for the privilege, and I had no funds. There was nothing for it but to appear at rehearsals. If there was a shortage of percussionists (which was usually the case) then I would ask if I could play. When I was invited to become a fully paid-up member, I then confessed my plight. In response, rules were bent and regulations ignored, and I found myself playing for free in The Morley College Orchestra (MCO) behind the Royal Albert Hall, the Royal Amateur Orchestra (RAO), and eventually the London Senior Orchestra (LSO). Bus fares had to be found, so there were no refreshments for me during the half-time breaks. I did not mind at all; it was just great to be playing as much as possible. Eventually I got to know the other percussionists in the MCO and was offered lifts home on the back of a scooter. This orchestra consisted mainly of music students and young professionals. In the 1950s it was normal for the chaps to treat the girls for break-time drinks, but I found this very hard to allow and had to learn to accept these small, generous gestures as gracefully as possible.

Inevitably I had left things at home that I found I needed, so I was forever pestering poor old dad to send things on. Postage was far cheaper than replacing such items as a toothbrush, tin opener, photo frame, hot water bottle, and so on. My requirements seemed never-ending, but at least they were simple, and dad felt that he was being involved in my new lifestyle and never failed to comply with my odd requests.

Something very special happened during my first term at the RAM. The

MCO was transformed into the Hoffnung Symphony Orchestra (HSO). Gerard Hoffnung was the tuba player in the orchestra, but was far better known as the clever, observant cartoonist responsible for numerous small books caricaturing the vagaries of the classical music world. We had all played for 'The Maestro' in one shape or form and were constantly on the lookout for Gerard's wicked sketches of friends and colleagues. He had only to look around with narrowed eyes for there to be much speculation as to who would be his next victim.

November 13th was chosen for the 'Hoffnung Music Festival Concert of 1956' at the Royal Festival Hall (RFH). Billed as 'An Extravagant Evening of Symphonic Caricature', this was the show in which everyone wanted to participate. Malcolm Arnold's newly commissioned *Grand Grand Overture* was rehearsed almost before the ink was dry on the score, with the percussion team in charge of many pairs of cymbals, copious amounts of bells, massive gongs, cannons and rifles; a prodigious array of pitched and unpitched instruments. Solo parts were performed by vacuum cleaners and a floor polisher (which constantly tried to escape), which had their own special sectional rehearsal scheduled for 9.15am on the concert day. Programme notes eventually revealed that "The score is dated November 5th, and bears a dedication to President Hoover."

A diary entry from the week commencing November 12th read:

Dear Pa,
On Tues we had a very long rehearsal. I was at the RFH at 9.00am for a standing ticket, queuing for a friend (some had been there all night) but no luck. The RFH man was very kind though and let the Q into rehearsal. Malcolm Arnold wanted as many cymbals as possible. The fainting fiddler at the cannon shot was rehearsed - what a gag! The audience was fooled. Arnold is a mad conductor: he looks as though he'll take off and fly any minute, and his facial expressions are a treat. The cannon was tried twice and from then on you couldn't see for smoke or hear for coughing.
I'd had to ring up the Warden of the RAM to ask for permission to play at the concert (we have to have permission for all public concerts). He wasn't in, but his secretary said that she supposed I'd play whether allowed or not - so go ahead. The 15-foot bass drum [made for Verdi's **Requiem** *decades previously] was brought in after the carpenters had taken part of the door away. What a monster - of course we all had a*

46

*smack at it! We found lots of strange instruments in our dept. e.g. an electric police siren, 2 whips, 8 tambourines, an enormous set of shiny bells, Norman del Mar's lovely gong (I'm sure it's from the YSO), whistles, klaxons, knives and forks (!), cuckoo, football rattles and then all the usual stuff. A little man in dungarees stopped the rehearsal by coming through the orch. with 2 zinc buckets (London County Council), 1 containing water. Then another one arrived full of broken glassware from the RFH bars. We had a smashing time with them (you bet!) Composer Gordon Jacob conducted his funny variations on **Annie Laurie**. Scored for a most weird assortment of things: heckelphone, hurdy-gurdy, serpent, contrabass serpent, 2 piccolos, 2 bass saxophones, and the world's largest tuba (on wheels and warmed up by bellows), played by H.M. Hoffnung. Crazy! We listened from the audience and watched the Chopin tuba quartet. Hoffnung fussed like a baby and everyone got mad with him. I sat by Dennis Brain.*

At the concert the audience actually laughed! Yvonne Arnaud excelled herself in the piano concerto; she's a born comedienne. She held on a trill for about 5 minutes, then to get his own back del Mar held an ugly orchestra chord for a terrific length just before her cadenza. She beat on the piano, shouted, then started some knitting, which she eventually threw at him. I got a huge roar from the audience at my little xylo solo ['Half a Pound of Tuppeny Rice']. They gave her a basket of vegetables at the end and she gave a leek to her turneroverer.

*[The second half of the concert was a serious performance of Respighi's rarely played, massively scored, colourful tone poem **'Roman Festivals'**, which had taken weeks to prepare.]*

*For **Roman Festivals** I play the sleigh bells. The conductor told me that he'd follow me as long as I kept a steady beat as I usually do. At the concert he did his level best to make me smile, but it's hair-raising and 60 bars long. Dennis Brain played principal horn in this, Norman del Mar 5th horn, Malcolm Arnold 4th trumpet and Yfrah Neaman at the back of the 1st fiddles. What a distinguished orchestra! Dennis Brain actually played a 3-movement concerto on 2 lengths of hosepipe - that man is marvellous - of course he used his own mouthpiece. The thing that symbolised the whole concert for me was the sight of Dennis Brain quietly walking out of the crush of artists and going home by himself. Horn case in one hand and 2 coils of hosepipe in the other. I'd have given anything for a photo of him.*

Every member of the orchestra found a typed sheet on their music stands:
Hoffnung Concert: Sequence of Events

7.55 Orchestra take places

7.59 Leader enters

8.00 'Beecham' enters; orchestra rise respectfully; 'Beecham' opens score on conductor's desk and departs.

8.01 Mr Bean (manager of the RFH) enters and makes announcement

8.02 As Mr Bean walks off, Fanfare trumpeters (from Kneller Hall) enter from back, six from each entrance, and line up across top steps, with instruments

8.03 Francis Baines enters and conducts the

1) Fanfare (approx. 0'40'), which starts off with long 'Queen' roll to which the orchestra respectfully rise

After the fanfare F.B. leaves, the trumpeters leave and the orchestra sits

8.05 (Here beginneth Television) Malcolm Arnold enters to conduct the

2) GRAND GRAND OVERTURE. Before he begins there is an interruption by Yfrah Neaman. After the overture is finished the orchestra reposition QUICKLY for the

3) SURPRISE SYMPHONY, entry and departure of hotwater-bottlists to be arranged

(... and so on: not forgetting Gerard being given time to 'harangue the audience'! Then ending with:)

12) FESTE ROMANE conducted by Lawrence Leonard (no gags)

The list of acknowledgements in the programme included the following:
Subcontra-bass Tuba kindly lent by Paxman Brothers.
Big Bass Drum kindly lent by Boosey & Hawkes.
Vacuum Cleaners and Floor Polisher kindly lent by Hoover Ltd.
Hot Water Bottles kindly lent by Doultons Ltd.
Hosepipe kindly lent by Harrods Ltd.
Contrabass Serpent kindly lent by the Tolson Memorial Museum, Huddersfield.*
Gerard Hoffnung appears by kind permission of Madame Tussaud's.
Dennis Brain appears without the permission of Walter Legge.

* I had always imagined that all small local museums had collections of musical instruments until I left home, and then I realised how fortunate we

were in my home town.

The Interplanetary Music Festival was presented at the Royal Festival Hall in 1958, a further extravagant evening of musical caricature from Gerard's fertile imagination. His wheezy laugh and balding, portly figure was ever-present. More great names joined in the fun: Dame Edith Evans, Aaron Copland, John Amis, Owen Brannigan, Joseph Cooper, Ian Wallace, April Cantelo, Edith Coates, the Dolmetsch Ensemble and many others adding to the old team. Malcolm Arnold did his stuff again, a lot of hard work was engendered and both performances were sell-outs with everyone having a great time, so it was all the more shocking that within a short time Gerard died at the unbelievably early age of thirty-four.

The MCO had a large repertoire and was known for its adventurous programming. So, needless to say, I felt very honoured to be asked to play the second timpani part in Stravinsky's *Rite of Spring* at Chelsea Town Hall. My diary relates that the first person chosen 'backed out' and that I couldn't make head or tail of the piece! The noise in the rehearsal room was indescribable, but I managed somehow and even got a mention from a London newspaper critic: "I am sure that the charming young lady who biffed the timps in *'Le Sacre'* must have released enough aggressive energy to ensure her from any future fear of a neurosis."

One evening we arrived at the rehearsal to discover no less a composer than Aaron Copland on the rostrum. His quiet demeanour and American accent bemused us as we played through his colourful *El Salon Mexico*, with myself grinning all the way through the exhilarating bass drum depth charges. When Ralph Vaughan Williams (known by some as 'Uncle Rafe') was the grand old age of eighty-four he used to come into the Academy to listen to rehearsals of his opera *The Poisoned Kiss*. I remember him sitting with his legs dangling over the edge of the orchestra pit, fiddling with his hearing aid and smiling amiably.I described him as follows in a letter to dad:

He's a broad chap, with a stoop. He's not got much colour and his hair is thick and white. It's funny about his hearing aid because he goes around with it off and seems to turn it on halfway through a conversation.

He seemed a friendly old man. In fact, some time later, I found myself having tea with him (and lots of others) at a posh music festival featuring one or other of his rural fancies.

But it was a different story in those early days when I found myself at a chamber concert at Dartington Hall Summer School. Students had been sent from the RAM to be guinea pigs for an experimental New Music Group and, as part of the no-fee deal, we were allowed to attend any of the concerts if seats were available. One such recital was in the crowded medieval-style hall where my sharp ears picked up some whispered French between the pieces. When curiosity got the better of me, I half turned and was totally thrown to discover Mr and Mrs Igor Stravinsky sitting immediately behind me; he tiny and hunched in an overwhelming fur coat, she larger than life – an odd-looking couple. It was unbelievable to see such a legendary figure, and I was awestruck trying to imagine the amazing music inside that small cranium. How was it possible? Eventually I was to discover the joys, or otherwise, of working closely with the creators of the actual sounds we were playing – the awesomely great as well as the plainly incompetent. There were, indeed, such beings as real-life composers, something that I eventually took for granted.

Once I had settled down to life at the RAM, it dawned on me that something had to be done to redress its lack of percussion instruments. It is normal for students to have their own instruments, of course, but in the case of timpani and percussion these large instruments usually stay with the orchestra in which they are played and are supplied by the said orchestra. It was fine to use three hand-tuned timpani for the normal fare in all the orchestras – mainly non-twentieth-century music and incorporating many concertos to cater for the ambitious instrumental soloists amongst the student population. There was not much call for anything other than timpani, although the Academy did boast a large selection of tubular bells hanging in disarray on hooks in a basement corridor. This was a start, I thought, as I went downstairs armed with tuning fork and stepladder. But for the life of me I could not concoct anything remotely resembling a chromatic scale, so I eventually gave up in despair.

Thankfully, dad sent my cymbals by care of British Rail. He had made a sturdy, padded wooden case in which they were snug and totally safe. When I levered open the lid, I discovered that he had also incorporated cunning slots around the edge of the case in which he had stowed all the glockenspiel notes. The empty glock case followed later by cheaper second-class Royal Mail. I also had my triangle, castanets, sticks and beaters. The Academy boasted an ancient rope-tensioned bass drum, but there was no xylophone. I had found a tatty wooden-shelled drum masquerading as a snare drum, but without snares. This was the drum I used for practice purposes. Battle commenced as I tried to do something about this sorry state of affairs.

Dr Thomas Armstrong, the Academy principal (nicknamed 'The Farmer'), sent for me as he had heard that I had been complaining about the lack of instruments. He seemed a reasonable man and was very interested to see my cymbals. I had made no bones about the fact that I possessed a fine pair of Zyldjian orchestral cymbals. Unbeknown to me, he later wrote an article about them for a local newspaper. However, he could offer no solution to the problem apart from sanctioning the hire of a professional extra player for a prestigious college performance of Holst's rarely played *Choral Symphony*. When it came to the concert day, the hired player appeared, complete with his own xylophone, but he did not perform in the student orchestra. He was a theatre player of enormous girth and lovely sense of humour but, after taking one look at the awkward-to-play part and lack of space on the stage, he suggested that I carry on with the good work. So I played the xylo part, which I had learnt on my glockenspiel; smaller notes, but same fingering/sticking. Needless to say, we were both very happy with this arrangement. However, the situation got to even more farcical proportions when we were performing a new work by one of the student composers, as I noted in a letter to my father:

Dear Feyther,

... On Friday I only had a small rickety wooden s.d. stand and was waiting for Wendy (a fellow student) to arrive with her s.d. when Mr S (the RAM staff member responsible for orchestra and platform needs) asked me if I was playing in the new work.

"Yes, side drum."

"Have you got one?"

"No, but Wendy's hoping to get here in time with hers." Actually I'd seen another strange drum behind the stage and was keeping my fingers crossed.

"Come with me, we've got a Boy's Brigade drum that might do. Have you got a stand?"

"No - well only an unsafe wooden one."

He didn't have a stand, but offered me a shoulder strap to hold it with. I pointed out (with only the slightest hint of irony) that it might look rather odd, especially as I would be in academic dress! (A long white dress resplendent with scarlet sash across one shoulder.) Anyway I tried the drum but it wouldn't go on the stand, so I quietly took it back and got the

nasty little practice drum.
He then beckoned and said, "Can you keep quiet if I get another drum?
I'd get the sack if anyone knew I was doing this. These things belong to
the London Philharmonic Orchestra."
He unlocked a little door under the platform and got out a black case
containing a lovely s.d. and stand.
*I borrowed that - a treat to play on; even **my** roll sounded reasonable!*

I was constantly worried about how my father was coping, so we found ourselves in the ludicrous situation of trying to support each other from a distance. He sent me a ten-shilling note whenever he could, taped into a letter with stamp edging. I, on the other hand, darned his socks at the back of the orchestra and schemed about how to swell the funds. Foreign girls at the hostel were willing to pay 2s (10p) per hour for English conversation (albeit with a Yorkshire accent) and I had a percussion student in the shape of a young composer who needed to know more about the instruments and how to play them. This brought in another 5s (25p) per hour, but then I managed to get a job as a cleaner in the hostel. The pay was a mere 2s 6d (12½p) per hour, so for fifteen hours a week I was paid a total of £1 17s 6d (£1.75). Dad was earning under £700 per year, so another idea was to rent out a room in the house in Huddersfield. This meant that we would have to redecorate and smarten up some of the soft furnishings, and consequently I had a great time sending colour schemes and bits of fabric to my baffled parent. One of my more desperate ideas was to sell my long, thick hair. There was a nearby hairdresser with a notice in the window stating 'Hair wanted for wig maker', but on enquiring about this I was turned down because the unusual colour of my copious locks would be have been too difficult to match.

It was obvious that extra funds would be needed, so I made a brave attempt to win the Walter Stokes Scholarship. This was an open scholarship for all instrumentalists. My chosen piece was a composition for timpani and percussion written for final-year students at the Paris Conservatoire. Solo music written for timpani and percussion was practically non-existent in those days, so one had to make do with the little that was available. I found a willing pianist and worked cheerfully, having borrowed numerous instruments to make up for the shortfall at the Academy. The patronising and amused adjudicating panel listened with ill-concealed indulgence as they watched me work through my array of instruments, their insincere words falling on dismayed ears. I was awarded the fourth place out of twenty-two entrants. Eternal Optimism must have been my middle name as I tried valiantly for a whole year to persuade my local authority to help me with finances. These particular battles were in vain, but my gritty determination did not go unnoticed.

A number of established professional players were very kind and helpful towards keen youngsters. Eric Pritchard of the BBC Symphony Orchestra was my timpani professor, with Charlie Donaldson taking care of percussion lessons. Neither had ever heard me play in an orchestra but, in spite of this, I found myself being introduced to the BBC team and freelance percussionists as a likely future player. The *girl* thing always came into the equation, of course, but I was used to being teased and took it in my stride.

Quite unexpectedly a series of extraordinary coincidences arose, which changed my life forever. The famous percussionist James Blades came to The Academy to give one of his legendary lectures, but I only learnt of this after the event. Nevertheless, shortly afterwards a message appeared in my pigeonhole bidding me to see the Warden, who told me that Mr Blades had asked about "the girl percussionist with the fair hair" and "would she like to take part in the Dorking Music Festival orchestra for expenses, but no fee?" I was duly amazed at this and naturally agreed to anything that would give me more experience in an orchestra. Details were given to me and I accordingly presented myself on the day and at the appropriate time in Dorking. When I met Mr Blades, he looked puzzled and then said, "I don't remember you as the girl from the Academy"! It was only then that I realised that he had met my fellow-student Wendy (a second study percussionist, mentioned previously) and that I, in all innocence, had made a terrible blunder. Needless to say, it was too late to rectify this, so I played in the orchestra. Fortunately, the first piece was Dvořák's *Carneval* overture. I revelled in the tambourine part again, thanking my lucky stars that Jim Bradshaw had seen to it that I made a good job of it in the NYO two years previously.

I thoroughly enjoyed myself for the rest of the programme, and after the concert I helped Jimmy pack away his instruments into his big old-fashioned Rover. Everything had its exact place, all fitting like a glove, but it wasn't until I was just about to board the train in Dorking that I realised with horror that I had left my bag of precious cymbals behind, propped up against the stage scenery. At the last minute I managed to phone the hall and spoke to the caretaker, who told me that Mr Blades had rescued them and he gave me his telephone number. The next day I telephoned as early as I dare. Yes, they were safe, and I could pick them up at lunchtime at the BBC studios in Maida Vale. Much relieved, I turned up at the agreed time and, after being treated to a very good BBC canteen meal, I went into the studio where Lambert's *Rio Grande* was being recorded, a score that requires the percussionists to have their wits about them, as, among other things, they have a lot of exposed neat solo bits and pieces that blend in with the long piano cadenza. I had never heard of the piece, so when Jimmy asked me to play one of the xylophone passages I just played it. No problem. He then asked if I could do it twice as fast. That was fine also. Being a pianist helped enormously in such circumstances. I was then taken through my paces, apparently passing his little tests with flying colours. Dear Jimmy then said, "If you ever get a job and have no instruments, don't turn it down - get in touch with me or Sam, the manager at Booseys (Boosey & Hawkes' Instruments) and we'll fix you up"!

Other professionals offered help too. Gilbert Webster, the BBC Symphony Orchestra's principal percussionist, sympathised as he had heard that I had not got a grant, saying, "Well, kid, if you're ever desperate, don't pack it in - ring me up and I'll see what I can do." I confessed to him about innocently diddling Wendy out of the Dorking job, but he merely laughed and said, "You'll do. Sometimes you can see the women going slowly mad, but you won't, I can tell that. It's a fight, kid, but you keep it up, you're doing fine!" So, forgetting the cymbals turned out to be a good thing after all. Incidentally, I knew that the BBC Symphony Orchestra's second timpanist was a woman, Pat Brady, so that was one place at least where there was no overt sex discrimination. Some of the hard-boiled London players were intimidating, but Jimmy Blades was always encouraging, and said to me that he might sometimes be able to hand on a few amateur orchestra dates and, as he had always been lucky, he believed in helping others over their difficulties. His dictum was: 'Learn as you earn, earn as you learn.'

Dribs and drabs of work slowly began to come my way. On one particularly memorable occasion, I saw how the other half lived for the first time when I played for a performance of Mendelssohn's *Elijah* in a country church near Oxford, writing afterwards to tell my father about the wine in a decanter, sherry in crystal glasses (my first taste of this, which I did *not* enjoy), watercress with orange, boiled ham rolled around prunes, white wine and "oak beams everywhere"! I was unaware, as ever, of who was or wasn't famous, but was brought up short at the rehearsal by an angelic voice I recognised from my school days. I knew Isobel Baillie's voice, as she was a favourite with music teacher Miss Townsend. We were always listening to the record of 'Hear ye, Israel', with Miss Townsend drawing attention to the perfection of Dame Isobel's flawlessly placed notes, effortless phrasing and beautiful tone. Here she was for real - an old lady now, but I couldn't believe my ears.

The social whirl was not for me, but this did not mean to say that I had a miserable existence. We students were sometimes given guest tickets to the more obscure operas at Covent Garden when the audience promised to be thin on the ground. These were dished out at the very last minute and were the best seats in the house - front stalls - but too expensive and difficult to sell at £1 15s (£1.75) each. There would be a great flurry amongst my hostel pals, as they made sure that I looked smart enough to attend the opera. Clothes were borrowed and I was persuaded to wear make-up. There was a Morley College social and dance nearer Christmas, and I also found myself dressing up for the Coldstream Guards Regimental Dinner, my escort on that occasion being a flautist friend from Huddersfield. I went to the RAM Christmas Ball, but not as a guest – I was the Cinderella. In other words, at midnight I found myself playing a set of bells hidden on stage for the grand sum of 8s 6d (43p) while carols were being sung and a jovial Father Christmas was being dragged round on a sleigh pulled by students.

My lack of funds continued to be a problem. For instance, numerous people questioned me as to whether I was eating enough (the answer would have been "No" – but it was not something I would ever admit to). Help sometimes came from unexpected quarters: fees for the hire of timpani were mysteriously waived and I was given free drum-kit lessons by Max Abrahams, a generous jazz drummer who was very well known in his field, but sadly I had to admit that this was not my favourite occupation in spite of the fact that there was a great demand for 'lady drummers' at seaside venues. In spite of my impecunious state, I had long nursed an expensive ambition, as the following letter to my father reveals:

May 17th 1957

Dear dad,

I want a pair of timps for my 21st birthday, so start saving! Jimmy [Blades] has put me onto a pair he's let go to Boosey & Hawkes, and Sam, the boss there, says that J told him to let me have first refusal, and that he had to 'cut out the frills'. I can arrange to have them on hire purchase [dirty words in my family]. They are just like new and are £60. I have about £30 in a savings account, which I was told would be mine when I reached 21. It's no good being a drummer without drums.

This dream would eventually come to fruition, but not before I experienced a lot of angst and further stoical battles. My hoped-for grant from Yorkshire came to naught, and so, without any funds remaining with which to continue at the RAM, I returned home to lick my wounds at the end of the summer term. As I was a well-brought-up young lady, I sent a proper thank you letter to Jimmy Blades for all his kindness and support over the previous months. We had no telephone at home and what made me include my best friend's telephone number (with her permission I might say) I will never know, but this proved to be another crucial link towards my goal of becoming a professional musician.

4
We Have Lift-off!

I was halfway through painting a window frame at the front of our house, when my friend's mother hove into view panting, "There's been a telephone call for you, and you have to ring this number straight away. It's a Mr Blades!"

I was astonished, thanked her, gathered up a fistful of pennies and rushed across the road to the public telephone box. When I eventually got through, I found, to my amazement, that Jimmy was offering me a great opportunity to be part of a small UK orchestra playing for the José Limon American Dance Group, an offshoot of the *Martha Graham Dance Company*. It turned out that a player had been booked to be the percussionist for a possible long run, but it was soon discovered that he was not a good 'tuned' percussionist and the exposed xylophone solos in some of the complex South American music were beyond his skills. A week of embarrassing rehearsals had gone by, things had gone from bad to worse, and so, after much agony on everyone's part, it was decided to pull in a replacement player at the last minute. I received the news on the Thursday; the company was opening at Sadler's Wells Theatre on the following Monday, so time was of the essence. I was given a sketchy outline of the proposed tour, which started on September 2nd with fifteen performances in London, followed by Paris, Berlin, Poland, Germany, Belgium and Holland, and then to be continued anywhere in Europe where advanced bookings could be arranged.

There was almost too much to take in, but Jimmy assured me that there would be no problem about getting any instruments I might need – he would see to that. After phoning the hostel for accommodation and having a delirious conversation with my friends there, I packed on the Friday and set off once more to the Big Smoke where I was met at the station by the timpanist, Jeremy Montagu, who took me to his home for supper and to discuss what was required regarding music and instruments. The sense of unreality was heightened by the fact that the first course of our splendid meal turned out to be globe artichokes. Yorkshire was never like this, but somehow I managed and found them to be delicious, even if they did have a knack of producing more and more debris the more one ate.

After a late night of excited chatter, I found my way to Sadler's Wells

Theatre early on Saturday morning, where I was catapulted straight into a rehearsal. My sight-reading abilities were stretched to the limit, but the music was exciting and any difficulties were not insurmountable. Luckily the conductor, Simon Sadoff, was more tied to what was happening on stage than what we were doing in the pit. Sunday was a free day for the company, as the crew had to get the stage, scenery, props and lighting ready for the opening night on the Monday. This was just the opportunity I needed, so I found an empty dance studio, set up my instruments and practised all day until I had a roaring headache and spots before my eyes. At one juncture, Simon stuck his head round the door to remark that he'd never known a percussionist to practise before. I had brought numerous small instruments with me as well as many sticks and beaters, and Jeremy generously provided most of the others, with Jimmy pitching in with a super little xylophone. He lent this to me on condition that I had a crate made for it. This was no problem, as Giovanni, the company carpenter, kindly took it upon himself to do the job. Opening night flashed by in a daze of instruments and notes, and everyone seemed relieved and pleased that we had soldiered our way through everything without too many disasters. At the end of the week I had my very first proper pay packet, and could not believe my eyes when I realised that I was being paid as a principal and, in addition, there was a small supplementary fee for 'playing tuned percussion instruments'. I had never had so much money at one time, so Saturday morning was spent on Oxford Street kitting myself out for a variety of temperatures. Man-made fibres were becoming all the rage, so I was able to buy clothes that would travel reasonably well. We knew not where we would end up. Rumours had been flying, with Turkey, the Middle East and Scandinavia being tossed about as possible future locations.

Dad came to London for the final show at Sadler's Wells. I was very excited and talked nineteen to the dozen all day. Friends from the hostel also came to the performance, waving and grinning over the edge of the upper circle. The show went well and, after the rush to get everything packed securely, we all went for coffee before I saw dad off to the station to catch the midnight train back to Yorkshire. He had forgotten some socks I got him in the morning, so I trailed back to the crowded snack bar to give them to him. He looked so forlorn with his cup of tea and sausage roll that I rushed away quickly and found myself crying all the way back to the hostel. I was very miserable and didn't get to sleep until at least 2.00am It took forever to pack, but it was too late to turn back now. First stop – London Airport.

Everything to do with my first ever flight was a great novelty. This was the beginning of lots of 'firsts', as I described the BEA bus, airport, aeroplane, seating arrangements, food, air hostesses, taxiing, speed of take-off, dazzling sun above the clouds, a wrinkled English Channel, and finally the top of the Eiffel Tower in mist – everything was noted for dad.

Constantly working in a theatre was another novelty, but one with which I was to become very familiar. Curtains were 'tabs', I knew about upstage and downstage, wings and five-minute calls, learned about the clocks being set five minutes ahead of time, and then "on stage please!" It was all totally exhilarating. I discovered that the electricians and stagehands were known as The Crew, regarding them as a new breed, especially as they all had American accents. This worked both ways, of course, as being the baby of the whole company I soon became a target for good-natured teasing. Few tried to unravel my 'funny way of speaking', but many were often kind enough to lend a hand when heavy instruments needed to be handed over the edge of the orchestra pit rather than my having to lug them through narrow underground corridors and negotiate impossibly awkward steps, including iron spiral stairs.

I soon made my presence felt because, as an avid reader, I decided to create a travelling library. When the little xylophone was taken out of its crate, the magazines and paper-backed books used to pack it were rearranged in the empty crate with a notice on the lid proclaiming, "Please help yourselves, but replace any book borrowed with one of your own". Thus we had a continuous stream of books to keep our minds active throughout the whole tour; everything from trashy novels to classics in their original languages. Out of the twenty-one-piece orchestra, only four were women. Fortunately, cellist Maryse and I got on very well, although there was a difference of ten years in our ages. We often found that we were sharing hotel rooms. Ad hoc touring orchestras frequently consist of older players or non-established youngsters fresh from college. We were fortunate in having a good mix of musicians. Some were experienced theatre players, but also there were classical players, some nearing retirement age. A good stretch of well-paid work was not to be sneezed at in our overcrowded profession.

When I was in the NYO, James Bradshaw, the percussion professor, made it crystal clear that none of us was to state that he had ever taught us until he gave us specific permission to do so. When my last orchestra course rolled around, he solemnly announced to me that I could now name him as my teacher. I could not understand the full implication of all this then, but now it is clear: we had to be a credit to him. He also said to me, "If you ever go to

Berlin, then visit the Berlin Philharmonic Orchestra and give their timpanist, Herr Gerissimos Avgerinos, my best wishes, and tell him that you are one of my students."

At the time this seemed to be as likely as flying to the moon, but there I was, a mere two years later, after two weeks in gorgeous Paris, now embarking on a Berlin venture. Music is a great leveller with many tenuous and curious connections worldwide. It is rare indeed for a bunch of musicians not to have a common friend, teacher or colleague when meeting up with other groups of players. Maryse's father had come with the company as far as Berlin and the three of us went to a Berlin Philharmonic Orchestra (BPO) concert; tickets cost three marks (25p) each. Herbert von Karajan conducted Bruckner's Fifth Symphony. I noted that "the orchestra played it wonderfully – a marvellous and exciting performance, but a boring piece!" I went round the back afterwards to try to catch the timpanist, but no luck. However, I managed to arrange to see him the following day at the 10.00am rehearsal, and found Maryse with her fluent French hobnobbing with the leader (a Frenchman "so he must be brilliant!") and the principal cellist whom she had met at the Geneva Festival. We went for a drink afterwards, but it was difficult for me to keep sane when listening to German and French with only a smattering of English thrown in now and again. As usual, amazement was expressed when I said what my instrument was. We were taken back very late to the hotel in Friedrichstrasse (near to what was to become Checkpoint Charlie), but on the way we got lost and ended up at the border between the Russian and American zones. We were stopped twice by uniformed young men waving red lanterns and carrying rifles - an uncomfortable experience for naive and innocent Brits.

The following day I managed to meet up with the timpanist, who asked if I was Mr Bradshaw's daughter. When I laughed and replied that I was one of his students, he was suitably flabbergasted. Apparently there had been a big fuss when I had calmly walked into the BPO's rehearsal hall, but when I explained why I was there everyone calmed down and the players could not have been more kind. They took me onto the stage during the break, where I was invited to play some of the instruments, and then conductor Hermann Scherchen's secretary asked me if I could get her three tickets for one of our performances. I promised to do my best. (This proved to be impossible, so I never knew if they managed to pull any other strings after I telephoned with the disappointing news.)

In 1957 Berlin was still very war-torn, with skeletal wrecked buildings and piles of bomb-damaged rubble everywhere. It was impossible to imagine that Potsdam Platz near to our shabby hotel (standing alone midst collapsed buildings) had been in the heart of the city, and we were shocked when we saw the derelict shells of a huge railway station and the nearby Reichstag. Try as we might, none of us could imagine our Houses of Parliament in the same ruined state. Walking around was a real revelation. This was before the Berlin Wall had been built, so it was possible to stroll down Unter den Linden and through the Brandenburger Tor into the Russian Sector in East Berlin. It was very depressing, with mile upon mile of ruins. All the big shopping areas were totally dilapidated. There was still rationing for certain items, but if money was available it was possible to buy more luxurious goods from special stores - something akin to black market but within the law – but with prices at four times above the normal rate. Red flags were flying everywhere, especially from the apartments of party members in the main street, Stalinallee – soul-destroying and hideous, the buildings covered in cracked yellow tiles. Everywhere we looked there were shoddy, ugly apartment blocks that appeared raw and unfinished with their outer walls of uneven red brick. I was astonished to see women doing labouring work such as bricklaying, shovelling coal and mending street lamps. It was little wonder that few smiles were to be seen in this drab environment. We gradually saw more Russian edifices in East Berlin: war memorials, red flags, the huge abandoned stadium where the massive Nazi rallies were held, and Hitler's bunker. Berlin was an eye-opener for everyone in the company.

Everywhere we walked we were stared at, and when we returned from our perambulations a lady helped us by exchanging a one-mark note for a Russian five-mark note with which we were able to buy train tickets. Hard currency was at a premium. After one of the shows we went for a drink at a bar near the theatre where the English Opera Group were performing. Having done Britten's *Turn of the Screw*, some of their orchestra turned up, including Jimmy Blades, and then later on Peter Pears, Benjamin Britten and soprano Jennifer Vyvyan joined the group. A bouquet of huge chrysanthemums was donated to our table, and then, after much nattering, we all went home to our respective hotels. The next evening saw Jimmy and some of the others at our show. I was really glad that I had practised so hard – it wouldn't do to be a disappointment to him.

My trip to the timpani factory with Herr Avgerinos was a great success. He spent most of the day kindly showing me round the city, and after lunch he introduced me to his pet camera shop as well as music and instrument shops.

61

As prices seemed very reasonable, I bought a tambourine, a siren and a pair of hard cymbal beaters. All in all, a very pleasing day.

Poland also came as a big shock. People had queued all night for tickets for all of our shows, and everywhere we went we caused a mild sensation. In Poznan I had decided to go early to the theatre, but on the way I stopped to look into a bookshop window. As I stood there, I began to realise that a crowd was forming behind me. It slowly dawned on me that people were trying to see my clothes (a red mohair stole, white courtelle jumper, non-crease grey pinafore dress, nylons and black high-heeled sandals) and, as more and more stopped to see what the fuss was about, the traffic came to a halt and we had the beginnings of a major jam on our hands. No one spoke English, but everyone was friendly and intrigued by this creature seemingly from another planet.

I beat a hasty retreat back to the hotel, where I put on a coat and sensible shoes, and I eventually managed to arrive at the theatre in one piece. When the xylo came out of its case, one of the Polish stagehands mimed that he would like to look at one of the magazines, so I was only too pleased to hand him a *Woman* magazine. He stood in wonder looking at the colour photos, and in particular at an advertisement for perfume with the inevitable gorgeous woman and glamorous background. It was obvious that he could not take it all in, as he kept shaking his head and looking enquiringly at us, saying in essence, "Is this true?" When I gave a magazine to the young girl serving tea in our canteen, she burst into tears of delight and immediately hid it. We discovered later that Western newspapers and magazines were forbidden but worth their weight in gold, as they were used for copying up-to-date styles and women's fashions. Clothes were of very poor quality, and fashions were about ten years behind ours.

One of the problems we faced in Poland was trying to work out the exchange rate but, as there were two rates of exchange, this was nigh on impossible. Officially there were 25 zlotys to the dollar, but the black market rate was 180 zlotys to the dollar (or 60zl = £1.00 sterling), but in reality, since hard currency was at a premium, the rate could be as much as 300zl to the pound, which meant that it was almost impossible to deduce the cost of anything, particularly as prices changed week by week.

We were supposed to do all our journeys at night so that we could not see anything of the areas we were travelling through: endless, sparse birch forests, dingy, run-down villages and flat winter countryside as far as the eye could see. However, thanks to the bureaucracy's legendary inefficiency, in fact we saw plenty. We learnt that no one could leave the country, except for holidays, which was a farce as it was not possible to take any money beyond the borders. The only chance for Polish people to see outside their own country was to camp, taking all their food with them.

Polish food came as another shock to the system. Vodka may have flowed like water, but every main meal in all the hotels was the same: veal cutlets, plain boiled potatoes and peas with chopped, mixed carrots and turnips. Dessert was usually a piece of luridly iced cake or, if we were lucky, ice cream. It was not unusual for local people to stop us in the street and ask, "Amerikanski?" On being told, "No, British", they would get very excited, with much arm-waving, often accompanied by tears. Somehow they would convey that a relative had fought for the 'Breetish Air Force' in such places as 'Sousehampton'. Older people would stroke an arm or pat a hand, and we wished that we could communicate properly. Our American Dance Company was the first Western group to visit since before the war, so it is little wonder then that they brought in the crowds. We were a huge success, with packed houses every night.

A very enthusiastic audience turned up for the first show, with more people outside the theatre looking at us as we arrived. Halfway through one of my more awkward xylophone solos the lights failed, but from sheer devilment I finished a chromatic run and managed, by pure fluke, to land on the correct note. It was pitch dark, electricians were running about, and then the curtain was dropped down. Someone announced to the sympathetic audience that it was a general power cut and this was received with roars of laughter. The lights soon went up again, and during the interval everyone said how funny my efforts had been. In the second half, at the climax of one of the most dramatic dances, the lights failed again, to predictable groans from the audience. During dinner that night, a few of the dancers came over to us and congratulated me for the xylo effort, whereupon Simon, our conductor, stood me on a chair and crowned me 'Miss Percussion, Poznan 1957' and we all had a good laugh.

One of the joys of this tour was the opportunity to play and hear a great variety of music, from Vivaldi and Purcell to Poulenc and contemporary South American composers. I turned pages for Simon, who played the piano in Poulenc's *Trio for Oboe, Bassoon and Piano*. Only the first movement was used, but even now, whenever I hear it, I mentally hear the ghostly thump of tabs crashing down after the final bar of that movement. One day I was persuaded to try out some piano duets newly purchased by Simon. Not a one to refuse, I nervously agreed and, of course, thoroughly enjoyed the experience. Chamber music was bought in Poland and often little knots of players could be heard enjoying other repertoire. Scarlatti keyboard sonatas and Bartók's difficult *Gyermekeknek* headed my list, with some crazy Polish dances thrown in for good measure.

A visit to Auschwitz concentration camp was a sobering event. As a small child during the war I had no idea that such places existed, of course. Youngsters were kept in innocent ignorance even when questions arose. For instance, my mother noted that when a stray stick of bombs was dropped on Halifax I was told that the noise was that of "men mending trains". My puzzled disbelief soon turned to stony misery as we looked upon all the items left in the wake of the murdering Nazis. It was only then I realised why there was such antipathy towards the German language, often the only way to communicate for us.

Warsaw had been the first Polish city to be rebuilt after the war. Everything was restored as much as possible to what it had been. The curious aspect of all this was that areas such as the old city were newly plastered and freshly painted and somehow looked like lovely stage sets. We played in the Palace of Culture, a huge wedding cake-like edifice built by the Russians and truly hated by the Poles, but greeted by our American friends as, "Gee! A skyscraper!" Inside was the multi-purpose hall where we did our performances. This could accommodate an audience of three thousand, but with no pit, and no wings or facilities on stage for hanging scenery or 'flats'. As the crew struggled with many problems, some of us went on a city bus tour. One of the areas we saw was the levelled area of rubble that had once been the Jewish Ghetto, systematically eliminated during the battle for Warsaw. More pleasurable was a recital of Chopin's music by a leading Polish pianist, and then it was back to the hotel for my trouser-pressing service. I could work wonders with a damp towel and my little travel iron, and consequently 'my men' looked smart for the capital city performances. In a way I felt that I was thanking them for the unstinting help they gave me at the end of shows when lots of instruments had to be carted out of the pit and packed away for the next venue.

I was still starry-eyed when we moved on to doing exhausting and disorienting one-night-stands in Germany, Belgium and Holland. There were constant changes of programme, so one had to be on one's toes to be sure to have the correct music and instruments ready for 'curtain up' every night. Local television stations were quick to include some of the dances and dancers in their arts programmes, and we all became used to reporters pointing cameras and asking questions.

On the fourth Thursday in November, we again left the West and travelled by train across Europe to Ljubljana in Yugoslavia. There was a curious air of suppressed excitement on board the Trans-European Express, and the dancers, with whom we were now firm friends, seemed distracted and non-responsive towards the musicians. All became clear, however, when we were well into the journey, as an excited bunch of youngsters burst into the carriages with, "Come on, this way … Happy Thanksgiving!" The dining car had been requisitioned and for the next few hours we had a wonderful Thanksgiving party courtesy of all our American friends. They had gone to the trouble of having special menu cards printed and had tried to stick to traditional fare as much as possible. Wine flowed, and a very happy company eventually arrived yet again on the eastern side of the Iron Curtain.

Yugoslavia, another war-torn country, felt even more foreign to us. We were warned never to take photographs of bridges, customs posts and soldiers, and to "keep a low profile". There seemed to be little or no eye contact in these communist countries; no one smiled and there was an air of suspicion everywhere. On every landing in the hotel in Belgrade there was a plain wooden table where an elderly stone-faced woman sat, keeping an eye on the comings and goings of the hotel visitors. This was most unnerving, but we were told that it was simply a way of providing full employment for the whole population. We weren't convinced.

From Ljubljana we travelled by private buses for hours over the mountains to the Adriatic coastal resort of Rijeka, to a theatre with one of the largest stages in Europe. At one point in our journey the rough road ended abruptly and we found ourselves bumping over a dry river bed to join up with a new road some hundreds of metres further on. Luckily the tough tyres stood the battering and we eventually arrived safely, if shaken. The furthest south we went was to Sarajevo, which in December has a temperature of many degrees below zero. The river was frozen into waves and curious contours, sleighs and sleds were the normal mode of transport and we wore every scrap of clothing we could. I was enchanted by the eastern aspects of the town: men in baggy trousers wearing scarlet fezzes, veiled women, minarets, mosques and a souk to satisfy any market addict. I tried my skill at bargaining and eventually became the delighted owner of a copper coffee pot, which I had seen being made by a cross-legged, dark-skinned man in a tiny stall heated by a charcoal brazier. This was very exotic, made all the more so when we were

65

told that we were on the crossroads between Europe and Asia.

Then we headed back north again to Novi Sad, which was a small garrison town, packed with young soldiers. When we arrived at the theatre we were greeted by the sight of our crew sitting outside on rolled-up scenery flats playing cards. As we knew that it took a minimum of four hours to set up, we realised that there would be no performance that night. It turned out that the local theatre had also been booked by an amateur company and that there was no shifting them out of the building. After checking into the filthiest hotel I have ever encountered, we discovered that everyone was on holiday for one day, so we joined the young troops for an outdoor cinema presentation – an interesting experience, but one that meant nothing to us, as we did not understand a single word of what was going on. The next afternoon we gave a free performance for the town and the theatre was packed. Honour satisfied!

The tour provided a fabulous kaleidoscope of impressions: hard work, thousands of miles travelled, diverse customs, languages, countries and foods, and, last but not least, a sense of growing up. I learned to have more confidence in what I was doing, and on returning home from Portugal on Christmas Eve I knew that at least £300 waited for me in a bank account thanks to modest savings from the weekly pay. Freshly picked oranges, lemons, sweetcorn (never seen in Yorkshire), pomegranates, apricots, grapes and finally a jar of honey – they all travelled north with me in a new basket bought specially for the occasion. I arrived home with a suitcase stuffed with souvenirs: silver filigree jewellery, leather wallet and purse, silk scarves, carved boxes, the copper coffee pot, pretty glassware and pottery. We had a good Christmas that year and I doubt if I drew breath for days, determined as I was to share my adventures with dad and the rest of the family.

* * *

No more dithering. After Christmas I decided to try again in London. My first taste of being a real professional player made me long to be more independent. Three friends from the hostel also wanted to stretch their wings, so we searched around until we found a small flat to rent in less than salubrious Kilburn, a few miles north of the city centre. The little house in Leinster Road was typical of many terraced houses, and was split horizontally into three small flats. Two gay guys had a most charming bijou residence on the top floor, awash with subtle lighting and fluffy cushions; a very quiet brother and sister occupied a somewhat dreary flat sandwiched in the middle, and we four lively lasses had the ground floor. Fortunately, we all got on very well indeed. Cheerful Irish Chris from the attic region worked as a kitchen skivvy in Buckingham Palace, so there were times when he came home after posh banquets with such leftovers as huge amounts of thick cream, smoked salmon, exotic fruits and foreign breads. He would have been in serious trouble if his superiors had found out but, as he said, everyone did it. One night he failed to return home and eventually a distraught Barry discovered that he had spent all night in jail. Apparently there had been some junketing at the Palace, which had got a bit out of hand as it spilled over in a tube train. When the police arrived and asked for addresses, Chris gave his as Buckingham Palace and was rewarded with a night behind bars to cool his heels at Her Majesty's pleasure.

It was at this juncture that I decided to stop worrying about my future. I was not going to starve, come what may, so everything else would be a bonus. Bits of work fluttered in, and, when I was booked to go out of town on short ballet tours, another music student slotted in nicely for that period in the flat, paying the rent and practising on my newly acquired ancient upright piano. Our landlord was a volatile Hungarian, but I suspect that he had a soft spot for us, as he was very generous when it came to agreeing to some of our more individual requests. Mice had been spotted in the kitchen, so I persuaded Mr Bland to let us have a cat. Sandy Cotton-Evans-Smith-Smith was the grand name we gave our tiny ball of pale ginger fluff. He fitted onto the palm of my hand when we first got him, and spent most of his waking hours peering out from underneath the furniture with round golden eyes. But eventually he became a fine mouser, and was spoiled by everyone, including Mr Bland.

One big step for womankind occurred when I was invited to play at Covent Garden Opera House. I had been introduced to Reg Barker, the principal percussionist, by one of the BBC players. He was a lovely teddy bear of a family man, with children of about my age. Word had apparently got round about this skinny Yorkshire kid and I found that, once again, some of the well-established players were kindness personified. Reg invited me to spend the occasional weekend with his folks: son, daughter and wife Kitty. It was lovely to be part of that generous and warm family. We all had lots of laughs and any anxieties about the future were totally forgotten for a while. I was whisked off to the seaside for family picnics, feeling thoroughly at home with them and being included in a normal family if only for a brief time. Then one day Reg phoned to ask me if I would like to play at *The Garden*. Would I?! I turned up for a Wednesday afternoon matinee and found myself playing triangle underneath the stage apron, at the very back of the pit. No rehearsal, of course. The familiar ballet was *Swan Lake* and the conductor was flabbergasted to see me in the then all-male orchestra (with the exception of the harpist I guess).

My father had sent my old-fashioned sit-up-and-beg bicycle during my college year, so transport costs were cut as I cycled everywhere possible. It was quite a feat to take a bag containing heavy cymbals from Kilburn to Morley College in South Kensington, but nothing deterred me. Negotiating such hazards as Oxford Street and Marble Arch was a bit unnerving, but I certainly learnt to find my way around the city, part cycling, part walking. When I needed to move larger instruments around, I found a willing, tame taxi driver to help. He was a good-natured cockney, totally reliable and kind. Nothing ever fazed him – instruments came first, and then I was shoved into the taxi. We always managed somehow. During the summer, when work was not available, I dusted off my short black dress and presented myself as a waitress at a tiny omelette bar off Park Lane. At least I could have one decent meal a day and know that the rent would be paid. The result of this experience was that I became a dab hand at omelette making.

London was not my favourite place to live, as I felt totally at odds with the overcrowded streets, lack of countryside and general claustrophobic atmosphere during the summer months. Suddenly I had had enough, so, with a meagre budget of £10 and my toothbrush, pyjamas and plenty of sandwiches and apples in my bike basket, I was all set for an adventure. South seemed to be the answer, so I decided to explore the Cinque Ports.

At the outset of my escapade, typical British summer weather almost finished me off with torrential rain on the main road leading south out of the big city. However, a kind lorry driver spotted my predicament, stopped me, threw the bike into the open truck and took me like a drowned rat on to Tunbridge Wells, where a friend from college lived. This is where I learnt a very hard lesson. Having been brought up to "say what you mean, and mean what you say", I had imagined, without question, that this was a philosophy set in concrete, which everyone understood and adhered to. A rude awakening to the joys of greys, rather than the black and white I had always known, came, however, when I presented myself at the door of cello friend Alison's parents' house. Alison's "Do pop in for a cup of tea if you are ever passing" had been in my mind until her mother opened the door. Then, in a flash of horrified comprehension, I suddenly realised that southerners did not behave in the same way as northerners, and that dropping in unannounced was

68

unheard of. Covered with embarrassment, I made an ungainly and hasty retreat, licking my wounds as I ploughed on further south.

After that experience I was always cautious when dealing with anyone south of my own familiar territory. I managed to enjoy plenty of fresh air, stay in two very modest bed and breakfast cottages, visit three of the Cinque Ports, and still scrape together enough money to get myself and the bike back to London by train from Canterbury.

The Academy courses never covered how to deal with such things as tax, insurance, keeping track of life in diary form, or indeed anything useful appertaining to survival as a professional musician, although I had the foresight to join the Musicians' Union before going to the RAM, having discovered that all professional players were required to be members. When lack of work loomed large enough to make an oncoming rent day a worry, I steadfastly refused to go on the dole, but stayed at home, crossing my fingers for more funds to materialise from somewhere – anywhere. I got as far as applying for assistance, but when it came to it I could not face queuing up in that ignominious fashion with all the other poor souls. Starving seemed much more preferable for my personal dignity.

One day a knock on the door heralded a young woman who announced herself as the local tax inspector. In my naivety I thought that, as I was constantly on the breadline and doing nothing but domestic chores for weeks on end, I would not be liable for income tax. Not so. However, a curious coincidence let me off the hook. The young woman was from my old school in Huddersfield and only a few years older than me. She proceeded to give me a serious lecture, pointing out that ignorance was no excuse for not paying tax. "But I don't have any money!" I bleated. I knew that pleading absence of funds should not have cut any ice either, but on this occasion I was let off with a warning. Another lesson learnt.

Such was life in London. We went to anything that was free and queued for hours to see our heroes at the theatre and cinema – in the cheapest seats, of course. Once when Jimmy Blades asked me if I was doing anything on a particular Friday evening (he needed a player for an amateur orchestra), I replied that I was going to the Old Vic with my friends to see my idol Laurence Olivier in Shakespeare's *Titus Andronicus*.

"Oh, Larry's a friend of mine!" chirped Jimmy. I was deeply impressed, and even more so when he continued, "I did all his films for him, you know. In *Hamlet,* when the ghost appeared, we draped Vivien Leigh's fur coat over a bass drum and tapped through it to make the sound of muffled heartbeats."

69

He had already told me that he was responsible for the gong sound at the beginning of the J Arthur Rank films, and that the huge bronze instrument that appeared on screen was in fact a cardboard model. He recorded the sound every six months and no doubt made a fortune from it. (I was later introduced to the real gong and had the pleasure of playing it for myself.)

Once again, in early September, another ballet company hit the road and, once again, I was invited to be part of the orchestra. The Edinburgh International Ballet Company (conductor in Scotland, Charles Mackerras) began at the Edinburgh Festival, and then followed in the footsteps of the American company the previous year. The only difference was that when we arrived in Yugoslavia it was discovered that there were no funds whatsoever in the coffers. The company was bankrupt. The curtain was rung down for the final time and everyone was called on stage to be given the ghastly news. We were sworn to secrecy, and the very next day we sneaked out of the country on worthless tickets, leaving debts behind and salaries unpaid – our own amongst them. Unfortunately, the large instruments that had to be transported by the company were taken into custody by Customs and Excise and held as collateral for creditors. I returned to London having lost a large amount of money and without my instruments. The musicians concerned hired a lawyer, helped by the Musicians' Union, and we discovered where the instruments were being held. I went with my lovely, tame taxi to a warehouse in St Johns Wood and remember crying real tears, begging them to let me have my own belongings back. It was no good, and I went home empty-handed. Word got round about this, of course, and eventually, after being lent instruments by Jimmy Blades and others, I managed to retrieve the precious tools of my trade. By law, these should not have been impounded, but it took some time and expense for justice to be done in the matter.

Pantomime seasons brought long stretches of work for all, and I found myself playing for a huge production of *Where the Rainbow Ends* at the massive Stoll Theatre. Alicia Markova was the prima ballerina, with Anton Dolin as her partner. Witnessing bitchiness on the scale displayed here was a real eye-opener, with screaming rages, sulks, stamping of dainty feet, pouting and ersatz tears adding to the overall effect. We in the pit thought that it was great sport. There was everything in the production: animals, flying witches, lost children, snowstorms, transformation scenes. In fact, it was very difficult to keep one's mind on the music, especially as I had to be able to see everything so that I could get my sound effects to coincide with bits of stage business. A hotchpotch of music was used, from Tchaikovsky to Victorian-style aural wallpaper, and we acquired enough absurd quotations to last us a lifetime. It was a great surreal experience.

Touring the country was a curious way to earn a crust, with grisly theatre digs to endure and lots of hanging about in grim towns during the day. Musically speaking, we got through a wide repertoire. I played at the very end of the Carl Rosa Opera Company reign, the Festival Ballet and the touring Royal Ballet. It was good to be out of London, but musically the artistic standards left a lot to be desired. We shared accommodation with the dancers, and I was surprised to discover that all the companies had 'strong men' who were the ones who held up the climactic piles of dancers with such apparent ease. These guys also seemed to be the ones who would trawl through every newspaper at breakfast time and bemoan their fate. No jobs seemed suitable as they sifted through the advertisements, sighing and complaining. Other company members took this in their stride; it was a normal, everyday routine. We musicians looked on and thought our secret thoughts. Sunday, as on all tours, was the changeover day, and then we were on the move again, just like wandering gypsies.

During my time in London, my father made an effort to meet, as he put it, 'girl friends': ladies of a certain maturity who were footloose if not particularly fancy-free. He sheepishly introduced me to one or two new friends, but eventually popped the question to Alice, a quiet, independent woman of about his age. I was delighted when they married, but managed to avoid an appearance as bridesmaid, as I explained that my toehold in a precarious profession might be jeopardised if I refused work 'for whatever reason'. This seemed logical to me at the time, but in retrospect I realise that I was being deeply self-centred. Fortunately, the problem never arose, as I was without employment at the time of the wedding, and I was truly delighted that dad had found another soulmate; one who was to be with him over the next four decades.

In spring 1959, there was a job advertised in Birmingham. This was potential groundbreaking territory, as a percussionist was needed in the CBSO: a percussionist, not a timpanist, but one of the boys; a member of the 100% male team in any orchestra. As already noted, Joyce Aldous had made her mark many years previously as timpanist of the Hallé Orchestra and more recently Pat Brady had joined the BBC Symphony Orchestra. But women percussionists were not on contract in any professional orchestra in the UK. Yet again, I was encouraged to have a go, be brave and accept the challenge. I discovered much later that Reg Barker and James Blades had both sent letters of recommendation to the CBSO management. I sent off my letter of application, and was pulled in for an audition in early 1959 at the tender age of twenty-one.

5
CBSO Overture and Beginnings

Auditions for percussionists inevitably take on an air of the surreal, as the whole point is that a player should implement his art within the framework of the whole orchestra, not alone on a concert platform with only the timpanist and general manager in attendance, which is what happened when I duly presented myself at Birmingham Town Hall in February 1959. The fact that I was a female must have given much pause for thought, but I was oblivious to any of this when I arrived with my selection of personal sticks and beaters and a head full of memorised nasty bits from the orchestral repertoire. Xylophone, glockenspiel, vibraphone – 'tuned percussion' in general – held no fears for me as I was a pianist, but I was not comfortable with the snare drum. However, I knew that Don Thomas, the resident principal percussionist, was a good snare drum player having heard him often in the by-then defunct Yorkshire Symphony Orchestra (YSO). He rarely played much 'bird seed' (a theatre term for tuned percussion instruments – all that pecking) when he was in the YSO. Indeed, I guessed that he was uncomfortable with these instruments, as he always appeared on stage before numerous performances long before the rest of the orchestra, to practise any tricky corners with silent rubber beaters. I therefore staked my chances on the maxim of 'stick to what you are good at' by concentrating on the tune stuff.

Having done a quick appraisal of the array of unfamiliar instruments on the town hall stage, I played through my own selection of difficult bits and pieces from the repertoire, and was required to sight-read not only percussion parts, but also some timpani music. Fortunately, I was quick-witted and sailed through the careful selection without any trouble. The final task was to play the heavy orchestral cymbals, offering a range of dynamics, the control needed for pianissimo notes being far more taxing than that needed for a good, honest fortissimo crash. The piece on the music stand was Rachmaninov's Piano Concerto No 2: pianissimo cymbal writing that gently highlights one of his famous, well-loved tunes. This was to prove that I, as a slender girl, could do just that. Much was made of the novelty value of my femininity, however, and I had to field some blunt queries about how I thought that I would cope with working in a strictly all-male environment. The fact that Don was absent from the audition made me curious because, as the only percussionist on contract, he should have been present at all auditions for a second player. I eventually learnt that, although he was aware that auditions were going to be held, he was not told the dates and times of these events. It was not until much later that he discovered who had applied for the job and he had to accept the fact that, in this instance, the timpanist had had the final word, eventually presenting Don with a fait accompli. Having learnt that fifteen men had competed for the position, I was astonished to be offered a batch of concerts for a trial period with the orchestra. There were twelve in all, including a number of schools' concerts in Leeds Town Hall, one of my old stamping grounds.

Birmingham as a city came as a total surprise to me in early spring. I had imagined, no doubt with the majority of the UK population, that Birmingham would be grimly industrial everywhere – not so from the top of the No. 50 bus. It was very fortunate for me that my father's youngest sister and family lived five miles from the city centre in leafy Kings Heath, so at least I had wonderful support from my own clan, and a bed for the night whenever I needed one. Every garden was bursting with blossom and spring flowers, the city boasting many parks with fine, mature forest trees, flower beds and lakes. As morning rehearsals were customary on concert days, I often used the free afternoons to wander around, savouring the sights and sounds of the UK's second city. A free morning was always perceived as true free time, leaving the rest of the day for rehearsal followed by the concert. In my experience, however, a free afternoon was not so productive, as time was nibbled into with travelling back and forth to one's home. After coming down to earth domestically, one then had to get into the right frame of mind yet again, prior to the performance in the evening. Players fought long and hard over many years to change the practice of morning rehearsals and, with few exceptions, afternoon rehearsals are now accepted practice for Birmingham concert days.

1959 saw the beginnings of the regeneration of the city, with the innovative Bull Ring Shopping Centre at an advanced planning stage. The idea that one could shop in a specially designated area with a variety of undercover shops – the first such scheme in the country – was a novelty and marvel for the citizens. There were many mixed feelings, however, when some of the fine Victorian buildings were demolished to make way for a new Birmingham. Chaos reigned, but with some purpose. Brummies were totally phlegmatic about not knowing how to get from A to B on their own patch. I was bemused to observe and eventually understand the heavily accented chit-chat and banter that went on between total strangers during this period. An air of

74

subdued excitement prevailed and I was delighted to be part of it.

Meanwhile, it never crossed my mind that anyone would be the least bit interested in the fact that a young girl had appeared as a percussionist in the orchestra. Being a few weeks short of my twenty-second birthday, slim to the point of being skinny, with a mass of fair reddish hair and of medium height, I certainly did not fit the stereotype of a big butch guy playing all those physically demanding boys' toys. Nevertheless, on April 23rd 1959, after the twelve trial concerts, I was offered and accepted a contract to play sub-principal percussion. As far as I know, I was the first ever female to venture into a percussion team of a professional symphony orchestra, and was the baby of the CBSO for three years. At that time, incidentally, there were only eight women in the orchestra.

Crossing the great divide from being a mad-keen amateur into the realms of serious professionalism was a shock to the system, which took some time to come to terms with. Initially, the practicalities of this seemed insurmountable, but one inevitably got on with it, bit by bit.

In London I had managed to collect a certain number of items conducive to my life as an independent young woman. To my surprise, I discovered a burgeoning interest in cooking and so, remembering my mother's advice, I saved for the best quality possible within my budget and bought a set of copper-bottomed saucepans (still in use today) and various small kitchen tools. Sandy Cotton-Evans-Smith-Smith needed a travel basket and I needed to offload a piano and a pair of hand-tuned timpani. Advertisements on the RAM noticeboard did the trick for the musical items, and more suitcases and large holdalls were bought in readiness for a gargantuan packing session, after which we – the cat and I – travelled guard's van and third class respectively. A transfer to the local train for Sutton Coldfield, some ten miles north of Birmingham's city centre, got us to a taxi, and then we completed the final short distance to my new abode in the shape of a rented room in the garden flat of Daphne, one of the viola players in the orchestra.

My new landlady was a large middle-aged lady, unmarried and old-fashioned. Fortunately, she loved cats and was delighted to have Sandy – a quiet, pretty beast – as part of her little household. He was equally happy with his new home and the freedom of large Victorian gardens, often presenting us with many furry gifts thoughtfully dismembered into bite-sized portions. My room was very small, but I bought a cosy old wing chair in a house sale and, with family photographs and a few fresh flowers, made it into my very own space. Daphne had a very presentable baby grand piano, which she encouraged me to play, to the mutual benefit of the instrument and myself. It was not long after I arrived that a bright, chatty Welsh violinist also came and rented a room in the flat. Lexey was bubbly and positive. I had never before met anyone that was so confident about revealing her innermost feelings about most things, so it took some time for me to come to terms with her eulogies and overt enjoyment of nature: trees, sunsets, flowers, gardens, views – everything was discussed freely. We gritty northerners appreciated such delights but I, for one, had never discovered how to express in words how I felt about them. I learnt a lot from Lexey and we became firm friends.

No longer living from hand to mouth or having to worry about where the next cash input would be coming from was a great novelty. Now I was able to settle down to a proper life, one of irregular hours, but a more established, reliable existence. Naturally the rent had to be paid every week, and a big leap forward occurred when I discovered where the local launderette was. Some kind of normality was beginning to manifest itself.

Train was our main mode of transport into Birmingham, and I usually caught an earlier one than my string colleagues unless, of course, it was a non-percussion programme, when I was as free as a bird (and still being paid!) The contract stated that we were not allowed to play with any other professional group unless we had written permission from the management. Neither were we allowed to contact the press or media in any way. Teaching was allowed, however – a saving grace for players with families, being a regular supplement to the less than adequate salaries. Everyone had to belong to the Musicians' Union, and in my naivety I was bemused and amazed to discover that the orchestra had a shop steward, just like a factory. If anyone was too ill to go to work, a doctor's note had to be produced immediately; the only slight relaxation to this strict rule being if a wind player had to attend an emergency dental session.

My first undertaking was to look the part. Luckily, I already possessed 'short black'. No doubt it was very ageing for daywear, but it came home to me that I was now a *real* musician, with a wardrobe full of necessary black drag. A small case was bought for carting everything needed for out-of-town concerts, and I was ready for anything.

Most of the men wore suits, white shirts and ties for rehearsal. Casual wear was not the fashion for work. The only exception was the appearance of short-sleeved cotton shirts in summer, but only in extremely hot weather. Anoraks were becoming a popular novelty, but we had to think hard before we could recall that curious, strange-sounding name for a zipped casual jacket. If anyone sported a daring checked shirt, there would be sure to be comments from colleagues, probably with reference to cowboys, and it was not done for any of the women to wear trousers. My usual attire was a simple, smart dress, high-heeled shoes, discreet make-up and a neat hairsyle.

The nearest I got to being informally dressed was when I wore a chunky pullover and tweed skirt in an attempt to offset the bitter cold in cathedrals. Concert wear in these instances posed an entirely different problem. The men never wore dinner jackets on these occasions (neither was there any applause in a churches or cathedrals), so they could pile on the layers under their formal dark suits. Women were in 'short black', which could be anything from cocktail-style dresses to smart winter dresses, and we would gaze enviously at the audience muffled up in woollies and fur coats, our only assets being brightly coloured knee-length thermal 'long johns'. When we were getting ready in the confines of some tiny stone-clad room in a freezing cathedral, there was many a time when an impromptu Follies-style line-up with kicking legs, giggling and a flash of coloured underwear caused us to be late onto the platform, much to the curiosity of our male colleagues and the irritation of the orchestra manager. These winter endurance tests were nicknamed 'double-gusset days' by the CBSO ladies.

It took a long time to work out how to fit in sensible living: shopping, hair washing, laundry, piano practice, and visiting dad. Eventually, I developed a fine automatic pilot, which enabled me to count bars, often without conscious thought. In trickier scores, the fail-safe was always to keep checking with one's nearest colleague, mouthing, "Where are we?" Or, if one was solely accountable for the next entry, then the responsibility to play in the correct place was on one's own shoulders. In time, it was possible to relax a little as more music became familiar and I became more experienced at the game. Music is usually divided into sensible sections, normally designated by a letter of the alphabet or numbers. The end of a musical phrase is frequently the logical indicator for the next letter or number change, but, if the score is modern, difficult and complicated (like a Fair Isle knitting pattern?), we all need to concentrate intensely, ticking off the signposts with a visible twitch of a finger, keeping in discreet contact with each other.

As the music rarely appeared prior to a rehearsal, I was often in a state of anxiety and on my guard, because every time I opened the percussion folder there was something in it that I had not seen before. No one else apparently had any problems with the familiar repertoire in the changing programmes. But my constant anxieties had obviously been observed by colleagues, so much so that one day I was given an unforgettable boost by 'Rusty' (Albert Russell), a fatherly Yorkshire fiddle player. We spoke the same language, so it was a great comfort when he put his arm round my shoulders, gave me a hug and said, with a smile, "Eh, lass … don't look so worried, you're doing all right!" After that I was able to take a more objective overview of my own musical contributions to the orchestra, but still found it hard to come to terms with what I quickly perceived to be the very strange relationship that existed between my two closest colleagues.

There is a distinct division between timpani and percussion in a symphony orchestra; indeed, they are regarded as two separate sections. For instance, if a conductor asks for *percussion*, the timpanist (a section principal in the orchestral hierarchy) will sit in glorious isolation, the king of all he surveys and surrounded by his kettledrums, and will not expect to play. The remaining percussionists (headed by their own section principal) play everything else except timpani. All have been trained to play timpani and, if required by the music, will do so, but in those far-off days it was a rare timpanist who could be persuaded to cross the boundary to play any of the countless interesting instruments in the percussion department nearby, even for a doubling fee. It simply was not done.

Ernest Parsons, the CBSO timpanist, however, was an exception to this rule. As there were only two contracted percussionists, Don Thomas and myself, Ernie often chipped in uninvited with various bits of percussion from his position behind the timpani. My heart would sink when I observed a triangle hanging on his music stand, or a suspended cymbal lurking somewhere beyond the farthest timp. Don, of course, saw this as gross interference in his section (just the two of us), so I soon discovered exactly how blinkered and childish some seasoned adults could be. There was no love lost between the two of them and sparks often flew. I know now that the rest of the orchestra looked on with some amusement, as Ernie had frequently crossed swords with many colleagues. Something of an institution, he had been in the orchestra since its foundation in 1920 and thus he reckoned that he knew all that was worth knowing about the orchestra and expected to rule the roost as its Grand Old Man, as indeed he regarded himself. Nicknamed Snakey, Ernie was totally unpredictable – nice as pie one minute, and the next, for no apparent reason that I could ever ascertain, explosive, rude and unreasonable. This was very unnerving to one who had never encountered this kind of erratic behaviour before. Dark mutterings developed into bursts of scarlet-faced ranting fury, accompanied by the slamming of the flat of his hands on the drum heads and timpani sticks thrown onto the ground – never too far away for him to pick up again, I observed, but flung hard enough for an audible effect.

This situation was not helped by the fact that money was not often forthcoming for the booking of extra percussionists from outside the orchestra. The management cheerfully programmed pieces written for four or more percussionists, leaving the two of us to cope as best we could. I often found myself struggling to get around a ridiculous number of instruments. Holst's *Planets* suite and Rimsky-Korsakov's colourful *Scheherazade* and *Capriccio Espagnol* were particular nightmares, with Britten's *Young Person's Guide to the Orchestra* (YPG) coming top of the list for unbelievable stress. A composite part had been cobbled together for me for the latter, but it was never a happy experience. It was a case of valiantly trying to be true to the composers on little or no rehearsal time, and endeavouring to cover as much as possible of the percussion score – dodging from one instrument to another whilst attempting to look calm, as it would never do to worry the audience by our frantic antics. Ever afterwards I was usually the one in the team to be asked to cope with 'bits parts', for instance juggling with gong, tambourine and triangle on three copies of music: one copy = one instrument – a case of 'must always look serene and don't panic'! Unbelievably, I also became adept at playing bass drum and cymbals simultaneously, another indefensible economy measure. A cymbal was fixed on top of the bass drum, whereupon I played it with its partner in my left hand, the right hand holding a double-headed bass-drum beater, all the better to play drum rolls with. It was something of a circus act, which Sir Adrian Boult eventually spotted and immediately nipped in the bud.

On the rare occasions when an extra player was engaged, the management usually booked a theatre drummer from Walsall in the Black Country: Jim Beaumont. Jimmy was a small, cheerful, elderly man who owned a tiny jeweller's shop, specialising in selling and repairing clocks and watches. He would breeze into a rehearsal to be greeted by numerous colleagues who needed his daytime services. Anything requiring his attention would be stowed away in a battered leather briefcase, which stayed in sight on stage. We once heard a muffled alarm clock go off during a concert, but otherwise all remained peaceful. I had a habit of taking off my watch prior to performing, and if we were out of town I would pop it into Don or Jim's pocket for safe keeping until after the show, there being no pockets in my evening dress. One day Jim came into rehearsal and handed me my watch. He had taken it home and given it a good clean, not realising that I had only intended to park it temporarily in his pocket.

As Mr E. A. Parsons of Parsons Drum Co. Ltd, Ernie had numerous instruments to hand. Many of these were used in the orchestra, and indeed it was generally expected that players should supply as many instruments as possible. Whilst in London I had continued to expand my collection of instruments, so I now felt that I was making a modest contribution to the orchestra's stock.

One of Ernie's more bizarre ploys was to remove one or more of his personally owned percussion instruments from the platform between the rehearsal and concert. For example, his gong, stand and large beater could vanish in a fit of invented, inexplicable pique before a performance of Tchaikovsky's *Pathetique* symphony, where it was needed for the sonorous single gong stroke in the finale. This was something of a worry, to say the least, necessitating either Don or I hanging around like artistic guard dogs for the period in question, before the old man stomped off for his tea. Everyone seemed aware of these mood swings, and the general consensus of opinion was that they were very much tied in with the phases of the moon. In spite of all this, I was never comfortable referring to a man of his age and experience by his first name and, as a well-brought-up youngster would have preferred to call him Mr Parsons. However, I was now, if not exactly one of the boys, at least a real professional, earning a real wage.

Ernie Parsons was not alone in possessing a volatile temperament: Don had his difficult moments too, and this must have caused much speculation amongst my colleagues. Indeed, Rusty had drawn a cartoon of a pantomime horse pulling in two directions at once, with Don and Ernie's heads at either end. This was ridden by yours truly waving drumsticks instead of a whip. However, it was soon torn down from the noticeboard by one of the protagonists and sadly I never saw it. In printed concert programmes Don was identified as Donald V. Thomas. He always insisted that the V stood for Vesuvius and, had I been more mature, I would have seen this as a major clue to his character. Other fantasies of his were that he owned a lion and that he was the strongest fellow in the country. Built like a bulldog and of medium height, he was somewhat intimidating, but he could also be sentimental to the point of being maudlin, showing a very soft and protective side towards 'his section' should anyone have any reason to criticise our modus operandi. He also had a great love of music, but for some reason or other this was something he would never admit to unless he had had a few drinks. He lavished lots of affection on his large, eccentric boxer dog, which eventually had to be put down because of dangerous behaviour; after which there were four months of unexplained, impenetrable non-communication. I soon realised that, in his own way, he could be as moody as Ernie, veering from madcap behaviour to black, silent, intense glooms. One minute he would scoop me up, chair and all, and whirl me around the rehearsal hall, and the next I was in the doghouse for some enigmatic misdemeanour. "You KNOW!" he would snarl, and then he would stamp off without further explanation. This erratic behaviour was trying, exhausting, puzzling and frightening – I was too young to handle it, and yet also too stubbornly independent to ask for advice or help from those more able to explain his conduct. I felt that this would have been an admission of feminine weakness, so behaved in a stoical manner and kept my worries and opinions to myself.

By the nature of the job, percussion players are somewhat clannish. So much time is needed for setting up instruments beforehand and clearing them away afterwards that there is little occasion for them to socialise with other players except, perhaps, when we are on the move to another town.

When the orchestra played away from Birmingham Town Hall, whether at a rehearsal space in the city or at an out-of-town venue, the instruments were transported by two medium-sized removal vans. In 1959 the firm used was always the same: Brown's Removals, with 'Who's (sic) Van is This?' emblazoned on the side. Two cheery brothers were the driver and porter, aided and abetted by a pair of large retired policemen, Albert and Reg, who were general handymen and permanent fixtures in the orchestra. Folding music stands were carried in heavy metal ammunition boxes, whilst the music folders were carted in a large, square basket-skip with rope handles. Nothing was too much trouble as Tony and his brother lugged impossible shapes up inaccessible stairs, and they were always willing to add their muscles to the more awkward aspects of our job. For instance, division of labour was necessary when it came to moving the large concert xylophone. This awkward but fragile instrument had to be dismantled and crated whenever it left the town hall and then reassembled ready to play, the latter being the responsibility of players, after which the platform staff carried it onto the stage. A team effort was necessary – a cause of much finger pinching and cursing from Don and myself – especially if there was the coach to catch from some far-flung outpost after a tough concert. The men would heave things like tubular bells, timpani and bass drum, but for some undisclosed reason the line was drawn at the awkward, weighty gong, which we also had to bed

81

down in its crate. There was no respite if lots of percussion was needed. After all the heaving and lugging about of instruments and stands, we then had to play. I was expected to pull my weight the same as the men, and only once was there a near-disaster as the xylo frame collapsed on top of me when the two of us were trying to get it up the steps to the town hall stage in one piece, rather than in more time-consuming separate sections.

The quick thinking of a horn player averted one other potential neck-breaking disaster. I was trundling off the steep platform in Leicester's De Montfort Hall, loaded up with heavy instrument stands, when a heel caught in the hem of my long dress. Fortunately, I had the wit to yell and was grabbed by the said horn player, who hauled me back to safety. It was a very nasty moment. After that incident I went to see Eddie Edwards, the general manager of the orchestra (no chief executives in those days), and asked permission to wear evening trousers on the more lethal platforms. He was not happy at the prospect but, after quizzing me thoroughly about what these proposed evening trousers would look like, he reluctantly agreed to allow such a garment in his orchestra, but only if *absolutely* necessary. He also added the comment that, "If I had been manager at the time you had applied for the job, you wouldn't have been offered an audition as a girl playing percussion. But, as you do have the job now, and you're making a good go at it, good luck to you!" "Thanks a bundle", I said to myself. But at the time this was a normal response, and many a time I was criticised for "taking a man's job" – usually by older male orchestra members. A favourite taunt from one colleague whenever he saw me was, "WOMEN in orchestras!", accompanied by appropriate face-pulling.

I just took all this as part of life, and thanked my lucky stars that I was in work and doing what I would have done for love, but having the additional bonus of a weekly wage. This, by the way, was doled out as near to Friday as possible, depending on the orchestra schedule. The secretary from the finance department was escorted for the five-minute walk from the offices, and then names were called out in alphabetical order and small brown wage packets, containing real cash, were produced from an anonymous shopping bag. As a sub-principal player I earned £15 10s 0d (£15.50) per week; the rank-and-file players (or tutti as they are known now) earning the princely sum of £13.00 per week. To put this in a more realistic context, in the early 1960s four gallons of petrol cost £1.00, the rent for my tiny shared flatlet was £4 10s 0d (£4.50) per week, and I paid the enormous sum of £35.00 for a pair of new Zyldjian cymbals - the equivalent of more than two weeks' wages.

Before long I was able to acquire my first vehicle: a brand new Austin A35 van, which cost £420 including road tax. I paid half immediately and the rest in weekly instalments. Vans cost less than the equivalent A35 car, as they had no side windows and therefore were taxed differently. When it came to learning to drive, I asked around and discovered that the tuba player's son Roger, a fireman, was a dab hand as a driving instructor. We got on famously, and once I had mastered the basics there were plenty of colleagues living locally who were generous enough to sit by me as the legally required qualified driver as I gained more experience. My first driving test was a nightmare: the van stalled in a cloud of blue smoke (over-choked) and I nearly put the examiner through the windscreen as I came 'in on the downbeat' when his hand slapped the clipboard for the emergency stop: no seat belts in those days. I struggled nervously through torrential winter rain in the dark during a busy winter teatime, and failed the test. The second attempt, with the same examiner, did not include an emergency stop, but I passed with flying colours. In those days it was rare to see a young woman in charge of a vehicle, as only one in ten car drivers were female, so I became used to being stopped by the police in the dead of night wanting to know where I had been and what I had in the van. At the time I thought that this was amusing, but now I would resent the implication of dark deeds afoot.

As an onlooker, I had imagined that an orchestra was a starry-eyed bunch of dedicated other-planet souls, definitely not of this world. When I entered this apparently rarefied atmosphere I discovered, for a start, that the Birmingham orchestra consisted of musicians from all over the country - nay, the world. We had players from Australia, Holland, Germany, South Africa, Eastern Europe, and all corners of the British Isles. In fact, it was quite unusual to hear a Birmingham accent, but the Scots had good representation and numerous northern twangs made me feel welcome and at home. The CBSO was known as the jumping-off orchestra for the 'Big Smoke', in other words the bright lights of a London orchestra. I just felt very comfortable with the family atmosphere. Meeting the wives and babysitting for children of colleagues were all part of the overall scene.

There are many skills in a symphony orchestra, with numerous players having first-class talents other than their musical ability. I discovered that a qualified lawyer had reverted to his first love of music, we had mathematics and physics graduates, and more than one person was studying for a further degree from the Open University. Sitting on a coach for hours on end is useful for private study if one does not suffer from travel sickness, but hobbies were usually of a singular or solitary nature.

An occupation with such irregular hours was not conducive to joining activities such as evening classes, or regular team sports, as we could never be relied upon to finish a specific course of study or plan anything too far ahead. When I lived in Sutton Coldfield I managed to go to the local art school for pottery classes, but only because these were on a Monday, the one night in the week when we were very rarely required by the orchestra. This lasted for a year only, after which the class night was changed. It also dawned on me that one might spend a lot of time in a sedentary fashion, so I decided to take up horse riding instead. There were plenty of farms and stables nearby, so I took the bit between my, and the horse's, teeth and had a go. Lindy, my teacher, was just nineteen and we got on very well. The horses were enormous and made me nervous, but eventually I managed to stay on more than fall off and enjoyed my countryside experiences. (This intermittent hobby eventually came into its own when my daughter, at the age of nine, won an *Observer* competition, the prize being a ten-day holiday on a luxurious dude Ranch on the Santa Fe Trail in Arizona. We were wild cowboys on huge, roughly schooled horses – stop, start, left, right! – in cactus country. Galloping and vulgar whooping came very naturally to both of us, cushioned as we were by comfortable Western saddles. No falling off allowed.)

Gardening is a favourite creative occupation for many musicians, but even that can bring hazards. For example, I remember when the leader of the orchestra was told in no uncertain terms that he was "paid to lead a symphony orchestra and not to prune roses", after he had run a thorn into a finger and had been forced to take a few days off sick until he could play again. On another occasion, a viola player could be seen knitting tiny garments for his first-born, and one of the timpanists knitted wonderful designer numbers, his elaborate creations resembling some of the more adventurous modern music scores.

Within the orchestra we have inventors, writers, skilled photographers and DIY fanatics, with composing and teaching being normal sidelines for others, and of course the inevitable computer enthusiasts. Sports are often of an individual nature: indeed, some years ago, on one of the American tours, one of the cellists was cheered on in the Boston Marathon by many of his colleagues. Cycling is an obsession with one of the woodwind players, so much so that he takes his lightweight folding bike on every tour, be it to America, Hong Kong, Japan or further afield to South America. Swimming and gym workouts are healthy pursuits for a good majority, and some risk injury to hands and mouths in intermittent team sports. Life has to be lived. The orchestra fields cricket and football teams when time and schedules permit. Matches are arranged with other visiting orchestras and opera and ballet companies, or when the orchestra is away on tour. It came as no surprise when our football players were demolished in a 'friendly' match by the super-fit Royal Ballet team; they were far superior to our more sedentary symphony players.

After two years in Sutton Coldfield I moved to within four miles of the town hall, this being much more convenient. Moseley is a district that attracts a mixed population with every kind of profession, occupation, colour and creed. Many musicians lived in this stimulating area, and I was delighted to share a tiny flat on the ground floor of a tall Victorian house with Anne, a bass player in the orchestra. As she spent most of her time staying with her domineering bassoonist boyfriend, I often had the place to myself, together with the cat, of course. These arrangement gave her an address should her parents wish to contact her, and I very quickly learnt to be the soul of discretion. It was at this time that I began to experience a social life.

Every two weeks or so, huge parties were thrown, usually on Friday evenings. One nearby enormous Victorian edifice housed three massive flats and had an extensive garden and its own dark and murky frog-filled swimming pool. The flats' tenants included medics, architects and musicians, so there was always a good mix of young professionals at any gathering. Fairy lights were hung in the old trees and a band was pulled together from CBSO players and friends from the BBC Midland Light Orchestra. Hunks of strong cheese were plonked on the kitchen table, with whole loaves, and butter still in wraps. Nothing sophisticated here. Until this point in my life, I had never heard of a 'bottle party', and indeed did not like alcohol. As soon as this fact was discovered, it seemed to me that all the lads felt that it was necessary to change this state of affairs. I only came a cropper once when some cynical character spiked my orange juice with vodka. After that unpleasant experience I learnt to drink plain tonic water, and then everyone left me alone thinking that I was working my way down the gin bottle. The junketings went on late into the night, when in desperation the neighbours called the police in a vain attempt to curb our excessive noise. The other party venue was in a much smaller semi-detached house, also in Moseley. The cellist owner had painted the empty front room in unrelieved black from floor to ceiling, and this was where loud music, amorous designs and smoochy dancing took place. No one asked embarrassing questions, as we all knew the score when it came to entering the Gloom Room.

Life became a kaleidoscope of experiences as I became familiar with the day-to-day workings of a professional orchestra. Monthly schedules, or 'duty sheets' as they were known then, were dished out – an essential reference for everyone. These precious diaries covered everything we needed to know about rehearsal and concert times, venues, programmes, conductors, soloists, dress required and travel times. Whenever anyone observes that a local amateur orchestra can put on a concert "every bit as good as a professional orchestra", I take a deep breath and trot out a few facts and figures gleaned from any one of the scores of schedules I have kept over the years, and then leave that person to think it through. We perform in and away from our own hall, covering hundreds of miles by coach. We also make recordings for radio, television and recording companies, play for every kind of audience, perform in schools and attend many, many rehearsal days, and, yes, we have free days too; all this with private practice slotted in whenever possible. In the bad old days, travel days were noted as *'Free Day*: orchestra travels to Brighton', or wherever.

Two coaches were, and still are, used for out-of-town days. If one wishes to go by private transport, then it is a matter of self-funding and being responsible for turning up on time. If a coach is late, then it is a management problem and everyone can relax. There are always a large number of players who travel independently, however, sharing lifts and often creating a mini-convoy on well-worn routes. On one occasion I travelled as a pillion passenger on the back of a powerful motorbike when we were doing schools concerts in Leeds Town Hall. There were no motorways, so my cellist friend and I set off at the crack of dawn to go the pretty way through some of the wilder parts of the country, where, in spite of forward planning, we managed to run out of petrol in a remote part of the Derbyshire Peak District. Fortunately, there was a farmer nearby with a tractor, so somehow fuel was siphoned into the motorbike's tank and we were off on our merry way once more. I found this particularly unnerving, as I always liked to get to a rehearsal early for obvious setting-up reasons.

The next Yorkshire trip was to Sheffield, this time by coach. On this particular route we always broke our journey in the market square in Ripley, dashing to our favourite *greasy spoon café* for the obligatory cup of tea.

"Ello, luv, are you going far?" This from an ancient local, observing the gaggle of young brass players and myself enjoying our cuppas.

"No, not really. We're just playing in Sheffield." The orchestra coaches were nearby, suitably labelled for all to see.

"Oh, I see. That's nice. What time do you start then?"

"Half past two, on the dot!"

He smiled and pondered a while. Meanwhile, the orchestra manager had stuck his head round the door and called us.

As we rushed out to the coaches, the old boy waved a hand and called out, "Well, cheerio then – I 'ope you win"!

During holiday periods, our regular coach drivers were sent on more lucrative journeys further afield. This meant that we were fobbed off with the older, less reliable coaches and drivers who were unfamiliar with our forays into the delights of small Midland towns. Bedworth is one such nearby town, but in the early '60s was without a concert hall, so we used to play in a large secondary school hall just outside the centre. A disgruntled driver turned up to take one of the two coaches to the afternoon schools concert. In spite of all our efforts, he did not want to communicate, so we chatted to each other and let him get on with it. Nothing went right from the outset. To begin with, he ran out of fuel, but luckily the other coach was behind us and so was able to get a can of petrol from a nearby garage where we eventually filled up. The other coach left, after which our grumpy driver managed to prang a car in his angst to get ahead at some traffic lights. Details were exchanged and the atmosphere grew more tense as we ploughed on, only to lose our way on the byroads. Too stubborn to ask for directions, he managed to get us into a farmyard, whereupon the men got out and with difficulty manhandled the coach for a reverse retreat down the muddy track. After that he really got mad: time was getting short and Don and I were beginning to get agitated as the afternoon children's concert was one that set out to highlight the percussion section, and we had our music on board. The driver put his foot down and was immediately stopped by a police patrol car for speeding. We arrived to find that the concert had started and that Ernie was valiantly trying to cope with a rendition of Chabrier's colourful *España*, playing as much as he could remember and physically get to. It was a noble effort. Ah, but the day had not yet ended! It was discovered that the programmes for the evening concert were in the locked coach parked nearby. There was no sign of the driver, so the orchestra manager had to break in to retrieve them. A telephone call to the transport firm resulted in another driver being sent out to bring us home. This was perhaps as well, as Mr Miserable was discovered drowning his sorrows in a nearby pub. Needless to say, he was sacked on the spot.

In those days the coaches always started from and returned to the town hall with no pick-ups on the way, even when passing by the house of one of the horn players. This situation could not continue, especially after numerous problems trying to catch the midnight buses. Landing after midnight meant that we were into overtime, so there was often a risky race as we approached the city limits, with ironic countdowns from the more militant members of the merry band. The final straw came when one of the violists discovered that his car wheels had been removed in a supposedly safe city centre car park. Meetings were held and at long last the two coaches were given two routes, in and out, through the city from the outskirts. It was then a far simpler matter to agree on sensible, safe pick-up spots and peace reigned once more. Any aspiring members are always advised about the coach routes, and eventually little enclaves of CBSO players were established in specific districts in the city – something that remains to this day.

6
Early Daze

When I was at the Royal Academy of Music, we were told that if an orchestra ever employed us, on no account were we to speak to conductors or members of the management team: it was *not done*. These inhibitions lasted for many years, well into my career in the CBSO, and I was more than happy to comply with such unwritten rules. It was customary to address conductors, if at all, as 'Mr' or as in Boult, 'Sir Adrian'.

In the early '60s, players were referred to by instrument or as 'Mr' or 'Miss': none of the women was ever addressed as 'Mrs' even though there were married couples within the orchestra. We women kept our maiden names and so, for instance, I was always Miss Cotton, even when heavily pregnant. The men were named in the personnel list in the programmes by their initial and then surname or, if principal players, full first name and surname. If extra players had not been booked before the programmes were printed, they were always quaintly listed as 'A. N. Other'. The accepted etiquette within an orchestra during rehearsals is that the conductor speaks 'through' the principal of a section and not to an individual player. Any problems are then sorted out within the section with the principal as spokesman rather than across the orchestra. It stands to reason that, if there were as many as one hundred players on stage, chaos would reign if everyone had a say in what was going on. Rules are bent, however, when it comes to the percussion clan, as each player is responsible for many different instruments, usually resulting in our being addressed by whichever instrument we are responsible for at the time. There are times though, when we will appeal *sotto voce* to our section principal to "Speak to him, boss ..." if a finicky maestro is being particularly irritating or obtuse. It is then the duty of the percussion chief to sort out any problems with the conductor. Serious disagreements or misunderstandings between the conductor and players have a final line of appeal – via the leader. It is his or her job to smooth out more difficult issues and, if necessary, call a coffee break so that any breakdown in communication can be resolved *in camera*.

At first I felt that I was blundering from one schedule to the next, blindly taking each day as it presented itself, but eventually the irregular working days became more predictable as I became familiar with the overall work schedule. I became more comfortable with the large working group and soon acquired many nicknames: thirteen at one count (Phyllis, Margarita, Magorama, Ginge, Girlie, Young 'un and Mags, to name but a few). Harold Gray frequently introduced me to total strangers as, "Oh, this is Clanger", and was forever referring to our section in rehearsal as "Gentlemen of the Percussion" - just teasing.

Conductors came and went, but I soon realised that indeed the one constant figure in all this was Harold Gray, a much-loved local musician and the only conductor, as far as I could see, whom everyone referred to by his first name. He was the organist at Sutton Coldfield Parish Church and teacher and conductor at the Birmingham School of Music, and he played a major part in the choral life of the Midlands, especially in Birmingham where he conducted the Birmingham Choral Union for many years. A one-time secretary to Sir Adrian Boult, Harold was always there, come rain or shine, ready to step in at the last minute should a conductor fail to materialise for whatever reason and at whatever late hour. At one point Harold even took over the running of the orchestra for some months after the sudden death of general manager Eddie Edwards. Dear Harold was reliable, amiable, totally professional and loved for what became a fifty-year association with the orchestra, earning the highest accolade of all as far as the players are concerned – he never got in the way of the music. We always felt that we were in the same boat: he loved his music. Affectionate recollections abound at the memory of his almost inaudible, tuneless, breathy whistling of favourite melodies during rehearsals (left hand in his jacket pocket, baton parked, eyes on score and right hand twiddling fingers in the air), or the audible clunk of cufflinks at the almighty downbeat after a particular silent pause in Rimsky Korsakov's *Scheherazade*. And it only needed a bland straightening of hair above an eyebrow by an orchestra wag for everyone to grin in recognition of one of Harold's familiar mannerisms. In all the years I worked for him, I cannot remember him ever being less than courteous, although at times he could be tediously pedantic and alarmingly vague.

"Harold, does that ornament come before or on the beat?"

"Oh? ... yes! Er ... thank you, gentlemen," would come the reply, and off we would go again with no one any the wiser, but it somehow didn't seem fair to pursue the matter.

The nearest he came to putting his foot down was his oft repeated, mild request of "Follow me, boys!" or announcing, "Start again at the beginning, it saves going back." One of his more maddening quirks was the way in which he chose to show us that he was, after all, in charge. He would never reveal his rehearsal plans at the start of a day's work. Instead, he would vaguely plough through a piece and then announce, "We'll come back to that later, ladies and gentlemen." This frequently meant that we percussionists would find ourselves hanging around all day waiting to play through the final throes of a sparsely scored scrap of music, only to be told ten minutes before the end of rehearsal that we would not be needed, "thank you". No explanation would be forthcoming, just a vague smile and an unspoken "I'm in charge, and you are paid to be here" – understandable, but irritating nevertheless. All his years of loyal service to the orchestra were rightly rewarded by an OBE in 1974 and, on his retirement in 1979, Harold was awarded the title of Conductor Emeritus for life, much to everyone's delight.

Bread-and-butter fees for the orchestra came from schools concerts. We played for children far and wide, usually just doing as we were bid, but eventually a day arrived when we found it necessary to question seriously the work schedules.

Late one evening we travelled to Newcastle upon Tyne by road, and the following day we gave a late-morning schools concert in the City Hall. After lunch we boarded two coaches and sped to Leeds, where we did a late rehearsal in the town hall followed by a full evening concert. It was only when we were back on the coaches and homeward-bound that it dawned on us that in a single day we had given two concerts, plus had one rehearsal, and had travelled by coach from Newcastle to Birmingham via Leeds, some 218 miles. This, of course, was totally unacceptable, and ever afterwards it was the responsibility of a Players' Committee member to check the advanced work schedule and nip in the bud any future plans of this ilk. The management certainly got its pound of flesh on that occasion.

Years later, in the heady days of Rattle's reign, we realised that our working practice had changed little when, in 1992, we appeared at the prestigious Aldeburgh Festival. I noted that, "At the end of this working day the orchestra will have been nine hours on a coach (approximately 400 miles), done a ninety-minute rehearsal and a performance, returning home after the concert."

The Birmingham Education Authority paid out a substantial amount annually for its orchestra to spread music around the city. I soon discovered that the orchestra split into five sections and that each of these covered four junior schools every day for at least one week in May. This must have been a nightmare to organise, but somehow we all arrived at our destinations, often unable to remember if we had eaten lunch, or where we were in the day. Initially, I found that I was playing in Section A, in other words a small light orchestra (Harold at the helm), with Section B being a string orchestra. These large groups trundled around the city in coaches, and I often found myself on map duty at the front, clutching the Birmingham A-Z and trying not to get us lost. We took turns at this. Separate brass and woodwind groups travelled around in their own cars and a solo violinist was also sent to four schools a day, primarily to play for the youngest children. When it was realised that I was a pianist, however, it was decided that I should initially join the four string principals (including the leader of the orchestra, Wilfred Lehmann) as their accompanist, travelling everywhere crammed into an old-fashioned black cab.

The formula for our school visits consisted of a movement from a string quartet and then individual short pieces with piano – violin, viola, cello – after which we ended with another movement of a quartet. Interspersed in all this was a demonstration by Wilf, who explained how his violin was constructed and intrigued the children by loosening the bow so that they could see the hank of horsehair hanging free. As the others had been down this road many, many times, they did not bother to rehearse anything with me, and I found myself sight-reading some very awkward choice numbers. The viola principal, Sammy Spinak, took great delight in trying out all kinds of difficult pieces with me as his tame pianist. He would test my sight-reading skills to the limits with, for instance, a Hindemith Viola Sonata saying, "Let's try a bit of this, Girlie!" I felt that this was cheating and hardly conducive to encouraging a love of music in young children, but as a mere percussion player I dare not complain. Problems frequently arose when the school piano was so out of tune that it was impossible to use it with the stringed instruments. This meant that I would bow out gracefully, sit in the staff room and read a book.

One day, however, Wilf decided that it was about time that I earned my crust, so he thrust his violin at me and said something to the effect, "You've heard me do this often enough, so *you* have a go. Bob (principal second violin) will do any playing you need for demonstrating!", and then he temporarily departed. What he had failed to tell me was that his violin was a Stradivarius. The others informed me of this after my first effort, and, as I could not think of any way to avoid further 'demonstrations', I decided to be positive and savour the frisson of delight (terror?) when showing the children that superb instrument. Shortly after this encounter, Wilf asked me if I would rehearse with him as he was learning Walton's Violin Concerto and needed a pianist to, as he put it, "sketch in the orchestral part from a piano reduction". Oh, the innocence of it. I agreed, not knowing what I was letting myself in for, but I consequently found that every waking minute was spent trying to get my head and fingers round the difficult piano/orchestra transcription in the hope that I would not let him or myself down. I tenaciously slaved through it and confess to feeling a certain pride when I eventually sat in the audience to hear Sir Adrian Boult conduct the real performance in all its glory. The upshot of this was that when Wilf and his wife returned to his native Australia they very kindly gave me one of their music cabinets as a very generous thank-you present. I was delighted – another problem solved as the elegant cabinet neatly swallowed up large amounts of my piano music.

A light orchestra with only one percussionist was not ideal, so when a new violinist arrived who also happened to be a good keyboard player, she took on the mantle of pianist with the quartet and I reverted to my rightful place at the back of Section A. We travelled by coach, which set off from the city centre at 8.30am, or one blearily drove one's own car if the schools were within spitting distance of home. Instrument cases had been packed after the one and only run-through on the previous day, and a van loaded. This arrived before the musicians at the first school, with time being allowed for the stage to be set and folding music stands unfurled, the orchestra being totally self-sufficient in this respect. On arrival at a new school, as we doggedly piled out of the coach, we never knew what our reception would be like. Some schools resented the intrusion of a bunch of musicians disturbing their timetable. This was made patently obvious by the fact that there would be no one there to greet us, we had to find the hall ourselves, and our platform staff had to request chairs for the players. Children were marched into the concert in rigid silence and, as soon as the programme ended, they trooped out again and we were left to the delights of finding the next school on the list. Most of the schools, however, were very pleased to have a break in their usual routine and welcomed us with open arms and cups of tea. Favourite venues were the ones where small girls had made copious amounts of knobbly biscuits and were shyly standing around looking after our teatime requirements.

Some of the music we dished up to these children was tedious to the extreme, and one wondered who had dreamed up such unimaginative programmes for unsuspecting youngsters and often musically uninformed teachers. This state of affairs would eventually change as arts organisations recognised the old adage that 'interest' has to come first before 'education', and that we should try to meet everyone halfway with something familiar. But in those days the fare was purely classical and rarely of the children's own century. We flogged through bits of Beethoven, Grieg and Dvorák, a dreary *Sleeping Beauty*, a non-merry *Merry Wives of Windsor* overture, acres of Mozart and scraps of well-worn ballet music. It was mostly lacklustre with the occasional nightmarish highlight, such as a snare drum being unseated and pulled over onto the glockenspiel with a tremendous clatter. That woke everyone up!

Worse than school visits were the Junior Schools Music Festivals in early summer. The city was divided into geographical areas, each of these supplying schools to perform the same programme with items from recorder groups, music and movement, simple choir pieces based on nursery rhymes, folk songs or arrangements of children's poems by the city's Music Adviser: a cornucopia of juvenile bits and pieces. By the time the final show bit the dust in the town hall, Birmingham's professional symphony orchestra had rehearsed and played these bland programmes twelve times, so it was understandable that morale was very low indeed.

One of the perks for the Music Adviser was that he got the opportunity to conduct a real orchestra in one or two short orchestral items. This was translated as him 'playing with (and over-winding?) a very expensive train set' by the more cynical members of the band. Unfortunately, music advisers were often blessed with delusions of grandeur, as the acquisition of that little white baton immediately went to their heads. One such adviser was charmless to the extreme, treating the players like recalcitrant school kids and with poorly disguised contempt. We were required to play Liadov's delightful *Musical Box* in one of the music festivals: a little gem scored for woodwind and glockenspiel. To us, the pattern of notes was simple, but the maestro of the day was incapable of conducting one beat per bar. He had problems with the fact that the accented pulse went across the bar lines, giving a delightful mechanical lilt to the musical box (*one* two *three* /one *two* three /*one* two *three* /one *two* three, and so on ...). In no time our volatile principal flautist cracked, stood up, angrily waved his flute and protested, "Why don't you just go home, take your liver pills and let us get on with it!" There was an imperceptible pause before the full score was hurled to the ground and the boss-man stomped angrily off the platform. As he went, Tony the flautist craned his neck round and grinned at me, and we then started the *Musical Box* with the first few bell-like glockenspiel notes. We wound up the musical box and then let it run down, letting it get gradually slower and slower before the final tiny tinkling notes ended the piece. Who needs a conductor? We certainly did not have one for that part of the concert, and sighs of relief could be heard all round from the musicians.

The other memorable effort was from the principal percussionist of many years, Doug Milne. Another Mr Big from the Education Department seemed unable to beat time quickly for some reason or other, so everything took on the air of a dirge. Doug managed to curb his irritation until we came to play the 'Farandole' from Bizet's *L'Arlésienne* suite. This is a lively dance, which starts with a solo drum beating out a simple, quick, four notes to the bar. All we got from the rostrum was a laboured directive bearing no resemblance whatsoever to the composer's metronome markings. A plan was hatched and the woodwind players promised to follow the drum. When it came to the concert, Doug put his head down and cracked off at the correct tempo, hidden by his music stand. There was nothing the conductor could do apart from mouthing, gesturing, turning scarlet and otherwise looking apoplectic. Woodwind valiantly followed suit and an exciting time was had by all. The audience loved it, but, immediately the interval arrived, Doug was summoned to the Green Room to account for his behaviour. "Oh, I thought that you were beating one in a bar" was the innocent rejoinder when he was questioned by the egotistical part-timer. There was no answer to that.

In the early '60s there seemed to be numerous soloists who did not perform from memory, and, since percussionists were not often required for concerti, I found that I was always the one to be given the dubious honour of turning pages for them. My worst nightmare came after an overture one evening at a town hall concert, where a capacity audience was in attendance to hear a favourite violinist. I had already changed out of my concert dress and was ready to fly the coop when a breathless orchestra manager burst into the room with, "Get changed, you're turning pages for Campoli. Quick, quick!" Using the score had been a last-minute decision by the soloist, and there was no discussion as I hurriedly threw my evening skirt over a tweed skirt and street shoes. There was an expectant hush in the hall as I self-consciously edged through the orchestra to the front of the platform, pink in the face and just a little flustered. Neither did it help to hear little whispers of "Give us a song!" and "Do you come here often?" and suchlike from amused colleagues. The platform staff had hastily found a chair for me, which turned out to be one of the town hall's huge Edwardian horsehair and carved oak horrors, normally parked in our band room. These monstrosities must have been the most uncomfortable chairs in the entire world and, without a piano to hide behind,

I felt like Alice in Wonderland perched bolt upright, waiting for the soloist. I had never turned pages for a violinist before, so I sat there worrying about which side to approach the music from and eyeing the music stand with suspicion. I knew this stand of old. It was one of the 'travelling' stands which, given half a 'chance, would collapse in a folded heap. When the soloist Campoli entered, it was to tumultuous applause. He took his bow and then, during the long orchestral tutti before his first entry in Elgar's Violin Concerto, he turned to me and whispered, "Can you get the stand a leetle higher, dear?" I half rose, heart sinking, and as gracefully as possible fought with the stand. It was no good, the wretched thing would not budge, so I'm afraid that he had to put up with it being less than a perfect height for him. Not having seen the part before, I was not sure when the cadenza came as one dared not take one's eyes off the part to look ahead. This precipitated a cliff-hanging situation: whether to whip the page over, only to find that the soloist was ploughing into the cadenza regardless; or not to whip the page over, in the hope that the cadenza was committed to memory. How dare a mere page-turner presume that the soloist needs the music for the cadenza? All this went on in my mind during the music.

Turning for a violinist is very awkward: one is always in the way, with the added worry of having to handle thin and insubstantial music likely to fall off the stand anyway. Somehow, though, the pages got turned as unobtrusively as possible, my eyes out on stalks and counting bars under my breath whilst following the notes, to cover all contingencies. At the end, the audience went crazy. There were grins all round and genuine acknowledgement from the players too. I sat still, applauding and feeling very self-conscious as the soloist gestured for the orchestra to take a bow. He went off the platform, and when he returned for his second accolade he turned to me, held out his hand, and graciously got me to my feet for a special 'thank you' in front of the crowd. I grinned, went scarlet and was delighted. It was worth all the angst to be involved in that particular performance, and to meet such a charming and well-loved soloist.

Another nightmare I recall was that of turning pages for a tense and temperamental pianist who was giving the first performance of a fiendishly difficult concerto. My presence went by unacknowledged, the soloist having enough to do trying to sort out the myriads of notes on every page. As the part was sometimes written in three staves, there was only space for one or two bars of the complicated stuff across a double-page spread. This meant that I was half standing throughout the piece, alert and ready to zip over the pages every few seconds. Being a percussionist was, for that performance, a godsend. There was no time to follow the actual music as it flew by and spread itself across the whole of the keyboard. One hundred per cent concentration was the name of the game as I counted the beats and bars through gritted teeth, checking on the rehearsal numbers whilst handling the whiplash page-turns. I have a feeling that this was one of those times when we gave the first and last performance of a piece, both rolled into one, as I doubt if it has ever seen the light of day again since that inauspicious premiere. At the time it certainly seemed like a fight to the death, and to this day I cannot remember whether the orchestra or the pianist won. The audience applauded, our hero stood amidst perspiration and exhaustion – and his brave page-turner sat back and thought that there must be an easier way to earn a crust.

It looks so easy, doesn't it? Someone sits by a soloist calmly and unobtrusively turning the music pages. He or she vanishes at the end of the performance and no one thinks any more about it. Be not deceived. This is one of the most terrifying jobs anyone can be asked to do on a concert platform. The responsibility is enormous, with the need for conspicuous calm, serenity and quiet confidence. The soloist has to be able to trust those page-turns: not too early, and certainly not too late. Each one has to be perfect, and they have to be inaudible. It is not easy to rise gracefully, reach over the piano keyboard and turn dog-eared, collapsing paper with any kind of cool composure. Oh, and another thing – one has to be *nice to be near*, but not over-perfumed. There is nothing more calculated to sap one's confidence than the soloist whispering (immediately prior to beginning some pianistic marathon) that the carefully chosen, subtle perfume is 'off-putting'. Yes, it happened to me, but I am pleased to say that I was not the unfortunate soul who had a large buckled belt fall off onto the keyboard during a high-powered and serious Radio 3 live piano recital. Oh, what an embarrassment. For the page-turner, then, no large sleeves, no dangling jewellery, no bright colours, and certainly no large cufflinks. This is definitely a crucial supporting role, should it be recognised at all. Oh, yes - and how or when does one arrive on the platform for chamber music or a solo recital? I usually stalk onto the starkly empty stage with attempted dignity, clutching music and praying that I have remembered all the repeats and back-to-the-beginnings in the minuet and trio movement. Sometimes a prior stage entry is not possible and the only solution is to shadow the soloist, slinking smoothly into the seat provided. Then, of course, the hapless page-turner is stranded at the end, feeling self-conscious sitting by the piano, or worse still by a violinist's lone music stand and applauding with a fixed smile. One feels as large as an elephant, when all one wants to be is a shy, retiring flower.

Occasionally, pages have to be turned by and for colleagues during orchestral concerts. There was a never-to-be-forgotten nightmare during the exacting solo violin part in Strauss's *Ein Heldenleben*, when the number two violinist turned two pages in error for the leader. He, of course, was well into his stride by that time and ploughed merrily on, playing what was in front of him with growing amazement. Half the orchestra realised what had happened, so jumped the appropriate pages accordingly, whilst the leader hopped back to where it had all begun to unravel. Needless to say, there was a glorious shambles and it all ground to an ignominious brief halt. A quick pause, stock taken and off again. I wonder how many in the audience noticed? We in the percussion clan often have to lean over to do a great 'boarding house reach' (pass the salt?) to turn some impossible part for a colleague. Contemporary music in particular is laced with personally pencilled instructions such as "Turn for snare drum" or whatever, or the offending bits from the top of the left-hand page are scribbled out in the gap at the bottom of the previous sheet, to be squinted and wondered at by others that follow. The most exciting efforts come when the pages are all attached to each other in concertina-style. This is supposed to enable the player to unfold three sheets at a time across one music stand. The only trouble with this is that, if anything goes awry, there is trouble to pay, and a heap of unfolded paper on the floor!

Something as simple as pages being turned can give a clue as to how the music is about to proceed. For instance, at the end of a slow movement the conductor may pause, take stock, and then continue with a blazing finale to the end of the piece; or, he may go straight into a last movement without any pause at all. It is as well for everyone to have been informed about this, as it would not do for the players to be caught out. The 'inside' string players (not the ones nearest to the audience) have the responsibility of continuity in this respect, so if they lean over to do a quick turn a few bars before the end of a slow movement, one can usually guarantee that the conductor will dive straight into the next movement without any perceptible gap. However, some egomaniacs on the rostrum regard this as "I'll show them who's the boss!" territory, changing their minds during the performance and throwing all prearrangement out of the window. One has experienced conductors who have deliberately put down the baton after everyone is prepared and tense for a final onslaught (all pages turned, fiddles at the ready), slowly and deliberately mopped his oh-so-artistic brow and then, as soon as the players relax, the baton is whipped up again and "Look who has the final say!" is written clearly for all to see except, of course, the dear, trusting audiences, who rarely notice these power games and who just believe all the glory that they read in the programme notes and newspapers.

Long stretches of working days were normal. Indeed, I remember that in one busy patch eleven full days had been scheduled without a break. Travel days, as previously mentioned, were regarded as 'free' days by the powers-that-be; hence, 'Free Day: orchestra travels to Cardiff.' Such long trips (pre-motorways) were to enable the orchestra to stay overnight, the cost of which being offset by schools concerts the following morning (Leeds, Newcastle, Bristol, Swansea, and so on). Then, of course, we were back on track with a full afternoon's rehearsal, evening concert and return coach journey. One such return trip from Bristol was ever memorable, not only by the fact that we stopped off at a huge roadhouse-style pub for refreshment, but that I had a bizarre stroke of luck. A curious incident occurred in the bar as we watched a customer playing the fruit machine (for all he was worth, it appeared). He observed us watching and beckoned me over to the machine with, "Can you come and stand by me, love? You have a lucky face." This naturally was greeted by ribald remarks from my friends, whereupon the machine was activated and our gambler pal promptly won the jackpot! Coins poured out and scattered everywhere, there was a great shout and I was rewarded with a fistful of sixpences, much to my amused embarrassment.

It had never occurred to me that being a professional musician needed physical stamina. However, I discovered that I had the enviable knack of being able to take catnaps during hectic days, after which I would wake up bright-eyed and furry, ready for the off again. Underneath the band-room table is a good spot for this, as one is out of the way but still able to hear the general murmur of pre-concert preparations and be awake in time to gather wits, tidy hair and switch into concert mode.

The concept of actually 'going to work' when I presented myself for a day of music making took some time to get used to. My many musical heroes were casually referred to with cool familiarity by colleagues, and titles of pieces became truncated to the point of flippancy – after all, it is far simpler to refer to Rachmaninov's *Rhapsody on a Theme of Paganini* as Rach-Pag and, of course, YPG was Britten's *Young Person's Guide to the Orchestra*. It did not take long for me to catch on and use the well-worn names for these and many other pieces. Any coffee break, coach journey or gap between rehearsal and concert became an opportunity for the swapping of tall stories, character assassinations, analysis of current rehearsals and performances, gossip, rumours and the normal chit-chat between friends. There was little time as a new girl to peep over the parapet to see what the rest of the world was up to. An orchestra can be as insular as individual members require it to be, often replacing an extended family in the case of musicians who devote their life to the art. Many musicians remain single, married only to their chosen demanding instrument.

One important matter of which I was totally ignorant when I joined the orchestra was the process by which principal conductors came and went. At the time there was heavy speculation over the demise of the most recent principal conductor of the orchestra: gentle Andrzej Panufnik: "Did he fall, or was he pushed?" I had signed a contract in spring 1959 at the end of his short reign, but dark mutterings were the only clue I had about how the players felt about the present situation.

Many had felt musically frustrated, as he often used a tiny orchestra, leaving the majority of his players wondering why he had taken up a position with a full-sized symphony orchestra. Extra free days were always welcomed, of course, but, perversely, if players were not required to play in the quasi-chamber concerts, the morale of the whole group fell. It was inevitable that some were happy as they were artistically involved, but others felt musically stranded.

After Panufnik's resignation, Meredith Davies, the assistant conductor, was offered the top job, but was unsure about assuming such a heavy responsibility and so asked the management to appoint an eminent conductor for the 1959-60 season. More stability was badly needed, morale was low, and everyone needed a musical boost for self-esteem.

The inspired choice for the rescue job was Sir Adrian Boult. He fitted every criterion for success and, when the news eventually broke, the dispirited atmosphere in the orchestra lightened considerably.

* * *

Sir Adrian Boult had been the director and conductor of the orchestra from 1924 to 1930, after which he took over the BBC Symphony Orchestra. As someone who had already been part of the Birmingham scene, he was now happy to accept the post as conductor for the stopgap year until the position could be filled permanently, and described himself in a letter to John

Waterhouse of the *Birmingham Post* as, "Only a carpet-bagger … an elderly umbrella to keep, if possible, some of the rain and snow off Meredith Davies" (now the deputy musical director). He undertook ten concerts in the Birmingham winter season, plus a number of out-of-town engagements.

I found myself playing for him in May 1959 soon after I joined the orchestra, but, in spite of trying to be adult about the experience, I was always on edge and scared of him. The shock of seeing a young girl at the back of a predominantly male orchestra prompted one or two pithy comments from the rostrum. One of his favourite observations was his regular opening gambit of, "Oh, percussion, you look like a happy family at the back there." I was never quite sure how to take this, but it always produced a laugh from the orchestra. He probably found it as difficult to come to terms with my presence as I did with his.

At the age of seventy, Sir Adrian was a fine figure of a man: very tall, smartly dressed, with an upright military bearing, resonant of voice and with a short fuse for irritation and impatience should a player not immediately meet his exacting standards. As far as I could see, this was a very different person from the genteel archetypal Englishman I had encountered putting the NYO through its paces not many years previously. He would enter a rehearsal room without any preamble or fuss, formally greet the leader, acknowledge the orchestra and then slowly and deliberately take up his exceptionally long baton and, on the dot of the starting time, begin to conduct the first piece. It mattered not one jot if the orchestra was ready – he had started, often accompanied by a glare from those hooded eyes and a booming, "Oh, DO come along!" Everyone quickly responded and the day's work began.

It was made clear from the outset that he disapproved of smoking in rehearsals. However, this did not deter the many hardened addicts and, as usual, a pall of smoke wreathed its way over the heads of the players. This was customary, and indeed most people did smoke. I watched with fascination as horns tucked half-finished cigarettes into a convenient crook in their instruments, or precariously balanced glowing dog-ends on the music stands. My colleague Ernie Parsons could smoke a cigarette halfway through without dropping any ash at all, the resulting grey mess when it eventually fell causing much 'tutting' and an audible dusting down of timpani heads. If the town hall was particularly draughty, Don would hold his cigarette in the air and, should the smoke blow horizontally towards the front, I would be despatched to the back of the organ to close the roof doors. This was a regular occurrence. My abiding memory of conductor Hugo Rignold is of his chain-smoking through rehearsals, cigarette between yellowed fingers, squinting against smoke whilst studying the score. One South American conductor regularly called for "five minutes for a leetle cigaretta!" Great clouds of smoke were emitted in all dressing rooms, band rooms and on all coach journeys, so that on our return from wherever and at whatever time of night or early morning, I would throw every stitch of clothing into the laundry basket before immersing myself in a hot bath and washing my hair.

As Sir Adrian had conducted the orchestra for many years previously and for numerous recent concerts, he knew several of the individuals in the orchestra, and I listened with amazement as the principal flautist made comments and suggestions during rehearsals, not realising that there was a certain rapport between the two men. "Please could we have more 'ups and downs', Sir Adrian?" Boult initially looked furious at this none-too-serious criticism of his sideways-sweeping beats, and then he relaxed, half bowed and said, "Certainly, Mr Moroney." These two were old sparring partners.

As is often the case with conductors, Sir Adrian suffered with back problems, and it was common knowledge that he wore a back support when he was working. This no doubt gave rise to his uncompromisingly upright stance and to some extent his deliberate, measured stick technique. Orchestra breaks would often find him sitting quietly studying a score or chatting to musicians with a glass of milk to hand – the very epitome of dignity. This illusion was somewhat dented, however, during one rehearsal in an exceptionally grubby old school hall. An unusually energetic upward sweep of the baton resulted in a Statue of Liberty-esque Sir Adrian remaining rigid with an upraised arm. He had got stuck, something ghastly having happened in his back. He bellowed to the front desks of startled players, "You'll have to get me down!", whereupon they downed tools and manhandled him to the less than pristine floor. A break was called, we tactfully withdrew and rehearsal was cancelled for the morning. Old trouper that he was, Sir Adrian was there for the following rehearsal, somewhat subdued, facing an angelic and accommodating orchestra.

Styles of playing change through the generations, of course, but there were times when Sir Adrian insisted on sticking to the composer's instructions even when they were no longer relevant. For instance, before a note was played in Elgar's *Enigma Variations*, he always barked, "Percussion, have you got your metal beater?" Elgar's instruction in the finale is for the suspended cymbal to be struck with a metal beater. As we now use modern cymbals and not the thick, heavy military monstrosities of Elgar's original orchestra, a metal beater is not only unnecessary, but would damage present-day instruments. The simple solution was to paint a wooden drumstick with silver gloss paint. When the expected query came from the rostrum, this was held up for him with a meek reply of, "Yes, Sir Adrian!", and he was happy.

As previously noted, my contribution to the instrument stock was, among other things, a fine pair of seventeen-inch-diameter Zyldjian cymbals, not enormous by orchestral standards, but the very best of their kind with a full, rich tone. The orchestra possessed a much larger pair of thin, inferior cymbals, which when played above forte had a habit of turning inside out like an umbrella in a storm. Quiet notes sounded like coughs or sneezes, earning the player many a "bless you!" from nearby horn players.

One day we were in the thick of an exciting rehearsal when Boult stopped, looked across the orchestra at me, paused and asked in a very deliberate way, "Is that the *largest* pair you've got?" Sniggers from the assembly; faint puzzlement from me. "Show him the big ones," whispered Don, whereupon I grabbed the nasty, thin cymbals and held them up high at the same time as Boult boomed, "SHOW me!" There was proper laughter this time, yet I was still in the dark as to what the joke was until he qualified his last comment with, "I want you to be known as the young lady with the LARGEST pair in the Midlands!" – then the penny dropped. I flushed scarlet and, when the laughter died down, a break was called and I endured endless teasing from my colleagues. This little anecdote has echoed down the profession for decades, as it was told afresh by players and conductors who did not realise that I was the player in question until they saw my knowing grin.

As a raw youngster I was on a very steep learning curve, trying to keep a grip on difficult situations with dignity and intelligence. A big test came with Holst's *Planets* suite. I had a vague idea what to expect but had not seen the music, and when Don was off sick I found myself alone at the first rehearsal, playing, among other things, the unrelenting snare-drum part in 'Mars Bringer of War'. After the loud first section, there is a menacing quiet passage with accompanying scary, quiet snare-drum patterns. Not having heard any of this before, I made heavy weather of it and messed it up. Sir Adrian was steely but patient, and somehow we managed to get through it without my losing my nerve altogether. By the time it came to the concert, I knew the part from memory. Shaking with nerves, I adopted a head up and straight back pose – don't let the old man know. At least he did not yell at me as he did at the offstage, supposedly ethereal, wordless women's voices dying away into the distance at the very end of the piece: every rehearsal shook with a roar of

"Shut the door!" as the poor souls crept further and further away down the back steps behind the platform, losing all contact with what was happening in the real world.

Then there was the time when I dropped a heavy triangle with an almighty clatter (the nylon fishing line holding it gave way) in the split second after the end of a piece, but before the applause broke. Not one of us moved a hair, but Boult knew who was the culprit. We also did a concert that included Grieg's 'In the Hall of the Mountain King' from *Peer Gynt*. On this, my very first performance of the piece, I was playing the bass drum and somehow miscounted at the end of the final long crescendo, managing to put in a very loud solo note after everyone else had finished. This was met with delighted grins from my colleagues, but for the life of me I could not tell why they were so happy. As I came off the stage, I was greeted by "That was great", "You show 'em girl", and such like. Don took me on one side and gently pointed out my misdemeanour. I was truly mortified and had to be dissuaded from going to the Green Room to apologise – nay, grovel – to the big boss.

One summer day the rehearsal began with a violin concerto, but unfortunately Ralph Holmes, the soloist, was making creaking noises with his every movement on the wooden platform staging. This drove Boult mad. Rehearsal came to a grinding halt, whereupon he yelled out for "Water! Water!" The orchestra manager came running and was duly despatched offstage. We then watched with amazement as the old man grabbed the proffered Parks Department watering can (resident in the town hall for the floral decorations therein) and proceeded to water the stage where Ralph was standing. It did the trick, with no more squeaks from then on. Rehearsal continued as though nothing untoward had happened.

Another memorable experience awaited me in the shape of Mahler's Fourth Symphony. I had never heard any Mahler, and imagined that it would be heavy, Wagner-like, indigestible and far too long. Don had told me that there was nothing to worry about, with no alarming technical problems. He handed me my music and I saw, to my astonishment, that I was to be playing sleigh bells. Up to this point in my career, sleigh bells denoted one thing only, and that was Christmas. The symphony begins with gentle solo quavers played on *schellen* (sleigh bells). That long baton came down for the first bar, I began, and then, as nothing else seemed to be going on, I stopped, looking puzzled. I don't suppose that it would have crossed Boult's mind that any one of his players had no idea what to expect in this music, but that was certainly the case with me. He looked up and tetchily growled, "Go on, GO ON!" After that ignominious beginning, my first experience of Mahler's music was that of delight and enchantment, especially when I realised that Joan Sutherland was the soloist in the last movement, and I was being paid for the pleasure of hearing her. Sadly, it is difficult to remember any personal impressions of how Boult interpreted any of the music we played, as I was far too wrapped up in my own inadequacies. As a mere beginner in the game, I had no yardstick for comparisons and suspect that in my ignorance everything I heard was, in my opinion, one hundred per cent acceptable and fine by me. Indeed, when I was aware of the everyday comments from colleagues, surprise was my uppermost emotion if these were in any way negative. I saw myself as a mere triangle player and it was not my place to think beyond playing the instruments and doing my best. The music spoke to me loud and clear, however, and I was never shy to give voice about favourite (or otherwise) pieces.

Throughout a long career one fields questions about what we musicians think about specific pieces, often those by contemporary composers. My answer is always the same: "I have to try even harder if I don't like the piece, but it has to be well crafted and one hopes that it is screaming to be let out." If the workmanship is shabby or uncaring, then it takes only a short time for the musicians to lose interest. We try our best, but there is always an extra shine if the music is to our liking for whatever reason, but we are allowed to say that we do not like a particular composition. No one seems to have inhibitions about giving vent to their opinions in, say, an art gallery – "I couldn't live with that thing on my wall", but when it comes to music one is aware of a certain reticence in giving an opinion about something so transitory.

Winter brought the inevitable pea-souper fogs. The city was not to become a smokeless zone for some time, so these were a regular feature of life. In 1960 I was a novice driver travelling into the city centre in Fred, my little A35 van. One January day we had a morning rehearsal with Sir Adrian and then I returned home the ten miles to Sutton Coldfield. Mid-afternoon brought the first few whiffs of fog in the still air, so flatmate Daphne and I decided to go early by train for the evening concert. This was not to be, however, as the trains were cancelled in the late afternoon. So Plan B was put into action. Armed with large torches, we set off in the van, giving ourselves plenty of time, or so we thought. The familiar route was totally obscured, with every junction and roundabout becoming a nightmare as Daphne walked in front of the van with a torch, trying valiantly to keep us on track. It was freezing cold and I spent most of the trip with my head stuck out of the window trying to find the kerb. In those days there were no roadside lines to follow, poor street lighting and very little traffic in such conditions. It really was a case of not being able to see a hand in front of one. I know, because I tried. We eventually reached the town hall at 9.00pm, dashing through the door in time to hear the beginning of the last movement of the Vaughan Williams *London Symphony*. Still in my day clothes, I rushed onto the platform just in time to play my first entry, earning myself a relieved look from Don and a twitch of an eyebrow from Sir Adrian. Even the hall was thick with fog, and there were more people on stage than in the audience. An all-pervading air of gloom permeated the place, but I was soon to discover the real reason why: our dear colleague Rusty (Albert Russell, violinist, watercolour artist and cartoonist) had collapsed and died after running to get to the concert in time and he had been laid out on the ladies' band-room table (with no one there to prevent any latecomers from bursting in). One might have expected such exceptional circumstances to be a good enough reason to cancel the concert, but no, the show must go on. As it was, it took more agonising hours before anyone returned home again through the noxious weather. Two weeks later, records trumpeted the wettest weather for 72 years, and yet, despite widespread flooding, the intrepid orchestra arrived for an engagement in Kidderminster, only to find rowing boats sculling around the town hall there. After that it was a case of 'Home James!' and a free evening for all.

Sir Adrian's tenure ended in June 1960. He was then invited to become the CBSO Society's Vice-President, but continued to appear as a guest conductor until his final concert with the orchestra at the grand old age of eighty-eight, when he was helped onto the platform and sat to conduct the Elgar version of the National Anthem in Worcester Cathedral. This was an emotional time for all of us, as we knew that it marked the end of an era and that we would never play for the old man again.

7
New Broom

When it was realised that the next musical director was to be Hugo Rignold, a frisson of interest and anxiety ran through the orchestra, especially amongst the strings. In orchestral circles he was known as a martinet, hard worker, and an ex-'jolly jazzer', as one player put it. This latter designation lent a faint air of mystery to a character seen by some as not altogether a one hundred per cent classical musician. He had been the lead violinist with Jack Hylton's light orchestra in London, moving on to found the Cairo Symphony Orchestra during the war whilst serving with the RAF in the Middle East. Other conducting engagements followed, though on demobilisation he was for a time principal viola in the orchestra of the Royal Opera House before becoming a full-time conductor. We were also aware that he was an orchestral trainer par excellence, if not an actual bandmaster, and we bore in mind his notorious reputation as someone not afraid to clear out what he perceived as dead wood in the ranks. The Liverpool Philharmonic Orchestra had been through that particular hoop when he had been their conductor for six seasons some years earlier.

I listened to all the discussions with fascination, as I remembered 'Riggy' (as he was known by the players) from when he had conducted the NYO. My subsequent impression of him was, thankfully, totally at odds with how he had seemed to me as a raw teenager. Here was a man with firm ideas about the music under his care, and how we were going to communicate without too much friction. He was always the boss; there was never any doubt about that – a true professional and stickler for his way of doing things. Neither was he as avuncular as his other nickname, 'Uncle Hugo', would have us believe. When he got mad there were no holds barred, and no one was immune from his wrath.

Initially, rehearsals were constantly being interrupted by a look of mock surprise and a lesson on how to interpret his beats. It was essential that we all agreed on where the sound was going to come at any given indication from the baton; he needed a disciplined framework in which to work. Time after time we followed that deliberate, slow downbeat, the stick coming to rest on his outstretched left index finger. "Here's your beat; all you have to do is to follow it. Thank you, ladies and gentlemen." The chord had to come just *there!* For instance, if he were not satisfied after numerous attempts to effect a clean entry, he would say, somewhat peevishly, "What's the *matter* with you all?" This soon became a mantra to be trotted out down the years by all and sundry, and it was always delivered in an exaggerated imitation of Riggy's slightly unctuous nasal voice. String players remember another of his favourite phrases during sectional rehearsals: "You're all leaders." He wanted everyone to play at the point of his stick and became even more irritable after we had had a spell with guest conductors. Whatever we did was never good enough and at the first rehearsal he would peer through his personal tobacco haze and enquire, "What's happened to MY orchestra?" Back we were, directed to the basics of that deliberate, straight downbeat.

As standards began to improve, Rignold drew in bigger audiences, and the orchestra's morale rose accordingly. Interest grew as different works appeared in the music folders, and an ever-expanding repertoire added greatly to the enjoyment of the job, not least a first never-to-be-forgotten exposure to Ravel's wonderful *Daphnis and Chloë* score. Five extra percussionists were employed for this, and I revelled in the glorious music and the excitement of working within a large section.

In spring 1962, there was much press coverage of the fact that the brand new cathedral in Coventry was almost at completion point. Contemporary artists had been commissioned to create unique works of art for this amazing building and the CBSO was given the honour of playing there for the premiere of Benjamin Britten's *War Requiem* on May 30th. We were all starry-eyed at the prospect of such a unique occasion.

None of us had ever encountered such a huge and complex work before, and we were all intrigued by the fact that it called for uncommonly large and varied forces requiring three conductors. Britten took charge of the Melos Ensemble, a chamber group of high-profile London players mainly responsible for accompanying the specially chosen three solo singers for whom the parts were written: Russian soprano Galina Vishnevskaya, German baritone Dietrich Fischer-Dieskau, and English tenor Peter Pears. Unfortunately, Vishnevskaya was not able to take part in the first performance as her husband, the famous cellist Rostropovitch, was out of favour with the Russian authorities, the consequence being that both were denied exit visas from the USSR. Soprano Heather Harper, whose sister Alison was a CBSO cellist, was pulled in at the last minute; an inspired and splendid replacement. Britten was present for all rehearsals, but Meredith Davies conducted the large symphony orchestra which accompanied a huge choir, and an unseen choirmaster was in charge of a boys' choir hidden somewhere in the organ loft. At the final rehearsals, when everyone took part, we only ever heard their disembodied voices floating down from the rafters.

The timpanist, five percussionists and a large brass section were called for a sectional rehearsal in the cathedral in advance of the big day. It was spring and the weather was unsettled with fitful, scudding dark clouds interspersed with shafts of sunlight. All the brass players were needed first, so when we returned from our cups of tea we stood outside with our backs to the strange, livid daylight and looked down the body of the cathedral towards the altar through the massive, engraved glass window. Even after all these years, hairs stand on my arms at the memory of seeing the gleam of brass instruments in shafts of light, with Britten perched on a tall percussion stool taking the rehearsal, and the ethereal sound of those unique, cascading fanfares. After being rooted silently to the spot, we somehow managed to present our security passes to the doorman and walk slowly down the nave towards that powerful new sound.

Added to all this was the fact that the cathedral was as yet unconsecrated. It was an exceptional experience to be in such a building. There was noise – lots of noise – of workmen and cleaners. Carpenters were beavering away as great energy was being expended in building a scaffold tower to hold television cameras. After showing curiosity about the timber being used for the Bishop's throne, I was given a small offcut of what proved to be an unusual African wood. (My dad subsequently made two tiny Coventry 'crosses of nails' from this. One is now in a time capsule beneath the CBSO Centre in Birmingham and the other is in Coventry Cathedral as part of a public display.) The mirror-glossy black marble floor was being cleaned by an army of stalwarts, as were lines of embedded new pennies, bright and shiny. It was explained that they were there to keep the processing choir straight, and were quickly dubbed 'Sir Basil's pence' by an orchestra wit; not an original phrase, I suspect. Sir Basil Spence, the architect, was frequently seen strolling around the cathedral during our many rehearsals, usually talking to important-looking people and watching with interest as final elements of this fine building slowly came together before our eyes.

I was intrigued to know what such a huge musical enterprise looked like on paper, so I sneaked up to the front during a break to peer at the massive full score written on oversized manuscript paper. This was opened out and secured onto a large sheet of hardboard firmly fixed to the sturdy music stand on the conductor's rostrum. I was duly awestruck and, together with all my colleagues, realised that we were in the uniquely privileged position of taking part in a very special first performance. During rehearsals everyone got used to seeing the composer flitting in and out between the musicians, tweaking mistakes in the complex parts or slightly adjusting dynamics. There was a wonderful feeling of being involved in something exceptional. Britten was indeed a master of his craft. For instance, the string bowings at the end of the piece are visually riveting, emphasised by a relentless snare drum beating the same rhythm. His percussion writing is thrilling indeed, creating tingles down the spine for all of us. One particular moment always stands out for me at every performance. At the beginning of the Sanctus, the spine-chilling bell-like notes must **not** be together, but must 'sound like echoes from ages past', getting louder and louder and more and more unremitting, until they resolve into single, merciless chords. This was at the insistence of the composer during the very first rehearsal.

"Tingles down the spine" is how violinist Philip Head describes the experience of hearing Dietrich Fischer-Dieskau singing alongside Heather Harper in the new cathedral of a city with such haunting wartime connotations.

No applause after the performance by request of the composer.

This was printed in the programmes at the end of the work. The thought-provoking words and music spoke volumes, and any applause would have been a superfluous travesty. Everyone present that evening remembers the deafening silence as the final notes died away. No one moved, and many were in shock. Tears were shed that evening, as the solemn row of bishops slowly processed away from the stunned assembly.

Nowadays, of course, performances of the work in concert halls generate thunderous applause, but there are those amongst us who regret this and remember it all so differently. This matchless first performance remains one of the highlights of my long playing career.

Throughout my early days in the CBSO, as mentioned earlier, there was a constant underlying unease between timpanist Ernie and percussionist Don as they jostled for supremacy, with eruptions and childish name-calling finally coming to a serious head one day on the steep concert platform in Leeds Town Hall. The old man was arranging his timpani, Don was minding his own business organising our set-up, and I was sorting out the music prior to putting it onto the correct stands, when suddenly they both exploded into roaring verbal abuse. I first became aware of problems when I heard a muttered, "You aren't the **man** for it!" from Parsons. Don responded hotly with, "Don't you DARE say that to me! You're just a frustrated old fool!" As soon as I realised what was happening, I dumped the folders, but I was too late to prevent Don from half-heartedly slapping Ernie on the face after a warning not to repeat what he had said, "or I'll smack you!" This was a red rag to Ernie's bull, and a nasty situation became positively alarming as Don pulled him over a timp, which promptly fell over. (If loosened, the legs of a hand-tuned instrument disappear inside the shell, the whole thing becoming totally unstable.) I yelled at the top of my voice, and one of the orchestra attendants came running, but not before Don had dragged Ernie onto the floor and was attempting to strangle him, whereupon I wrenched Don away by his hair. This brought him to his senses and they were physically yanked apart. By this time, of course, there was a crowd of shocked onlookers, and I was clutching a clump of Don's hair and trembling like a leaf. Parsons went immediately to complain to Rignold, but the curious outcome was nil, as no one else reported the incident further. The majority of our colleagues reckoned that Parsons had 'had it coming to him', as he was constantly behaving in a malicious and underhand manner, and was heartily detested by many orchestra members. I wanted no part in their stupid quarrels, there being even less love lost between that malevolent old man and myself ever afterwards. Unfortunately, though, Don's temper was to become his final downfall, when he crossed swords with Rignold.

We were scheduled to rehearse Kabalevsky's lively *Colas Breugnon* overture in the town hall, and Don had taken the parts home to sort out and mark. There is a tricky xylophone part in this piece; one that most percussionists are familiar with as it is audition material. So, when Don failed to arrive, I was unable to play as there was no music, but on the second run-through I made an attempt to play the xylo part from memory. Riggy stopped the orchestra, looked up, and said with steely calm, "Where is Mr Thomas?" I began to concoct a suitable reply when suddenly Don burst onto the platform, resplendent in cycle clips, red in the face and sweating profusely.

"What time do you call this?" boomed from the rostrum.

Don glared, threw the music onto the xylo and then stuck out his chin, staring belligerently at Rignold, and, without a hint of an apology, he snarled, "Anybody can be late, you know!"

My blood ran cold. Deathly silence followed …

"GET OUT! Who the hell do you think you are?"

Don immediately stamped off the platform and never came back, then or ever again. He was sacked on the spot.

Arthur Baker, the new general manager, was landed with this problem and also the one of telling me that I was now the temporary principal percussionist. Rignold subsequently decreed that I was to be paid an extra £2 per week for taking on this onerous responsibility, but it was not a happy situation.

Telephones in the early '60s were not the commonplace necessity that they are nowadays; indeed the CBSO management had to communicate with me by telegram in extremis, as it was some time before I was elevated to the status of telephone owner. I was now responsible for the organisation of all the percussion requirements, which was not helped by Parsons crowing with evil delight from behind his timpani. Thankfully, a lot of help was forthcoming from Jim Wedge, our orchestral librarian, who saw to it that I received the music in good time so that I could practise any difficult passages, sort out who was to play what, and note instruments to be hired if not owned by the orchestra. I had to make sure that extra players were booked in time for large works, and that the instrument lists were correct for the van men and platform staff. It seemed to be a never-ending catalogue of all the awkward percussion music in the orchestral repertoire, with myself getting more and more stressed and hassled.

I managed to weather our own Promenade Concerts – a feature of which, incidentally, was a fountain complete with goldfish. There were different programmes nightly, except for Sundays, each with a single-run-through style rehearsal on the day, the concerts being repeated in other Midland towns. After a blissful holiday fortnight, we were once again heavily involved with the annual Three Choirs Festival. The new concert season began in early autumn with even more challenging programmes, including a terrifying blooding with Ravel's *Boléro*, where Riggy seemed to dwindle away to nothing through my haze of nerves at its beginning, after which we embarked on my biggest challenge to date.

Variety is the spice of life, I am told, and this is what I find appealing about playing percussion. We need to be on our toes to tame a vast range of instruments covering many techniques. Certain instruments inevitably become our most preferred and, conversely, we all have our least favourites. For many years I have agonised about, and fought a losing battle with the snare drum. This neat military instrument is deceptive to the casual listener, but it requires a formidable technique for its correct execution. Many hours of my life have been spent trying to overcome the problems it poses. Every roll (other than a continuous long roll) should be of a specific number of strokes, and all 'flams', 'drags', 'ruffs' and other individual drum ornaments must be played with precise accuracy; there is no hiding place for a conscientious player. Practice became a mesmerising agony of endless repetition as I fought to control hands and wrists, but I was never comfortable with the instrument and always felt hideously self-conscious when playing it.

For me, the nightmare of all nightmares came in the shape of Nielsen's Fifth Symphony in October 1962. The composer requires a snare drummer to try to annihilate the rest of the orchestra as he/she overwhelms everyone with an ad-lib tour de force. A germ of an idea is developed into what becomes a terrifying aural thrashing, which eventually dies away into the distance. Harold Gray, the conductor, was most encouraging – smiling and urging on my brave effort during rehearsals with a very Brummie-accented appeal to "Gow *ber*-serk, Margaret, gow *ber*-serk!" In the performance I went as crazy as I was able, but much prefer to hear others giving their all in this particular piece: I know my limitations.

During my starvation year in London I had met many musicians and, now that I was responsible for booking extras for Riggy's more adventurous programming, I was able to recommend freelance percussionists for work with the orchestra and, when it was necessary, look beyond the Midlands. During the bitterly cold winter that year (1962), we were scheduled to perform a new work commissioned by Rugby School (of *Tom Brown's Schooldays* fame). Sir Arthur Bliss, an old boy of the school, was the distinguished composer. Master of the Queen's Music is a fine title and I had to pinch myself when I realised that we were going to meet and play for the man himself. Rumour had it that Sir Arthur had a short fuse, but when he arrived to take a preliminary rehearsal of his new work he could not have been more charming and accommodating. Small, smiling, with an Edwardian turn of phrase and pronunciation, his white moustache twitched when he looked up to see me rushing about trying to fit in all the notes for him. After stopping the orchestra he announced, "My **dear** young lady, you are very busy – I think you are wonderful!" and then he asked, "Are you going to manage all that alone, or shall you have a friend to help you?" I blinked, smiled and replied, "Yes, Sir Arthur, we have another player coming tomorrow." He beamed and responded with, "Oh, *splendid* ... I hope he's a big, strong fellow." What I was unable to convey was that the extra player in question, Charlie, was a very good theatre-pit player but was also a dwarf. He loved playing with a full symphony orchestra, but it was only rarely that he was booked because he could not share music stands, or share such as a xylophone or glockenspiel, as they were too high from the ground for him to reach. Having had Bliss's music for some time, I realised that it was perfectly possible for two players to be more or less independent in all but small, hand-held instruments, so Charlie was engaged.

On the day of the concert, Charlie and I were not required for the beginning of rehearsal and we managed to find a tiny, uncomfortable classroom, resplendent with a one-bar electric fire. As we were trying to get warm, I heard a fussy "Oh my fur and whiskers!" approach down the bleak corridor (Bliss always seemed to me to be a quaint cross between Peter Rabbit and Queen Victoria). In came Sir Arthur, blowing on his hands and stamping his feet. "Don't go, don't go. Please stay and keep warm!" Yes, of course, we at once realised that this was his room. I introduced him to tiny Charlie and, gentleman that he was, Bliss never turned a hair. After a decent interval for chat, we retreated to our rightful place in that dreary building. Suffice to say, the concert, and in particular the new work, was a roaring success. Somewhere in all my scraps of paper there is a note from Sir Arthur altering a freshly penned tambourine part – "It just didn't work … don't you know! A.B".

Ever after my first encounter with that lovely man, he always came backstage to say "hello" to his "dear young lady", and after I had my first child he spotted me at the back of the orchestra as an extra player. In no time at all he was there again, shaking me by the hand and saying in his distinctive tones, "How lovely to see you. I hear that you now have a **dear** little baby."

November brought another outcry from Ernie Parsons as Remembrance Sunday loomed. We were rehearsing in the town hall on the previous Saturday when suddenly there was a great clatter at the back of the orchestra. Parsons had stormed in, hurled the wooden timpani covers onto the ground, thrown timpani sticks around and slammed his hands on the drum heads. "Don't you know what day it is?" he yelled. Everything ground to a halt as he continued with, "The trouble with this orchestra is that no one has any respect any more. This orchestra is full of …" He then proceeded to list the types of foreigners in the orchestra who supposedly had no respect, ending with, "… Poles, Mexicans and Jews!", shouting at the top of his voice. There was a stunned, appalled silence as he furiously gestured for everyone to stand for a minute's silence, halfway through which a little voice from deep within the violins ventured, "But it's Saturday, and not November the eleventh", whereupon the conductor, Meredith Davies, quietly suggested that Mr

Parsons should "put away his toys" and that we all should "continue to play orchestras - thank you"!

It was a great relief to go home to Yorkshire for the short Christmas break, after which we spent time between Christmas and New Year putting recordings in the can for future BBC use. Venues for these stalwart efforts were always in large, cold school halls in the outskirts of the city. All heating had been turned off for the holidays, and there was never anywhere to eat nearby, so once more it was a case of taking sandwiches and flasks of tea.

January 1963 brought the biggest freeze for years. Copious amounts of snow fell, so much so that the entire country became locked into a surreal frozen world. Water in the deep underground pipes that serviced our tall, narrow Victorian house soon became frozen solid. Power and telephone lines came down, public transport ground to a halt, heating was non-existent in many public buildings and we had to learn how to cope. Fortunately, the town hall functioned as normal, so I did no more but pile all my daily washing-up into a large bucket, load it into my van and process it in the town hall cloakroom: plenty of hot water there. Every day I brought home containers of fresh water, which, added to the water from standpipes at the end of the road, was sufficient for basic needs. Eventually even these standpipes froze and we had to rely on regular early morning visits from a council water tanker. We left clean buckets in the porch, but if we heard the handbell summoning us to the tanker we queued and swapped tales with our neighbours. Very primitive! But it was also rather friendly, so much so that when I presented myself at the flat of friends for a prearranged bath, total strangers took me in next door as my friends had gone out, having forgotten about our plans. Our house was the first to be without water and the last, six weeks later, to have the council workmen come round to put a shot of electricity through the pipes to free them. We were told that this was highly dangerous but the only way that they could think of to ease the situation. The whole episode was something of an adventure.

I was not happy in the responsible position as principal percussionist, so eventually I went to see Riggy for advice. It was duly decided that the job should be advertised and a new principal employed as soon as possible. My sanity was saved. One of the players we had been engaging regularly as an extra was a gentle Londoner, Douglas Milne. We had met briefly when I was a student, as he occasionally played with the MCO. His regular job was as a dance-band drummer (Quaglino's restaurant and club in the West End), but he also did a lot of extra work with the Philharmonia and other London orchestras. He was a perfect gentleman, an excellent, reliable all-rounder, skilled sight-reader and superb snare-drum player. Doug applied for and, after a comprehensive audition and numerous trial concerts, accepted the job in February 1963, much to my relief and delight.

March saw the orchestra on its first tour abroad with Riggy for thirteen concerts in Germany and Switzerland. Continental travel with a large group of musicians is nothing like being on holiday, of course, and this tough tour was not without incident. Over the years, one learns little tactics for overcoming the stresses and strains peculiar to the job, and very early in my career someone gave me sound advice, which I still take heed of to this day: "Whenever you get the opportunity to eat, sleep or go to the loo, take it whether you think you need to or not." We never know what is round the corner in our irregularly structured timetable. Exactly!

We all had reason to ponder on this recommendation on one of our journeys when, after a very early start, we encountered a freak snowstorm as we approached Ulm in Germany at a point where the autobahn splits into two halves. Each resulting one-way section negotiates a line of hills before joining together once more. Drifting, knee-deep snow covered the road and surrounding countryside, bringing everything to a grinding halt and causing a traffic jam of gargantuan proportions, with steep hills on one side and a long drop on the other confining the crammed lines of vehicles. There were no toilets on the two coaches and so, when it came to desperation point, emergency measures had to be instigated. The chaps were fine – they just did their little boy thing behind the coaches, but we women had to be more ingenious as tears and agony threatened. A tent of coats was made at the side of the coach and, as they say, "When you gotta go, you gotta go!" Not the happiest of situations, but the best solution in the circumstances. Soon after that episode, hunger and thirst set in. Some of us, hailed as wise virgins by the rest, had brought meagre iron rations for the long journey, as one can never be sure of when or where the next meal will come from. We frequently find our activities crossing over mealtimes. A large block of chocolate, a solitary apple and a handful of raisins were divided and sent round the ravenous company (not forgetting the driver); other titbits appeared, and then hysteria set in.

Bass players on board began the nonsense by singing their variation in *Young Person's Guide to the Orchestra* and percussionists and others joined in with the tambourine 'splats' between the repeated phrases, after which the whole thing took on the air of a mad party. Our German driver watched in astonishment as we played noisy games of charades with much joking and laughter. German symphony players no doubt behave with much more decorum and gravity. At one point I got out for a little walk, fresh air (lots of smokers on board) and change of scenery, resulting in an invitation to partake of a cheering cup of tea by an English family also in the line-up in their cosy camper van. As the queue began to move I returned, triumphantly clutching a pack of biscuits donated by our compatriots. After much more laughter, we eventually arrived exhausted in Ulm. Half an hour was the allotted time we had in which to buy portable food and ingeniously designed single pouches of soft drinks. At home our 'pop' only came in large unwieldy glass bottles with hefty screw tops: plastic bottles and bags had not yet entered the UK domestic scene.

It was discovered that the VIPs' large black chauffeur-driven car, for orchestra manager, conductor, Jennifer (Hugo's daughter) and the young Japanese violin soloist (she of wiry sound, dubbed Ko Ko Tin by the players), had made a small diversion at the point where the autobahn split. The driver needed to pop home briefly to a nearby village, thus no one in the staff car was aware of the snow problem until it became obvious that the orchestra was missing as they waited in vain for us to arrive at the concert hall in snowless Friedrichshaven.

Two hours after the concert should have started, the patient audience was beginning to leave the concert hall, but as we appeared they immediately formed a line and applauded as we stumbled wearily off the coaches and straight onto the concert platform in everyday dress. A part-programme was given by very zombified musicians, after which we went to our hotel to be greeted with upflung hands and generous hospitality from the proprietor's wife as she ushered us to tables, immediately plying us with delectable home-made soup and a splendid meal.

I discovered at that point that my friend and room-mate, Barbara, had been struck down with flu. She was packed off to bed with a hot-water bottle, eventually managing to struggle along with the rest of the party until she was fit enough to play again. Luckily no one else caught the bug this time, but on other occasions we were less fortunate. There have been other tours when programmes had to be adjusted to accommodate a decimated orchestra attacked by virulent bugs.

Thus began the 'join an orchestra and see the world' part of my career, as touring became part of life with this very busy professional symphony orchestra.

* * *

Working conditions in the '60s and '70s were not ideal. The orchestra had no home of its own and had to rehearse wherever halls could be found that were capable of housing up to a hundred musicians, chairs, music stands and general paraphernalia. These ranged from the low-ceilinged YMCA building in central Birmingham to spartan school halls, which could only be used during school holidays. In the latter there was rarely any heating and there were no refreshments; neither were the orchestra coaches on tap, as we were working within the city limits. Not everyone was a car owner, therefore it was either a case of getting to the outskirts for BBC recordings (for future broadcasting, when the orchestra was otherwise engaged during the busy concert season) either by bus or begging a lift from a colleague. These particular sessions were done on a rehearse/record system, therefore quick wits were a great asset, as there was usually only one chance to get it right before moving on to the next bit of the score.

As the Town Hall cost more than everywhere else to hire, we only did our final rehearsals in situ on the day of the concert, where Rignold was a stickler for making sure that we overcame the difficult acoustics. We percussionists were behind the second violins on the curve of the stage, and consequently there was a deceptive time lag, which was not apparent to us. The crunch eventually came for me when we were playing Ravel's *Mother Goose* suite. I was doing the oriental-style xylophone solo, trying valiantly to look at the conductor as well as keep an ear on the woodwind and an eye on the music and instrument. A quiet "Follow the stick, Miss Cotton!" pulled me up sharp: Riggy at his most unctuous. Trained never to speak to conductors across the orchestra unless absolutely imperative, I looked at him bleakly and half-nodded. The next attempt resulted in the same response from the rostrum; I was still evidently at odds with the flutes. In the deathly quiet that followed, I nervously ventured, "I'm sorry, Mr Rignold, but I can't hear what's wrong, and as far as I can tell I'm with your beat." A quizzical look was the response, and then slowly, "Shall you and I do it together?" My heart sank, but, as I had practised this bit at home with my eyes shut, I looked him straight in the eye and followed his every move, not looking down at my busy hands. Luckily, there were no wrong notes and at the end of my grilling there was a cheer from the orchestra, dispersing the tension; smiles all round. "Thank you, Miss Cotton." Ever afterwards he left me alone, but I always remembered to anticipate the beat by a whisker whenever we stood in that position on that particular platform.

Riggy had very firm ideas about his players, becoming terrifying in his quest for perfection. My new colleague Brian Heritage became completely unnerved, as cymbal playing was not his personal forte, and Rignold made no bones about how he felt about that. Doug was asked to give his sub-principal player anything except cymbals in the boss's programmes. Dear Brian, confidence truly sapped, was determined to overcome his army-style playing. The two of us did no more than take two pairs of cymbals into the town hall an hour before a rehearsal. Then I stood in the balcony and Brian on stage, and we spent a mesmerising time playing loud cymbal crashes at each other. Eventually he relaxed enough to get a decent, unselfconscious sound and subsequently laid the ghost to rest, although he never played cymbals for Rignold again.

Douglas was a very conscientious boss, carefully marking the parts for each player in his section, with nothing left to chance. We were, however, consulted as to what we would like to play, as we all had personal favourites and pet hates. I loved a hooligan tambourine part, and neat triangle writing was a delight. Great cymbal parts were a joy, and any underpinning by juicy bass-drum scoring was something to be gloated over and revelled in. The more experienced I became, the more I was able to relax and enjoy what I was doing. We all had fun with the 'toys' – kept in a 'toy box', naturally. These were, in essence, sound effects created by every kind of whistle and siren, popgun, starting pistol, many kinds of animal bells (sleigh, camel, cow bells of all sizes), coconut shells, hooters, ship's bell, rain sticks, large wind machine, and a great sunshine variety of Latin American instruments.

"When in doubt, leave it out." This was good advice from my teacher at the Academy and was subsequently qualified by the equally valuable notion of, "If you are going to make a mistake, make it a good one." There is always a point of no return with a large pair of cymbals and, once reached, it is a case of "go for it!" and don't wince or pull faces. There's no hiding place in such circumstances, but you might *just* get away with it. Not so, however, with my very first exposure to Shostakovitch's Fifth Symphony at a concert in the town hall, with Riggy carving. My calculations went awry, as I inadvertently counted one line of rests twice in the slow movement. I was concentrating hard when I realised with horror that a solo glockenspiel note was upon me. The blood drained from my brain as I realised that I was too far back on my chair to leap gracefully to my feet, by which time the second solo note was there too, which also escaped me. The moment had gone, and there was

119

nothing I could do except crawl down to the conductor's room to grovel with apologies at the end of the concert. When Rignold realised who was coming though the door, he yelled, "What the hell were you doing? Get out! GET OUT!" ... I got out. We all make mistakes. The next day I was mortified to see that the *Birmingham Post* critic had spotted "the two missing bell notes ..."

8
Mrs Brown

In my quieter moments, I thought long and hard about the future. It was assumed by friends and family that I was meeting lots of fascinating people, but it was not like that at all. An orchestra is a large working group, arguably the largest under the thrall of a single person in one room, and audiences come in all shapes and sizes: plenty of people there. But I realised that I had embarked on a rarefied lifestyle, and soon became aware of a great divide between players and listeners.

Birmingham Town Hall sported a basement bar, but there was no particular provision for the orchestra. The only concession for the players was the ministrations of a cheery barman near the door end of the long public bar. The chaps usually managed to tear down to the bowels of the building during the interval before the audience found their way through the crush. The ladies, on the other hand, had a much more civilised set-up as there was only a handful of us, so a tray of coffee was brought to our band room. A small clutch of diehards went downstairs after the concerts, but most preferred their own particular watering holes in the city away from the concert-goers. The only serious exception to this was at the end of the season in summer and at Christmas, when our in-house conductor, Harold Gray, generously treated all the orchestra to a drink at the bar: then the place was full. In spite of all this apparent camaraderie during an evening performance, it was a brave admirer who would venture to speak to a member of the orchestra. We were resplendent in black evening dress, busy talking to each other, as you cannot discuss the merits and demerits of a performance whilst on the stage, and thus were seriously, if unintentionally, unapproachable. Professional orchestral musicians must take the top prize in quick changes in and out of formal and informal outfits. At the end of the concert it is a case of instrument packed, removing white ties at least, out of the building and sinking the first pint before the audience has had time to think, never mind leave the premises.

Concert-goers often had favourite seats, and I soon realised that we percussionists were at the mercy of regular audience members sitting immediately behind us on the choir seating in front of the organ. I slowly became aware of a very odd, scruffily dressed, older man who always sat immediately behind me. It didn't take a genius to work out where specific

121

players would be, and he always seemed to turn up immediately opposite my music stand. When we were waiting to play, we sometimes perched on the edge of the staging behind us as there were no tall percussion stools then, but it took some time for me to catch on that nudging feet were often in the way of where I was going to land. When the penny eventually dropped that this was a deliberate manoeuvre, I was duly horrified and upset. One night, as I hurried off the platform, Reg, one of our lovely platform attendants, saw my flushed face and rushed to the rescue. "I'll kill him," he roared. And I really thought that he would, but never discovered what happened. My protector saw to it that it was the last time there was any such problem, and from then on 'Feet' kept well out of my area.

In later years, my percussion colleague Annie (Oakley) had an admirer, who eventually included me in his attentions. For years we never knew who he was, but amazingly expensive gifts would appear anonymously at the town hall: silk scarves, porcelain figurines, crystal glassware, French perfume, and all from the same smart department store in Birmingham. The store assistants were apprised of the situation and eventually anticipated our appearance after St Valentine's Day, summer holidays and Christmas. Fortunately, we had managed to persuade them to exchange any unopened perfumes for some that were more appropriate to our personal tastes. These presents were sometimes accompanied by stilted, short notes written in block capitals, giving no clue whatsoever to the sender. Eventually, after many years of this and the frustration of never being able to thank our benefactor, we uncovered his identity. John, a loner, living with mother and working at the big car factory in Birmingham. He only liked loud music – preferably with lots of cymbals - and when Simon Rattle came on the scene he decided that Simon was not for him. A one-man campaign was mounted, and Annie became the recipient of many long, semi-literate, weirdly rambling letters – no joined-up writing there. Eventually all this stopped, and we discovered that John had died. We had tried to say "hello" and be civil, but the situation was fraught with his crippling shyness and our acute embarrassment.

We musicians sit or stand (as the case may be) in the orchestra and think nothing of it, but of course in time it is brought to our notice that some audience members regard us as rare beings. Playing music is seen as an exotic way to earn a crust, and I have to confess that I agree. My career has been laced with many a grin, and whispered comments to each other that "we are being paid to do this". When connections were made with members of the audience, I, for one, was amazed to discover that people out there have favourites in the orchestra and always look out for them at every concert. One young man took his courage in both hands and approached me to confess that he was very happy when he discovered that I was playing and that he thought that I always "looked so serene". ME - serene! I must have been doing something right. That, along with "Maggie Cotton enjoying herself as usual!" from the *Birmingham Post* music critic (later to become my boss after I retired from playing), was one of many observations made by our regulars. All this was encouraging and gave one an even greater sense of responsibility, not only to the composer but also to the paying public.

I went out with one or two young men from the orchestra, but made a conscious decision to try to meet contemporaries from outside the profession. As I was not sporty and did not belong to a church, this problem merited serious thought. I could not envisage not being married and not having children, but at that time such aspirations seemed remote to the extreme. "If I'm not married by the time I'm thirty, I'll emigrate to Australia." At least I then had a timescale to work to. Having made enquiries about how to go about meeting people, I discovered the Inter Varsity Club (IVC), and it was just the job. No one expected full-time commitment and there were plenty of diverse activities on offer, from sailing in Wales to gourmet evenings at posh restaurants, where I eventually learnt to appreciate and enjoy wine.

I was very sensitive about my chosen profession and dreaded the tentative query of, "Well ... er ... and what do you do for a living then?" The temptation to reply, "Elephant trainer, jet pilot, deep-sea diver" would be reluctantly shelved, and I would take a deep breath, size up the potential shockability of the questioner and usually resort to saying that I was a teacher. If pressed further, I might just mutter "music – piano" and then rapidly change the subject. It was an unusual person who would dig deeper, but if this was the case then he would be told the alarming truth if I thought that he could handle it. I would confess to playing in the orchestra, giving it its full title, as few in those days seemed to recognise the initials CBSO. This admission usually elicited one of two responses: either, "Oh, how interesting, I didn't know that the piano was an orchestral instrument", in which case I had to come clean and explain my real calling, by, "I am actually *a percussionist* – you know, drums and all those things at the back"; or, if the enquirer admitted to knowing nothing about music, I would rapidly change the subject, hoping for an end to the questions.

At the time I joined the IVC I was worrying how to dump a particularly tedious, clinging and boring viola player boyfriend. Being the only professional musician in the ranks of the IVC, I magnanimously offered to do a live musical evening with real music, rather than one consisting solely of recordings. This obviously caught the imagination of many members, and I found myself inundated by keen musical types in my tiny flat in Moseley. The dying throes of my relationship with the dull boyfriend were a huge success: dreary music played with certain flair and, dare I say, great relief on my part, as I accompanied him on the piano. One of the listeners disappeared during the evening, only to turn up later clutching an armful of coffee mugs. I did not realise it at the time, of course, but Geoff Brown was to become the father of my children. Typically ever practical, he had spotted that I did not have enough mugs for the crowd in the flat and so he had nipped out to his nearby splendiferous bedsit to remedy the problem. I was suitably impressed. We met in May 1963 and were married in October of that year.

The day set for the wedding celebrations was a Friday and we had planned to tack on the Saturday 'free day' for our honeymoon. Our plans came to the notice of the CBSO management, whereupon I was granted a whole week in which to celebrate my marriage, eventually realising with amazement that we had set a precedent for any future time off for nuptials within the orchestra. A photographer from the local paper was sent to cover the occasion and we were then truly set on the road to married life.

Geoff initially took my job in his stride, although he was somewhat nonplussed to discover that in the first fourteen weekends of married bliss his wife was working on eleven of them. At the outset of our life together, even before we tied the knot, I had spelled out the fact that I was not going to give up music: it was more than a mere job; more a way of breathing and living. This sounded sentimental and sloppy coming from a down-to-earth Yorkshire lass, but it was true nevertheless. My dear husband found this hard to come to terms with and I suspect that he was often jealous of my relationship with the orchestra – something he could never be part of.

One initial problem was that of my name. Yes, of course I was Mrs Brown, but I was also Margaret Cotton, later to be known as Maggie as I never did like my first name. Geoff was somewhat affronted when he realised that I intended to continue to use my maiden name; neither did my flippant suggestion of a double-barrelled Brown-Cotton meet with his approval. I was adamant, however, and when explanations were necessary to his family and friends I gritted my teeth and doggedly enlightened them. When I went to my bank to sign forms and order items in two names, the old-fashioned bank manager succeeded in conveying a deep disapproval of what he saw as an unconventional approach to my new wifely status, so much so that I immediately closed my account and changed banks. We still lived in a male-dominated world. However, I was still known as Miss Cotton in the orchestra: this was the norm in the music profession, and indeed in the arts as a whole.

Weekend work was a very important and a regular money-spinner for the orchestra. Unless N.R. (Not Required) by the programming, we were all involved. On Sundays the orchestra slogged to London to play at the Royal Albert Hall (RAH), my least favourite venue of all. Backstage stank of diesel, or were they coke fumes? It was grubby, airless and boiling hot. We reckoned that the London County Council must have had a job lot of grey paint donated by those who painted battleships and, together with dark maroon, a more gloomy colour scheme could not have been invented. The overcrowded band rooms are below ground, with toilet facilities yet another floor below, down stone steps into subterranean, tiled troglodyte regions. The orchestra refreshment area is another cave with insufficient seating and a tiny bar selling overpriced, disgusting coffee and, in the bad old days, instant tea with powdered milk. The wise ones amongst us arrived armed with flasks of decent beverages, and home-made nosebags stuffed into overfilled gig bags. For those brave souls who always go out to eat between rehearsal and concert, it is a long trek from the RAH to find any kind of fodder, but at least it breaks up a very tedious day. We discovered that American package-holiday firms delivering eager tourists to our shores always included a 'Sunday Spectacular – popular classics at the World Famous Royal Albert Hall'. Posters trumpeted, 'Tchaikovsky Night': '*Swan Lake* ballet music, Piano concerto No. 1, Overture 1812 with Cannon and Mortar effects'; or 'A Night in Old Vienna' and suchlike. We played Grieg's Piano Concerto, Dvořák's *New World Symphony*, Mendelssohn's *Hebrides* overture and similar, until we wished that we were drowning in Fingal's Cave.

These zombifying programmes suited the promoters as they pulled in capacity audiences for every concert, but they did nothing for the standards of playing or morale of the players. And once more I came across a conductor who just could not resist making a crack when he saw me playing cymbals in rehearsal. As Viennese nights are long slogs, we percussionists would ring the changes with the instruments, if only to keep ourselves sane. It's not the loud stuff that is taxing, but, for instance, something like the *Radetzky March* is a killer. Super control of cymbals is required as they play continuously. Much is at a quiet level, with no time to park them to ease the ever-growing knife pain between the shoulder blades. If this inevitable piece is repeated, the bass drummer and cymbal player often swap instruments. Whenever conductor, Vilem Tausky, saw me pick up the cymbals he would say in his laconic, thin voice, "Go on deeearr, HURRT yourself", in that East European accent of his. Ha ha! Funny man. I hated him for it, and thought sourly, "Just you put your head between these cymbals ...", and would secretly mutter, "You wouldn't get away with saying that to a man, and, anyway, a woman would no more 'damp' the sound on her bosom than the guys." That was the implication and we all knew it. His nickname was The Bouncing Czech.

We would arrive mid-afternoon for a rehearsal, and if it was Tchaikovsky's turn we would plough through the inevitable First Piano Concerto, usually with some young hopeful as soloist, then skim through the more awkward bits of the *Swan Lake* ballet music, after which deep breaths were taken for the onslaught of 1812. By this time the cellists were in a state of nervous anticipation for the exposed introduction, and then we were away. However many times I play any piece by Tchaikovsky, I always count the bars most carefully. Even now, as a very experienced player, I find that he has a few tricks up his sleeve, and it wouldn't do to hazard a guess at some of the curiously deceptive entries; certainly not with a monster pair of cymbals or even a cannon to hand.

One Sunday a friend came to collect me after rehearsal and I found myself having a civilised meal in a real house with a real family. This was bliss. I chatted to an ancient aunty who quizzed me about my London visit. When I said that I was playing at the RAH nearby, she was duly impressed, and then she looked anxiously at the clock which was creeping nearer to the 7.30pm mark.

"Shouldn't you be going, dear?" she enquired.

"Oh, no it's all right," I replied jauntily. "I'm only in the overture." As soon as I had said it, I qualified this apparently ludicrous answer by adding, "It's 1812 and at the very end of the concert."

"Oh how interesting, dear – and I suppose you are the one who makes all those horrid noises?"

When the chortling had died down I looked hard at her and responded with, "Well yes, in fact I am!"

At that point I decided to withdraw and strolled back in time to hear strains of Pyotr Ilyich's popular efforts seeping through the artists' entrance. I had not been required to appear at the rehearsal, as conductor Hugo Rignold took my impending contributions to the evening's jollities on trust, so invariably I turned up after the interval, often after 1812 had actually started. It is a long

Arthur and Renie Cotton, 6 November 1932

Butter wouldn't melt, Margaret aged 5

"Your Margaret's such a toyboy", aged 10

Holiday snap. Arthur, Renie and Margaret, aged 15

1953 Huddersfield Youth Orchestra in BBC studio, Leeds.
(Miss Brearley looking on). Conductor: Wyndam Williams

Big transition to National Youth Orchestra of Great Britain,
in Amsterdam's Concertgebouw 1955. Conductor: Hugo Rignold

High jinks at the CBSO Proms 'Last Night' 1961 (Photo: Birmingham Post)

Left: Birmingham Town Hall, Don Thomas playing cymbals. (Photo: Birmingham Post)

Above: Smoking in rehearsals; Ernest Parsons (Photo: Shropshire Magazine)

As soon as a wedding photo is taken, it becomes dated! Margaret and Geoffrey, 18 October 1963

We were blessed with one of each. Alistair 11yrs. Fiona 9yrs (1975)

CBSO percussion and timpani, 1968

Sir Arthur and Hugo Rignold discuss
a technicality during rehearsals

Louis Frémaux danced on the rostrum

The bright green 'Flying Shamrock' ready to take off from
Birmingham's Town Hall

Royal Festival Hall, 1968

Above: Berlioz:
Symphonie Fantastique

No-win situations with bells! Photo: Alan Wood

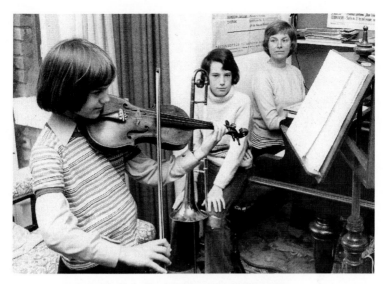

Musical offspring. Photo: Birmingham Post

Above: Kenya visit, 1985. Kyalo (sponsored child) at home with mum, Esther.

Right: Water tank, "Builted by orchastre" from money raised by generous donations and musical events

Victorian House Party. Fiona, Maggie, Anne Steele, Felix Kok

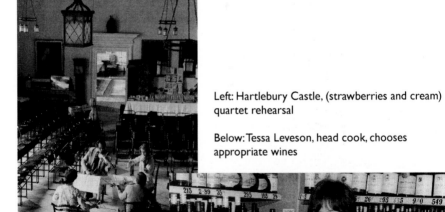

Left: Hartlebury Castle, (strawberries and cream) quartet rehearsal

Below: Tessa Leveson, head cook, chooses appropriate wines

stretch before my first entry, so this was no problem.

My first task was to find the electrician. We greeted each other as long-lost friends and then, with me clutching my music, we began our long trek to the top of the building, through mysterious narrow corridors, up constricted stairways seemingly sandwiched between walls, finally emerging to stride over the outstretched legs of the audience sitting on the floor in the uppermost gallery ('Standing Room Only'), before unlocking the last small door to the roof space above the orchestra. It is as well not to suffer from vertigo in this chosen career. In spite of having played the wretched piece many, many times, my heart always thumped when I heard it from offstage. It was the feeling of inevitability that always got to me – the trapped-in-a-time-warp, 'here we are again' syndrome.

There are sixteen 'cannon shots', which are activated from four galvanised iron tanks secured into the curve of the roof high above the orchestra. Nowadays, I am sure that no such crude methods are used, but this is how I remember my RAH adventures in the early '60s. Each tank contained four maroons, which are normally used as distress signals at sea, their detonator cables leading to sixteen ordinary light switches on a wall-mounted wooden board. My job was to stand behind the electrician and tap him on his shoulder so that, at the appropriate moment, he would pull a switch, thus activating an almighty explosion. This was not as simple as it sounds, as the orchestra was far, far away, conducted by a tiny, gesticulating black dot, and, by the time the sound had reached us from down below, the moment had already gone. It was therefore a case of anticipating the shoulder taps with the hope that the resulting clangour might come somewhere close to the beat that I could not see and the music that I could not hear properly. At one juncture, I ventured to suggest that he probably knew the piece as well as, if not better than, me. He gave me a steely look and said, "You're in work aren't you?" I took the hint, realising that he, as a member of the Electricians' Union, and that I, as a member of the Musicians' Union, needed to cooperate in this, the consequence being that both of us were being paid to work together at the same job. My colleague's ears were far more tuned in to what was happening than mine. "That's two gone from that tank," he would mutter lugubriously, as we reeled back from a particularly loud explosion. I then had to work out where to place the remaining shots for best effect, being determined to use up all my ammunition. Eventually I returned to the relative sanity of the band room, keeping a very low profile as friends and colleagues grumbled past me: heads ringing, eyes glazed. Rumour had it that the electrician's name was

Albert Hall, but I could never pluck up the courage to quiz him on this.

Better even than the RAH affair was a performance we did in Hull some years later. It was the time of many Irish bombings and the country was in a jittery state, so much so that the police visited nearby shops to warn them that the explosion at four o'clock would only be the CBSO rehearsing 1812 and nothing more sinister. This was the first time that the piece had been performed in the City Hall, so extra care was taken in the placing of the explosive devices. At a slightly lower level and at right angles to the main hall there is a large Mayor's Parlour behind the platform, used as the men's changing room and also our tea room during the orchestra breaks. I went backstage to inspect the set-up. Sixteen brand new dustbins containing explosives, each with a covering of chicken wire – in case any red-hot bits might escape onto the carpet – had been wired up to a single cable. Police and firemen resplendent in helmets were in attendance, and we were in business. I was at the other end of the cable with a plunger-type switch, and able to view the conductor through a tiny 'electrician's window' behind the orchestra. So far, so good. There was a try-out at four o'clock, as planned, and everything went well. When it came to the evening I let fly with a carefully placed blast, after which I was horrified to discover that there was no further response from my frantic attempts to activate the plunger. It was evident that somehow a fuse had blown, so I could do no more but tear downstairs to find the electrician, and hopped about whilst he changed the fuse in the plug, arriving back in my eyrie just in time to hear the final throes of the piece and the audience going crazy. But I knew that there would be an encore of the finale, and that I still had fifteen explosions up my sleeve, as it were. When it came to it, I had a field day fitting in more than expected by the old hands on stage. Plaster flakes fell from the ceiling, the hall filled with smoke, the audience was delirious with shell shock and delight and I rushed backstage to thank the electrician before my staggering colleagues could catch up with me. The Mayor's Parlour was also obliterated by smoke, added to which there was a great deal of sweeping up going on. I looked heavenward and discovered that numerous glass ceiling panels had been demolished. Ever afterwards when we played in Hull, I visited the Mayor's Parlour for old time's sake, looked up to inspect the new, but ill-matched glass panels and thought to myself, "Hmm, I did that, with a bit of help!" Any self-respecting percussion section has a fund of stories about the dreaded 1812: we were no exception.

Summer time brought no relief from forays to London, as this was the time for outdoor concerts, resplendent with fireworks and unspeakable noise. Nearer home we play in the grounds of Warwick Castle, the racecourse in Worcester and a local park in Birmingham. Each has its own individuality, but all are near water. Myriads of insects delight in these rehearsals and concerts as they zoom relentlessly amongst the perspiring players. Irritating bites exacerbate the misery for everyone, but particularly for those with hay fever, who spend all their time trying to stifle sneezes – especially problematical for wind players. Summer zephyrs playfully remove music from music stands – this is when the librarian hands out clothes pegs along with the music – and the slightest scrap of sunshine can be guaranteed to dazzle the players to distraction and wrong notes. Music blows into the water and has to be dried out over the huge spotlights at the side of the concert shell, peacocks screech into trees and waterfowl pedal furiously on the water to get away from the strange noises in their domain. We watch in fascination as a constant stream of people move about during the music: children are allowed to run around screaming, teenagers hurl insults and, as darkness falls, tables, chairs, candelabra, bottles of wine and posh picnics are unfurled at the more affluent venues. A late start is de rigueur, as the final item is always teamed with a splendid show of fireworks. Needless to say, the orchestra is never able to see any of these, but interest flared on one occasion at the York Festival when some sparks fell dangerously close to the orchestra's parked instrument van. Seeing the haste with which one of our platform staff rushed over to drive it away in a cloud of blue exhaust fumes was a peripheral entertainment for the players, before we gathered wits, instruments, bags and baggage and pushed our way through the crowds to find our two coaches, grab seats and gratefully leave it to the drivers to take us safely back to base – this, of course, after the percussion players had packed away all their gear. There have been times when we were left behind; then it is a case of waiting for a long time whilst the platform is cleared and instruments are stowed safely before we cadge a lift on the massive van, hoping to be dropped off reasonably near a taxi rank, late-night bus stop or possibly close to home.

As the outdoor, or 'muddy field', concert season grew nearer, there was a heightened interest in daily weather forecasts. We already knew that, if Brits had paid for tickets, they came to outdoor concerts regardless of inclement weather, but we always lived in hope. I can remember only one instance when we spent all morning travelling to south London to play at Crystal Palace, every inch of the way being bedevilled by deluging storms. But it was not until we actually arrived at the venue to observe deckchairs full of thrashing rainwater that we turned tail and headed back to the Midlands. At least we had a free evening at home, and we'd had a lovely coach trip that day, hadn't we?

My life was changing for the better. Not only was I now happily married, but also, with the advent of a new principal percussionist, the job was much more fun. We worked well as a team – albeit just two players – and I became even more delighted with every aspect of being a professional orchestral musician, working with people I liked and respected and being accepted as an equal by most of my colleagues.

* * *

Married life was a great novelty for both Geoff and me, as was to be expected. He had recently reached the grand age of forty, whereas I was a mere twenty-six and was only too delighted to be fussed over and looked after. This seemed a fair exchange for my dogged, fierce independence. I admired my husband's intellectual prowess as a lecturer in Occupational Psychology at Birmingham University, and, although he rarely said anything of the kind to me, I was assured by his two sisters that he was very proud of my achievements in the music world. However, I felt that all his university friends were far more intelligent than me, so at social gatherings I usually said very little, instead listening with admiration and envy at everyone's apparent ease of debate, discussion and heated arguments.

As I now had a domestic audience, as it were, I began to be a more adventurous cook. Geoff had his own bachelor repertoire of dishes, but he was only too pleased to be my guinea pig when it came to experimenting with such strange foreign foods as coleslaw salad, yoghurt (which had to be specially ordered from the local dairy once a week), numerous pasta dishes, cheesecake, Maryland fried chicken, unfamiliar pulses, and such like. Peppers, garlic, fresh ginger, melons, avocado pears, exotic pineapples: all were now available if one knew where to look. Indian and Chinese restaurants were becoming more and more popular and, on high days and holidays, we would treat ourselves to throat-clutching vindaloos of questionable meats, or eye-watering Chinese mysteries full of monosodium glutamate. Visiting these restaurants took on an element of adventure, particularly as it was rare to find a proprietor or waiters who could understand, never mind speak, English. New gadgets constantly appeared in the shops and we were only too eager to try them, making such daring purchases as an electric frying pan, a dual-control electric blanket, large chest freezer and an expensive, top-of-the-range electric mixer. After our first child, Alistair, was born in late July 1964, I sacrificed my beloved van, Fred, to fund a new-fangled automatic washing machine, when everyone else was perfectly happy with a twin tub. We were in the swinging sixties after all, even if our aims were more domestic than personally self-indulgent.

We took out a mortgage on a large, cold, graciously proportioned Victorian semi-detached house in pleasant Moseley, opposite a favoured school. The long, narrow back garden was slowly tamed; Geoff did miracles with DIY; we stripped the doors down to fashionable oiled pine; massive storage heaters were installed as central heating was out of the question; and I beavered away making curtains from the most up-to-date, colourful, patterned material whilst wearing my Mrs Brown hat.

I cannot remember our ever discussing whether or not to have a family, as this was such a natural progression in life; even so, surprise and delight were equal emotions when I realised that I was pregnant. Before our son Alistair was born, I had many grand theories on how to combine motherhood with a demanding career but, needless to say, after the baby arrived I came to my senses. Being a mum is a tough job. Uncle Hugo was somewhat upset when I finally gave in my notice, especially as he had offered me generous maternity leave in the hope that I would return to the fold. I received the following letter written on my birthday:

April 16th 1964
To whom it may concern
Margaret Cotton has been member of my percussion section for the past three and a half years, and has always been reliable and responsible in every way, with the highest playing standards and versatility in the wide range of instruments she has been called upon to play.
I have no hesitation in giving her the strongest possible recommendation and am indeed sorry to be losing her as a member of my orchestra.
Signed Hugo Rignold

This was not to say that much changed in the way of available work, however, as I was always on hand to do any extra work so long as I was able to make sensible domestic arrangements well ahead of the engagements. The money came in handy too, so we were able to employ a treasure to help clean our large house. She lived nearby and was also delighted to help look after the baby when parental timetables clashed. Geoff had a reasonably flexible calendar as a university lecturer, and he loved being a dad, so he was only too happy to take on child-minding duties whenever possible: a rarity for the male-dominated times in which we lived.

My replacement, as sub-principal percussionist, was aforementioned Brian, the cheerful, devil-may-care, ex-army band drummer, who slotted in nicely, and stability reigned once more in the orchestra's kitchen department. Ernie Parsons was omnipresent, in his timpani lair, but his days were numbered as we all discovered when the orchestra gave its first performance of Stravinsky's taxing *Rite of Spring* in May 1965. The flexible malacca canes of his old-fashioned timpani sticks were forever catching on the rims of the drums as Ernie (The Rim-shot Kid) slouched lower and lower behind his instruments, muttering and cursing as he struggled with the difficult rhythms. "Rims Mr Parsons …. rims!" became a very familiar shout from Rignold when he heard this, and we would cringe accordingly. It was soon evident that the old man could not cope with the *Rite*, particularly at one difficult juncture, forever known as hellfire corner by future generations of CBSO players, so at the eleventh hour the timpanist from Covent Garden Opera House was imported to play in the concert. We all heaved a sigh of relief, and Parsons finally left the orchestra: a sad and ignominious end to a long career spanning 45 years, but I, for one, shed no tears.

Ernie's successor was Howard Bradshaw, the nephew of my professor in the NYO. It was such a novelty and relief to have a young player sitting in that prominent and vitally important position. We were a good team at the back there, and at last there was overt enjoyment of the music as we relaxed, smiled and got on with the job. Howard certainly had the bloodhound appearance of the Bradshaws, his rather jowly jawline earning him the nickname of 'Chops'. Doug (percussion principal) had a fund of cockney phrases to hand, and passed on appropriate everyday rhyming slang, much to the amusement and curiosity of our colleagues: we were a very happy section.

In early September 1966, my bouncing daughter Fiona was born, so I had more than my hands full trying to be a perfect mum with a new baby and toddler. Au pair girls were the answer as far as we were concerned, as it was obvious that if I wished to keep up with my playing in whatever capacity we needed more domestic backup. Personal recommendations were responsible for our finding lovely young women who fitted in with the family. They were very happy in Birmingham and attended English language classes, made friends and were a huge success. (To this day I am still in contact with two of my German 'sisters/daughters'.) Our house was a happy home and Geoff and

I were delighted to be blessed with 'one of each flavour' as I put it, and from the outset we agreed on a strict house rule that both parents would never be away from Birmingham at the same time – eventually being broken only when both offspring were well into their teens.

It was hard work to juggle my professional and domestic lives, but after concerts I learnt to sit in the car in the drive, taking time to remove my Margaret Cotton hat and revert to the Mrs Brown role before walking through the door and back to domesticity. There were times when my husband made it abundantly clear that he did not want to hear about the trivia of playing in an orchestra. He was very much the head of the household and in the unusual position of having a wife who did not fit the norm as far as a career was concerned. Trying to be the little woman at home was not easy, and I struggled to hide the fact that certain chores were to me deeply boring. Geoff was somewhat shocked to discover that I detested ironing, which I described as rubbing hot metal over crumpled cloth. His attitude was that of astonishment because, as he put it, "You should enjoy ironing my shirts, as you are looking after your husband." He has since denied all memory of this, but that comment was a watershed in my attitude to tedious domesticity. I kept quiet, did what was required of me, but whenever possible was only too glad to see that someone else was paid to do the jobs I hated. "If I had been meant to dust furniture and wash floors, I would not have been a musician", was my illogical and stubborn argument.

Alistair knew that mummy 'had a big orchestra', but it wasn't until he went to school that he discovered that not all small children have a full-sized concert xylophone parked in their bedroom. From an early age, our children were surrounded by music. I was a great one for singing in the car, encouraging our au pairs to join in, teaching the children Icelandic or German nursery rhymes as the case may be. Geoff had a great collection of jazz records, and classical music flowed from the radio, but life was so hectic that I stopped playing the piano in any serious way, only trotting out nursery rhymes and children's fun pieces when required.

The CBSO was still regarded as the stepping-off point for London orchestras, but now that Rignold was firmly in charge there were more adventurous programmes to grapple with, and many more players seemed happier to settle down and stay in the orchestra instead of moving on. I was in the enviable position of being able to accept or decline as much or as little freelance work as I wished, and suspect that there were colleagues who did not realise that I had done a sideways move, no longer being on a full contract.

In the mid '60s, old traditions changed. Applause became more acceptable in churches and cathedrals when performing before an audience rather than a congregation, and the orchestra stopped playing the National Anthem at the beginning of each and every concert – it was subsequently only played for the first and last concerts in the season, or in the presence of royalty. But before then it had always been the tradition that the full orchestra would come onto the platform to perform this task before every performance. Timpani and snare drum would begin with a cracking roll, after which the usual cymbals (and bass drum if an extra player was available) would highlight the final patriotic climaxes of the piece. If a short overture followed the anthem, then players superfluous to the scoring would be expected to sit on stage until the end of the piece. Then, and only then, were we allowed to leave. Full choral versions were trotted out when a choir was on the platform, but thankfully singing only one verse. Britten, Elgar and others had made arrangements of the piece, but normally we played the standard version. No one bothered using music: it just happened. On the only occasion that the orchestra played in Perth, Scotland, the management realised that two percussionists were being paid train fares, accommodation and allowances to appear for the anthem only. The consequence was that ever afterwards the style of the anthem was dictated by the scoring for the first piece in the programme, giving percussionists the occasional bonus of a free day. (Now the anthem is played exclusively for royal occasions, with only the old-timers playing the familiar harmonies from memory. The youngsters in the orchestra have no experience of this and many need to use the music: indeed; an American-born timpanist never got the bass-line correct as he blundered quietly through the oh-so-familiar routine, much to the amazement and amusement of nearby colleagues. No one said a word!)

Whenever a photographer came to do his stuff during rehearsals, a notice went onto the orchestra noticeboard some days before the event to warn us, whereupon we made a note to appear tidily dressed for the occasion. Not so later, when the orchestra was constantly being inundated with cameramen during the Rattle years. Some we eventually knew well enough to address by their first names, as we became more and more blasé with regard to media attention.

If a woman soloist appeared with us, it was the assistant concert manager's job to phone her agent to discover the colour of her evening dress. This was done so that the bouquet being presented at the end of her performance would not clash with a personal colour scheme. Such detail! It was rare for mere mortals in the orchestra to meet soloists, but there were times when, as percussionists not required for certain concerti, we found ourselves calming nerves backstage, making appreciative noises and admiring pretty evening dresses.

I recall a well-known TV heart-throb narrating Prokofiev's *Peter and the Wolf* for the first time in his life. Rehearsal had gone reasonably well, but prior to the performance he of the long lashes and dreamy eyes was jittery with nerves, pacing up and down backstage in a stew of indecision about which tie to wear. I did my mum thing, calmed him down with chatty trivia and, before he knew it, he was on stage with a smiling orchestra and bowing to an ecstatic audience. The first thing he did when it was all over was to find me in the women's band room and give me a smacking great kiss in front of everyone. I was the envy of all the women after that little effort and threatened not to wash my face for days.

As I began to accept more and more freelance work with the orchestra, it was decided that an additional percussionist should be employed as the number three player. I was offered the job, and Geoff and I agreed that I would go back on full contract for a trial year. However, we soon realised that this was not an ideal situation in terms of family life. In spite of having wonderful help from our au pairs, Alistair, still of preschool age, showed signs of being less than happy with mum not always being to hand. We all found that the situation was too stressful at times, so it was decided that I would tender my three months' notice once more and continue to be the local extra. This gave me the scope to play with my favourite orchestra and I still felt very much part of the team, but with the added flexibility of being able to say no when necessary.

Uncle Hugo's final fling with his orchestra was to take us on tour behind the Iron Curtain to East Germany, Poland and Czechoslovakia, in May 1968. This was the first time I had been away from my family, so I used my imagination to try to convey the passing of time for my young son. It was very important for him to know that mummy would be coming home and that I had not gone forever, so I made a large, colourful chart for the wall with blank spaces for postcards. The appropriate number of jolly postcards equalling days away were written, and then a numbered card would arrive daily from me, which Alistair could find amongst the legitimate mail and stick on the appropriate space on his wall chart. This worked well, although my arms constantly ached for my children: something I never imagined would happen, and for the first time in my adult life I was homesick. Geoff took the time off work to be at home full-time, although we had a very capable and loving au pair girl living with us. Fortunately, little Fiona was too young to understand what was happening.

The merry band flew from London to the very centre of West Berlin, arriving at Tempelhof airport where, after the usual scrum for luggage and tedious passport scrutiny, we found ourselves in a coach park area behind wire netting at Checkpoint Charlie. Our coaches were on the other side of the great divide, with the three drivers, fingers threaded through wire-netting fencing, waiting for us to move through to drab East Berlin. As someone said when we viewed the ugly, empty streets and war-ravaged buildings, "Plenty of parking spaces here!" All the hotels favoured dreary colour schemes, leaving us to wonder if cheerful paint cost more than ubiquitous beige, brown, grey, black and sludge. A small entrance lobby was the only place where one could meet up with friends after making prior arrangements before disappearing behind closed doors to unpack. Otherwise one contacted the front desk to find out room numbers – it was all too easy to be left behind. Once more we experienced problems with exchange rates: official, tourist and black market. Whenever any of us went beyond our hotel, we could guarantee an approach from furtive characters trying to buy our hard currency.

Our concerts sold out throughout the trip, with many people eager to speak to us, often about wartime experiences. In Warsaw we played in the huge, dark Philharmonic Hall, beginning the concert as usual with both national anthems. After the Polish anthem had died away, I noticed numerous people in the audience wiping away tears. I ventured to mention this to our interpreter, whereupon she told us that they had never heard their anthem played so slowly before, but that it was very moving. The older members of the audience no doubt reflected on the significant poignancy of a British orchestra playing this very special music for them in their rebuilt capital city.

Travel by train was during the hours of darkness so that we could not see our surroundings in either countryside or the towns we passed through. It was different during the day, however, as we found ourselves lurching along in uncomfortable buses. Luxury coaches were only in our dreams. These boneshakers stank of sour gasoline, and were dirty and slow. We could see filthy, choked rivers and polluting factories as well as massive, seemingly endless fields being weeded by rows of people wielding simple hoes. Villagers of all ages were collecting leaves from trees lining the dusty roads, and we discovered later that these mulberry leaves were being used to feed silkworms. Sundays saw many in national costume but, in spite of 'Sunday best', villagers were busy with such tasks as clearing out overgrown ditches, sweeping pathways, trimming overgrown trees, tidying massive piles of wood and other such country chores. Churches were much in evidence, but we were told by our interpreter that many had been closed for worship and now were only used for the storage of fodder, farm machinery and suchlike.

Travelling south through Silesia, we were aware of hundreds of tanks massing in the forests near the Polish-Czech border. Innocently, I vaguely imagined this to be the equivalent of army manoeuvres at home on Salisbury plain, but of course this was a deadly serious situation in Eastern Europe. Our three coaches bowled along, stopping at the Cieszyn border crossing, where in the spring sunshine we waited for what seemed like hours. Barbara and I leaned over a wall to watch the river down below, and as we stood there I felt a hand on my shoulder, turned, and there were the Rignolds – the boss with daughter Jenny – as white as sheets and gabbling with relief to see us all. Their VIP car had become separated from the orchestra coaches and had been pounced on by local police. Protestations from the driver were to no avail, passports were removed and their owners searched and subjected to two hours of detailed questioning in a soundproof room before being released to continue their journey.

A few days after our return home, tanks rolled into Czechoslovakia. The Prague spring was over, and the Russian winter had resumed.

* * *

Hugo Rignold's final concert in July 1968 ended with Berlioz's *Symphonie Fantastique*. This piece is fraught with danger, especially in my case as I played the unenviable bell part in the last movement. As usual, I counted through gritted teeth as the cellos rumbled through the final cue before my first fortissimo bell entry. Horror of horrors, Rignold indicated my solo entry a bar earlier than anticipated, but I stuck to my guns and came in after what I was sure were the requisite number of tacet bars. Once committed, one has to continue, which I did with little conviction, but, as I could not hear the rest of the orchestra clearly because of the noise I was making, I had no choice but to follow my prescribed path. After my contributions, I sat and trembled, wondering who had got it right, or otherwise. My colleagues assured me that Mr Reliable had indeed made a blunder, and "good for you, you stuck to your guns!" Ah well, I thought, it makes up for absent glockenspiel notes in the Shostakovitch symphony. These still rankled.

Later that night, after we had gone to bed, the telephone rang. I said casually to Geoff, "Oh, that'll be Riggy apologising – ha!"

Off he went to answer it, and then came the words, "It's Mr Rignold, for you."

"I'm SO sorry for tonight. Thank you for what you did … you saved my bacon!"

He then told me that he had not been able to phone earlier as he had immediately been whisked off to a posh reception, and that he was leaving Birmingham at the crack of the following dawn.

Another page closed and, so far as the players were concerned, no one knew when the next would open, or, even more importantly, with whom we would be working in the future.

9
Gallic Charm

The grapevine was alerted and the hunt was on for a new principal conductor. Meanwhile, the orchestra rubbed along quite nicely. Harold Gray, assisted by numerous guest conductors, held the fort. Finding and securing a suitable candidate necessitates contacting various conductors' agents, an inevitably long-winded operation, but any conductor worth his salt will usually be fully employed and probably tied in to a long contract with an orchestra. Up-and-coming eager youngsters rarely have enough experience, are often untried in the profession, and are unknown by the paying public, so the overall process can take years to come to fruition. Meanwhile, the orchestra's mood swings erratically between deep gloom and heart-thumping optimism, but all seems calm on the surface, with only occasional flurries of overt tension provoked by speculative articles in the local press.

Telephones became red-hot as CBSO players contacted friends and colleagues throughout Europe and beyond. Names were bandied around and hopefuls came as guest conductors to be analysed and picked over by the musicians they attempted to court. The chairman of the Council of Management, the leader and members of the orchestra's management team visited distant concert halls to listen to applicants working with other orchestras, eventually reporting back their findings to the Players' Committee. Ensuing orchestra meetings were many and vociferous; this was an anxious time for everyone.

I doubt if it would have been possible to employ anyone more different from Rignold than Louis Frémaux. He had thoroughly charmed us when he came as a guest, wooing the audience into the bargain with his carefully selected party pieces. An added glamour was the fact that he had been a member of the French Resistance and had served in Vietnam with the French Foreign Legion. Our imaginations ran riot as he blew into our lives like a breath of fresh air, accepting the offer of a contract and duly becoming our principal conductor as we celebrated the CBSO's Jubilee Season in 1969-70.

At the age of forty-eight, Louis was young as far as conductors go. He had conducted orchestras in Paris, Monte Carlo and Lyons, earning his stripes with over thirty recordings and offering a very different repertoire to that of Rignold. We never discovered if he actually played an instrument and this remained an intriguing mystery throughout his tenure with us, but posed no particular problems. The orchestra had excellent principals and a first-class leader, so any technical difficulties were resolved with little fuss. Slim, lithe, with a lively stick technique, Louis soon became a favourite with our audiences. He *danced* on the rostrum and once again we found ourselves studying every facial expression and gesture of our very own conductor. There was much speculation amongst the troops about his hair, for instance, as it was never possible to see how it connected with the scalp, looking as it did like a frizzy, carefully fluffed-up mat draped on the top of his head. There was never a single strand out of place, so we assumed that hair lacquer was very much part of the scene in his dressing room. Not for Louis the gesture of running his hands through his hair in desperation, as some were wont to do. A wide, ready smile lit up deep-set, currant-bun black eyes, and he had a splendid repertoire of truly French gestures soon to be imitated by one and all in the orchestra. My favourite was the shrug: head tilted slightly, shoulders up to the ears, hands spread wide, pursed lips and eyes rolling to the skies. We loved it. He was very keen to improve his English, and to his credit he told us that he tried to learn more vocabulary every day by writing down new words on a small blackboard in the hallway of his flat, so that he could take in fresh ideas on the way in and out of the house.

Even so, there were many bits of his fractured English that we found delightful and consequently no one attempted to correct him. When things were not going well, or when he became hot and bothered during rehearsals, the English would fly out of the window and he would do an obtuse *'elpless Frenchman* act, which drove us mad. One of his more irritating traits when we were trying to interpret some of his flowery efforts was the 'I 'elp you!' syndrome. This always manifested itself in a frantic subdividing of the music for one or many bars. If, for instance, he could not get a smooth flow in a slow passage, he would chop up a perfectly good, slow four beats in a bar to eight fiddly, agitated stabs, totally ruining the style of the music and compounding the problem even further. As far as I was concerned, when he ventured down this path I avoided looking at him altogether, which somewhat negated the whole object of the exercise. During some performances we had the added delight of watching whilst Felix, our distinguished leader, tried tactfully to persuade Louis to indicate a tempo change to two beats in a bar by the more acceptable 'V' sign rather than his preferred method of 'two fingers' with his palm facing inwards. He never seemed to get the hang of this. (Felix had once faced a similar embarrassment in Rignold's day when the maestro arrived on stage with his trousers undone at the flies. After much face-twitching and half-gestures from the front desk, Riggy eventually got the message and we were further entertained as we watched him struggle to keep conducting, fasten old-fashioned buttons, and try to appear as nonchalant as possible!)

Louis soon became a hit with all our audiences. Standing ovations were almost commonplace, but were nevertheless exciting novelties for Birmingham musicians. We relaxed, enjoying a wider French repertoire than with previous conductors. A number of older players retired, leaving room for a younger generation and the adoption of a more liberal attitude towards the inclusion of women. One of the new recruits was Liverpool-born percussionist Anne Oakley. I had met her on previous occasions at the BBC in Bristol, where she was a member of the BBC Training Orchestra, and recommended that she should be offered work as an extra player when we were fielding a full team for Louis' exciting programmes. Anne (to be known as Annie some years later) replaced me after I had handed in my notice for the second time, following my unsuccessful year trying to be a full-time mum and professional orchestral player. As she managed to rent a small flat near to me in Moseley, we shared lifts to work and became good friends, inside and outside the orchestra.

Audience numbers grew as word got around about the exciting CBSO concerts. Rignold's discipline and technical expertise had certainly paid off, but, when Louis' French flair and personal charisma were added, there was a perceptible rise in enthusiasm all round. Fine soloists were attracted to the orchestra along with distinguished conductors, standards soared, and once more we found ourselves touring Eastern Europe in the spring of 1972.

* * *

In May we left a chilly, windy Birmingham, but stumbled into a dry, oven-like 27°C at Bucharest airport some hours later. Thankfully, I had flung a cotton dress into my case at the very last minute, but others were not so fortunate with their choice of clothes. Nick, one of the percussionists, spent the whole of the tour in a striped tee shirt of mine - fortunately it was easy to wash and dry. As expected, the decor of the hotels was dreary and the workmanship shoddy, the whole effect being somewhat scruffy and dirty. No single rooms were available. Personal space was therefore at a premium and friendships foundered or were strengthened by enforced togetherness. Fortunately Barbara, my long-standing fiddle friend, and I shared not only

141

rooms but also the same sense of humour, a real bonus in such circumstances.

I immediately noted down differences, such as: real straw drinking straws; Turkish coffee thinned down with warm, watery milk and tasting burnt and truly disgusting; freshly squeezed lemon juice to drink, diluted with iced water and sieved through coarse, gritty sugar lumps held between the front teeth; wide tree-lined French-looking boulevards; and burly workmen wearing tiny tip-tilted straw hats, companionably holding hands walking down the street. Women laboured on the roads – sweeping, planting shrubs, pruning roadside trees, slaking dusty pavements with hosepipes, shifting loose granite pavement cobbles, or engaged in general manual work. I was fascinated with the foreignness of Rumania, thoroughly enjoying my strolls and indulging in my hobby of people-watching.

My diary at the time notes:

There seems to be a very interesting mixture of very dark-skinned, black-haired, Turkish types, to brown-haired and light-eyed Slavs with flattish faces and high cheekbones. Middle-aged women wear grey or dark skirts, flat shoes, wool socks, and incongruous light coloured crocheted tops or thin shirt-blouses. Little children wear thick tights or leggings (boys and girls, even in this heat!), often with grubby velvet or sateen tops for little girls. Tiny babies look boiled, stuffed in their wintry wrappings in small wickerwork prams, with only scarlet faces to be seen, poor things.

We were told that the concert hall was part of the Palace of the Republic - plenty of red flags in evidence here – designed for President Ceausescu for when he addressed the party faithful. Indeed it was somewhat unnerving to turn round during the rehearsal to discover an armed soldier looking on. However, after rehearsal I was solemnly presented with a full-blown yellow rose by one of the rifle-toting youngsters.

I further noted:

All the walls of the 3,000-seater hall are covered in shabby turquoise velvet. Dull and muffled to play in. An enormous stage, wide and flat with velvet-covered wings. We (percussion section) sat out front to listen during the piano concerto in the rehearsal. The piano sounded frightful – very sharp and 'canned'. Apparently it was tuned to A450, so our oboe's A440 sounded hideously flat.
We saw eight microphones in the orchestra, and a young woman stalking

about with a walky-talky radio, obviously balancing sound. As a broadcast was scheduled for the concert this seemed reasonable. However Brian (one of our 'extras'), sensitive soul, said that he could feel the music vibrating through his chair. After investigation we discovered that every chair in the place had a microphone in the back and that the whole stage was wired up to pump the sound out through to the auditorium. This ploy was an attempt to put some resonance back into the totally 'dead' hall, so therefore the orchestra sounded ill-balanced and canned. The woman in question spoke very highly of the method and probably found our attitude as perplexing as we hers. We mentioned how loud the cellos sounded in one solo passage to which she replied, "Yes, they have just been turned up!"

Everything ran smoothly until we eventually moved on to Belgrade late one evening, where it was discovered that, as an American, timpanist James Strebing did not have the necessary bits of paper to satisfy the customs officer on duty at the border. James was waiting for his British citizenship papers to come through and therefore only had a temporary International Travel Document instead of a full passport. Soon two of the orchestra and the agent's representative found themselves endlessly arguing with officials in German, their only common language. The first coach had departed, completely unaware of the problem. In the second coach we waited and waited in no-man's land, getting hungrier and hungrier as the British stiff upper lip set in. After two hours our coach driver insisted that we continue, so Maurice Handford, our associate conductor for the tour, and concert manager Beresford, stayed behind, finally managing to contact the British Council and Embassy. Eventually the problem was resolved in the wee small hours and the orchestra had a timpanist once more. James took it all in his stride: no ruffled feathers; no comment.

All the concerts went well. We were showered with red carnations and duly appreciated the enthusiastic, rhythmical applause at the end of each performance. In spite of hectic timetables, we always have some scheduled free time, which makes it possible to see something of the countries we visit, or wash our smalls, sleep, trail round the shops, meet friends, do the cultural trips round art galleries or go to local concerts. One such treat for some of us was to hear Tito Gobbi sing the role of Scarpia in Puccini's *Tosca* in Budapest. We had played on stage at the opera house the previous evening, but then it had been transformed into a concert platform with a plywood backdrop of painted panelling. Behind this we had discovered an enormous stage reaching far behind our small area and crowded with scenery and props for the opera. We thoroughly enjoyed an unforgettable performance, although the printed programme was impossible to understand. Luckily, I knew the plot of *Tosca*, having played it with the Welsh National Opera.

Our hotel was miles outside beautiful Budapest, so the two coaches travelled back after the concerts in two shifts: one immediately after the concert; the other nearer to midnight. One night a group of us opted for the late coach, as we had been recommended a real gypsy restaurant on the banks of the Danube. This turned out to be a tiny cellar dive with a whitewashed, arched roof, simple, plain wooden tables, and lively with local people. As soon as we walked through the door, the fiddler spotted Phil Head's violin case. When he had finished his piece, he came over to us and with mime and much laughter we managed to communicate that we were a bunch of professional musicians. Phil did no more than unfurl his violin and walk around the tables, grinning and playing *'The Irish Washerwoman'*. This was greeted with roars of approval from one and all, after which we were plied with generous quantities of spicy food, starting with paprika-laced carp soup and rough red wine. Dressed in hand-embroidered, full-sleeved white shirts, green satin boleros, red cummerbunds and black trousers, the musicians comprised two violins, viola, double bass and cimbalom. As soon as their boss realised that he had foreign colleagues in his audience, he gave a virtuoso performance that included many, many spectacular trick effects. He loosened the hair of the bow and played the fiddle between hair and stick, and then he played it behind his back, or switched from hand to hand without any perceptible pause in tempo or style, and at one point he loosened a single hair from the bow, tied it to the E string and played eerie 'mouse music', high and squeaky – way up in the rosin – harmonics to die for. The more we encouraged him, the more outrageous and breathtaking his performance became. But all too soon we had to go, and it was with great reluctance that we left for our Cinderella coach. We were pleased to note, however, that some of this had been captured on tape by our tame BBC reporter, who was compiling a sound picture for a local radio broadcast on our return to England.

A notable feature of this tour was that we often found ourselves playing in the very halls that had hosted first performances of some of the world's greatest music. Composers such as Liszt, Smetana and Dvorák haunted us, but then our own Birmingham Town Hall can boast performances from a number of top names too: Mendelssohn, Elgar, Sibelius, Dvořák, to name but a few.

Throughout our journeying, we were very aware of differences between our cultures. There was little or no smiling to be seen, and we were shocked by the fact that there was a constant feeling of people looking over their shoulders. Men in heavy black overcoats stood around in the corridors and by the doorways in hotels and concert halls – silent, stone-faced and unnerving to say the least. Our final concert was in Košice, a small Czechoslovakian garrison town by the Russian border. One of my tasks on this tour was to find a Czech crystal brandy glass for my husband and so, as I was not required for the rehearsal, I asked for help in my quest from our polite interpreter. He was a diffident young man, a mathematician, a computer programmer (something I checked on, as I had never heard of such a profession) and translator in his spare time; married and with a young family. His English was excellent, with a good vocabulary, but when he spoke to us he always seemed nervy and a little anxious, added to which his conversational skills were somewhat rusty. The shop we were taken to was a very basic department store, but I had plenty of choice from the cardboard boxes stacked on trestle tables, and selected some heavy crystal fruit dishes and a brandy glass. Rain poured down, but he very kindly took me to the food hall where I bought local smoked sausage with the remainder of my Czech currency. We were drenched and, after tramping back through the downpour, he shot off to have a meal at home before appearing on duty in the evening. As a little show of gratitude, I found Gloomy Joe before the concert and gave him a pack of unopened, new tights for his wife. From the reaction I got, I might have handed him a live hand grenade. He went red, mysterious, shifty and edgy all at once and hurriedly secreted the packet in his inside jacket pocket. He then physically backed away as I gabbled embarrassed near-nonsense to try to cover his discomfiture. After this small cloak-and-dagger episode we never saw him again.

It was decided by everyone that the hotel was bugged, and we discovered that another of our interpreters had been interviewed by the police for 'criticising the state' – probably prompted by a flippant remark from one of us. Everything took an inordinate amount of time, from ordering food to the stamping of passports, and everyone seemed to be constantly scrutinising everyone else. So it was with a certain feeling of relief that we returned home to our own country, with no travel or currency restrictions, freedom of speech and no sense of Big Brother constantly watching over us.

The orchestra was on a very exciting roll with Louis in the early '70s. Numerous recordings had come our way, but no more tours abroad were planned. In spite of a perceived memory of an all-French repertoire, our musical diet was very varied as we experienced a wide range of music, from flamboyant recordings of Walton to pre-Rattle Mahler blockbusters and reams of triumphant Beethoven delivered in Festival guise. Many big names were attracted to the Midlands and we found ourselves playing with such international stars as father and son Oistrakh, Elizabeth Schwarzkopf, Emil Gilels, Victoria de Los Angeles, Menuhin, Isaac Stern and Tortelier, and working closely with composers such as Arnold, Britten, Tippett, Bliss and Walton. Guest conductors came and went, some from the 'old school' and others with exciting, innovative ideas.

In 1974, Louis and Gordon Clinton, distinguished baritone and principal of the Birmingham School of Music, had the bright idea of creating a CBSO chorus: a stable 'in house' choir. Auditions were held, an upper age limit pinned at 45 years and, in spite of the fact that Birmingham boasted other fine choirs, the orchestra's own singers were to become renowned for their exemplary expertise, musicianship, and wide repertoire – on tap for everything from Messiaen's newly introduced works to the enormous, hall-filling Berlioz extravaganzas. (In 1995 the Chorus was renamed the City of Birmingham Symphony Chorus, a term much more understood overseas. With the further creation of an affiliated Youth Chorus, it is now recognised as one of the finest choirs in Europe, accepting invitations to give concerts in its own right and taking part in foreign tours worldwide, including performances and recordings with other orchestras such as the Vienna and Berlin Philharmonic orchestras.)

School visits came to an end as times changed, much to the relief of the players, but it was still imperative to encourage young people to take an interest in our music, and to this end the CBSO tied in with a local radio station to host highly successful, lively shows fronted by extrovert flautist Atarah Ben-Tovim. Also in the mid '70s a brash, flamboyant American, Robert Mandell, was engaged to conduct a series of Family Proms. His jazzy kaftans and glitzy pendants went down well with youngsters in the audiences, but Bernstein's erstwhile assistant took more and more risks as he bullied and sniped his way through rehearsals.

Matters eventually came to a head during a final rehearsal for one of these concerts, at the beginning of a fun Latin American number. This required colleague Annie (Oakley) and I to start the piece with maracas and claves. Unfortunately, we were unable to sort out what he was trying to convey with his wayward beat and so, after hesitating, we both stopped playing: no angst – just smiles and querulous looks. Taken aback, Mandell snapped, "What do those two stupid bitches think they're doing?" Shocked silence ensued, whereupon Margaret, the quietest viola player in the world, got to her feet, looked over to the horns, one of whom was the Musicians' Union (MU) steward, and said, "Are you going to let him speak to our percussionists like that?" I think that this reaction from such an unlikely source possibly shook the orchestra even more than the conductor's intemperate outburst. Annie and I were, for once, struck dumb.

Co-leader John Bradbury immediately insisted that Mandell follow him from the rehearsal room, together with Doug our percussion boss, and the MU steward. We never discovered what was said in the confines of the conductor's room, but Mandell did not return to that rehearsal and we never saw him again. Another conductor was found at the last moment and, of course, the concert happened. The saddest aspect of the incident, however, was the loss of a potentially colourful resource in the search for more imaginative concerts for young people.

'Bread and butter' concerts were, yet again, the Hochhauser Sunday extravaganzas at the Royal Albert Hall. On these dates, playing standards dropped alarmingly as an exhausted, zombified orchestra churned out predictable pop classics at a cheaper rate than the London orchestras. Arthur Baker, our general manager, had an eye for the money-spinners as well as more prestigious dates.

There was very much an 'us' and 'them' attitude prevailing at the time between the management and musicians. Office staff were told not to fraternise with players, in spite of the fact that there were previous student connections and long-standing friendships at stake. Baker was a tough control freak: handsome, debonair and confident. He was very much in charge and also had a reputation as a ladies' man, his covert peccadilloes in the office being observed with great interest by the musicians, but with dismay by non-involved office staff. The fact that his lady-love was a colleague in the administration department was not conducive to openness and trust within the general support staff. She became perceived as a glamorous spy in the camp, inadvertently engendering and exacerbating overall feelings of suspicion and unrest in the majority of the workforce, both onstage and backstage.

147

Louis had an agent in France, but, when Arthur Baker became his agent on home ground, alarm bells began to ring in the players' minds. We felt that Baker's energies should primarily be for the good of the orchestra and that, if he had the welfare of the music director at heart as his agent, this would inevitably create a serious conflict of interests. For example, news percolated through to the players that the CBSO had been invited to take part in a Bruckner Festival in Austria, perform in Hong Kong, and be the orchestra in residence at the Three Choirs Festival in Worcester, all of which were turned down by Baker on account of the fact that Louis was otherwise engaged – not with the CBSO. Disquiet on our part was noted and conveyed to Baker by the Players' Committee, but was promptly quashed. The next step was for the players to lobby the Council of Management, but Baker's strong character and articulate reasoning meant that the Council was effectively rubber-stamping every managerial proposal. In spite of an orchestra representative being an observer in Council of Management meetings, we felt that lines of communication were being blocked and that Baker regarded mere musicians with condescension and disrespect, to be kept on a concert platform to play the dots and nothing more. One of his well-worn quotes was that we were all 'musical bricklayers'; obviously a favourite notion of his, as he declared at a posh reception, "I regard musicians as bricks in a wall. When one falls out, I just get another." I was the dumbfounded recipient on that occasion.

No doubt Louis was relieved to know that a strong character was there for him to lean on, as there were times when he felt, rightly or wrongly, that his position as music director was being eroded. Trust between a conductor and his orchestra is a precious and essential commodity, but, when problems arose, Louis was dismayed to realise that his disparate bunch of bright musicians would question, discuss, examine and analyse every situation. One suspected that he was not accustomed to this approach from any of the French orchestras. Naturally the management dealt with the everyday running of the ship, but if there were any artistic difficulties, particularly during performances, then we felt that it was crucial for all to be open about what had occurred, enabling everyone to move forward in trust and honesty. Unfortunately, certain concerts stay in the memory as low points in the orchestra's history, often more for their consequences than for the occasions themselves.

One such was a disastrous performance of Stravinsky's *Rite of Spring*, which we were playing at the opening Thursday concert of the orchestra's 56th season in 1975. The BBC was broadcasting the concert live, so it was essential that the many microphones were placed advantageously for clarity and balance in the difficult acoustic of Birmingham's handsome town hall. Naturally this took place in the rehearsal, with woodwind players being moved a little here or there, until everyone was happy. There was a piano concerto in the first half of the concert, so after its removal from the platform there was the usual shuffling and settling down before embarking on the rigours of Stravinsky. All was going well until suddenly disaster struck in a particularly tricky area. Louis had miscounted or misread his score and proceeded to panic. As his wayward beats became more and more vague and impossible to follow, some simply stopped playing. In what seemed like a lifetime, a few carried on regardless, but the texture unravelled like an old sock. At that moment, I was turning pages for Doug, my boss, who had the onerous task of playing the huge bass drum, with two linchpin fortissimo depth charges in the offing. Everyone secretly relied on these two notes, but, in spite of a few stalwarts ploughing away on front desks and a brave principal clarinet, there was little to go on either visually or aurally. Doug's first cue was delivered with great aplomb, but unfortunately in the wrong spot; the second, however, arrived loud, clear and spot on. Threads were thankfully gathered up and we were back on track again. The incident affected only a few bars of music, but shook everyone to the core. The next day happened to be a free day, so there was much telephoning and reflection: "What on earth did it sound like?" "Did the audience notice how bad it was?" "Will we ever hold up our heads again?" and that sort of thing.

On the Saturday we had a late rehearsal in Worcester Cathedral, and one could have heard a pin drop as Louis came in to take the session. He said not one word. All it needed was a courageous "sorry" or something similar; but no. After rehearsal he actually took the bassoons to task for having changed their platform position for the Stravinsky. We were all in it together, but he transferred the blame to others who were not able to vindicate themselves. Everyone makes mistakes, and it would have been so easy for him to have redeemed his status with his orchestra by making a basic apology. Many of us felt that this unfortunate incident was the end of a long nine-year marriage and the beginning of deep mistrust on both sides. We felt that when Arthur Baker became Louis' agent, the orchestra had definitely become second fiddle to the needs of the maestro.

It was during this time that Louis came into a rehearsal and announced, "I 'ave something to tell you." There was a pause, and hope flickered in the minds of many of the players. Then followed, "I 'ave been invited to become

149

the conductor of the Sydney Symphony Orchestra, but ... don't worry, I will not leave you!" As one of the violinists said later, "It was the biggest anticlimax in the history of the world"! The ultimate crunch came, however, when Louis and the management ignored accepted custom and practice over the seating of extra musicians not on full contract with the orchestra.

In those days, whenever a player was absent for whatever reason, other members of the section (usually a string section) moved forward to fill the gap, with each player being expected to address the music with which they were confronted; front-desk strings often being required to play solo strands within the score. (This was precisely how I had found myself unwillingly being pushed into the situation of playing the principal percussion role for months, all those years previously.) The string pecking order consisted of a principal and co-principal on the front desk, with the players behind being ranked as numbers three and four, and so on. The two front-desk positions are the top-dog seats, carrying with them prestige within the section and an appropriate sitting-up-fee for those who move forward to compensate for any extra responsibilities entailed. All other players were known as rank and file (now known as tutti players).

The principal viola player had recently left for the bright lights of the Royal Opera House, others were off sick, and a rank and file player thus found herself sitting on the front desk for a week as the number two player. Frémaux, however, decided that the then rarely performed work (Tippett's *Ritual Dances*) needed a player of higher calibre in such a prominent position, and so instructed the orchestra manager to engage a recently departed sub-principal viola player to slot into this front-desk position. This duly happened. As non-CBSO players always sat at the back of the section, there were immediate objections to what was perceived, rightly or wrongly, as a cavalier rearrangement of the first desk. Consequently, during the lunch break an orchestra meeting was held at which a resolution was passed that "the orchestra would not play unless the incoming player was moved to the back of the section". Without immediate management support, Frémaux had to accept this humiliating situation, which further intensified unease and mistrust between all parties.

On March 9th 1978, at the end of a depressing meeting in the bar at the town hall, the orchestra passed a vote of no confidence in Baker's management. A letter was subsequently handed to the chairman of the Management Committee, George Jonas, along with a dossier of disquieting background material gathered over the previous months. A further meeting was convened with the whole orchestra where, after much airing of grievances, the vote of no confidence was grudgingly withdrawn on condition that George put the orchestra's complaints to Arthur Baker. Nevertheless, it was mutually agreed that Baker's position was totally untenable. As a result, he offered his resignation on March 16th, which was accepted. (More formal histories and accounts of the CBSO have given the official line on the Frémaux debacle, but as a member of the orchestra I believe that the time is long overdue for we musicians also to air our opinions on the sad situation.)

As soon as Frémaux was apprised of what he described as 'a revolution', he vanished from the scene, apparently unable or unwilling to appreciate that the clash was not primarily with him, but with overbearing management. Rehearsal the following day took place without a conductor much to our puzzlement, and he was not to be seen again with the CBSO from that day to this. In spite of many attempts to contact him, it was made perfectly clear that there would be no communication in any way with the players. His telephone was not answered, knocking on his door had no effect and he even went to the trouble of blocking off the letter box to prevent any contact by hand-delivered letter. Baker agreed to attempt to redress the damage done by finding other conductors to replace his client during the months in which Frémaux's contract was supposed to continue.

Our orchestral contract states that contact with the media is not allowed and, as any breach of contract meant instant dismissal, it was more than anyone's job was worth to speak to the papers. All players were effectively gagged, with none being able to give our angle on the affair. (This remains the case to this day, even in the case of this ancient history as far as players still in the orchestra from that time are concerned, but I am no longer constrained by a contract.) We musicians closed ranks as shock waves began to reverberate in the profession, frustrating the press by an overall silence. Paul Smith, chairman of the Players' Committee, was the only player allowed to quote on Frémaux's disappearance, saying, "We literally had no inkling about this. The first we knew was what we read in the newspapers. It was a complete bombshell!"

George Jonas valiantly attempted to persuade Louis to change his mind, but to no avail, and all too soon a letter was received from Frémaux asking to be released from his contract with immediate effect.

On March 21st, the *Birmingham Post*, under the heading of "'Unsettled' Louis Frémaux to Quit" trumpeted:

A surprise request to be released from his contract comes hot on the heels of a dispute between members of the CBSO and general manager Arthur Baker.

The *Birmingham Mail*, in their report of March 29th, memorably did not castigate the players, saying:

This was the first mention of the dual managership for engagements with other orchestras", but "it was not a particular cause of the dispute" [sic].

On March 30th, further comment was made in the *Birmingham Post*, by Barrie Grayson:

If Louis Frémaux and Arthur Baker, with the backing of the Management Committee, have decided that change is necessary for the further good of the orchestra, then one wishes them well. If there has been a drastic hatchet operation which could leave the orchestra truncated and in limbo for the next season, then a change would be nothing less than deplorable. The future of the CBSO must be made known for the morale of the players, Arts Council and Birmingham ratepayers.

As the maestro still had 16 months of his contract to run, there was a serious possibility that he would be sued for breach of contract, for walking out and leaving the orchestra in the lurch. We felt deeply betrayed by the one person who needed to be strong, but whom we now realised never would be.

On April 1st (a noteworthy date!), Frémaux issued a somewhat unabashed and condescending statement to the press, which was reported in the *Birmingham Post* under the heading "Frémaux stays – CBSO":

... he stated that he was prepared to conduct the Birmingham and London Prom concerts of the Berlioz Requiem, and that negotiations for War Requiem recordings continued [On the strict condition that a guest chamber orchestra would be invited to take part in the recording.] In April 1979 he was to take up his position as chief conductor of the Sydney Symphony Orchestra and would guest conduct with the CBSO ...

This was breathtaking in its arrogance and was received with derision and disbelief by the players, in the certain knowledge that the partnership between orchestra and conductor had irretrievably broken down. George was later heard to say that, as far as he was concerned, Frémaux would only conduct the CBSO again over his dead body. Regrettably, what had been a glorious chapter in the history of the CBSO closed on a sad and sour note.

Incidentally, in 1995 there was a warm welcome for Frémaux from a generous audience when he appeared at Symphony Hall with the National Youth Orchestra of Great Britain. This prompted speculation as to the possibility of a guest appearance with the CBSO – a 'let bygones be bygones' approach perhaps? Players were lobbied for their thoughts on the matter, but it came as no surprise when deep feelings of bitterness arose once more and many of the old guard declared that under no circumstances would they ever play again for the man, contract or no contract.

As far as many of us were concerned, the saddest aspect in all this was that the players had no public voice, so therefore were castigated as the villains in the minds of many of our faithful concert-goers. "What have you done to poor old Louis?", "Can't you all shake hands and make up?" and "Why are you trying to get rid of your conductor?" were the sorts of comments and questions that came thick and fast, but we were effectively silenced by the contract, feeling sore that we were unable to put forward our reasons other than what could be gleaned from the limited and sometimes scurrilous press coverage.

On June 23rd, *Private Eye* eventually kicked in with one of its more bizarre fairy tales (as if the music profession was not aware of the death of one of the great conductors of the day):

Having successfully ousted their principal conductor Louis Frémaux, the leftist firebrands of the CBSO were looking around for someone to replace him.
After a lengthy debate they finally decided that Rudolf Kempe had all the right political and musical qualifications. However, one slight drawback then emerged. Maestro Kempe had been dead for some time.

As expected, morale was at the lowest ebb possible, but again the show had to go on. Fortunately, we were nearing the end of our subscription series, but replacement conductors still had to be found and musicians auditioned to fill the gaps left by those who had resigned in despair or disgust. To his credit Arthur Baker worked hard to replace Frémaux where necessary, acting as manager until the end of the concert season, when he finally left in summer 1978. George Jonas, helped by Harold Gray, headed a splendid team of positive minds, who linked with the MU and Players' Committee, and the ship stayed afloat – just. The players remained dumb and miserable, and once more the hunt was on, this time for a conductor for the impending Beethoven Festival in May. By some wonderful miracle, the right man was found for the job. Erich Schmid was an amiable, elderly Swiss conductor of the 'old school', someone with whom we had never worked, but who had appeared with other British orchestras; and the prognosis was good.

I was only involved in the *Choral Symphony* and so I was somewhat surprised when I received excited messages from enthusiastic colleagues telling me that the old man was a perfect breath of fresh air. A number of phone calls drew me from my 'not required' state in Worcester to eavesdrop at a rehearsal, being intrigued by the excitement generated and needing to hear for myself. Sitting in the auditorium, I soon recognised that there was a wonderful rapport between dear Erich and the orchestra. He loved his Beethoven and it showed in every gesture, suggestion, phrase and sound. I noticed an elegant elderly lady sitting in the balcony and was encouraged by her smile to speak and introduce myself. Gentle Martha Schmid soon became a favourite with everyone, her charming presence at every rehearsal and concert helping with the healing process, along with Erich's intellect, deep understanding and loving interpretation of the master's scores.

From the very first concert of the Festival, it became apparent that the audience was aware of something very special happening. Word soon got around and tickets sold like hot cakes. Erich's magnificent interpretation of the Ninth Symphony was the only one in which I ever shed tears in the exquisite slow movement, and eventually grinned throughout the triumphant finale. Everyone was on a high at last, so much so that the CBSO Supporters presented Erich with an engraved silver box for stepping in and saving the day, not to mention giving us all the experience of a wonderful week of Beethoven greats. There were orchids for Martha, and red and white roses for the choir, orchestra, and every member of the audience. We were cheered to the rafters.

As the *Birmingham Mail* reported:

The audience stood, cheered and applauded through the most emotional demonstrations I have ever seen in this hall ... after the mighty climax of the Ninth Symphony had brought this remarkable Festival to a close.

With champagne from the [stand-in] management there also came the news that Erich Schmid will be back with us next season. And yet more cheers!

We were in a state of total bemusement over what had happened in a relatively short time, and Erich Schmid was rightly declared a hero by one and all. However, reality set in with a vengeance after the summer holiday break, with everyone cooperating as other guest conductors took over Frémaux programmes. The press remained frustrated; the players silent.

10
Worcester Move

Life rolled along both domestically and professionally in the '70s. I accepted most of the extra work offered with the orchestra, did some teaching and learnt to keep a low profile musically speaking, wearing my Mrs Brown hat at all times when at home. At the time, my professional persona seemed of little consequence behind my own front door, as Miss Cotton rarely came into the domestic scene. Then, out of the blue, for the second time during my time with the orchestra, a percussionist was dismissed on the spot. Greed or conceit had led a young player to skip a CBSO rehearsal in favour of a freelance engagement with another orchestra, naively imagining that no one would be any the wiser. However, as his name appeared in the list of players for the orchestra in question, it was only a matter of time before he was found out – in this case, almost immediately.

Once again I was invited to rejoin the orchestra as a full member. My children were eleven and nine years old and we had a totally reliable treasure willing to fit in with the household's unusual working schedules, and so, after a family conference, it was agreed that I should take up the sub-principal position with the orchestra, rejoining the merry band for a record-breaking third time.

In 1976 Alistair moved to a secondary school in the locality. This was the period when comprehensive schools were being introduced in Birmingham. We were not in the catchment area for the nearest school, and therefore the only solution seemed to be a smaller all-boys' school a bike ride away, through suburban side roads. A few boys from Alistair's junior school also moved on to that school, but inevitably this was a huge life-change for our quiet twelve-year-old. Our first impressions were good, but what we did not realise was that the school included a large intake of street-wise lads from inner-city clearance areas. The subsequent school terms proved to be an ever-growing nightmare for Alistair, who became increasingly silent and uncommunicative. Geoff and I became totally frustrated and deeply concerned as he hotly denied that there were any problems with his peers, but alarm bells rang when he came home with torn clothes and other more blood-stained signs of schoolboy bullying. The headmaster was contacted and we were assured that everything would be done to sort out the problem, if indeed there was a problem. "Your son is just the sort of boy we need in this school," we were told, but the school was not the sort of school our son needed.

After a lengthy family discussion about the predicament, a new life for all of us was soon to be launched. Alistair sat entrance papers for King's School, Worcester, and for Solihull School, and he was offered a place at both. He was one of the 10 successful applicants out of a total of 47 for Solihull, but we decided upon King's. Visits to Worcester and further dialogue with two colleagues, both of whom had sons at the school, confirmed our final decision, and the place at King's School was accepted. We were duly thrilled when our budding trombonist was awarded a Music Exhibition, a prize carrying with it a reduction of school fees by a third. Going down the road of public school fees had never been our intention, and so all contributions were of immense help. We were very proud of our talented son.

Major adjustments were made as we prepared for the wrench of a child going away to school, albeit as a weekly boarder. Alistair wrote to tell his grandparents about his new school and was very positive about the prospects of a move away from home: "Oh well, not long now. I will be at King's School from September 7th and am really looking forward to it. The house in which I will be living is opposite the cathedral."

I doubt if Alistair realised how deeply miserable his parents were after offloading the school trunk, tuck box, trombone and child. We drove back home, a mere 28 miles, in silence and tears. So far as we could see, the only solution was for him to come home every weekend, ostensibly for a trombone lesson. Weekly boarders were allowed home more than full boarders, but, even so, our family was split: Fiona missed her brother and I felt that we had betrayed our children.

After the initial settling down period, Alistair found himself playing in concerts and taking an active part in a very different school life. The only solution to parental misery and an unsettled family, however, was for us to move to Worcester, which we did in September 1978 about two days before term started. Fiona had gained a place at the Worcester Girls' Grammar School and thankfully we were a complete family unit once more. We sold one of the cars, and were to commute to Birmingham for nine years. I was fortunate that eight colleagues lived in and around Worcester, so we were able to share lifts for most rehearsals and concerts, and Geoff could walk to trains that delivered him into the centre of Birmingham and Aston University where he was now a senior lecturer.

The Brown family soon settled down in Lorne House, our new home in

Worcester, relishing the space of four reception rooms and the novelty, for us, of indoor sunshine. The tall, early-Victorian house consisted of the left side of a large property, divided in such a way that the other half, Worcester's Driving Test Centre, had the original front door complete with pillars and portico. Our entrance was far more modest, but we had a huge front room which I immediately designated for music. Geoff was delighted with the large custom-built workshop at the end of the tiny enclosed garden and, in addition, I had my very own garage in which to store instruments as well as our one remaining car.

I soon relished the delights of living close to town and dug out my ancient sit-up-and-beg bike with its useful shopping baskets. Son and daughter cycled to their respective schools, and Geoff could have his Sunday lunchtime pint in a choice of ancient hostelries nearby. Soft old Jasper, our black labrador, had nearby Pitchcroft racecourse to run on – "Don't let the dog go in the river!", there were goldfish in our minute back-garden pool, and a lively kitten was rapidly becoming a favourite character with all of us, including the dog. The trek to Birmingham was not as arduous as I had anticipated, as I realised that sitting post-concert in a car, discussing the evening's performance for forty-five minutes, neatly bridged the gap between professional and domestic lives. Schedules for strings and percussion did not always gel and so on those occasions I was independent, choosing to arrive very early and leave late after concerts, the dreaded instruments and platform arrangements always coming first. Then, of course, I had the advantage of not necessarily being required for all the items and, therefore, could often be on my way home as the rest began the second half. After out-of-town days I invariably slept on the coach, to wake bright-eyed and furry on my return to first base in Birmingham, ready for the extra drive home. My ability to sleep at any given time was viewed with envy by colleagues, particularly prior to a heavy concert, when they would discover a comatose body under the band-room table with note attached: "Please wake me with half an hour to go"!

When we arrived in our large Worcester house, there was the small matter of newly discovered wet rot, which had to be addressed before our mortgage could be secured. Drastic action was needed, and so I weeded out my instruments and sold those that were surplus to immediate requirements. My magpie collection of bits and pieces of Victorian jewellery had the same treatment, and a family decision was made to cash in on the needs for accommodation in the city during the Three Choirs Festival week in late summer.

Geoff and Alistair disappeared to a family cottage in the Cotswolds whilst Fiona and I did bed and breakfast for five guests in the house. The upshot of this adventure was a lifelong friendship with Fred from New York and some fascinating chats around the table with Jean Langlais, the distinguished blind organist and composer. He was a contemporary of Messiaen and told us many a tale of their exploits as students in Paris. We listened with round eyes as the coffee got cold, my role as landlady temporarily suspended.

Recently, a pianist friend and I concocted an entertainment/ demonstration/performance, showing the many fascinating aspects of the percussion family by way of an illustrated story, audience participation, arrangements of familiar pieces for piano and far too many instruments to fit comfortably in my estate car. This we named 'Sounds Interesting', eventually finding ourselves covering a wide area and playing for music clubs and schools. Paying guest Fred soon found himself unwittingly involved in the Three Choirs Festival, as he helped to lug copious amounts of my instruments to Worcester's small, modern theatre where I was playing for a very mixed family audience: toddlers to grandparents. Luckily, I seemed to have boundless energy, managing to fit in musical sidelines alongside a busy home life and, of course, the CBSO.

Our domestic life was a combination of school parent evenings, dinner parties, teenage discos, house guests, visits to friends and family holidays. Family communications were by way of a large house diary parked next to the telephone. "Put it in the diary" became a constant cry as our lives became more and more involved. Geoff regularly visited Berlin and London, and Fiona started a small but lucrative business. She had made herself a pair of bead earrings since having her ears pierced, after which school friends pestered for more of the same, and my entrepreneurial genes responded to the challenge of selling these attractive and unique pretties. We soon found ourselves travelling around the Midlands area, setting up a stall at many a weekend craft fair when my orchestra schedule would allow. A lot of effort was expended, but eventually Fiona bought herself a bicycle and an attractive old pine wardrobe for all her surplus clothes, went on holiday to Germany and found herself with extra cash of her very own all due to her enterprising ideas, ingenuity and hard work.

One evening, Geoff and I went to a concert given by an ex-leader of the CBSO, John Georgiadis. The Worcester Concert Club had booked him to do his gypsy music evening at a local school, so we went along to support him and hear his spectacular programme. The music was brilliant, but the venue was cold, fluorescently lit, and with uncomfortable seating and lukewarm instant coffee. All in all, it was a ghastly evening, as we all agreed when chatting backstage afterwards, trying to avoid groups of eager sycophantic middle-aged ladies telling John how wonderful everything had been.

The next day I related this sad state of affairs to Felix (Kok, our current leader and Worcester neighbour) as we drove to Birmingham, wistfully remarking, "Wouldn't it be great to go to a super chamber concert in a lovely venue and have food and wine, with the artistes and audience meeting together afterwards?" Little did I know that this was to spawn about sixty special concerts of great variety over the next eight years. Felix's immediate response was, "Yes! Let's do it!" In my innocence I thought, "Why not?", the upshot being the very first Worcester Music Group (WGM) concert in our local church, with Felix and his wife, pianist Ann (Steele), giving a recital. We even went to the trouble of moving my grand piano to the church. A new friend and professional caterer, Tess, and I were committed to providing hot food for about 75 people, and Geoff and Tess's husband, Peter, found themselves dragooned into running a simple wine bar. Daughter Fiona became an invaluable ally, helping on the domestic front, but Alistair was convinced that we were all raving mad and would have nothing to do with any of it, absenting himself from the scene when concerts were in the offing and musicians were in the house working hard in the music room. I loved to hear rehearsals under my own roof as I prepared food for all of us to share, the bonus to me being the inevitable musical shop talk throughout.

Players from the orchestra often form little groups of friends so that they can enjoy the intimacy of chamber music, something that enables them to hear their own efforts without being overwhelmed by a welter of orchestral scoring, and a well-loved form of relaxation and a release from the rigours of orchestral constrictions. In particular, I envied the string players their vast *other* repertoire. There were times when, as a jobbing pianist, I was allowed to run through bits of programmes being prepared by friends, but felt very inadequate as I am essentially an amateur in keyboard skills, particularly at that time in my life when family commitments were far more important than keeping up with piano practice. All music students play together in small groups, but when one joins a large professional orchestra such opportunities are less frequent. We discovered that we were filling a gap as we provided a platform for what was essentially self-indulgence. A basic fee was paid – rock bottom Musicians' Union rates – covered initially by ticket sales and subsequently by sponsorship from various sources. If I did not play in a programme, then at least I was able to request favourite pieces. Though the core group was Felix's Worcester-based string quartet, we also invited singers, instrumental soloists, actors, jazz musicians, handbell ringers, Indian dancers and talented youngsters to take part in Worcester Music Group offerings. Much care went into the substantial refreshments afterwards, and I soon realised that if I was playing in the concert then I could not have anything to do with the catering at the end of the performance. Willing volunteers took over my self-imposed duties and everything ran surprisingly smoothly.

At the outset I found myself on the steepest learning curve I had ever encountered as I discovered what was needed to put on a concert of professional standards. I dealt with the printing of tickets, designing programmes, going everywhere in the locality to place posters and handbills, procuring a licence to sell wine by the glass, hiring china, cutlery and glasses, contacting the local paper for free publicity, arranging photo calls and local radio advertising, and discussing with Tess interesting food that could be served easily and eaten with a fork, there being not enough hands for knives as well as a glass. We kept everything as simple as we could, using the best possible ingredients for our home cooking. Wine was basic but reasonably decent, the first glass being included in the ticket to avoid gasping queues after the music. My biggest hurdle came when the local vicar asked me to write a few words about our new venture for the church magazine. This took forever, and on completion I presented it for Geoff's approval and was duly amazed when it passed muster and he pronounced that it was to the point, light-hearted, informative and very acceptable!

I soon discovered that many friends were only too eager to have a platform for their favourite chamber music, as was I when it came to taking part in Stravinsky's exacting *Soldier's Tale* with Felix's young son Nicholas conducting, and playing in my first and only performance of Bartók's *Sonata for Two Pianos and Percussion*, given in the depths of winter. Peter Donohoe and Martin Roscoe were the pianists, with myself and Anne Collis, a friend from London, the percussionists. We had spent a whole weekend in Birmingham worrying about the complexities of this wonderful score and arrived early in the ancient College Hall behind Worcester Cathedral on the Sunday of the performance. Lots of spicy goulash, 'Bulls Blood' Hungarian wine and sponge cake concoctions (very Eastern European) were at the ready behind the scene. Our select and depleted audience drifted in through freezing snow and I became seriously gloom-ridden as I heard one man mutter to his

161

wife, "Well, I'm only here for the Hungarian food!"

When I related this to Peter backstage, I said, "I can't bear to think that they are in effect going to *sit it out* so that they can then get their teeth into some decent hot food before going home. If only they could feel about this music as we do. I've spent hours and hours doing accessible programme notes with musical quotes for those who can read music." Oh, misery!

Peter, practical as ever, replied, "Then we'll have to tell 'em, won't we?"

A plan was hatched whereupon we marched onto the platform, smiling through trembling lips, before Pete told everyone exactly what we had been discussing behind their backs. We were going to lead them through our favourite bits of the piece, go away for five minutes, and then return and do a complete performance. The audience was flabbergasted and we were on the edge of our seats with nervous anticipation. Musicians did not normally speak from concert platforms in those days. It did not dawn on us until later that we had effectively done a warm-up routine for the punters; consequently, our rescue plan was a roaring success. Afterwards I asked the gentleman whom I had overheard before the concert if he had enjoyed the music. To my immense relief his face brightened and he confessed to having "enjoyed the evening a hundred per cent!" I then told him that I had overheard his observations before the concert began, and that our actions had really been for his benefit.

Prior to one concert, early on in our long run, there was confusion with wine tickets and concert tickets at the door. As I was the only one in a position to make an announcement about the mix-up, I steeled myself to speak to our lovely audience. Every thought flew from my head as I stood in front of anticipatory smiles, so I did nothing more than give a basic message with a few personal embellishments to make it more friendly. Of course, I had unwittingly hit on the ideal approach, and my little welcoming ditties became yet another feature of our very special evenings. Keep it simple, not too long, speak slowly and don't forget to smile!

As I became more confident in what we were doing, I became braver and cheekier when trying to find special venues in the vicinity. As a result, a local National Trust property broke strict rules and allowed concerts in the house, and we were invited to perform in large private houses. We also played in local churches, Worcester Cathedral, Pershore Abbey and the Bishop's Palace in the tiny village of Hartlebury. The latter became our annual set-piece summer venue for performances of Schubert's *Trout Quintet*, featuring smoked salmon pâté and local strawberries and cream. It was a special joy to drive early to this venue through the glorious countryside, knowing that a few hours later about a hundred people would be following on in anticipation of a special event.

All these extra musical activities had to fit in with the CBSO schedules, of course – not an easy task, so forward planning was essential. Most of the WMG concerts fell on a Sunday, but trying to read the orchestra's future plans was always something of a gamble. The middle day of three free days was usually safe, and somehow we managed. Occasionally, we also fitted in last-minute repeats of sell-out concerts if venue and cooks were available.

Irvon Sunderland, a retired judge and avid CBSO fan, became our industrious chairman. With a passion for music and connections in high places, he was tireless in procuring sponsorship, dragging me off to meet his bank manager whom he bullied into guaranteeing a modest annual sum for a number of years. I was very diffident about asking for financial help but eventually accepted that it was necessary, as ticket sales could never hope to cover the true costs of the concerts. I subsequently found myself in a daze, including the words 'sponsored by the National Provincial Bank' on all our publicity material. On those rare occasions when we had surplus funds, local charities found themselves at the receiving end of modest donations. Worcester's local bank manager became one of our most loyal supporters and thankfully kept our unpretentious affairs in order. I tried my best and, although I realised that I could never be a true businesswoman, somehow we succeeded in keeping our fiscal head above water for many delightful concerts during the next eight years. We all worked hard, had a lot of laughs, and played and heard a huge variety of music. WMG was an altogether pleasurable experience, remembered with affection by all participants and the many new friends we made from our ever-changing audiences.

11

A Silent Majority

Thousands of people attend our concerts, including friends, pupils, musicians, media critics, and the great musical public. Some, more fascinated than others, ask, "What is it like to play in an orchestra?" or "What is/was it like to work with Simon Rattle?" Others think that they know the answers. Our families have more of an inkling than others, but no one can ever be told the whole tale, as no one person knows all the answers. However, now that I am no longer a member of the CBSO I can at least try to give our perspective for those who are curious about the concealed world behind those white ties and tails. We, the silent majority, have tales to tell.

* * *

Edward Smith, from the Liverpool Philharmonic Orchestra, was shortlisted from four candidates for the position of the CBSO general manager, vacant since the demise of Arthur Baker in early 1978, and was appointed from the beginning of the 1978-79 season. He arrived to discover a good working team already keeping the ship afloat, with Beresford King-Smith, our concerts manager, in the position of acting general manager during the interregnum, aided by many hours of dedicated input from the Council of Management led by George Jonas, and a determined Players' Committee. The new manager's most pressing task was to direct the search for a successor to Louis Frémaux as principal conductor. Once more, eager guest conductors came with finely honed party pieces with which to woo the orchestra.

A buzz of interest spread through the orchestra when music's new blue-eyed boy, Simon Rattle, appeared as a guest at the tender age of twenty-three. Everyone had heard about this youngster, who at the age of eighteen had become the conductor of the Merseyside Youth Orchestra, not long after which he had added a conducting prize and an official position with the Bournemouth Symphony Orchestra to his growing achievements. Not everyone in the CBSO had the experience of playing for twenty-three-year-old Simon when he first came as guest conductor, giving an electrifying account of Nielsen's Fourth Symphony, *The Inextinguishable*. Only one day of rehearsal time had been allocated for the complete programme, the first half consisting of the meaty Brahms D Minor Piano Concerto with John Lill as soloist. A buzz of interest soon percolated through to those of us not required for that programme, however: here was someone to look out for. I had listened to the concert with great interest, going backstage afterwards to join in the discussions and speculations about this exciting newcomer on the scene. We were still bruised by the orchestra's recent trials and tribulations, so it was only natural that there was a feeling of reserve, apprehension and some nervousness when we were presented with new hopefuls wooing the orchestra with meticulously prepared, one-off programmes and honeyed words. Many orchestra meetings were held following the appearance of various guest conductors, and eventually a vote was taken. Some time later, it was announced that Rattle had been appointed as principal conductor and artistic adviser – by a very narrow margin, our big boss at the age of twenty-five. For the first time ever, the players had had substantial input regarding the choice of the next conductor.

On June 11th 1979, I wrote home to my father:

It looks as though our new conductor will be announced fairly soon. It's a state secret, so I can't say, but the orchestra seems pleased on the whole. He's an up-and-coming youngster about to take off – so let's hope that he takes us with him!

Acknowledged and renowned writers, erudite researchers, music critics and countless journalists have written thousands of words about Simon Rattle. There would appear to be no angles on Simon's career, personality, ambitions, achievements and musical genius that have not been probed, analysed, explored and questioned. Seemingly everyone has given voice, from world-famous soloists, conductors and composers to music agents, broadcasting and recording companies, teachers and mentors from Simon's past – everyone, that is, except the ones who come in contact with the man every working hour, namely the orchestral players themselves; day-to-day observers. This is not to say that players are dumb on the subject, of course. It must be remembered that the CBSO eventually worked with Simon for eighteen years, during which every rehearsal and every concert engendered speculation, discussion and scrutiny before, during and after the event. Occasional glimpses of the non-public aspect of being a professional orchestral musician would sometimes find their way into newspaper articles, but hardly ever from those other than the leader or principal players.

Orchestral politics were rarely aired by players, as they were then strictly monitored, with an authority figure standing by as minder – our Chief Executive or maybe the Chairman of the Board.

As previously explained in Chapter 9, orchestral musicians are silenced by the fact that the standard contract categorically forbids any communication with the media. This applies to this day. Consequently, it is only the brave who will allow themselves to be quoted, incognito of course.

* * *

It has to be said that not all were enthusiastic about the new appointment. Some audience members were very worried about our choice, wondering how he would have the nerve to 'tell old lags how to play standard repertoire'. He agreed, emphasising that one of his biggest worries was that of gaining the respect of the orchestra, but wisely observed, "When rehearsing with a new orchestra, it's advisable to have the coffee break as early as possible, so that everybody can discuss whether you're any good. The real truth is that the rehearsal is not a performance. They're as different an act as mending an engine and driving in a Grand Prix."

The *Birmingham Post* music critic suspected that desperation had set in and that the orchestra had jumped on a trendy bandwagon, pandering somewhat to youth culture. For instance, he was rightly concerned about Simon's aversion to Tchaikovsky and his non-connection with Tippett, but then every conductor brings with him a different repertoire, and perhaps, if we had known then about the shake-up in store for our future programming, Simon might never have been appointed. The decision had been made relatively quickly and, yes, there certainly was much more under the tip of young Rattle's iceberg, as we soon discovered. The press had a field day, suggesting that Simon's youth must be something of a handicap.

In July 1980, Harold Gray introduced Simon to the audience at the last night of the Birmingham Proms, our in-house pre-holiday jamboree, after which we heard that members of the town hall staff were somewhat miffed by Simon's negative reference on that public occasion to the lack of air-conditioning in our fine old hall. Eventually the players met him properly for the first time in September prior to a rehearsal. He stood by the rostrum in the deathly hush, as his old friend, Ed Smith, the orchestra's general manager, did the honours.

Simon not only took on the CBSO in our 1980-1981 Jubilee Year, but also

166

became a married man, bought a house in Islington and began a long-planned sabbatical year in Oxford to read English Literature and Philosophy. The new Mrs Rattle was the American soprano Elise Ross, someone we soon accepted as an attractive and friendly member of the family.

Simon's only engagement with the orchestra during the first term of his sabbatical year was for the Royal Concert at the Royal Albert Hall, attended by HRH Princess Alexandra, memorable if only for the fact that Tchaikovsky was on the menu in the shape of his popular First Piano Concerto. Tchaikovsky was not Simon's favourite composer, however, and throughout our eighteen-year partnership his works rarely emanated from Simon's baton. After this appearance, the BBC's *Midlands Today* programme snapped him up for an interview in which he announced: "I intend to stay as long as they'll have me – certainly I think I will have to be kicked out forcibly! I really want to build up a relationship and this can only be done with time ..."

During university holidays, however, Simon was much in evidence, and we would often see him in the empty hall during rehearsals with guest conductors, peering at a score and taking everything in. We looked with interest at this very young man. Much had been made in the press about the wire-wool mass of dark brown curls, deep-set eyes, slightly snub nose, formidable meet-in-the-middle black eyebrows (which fellow-Liverpudlian, Annie, was dying to get at with tweezers!) and an altogether elfin face: a gift for the cartoonists. Fresh-faced and of medium height, he looked like a young lad, but this impression was dispelled as soon as he spoke. We soon discovered that Simon's resonant voice could carry through crowds of people without the effort of any crescendo or fortissimo on his part. Specific mannerisms were relished, as were repeated catchphrases; everything about the man was being scrutinised by beady-eyed and inquisitive players. "My brain hurts," is still a comment to be heard even now. This familiar expression originated after his and our unsuccessful attempts to achieve an exact effect, turn of phrase or suchlike. A follow-up was often, "We need a caffeine fix!", after which the terrier attack would begin again when we were replete from our coffee break. He never gives up.

A matchless sartorial style also caused much curiosity, comment, and often amusement. There was a memorable day when he arrived dressed from head to foot in bright green, including socks and shoes. This outfit was greeted by good-natured laughter, much teasing, and the question, "Why?" The reply was, "Oh, I'm your little 'go' sign"! Our response was that we thought that he was doing a leprechaun job for a local pantomime. On enquiry we discovered that many of the more bizarre clothes came from the States. We all remember the conventional-looking anorak (from front view), which sported a huge multi-coloured Disney character on the back, or the overlarge bright yellow sou'wester-style zipped jacket, which earned him the nickname of 'The Mersey Ferryman', which was apt for this son of Liverpool. Overalls of a dreary grey with myriads of zips thankfully only made a brief appearance, as we suspected that he had probably been mistaken for a stagehand. Annie and I certainly enjoyed the fashion parade at rehearsals. Beautiful, muted, peacock-hued silk shirts with soft batwing sleeves gave plenty of scope for whirling arms. Collarless, velvety, overlarge tops in clear colours and crazy tee shirts covered in hand-painted ticks, squiggles or Picasso-like portraits – undoubtedly expensive, undoubtedly unique – all caused comment. An admirer made him an enormous knitted pullover of many colours, which featured in countless press photos and was worn at posh receptions after many a prestigious concert. When the going got hot, he would stop conducting, but continue to talk as he scrabbled over his head with both hands to remove a layer of shirt or top – up and over, a flip of the curly mop, still talking – to drape it rag-like over the rostrum rail, or drop it onto the floor as he concentrated on the score in front of him. We could not decide whether Simon had short legs or whether he deliberately chose too-large trousers, which concertinaed around the ankle area. Ties never came into the picture even for the most formal of occasions, apart from the necessary accessory with concert tails. Even these were given the Rattle treatment as he experimented with half and half: black and white, or patterned in discreet silver and white, extraordinary custom-made neckwear designed to surprise and cause comment. At one point I noted during one of my diary phases:

Simon wearing patterned bow tie. As we were going on after the overture he was waiting in the wings. "Oh, what is on your tie? We can't see from the back." A raised eyebrow and a reply of, "It's very tacky – like a 9 o'clock shadow!" On close inspection we discovered miniature outlined violins on a white background. Terrible!

Someone must have told him that 100% concentration on the music was impossible for us when he bounced on stage wearing one of his more outrageous creations for a concert, so eventually he reverted to boring old white again, much to our relief.

From the very outset, the music always came first. Rehearsals were electric, as ideas, suggestions, jokes, covert admonitions and his uniquely imaginative approach fired us with enthusiasm and, for some, exhaustion. Every scrap of time was used and at speed, and we soon realised that being let off early was never going to be on the cards. "If I end a rehearsal early, then it comes to be expected. When it doesn't necessarily happen, that's when disappointment creeps in." His rapier brain was always ahead of us, so much so that there were many times when instruments were not at the ready for the downbeat. "Hang on Simon!" became a cri de coeur from the back, as we swiftly abandoned sticks or instruments so that we could return to a previous page or repeat a phrase or even a single crucial note.

Every rehearsal included a minimum audience of Simon's mother, father and sister, Susan, and as time went by Denis (Simon's father) made himself known to players, chatting to us if we were hanging around backstage. In time we also realised that certain favoured soloists had become part of the Rattle family-style entourage, appearing time after time with the orchestra and becoming familiar to all of us. As far as I was concerned, this gave an air of comfortable informality as we listened to the easy chit-chat around the rostrum. And I, for one, began to listen with a fascinated intensity to what was being said in rehearsal. One's critical faculties were being tested. What was he driving at? Could I hear any difference as he tried time after time to influence the subtle tuning of woodwind, polish a tiny, neat rhythm, make sure that players played precisely together, and so on? Nothing was ever left to chance. Fortunately, for the most part, he left us alone at the back. We had feared the worst from an ex-percussionist, and I must confess that initially many of us (and not just the percs tribe) had gone down the road of, "Here we go again, some young kid teaching us how to do our job!"

Not everyone appreciated the intensity of the Rattle approach, however. Here was a self-assured, single-minded young man who always had to have the final word. Heavy pressure was on. The orchestra had from necessity to become familiar with the more intense approach to work. It was not until players from other orchestras came in as extras that we fully realised how our modus operandi had changed, our visiting colleagues forever commenting on how the pace at rehearsals had accelerated. Some of the old hands felt that too high a price was being demanded and that we should be allowed to remain a good provincial orchestra. Who were we to try for the moon? Comfort zones for some of the more senior players were being seriously eroded. A few players left, but most were only too delighted to get down to some thorough rehearsing once more. There was no denying that the atmosphere in the orchestra changed in those early days. He was a breath of fresh air for most of us, and we were more than willing to jump on the exciting bandwagon being driven so successfully by this very special person. He too was very positive about his new, large 'family', and in an effort to get to know us better he threw a splendid party in one of the biggest Chinese restaurants in the city centre at Christmas time. Everyone was encouraged to bring a guest. Dim sum and buffet-style delicacies were produced non-stop, and a good evening was had by all.

In the early '80s we found ourselves in Newcastle upon Tyne prior to giving a number of concerts at the Edinburgh International Festival. After a blockbuster performance of a huge Mahler symphony, percussionists spent some time stowing instruments, after which we found ourselves strolling back to the hotel with Simon. I ventured to observe that I was pretty amazed when we saw that he had discarded his full score for the performance. "It's not decent, Simon. How do you do it? Do you have a photographic memory?" A long pause followed, then a shrug and "No ... one thing just follows another." Another pause ensued, and then, "The paper gets in the way." He is totally reliable and always remembers a promised cue or helpful glance. This is a man who has an awesome mass of music firmly stored between the ears. When a new piece was introduced into our repertoire, we were fascinated to note how long it took for the paper to be discarded, noting that special final rehearsal when pages would remain unturned until the music had to be referred to, and then an appeal to the leader of, "What page are we on?" This was it! "Tonight it'll be without the score, what d'you bet?"

Day after day we looked at that face, and I suspect that I know the nuances of his mannerisms and many and varied expressions better than I know those of my own family. It is true that he never overtly loses his temper, but we always knew when limits had been reached. A shutter would descend and a steely, formal politeness would reign, most of us getting the message as the charged atmosphere darkened. Neither did one relish being at the receiving end of his penetrating laser 'death rays' scorching across the orchestra at some misdemeanour, covering a nanosecond in real time, but reverberating as shock waves and taking what seemed like for ever to subside.

It is a little comfort to realise that the Vienna Philharmonic Orchestra can also receive this treatment, as many of the CBSO noticed when watching a TV programme some time ago. The following day Birmingham telephones rang with, "Did you see THE LOOK? Back desk second fiddles – glad it wasn't us!"

* * *

When I first decided that music was the only profession for me, I realised that most young hopefuls looked up to the BBC as the ideal employer. Indeed, I had auditioned for the job of number two timpanist in the BBC Symphony Orchestra before I found my feet in Birmingham. BBC orchestras worked during office hours, with proper weekends, generous holidays, minimum travelling, access to sports facilities and canteens, comfortable studios to play in and, ultimately, were cushioned from the harsh world by a pension (something that we lesser mortals had to fight for for years after I had joined the CBSO). Such employment was eagerly sought after, particularly by musicians with families to support. Money from the licence fees was always available and jobs were totally secure, ending with compulsory retirement at the age of 65. Public concerts were infrequent but prestigious, with the main bulk for the BBC Symphony Orchestra hinging on the annual Henry Wood Promenade Concerts in London's Royal Albert Hall. But I had a sneaking suspicion that a job in the BBC might just be a little bit too cosy; too safe.

It was all the more of a shock, therefore, when in early spring 1980 we learnt that 'Aunty' BBC had decided to cut costs and axe five of the regional orchestras, including our own BBC Midland Radio Orchestra (MRO). One-third of all the musicians employed by the Corporation were to be replaced by more recordings and foreign tapes, the ending of their twelve-week contracts not leading to any kind of redundancy pay.

At the time that this bombshell was announced, the MRO's harpist, who was playing with the CBSO as an extra player, tearfully related to sympathetic colleagues how the termination-of-contract letter had been timed to arrive just prior to the annual summer break, giving, in effect, only a further eight weeks of employment. The absolute opposition of the Musicians' Union (MU) to these proposals was registered immediately, after which the BBC's director of personnel later commented that he was "surprised at the strength of the Union's reactions". Valiant attempts were made to negotiate other options with the BBC, but to no avail. They stonewalled for months, the original proposals simply being re-presented with no attempt made to discuss alternative ways of achieving what they claimed to be necessary economies. Ever more prestigious supporters unsuccessfully lobbied the BBC, but finally the MU had to declare that, as from June 1st, no members would be allowed to play for the Corporation until the dispute was settled. As every professional musician had to be a member of the MU, this would present serious problems to the broadcasting fraternity.

On the dot of midnight, part-way through a live jazz broadcast from the Pebble Mill studios in Birmingham, everyone stopped playing, packed away instruments, walked out and left the building. This was the beginning of a very interesting nine weeks for musicians throughout the UK.

Pebble Mill studios are set back from a wide, tree-lined, short dual carriageway, which joins two main routes south out of Birmingham. Large detached houses face the BBC building, so the first thing that happened was that every nearby household received an explanatory letter, or personal visit, begging understanding for what was to follow. Detailed rosters had been devised for picket lines to be manned continuously, throughout the night as well as by day. These consisted of small groups of bemused musicians lined up in fluorescent yellow 'MU Official Picket' tabards, covering the main entrances to the building. Our own hectic summer Prom season was soon in full swing, but to 'Keep Music Live' (our MU slogan) was of paramount importance, and with our help we knew that our friends in the MRO could go on holiday knowing that all was well under control back at The Mill. We were ideal candidates for inventing ditties, slogans and chants, which were set to music and cheerfully performed outside, with or without instrumental backings. Cash for a Hardship Fund was collected in suitably labelled black buckets, though we were dutifully ignored by all who entered the building, despite the fact that many had worked with the benighted MRO personnel for many years. Sadly, many long-standing friendships foundered, as musicians attempted to explain the reasons for the stand-off.

A local garage offered its washroom facilities, and the CBSO's principal bassoonist lent a small caravan. This was parked in the road outside the studios and was used as a dry refuge and 'nerve centre' on site. An MRO musician's wife had the franchise for a snack bar inside the building, so every morning we were treated to wonderful scalding coffee and hot bacon rolls. The large tray was carefully placed on the grass verge, as we had been told in no uncertain terms that the tiny retaining wall was BBC property and was not to be used as a seat or table. We were hardly in a jolly picnic situation, but everyone chipped in with special treats for those patiently waiting to explain the musicians' predicament to anyone who cared to listen. I usually managed to produce a bag of home-made biscuits or a fruit loaf – anything to help keep up our spirits. The local police were sympathetic to our endeavours and many other unions were contacted. We found to our amazement that there was overall sympathy with the musicians and what was happening to them at Pebble Mill, although I suspect that surprise was the overriding emotion when the outside world discovered that musicians could bite when pushed to the limits. Our efforts were probably regarded by many as as bizarre as being savaged by teddy bears.

I was astonished when we managed to disrupt beer supplies for the BBC Club by politely persuading the brewer's lorry not to cross our picket lines. The driver simply waved, grinned amiably and then turned the great juggernaut round to return to his Burton upon Trent brewery. Regular communiqués from all districts were produced and despatched to the members on strike, the newsletters being avidly seized upon and read with amusement and a great deal of interest. We in Birmingham were noted for disrupting milk and meat deliveries, but there was also a darker rumour with Birmingham roots alleging that we had been rather too aggressive at one juncture and had turned away a fire engine. The piano tuner declined to cross our picket lines, and the programme *Saturday Night at the Mill* had to be abandoned owing to noises off; brass bands and jazz groups being only too happy to play loud music on the wide grass verges outside the studios. Notices strategically placed on the two main roads flanking the scene of action also earned a continuous cacophony of supportive hoots from traffic driving in and out of the city.

Glasgow colleagues announced: "The butcher's van left meat on the pavement for the BBC to collect. We understood that, before collection could be made, two of the pickets' dogs had paid their respects to the meat." The Glasgow BBC was also treated to a ten-minute dirge from a piper and, furthermore, it was reported that, "The absence of pies and toast for Broadcasting House Glasgow means that the BBC canteen menu will be reduced by some 50%."

On Day 39, the general disruption caused was further illustrated: "We have received a report from a Transport and General driver which seems to indicate that the management of TV Centre are pretty desperate to get their hands on their smoked salmon. They are having it delivered to Kensington House and then smuggle it into the TV Centre in taxis at night. It really is tough a the top."

The BBC Henry Wood Proms were in dire straits, as no British musicians would perform, added to which some of the foreign orchestras cancelled their London appearances, notably the Concertgebouw Orchestra and colleagues from Sweden, and promenaders switched allegiance to the series of Wembley

Proms conceived and organised by the BBC's own Symphony Orchestra. The BBC was losing an average of five hours live music a day, which had to be replaced by 'needle time', and the Royal Albert Hall Proms were eventually cancelled for the first time in their history.

Our official dispute lasted for nine long weeks. The hardship fund garnered £85,000, donated by the great and the good, music lovers and working colleagues, with massive support coming from very many famous artistes throughout the profession, generously giving their time and expertise to the furtherance of better working relations between the broadcasting company and musicians. Throughout these trying and unique times, concerts were given, rehearsals attended, yawns smothered by those from the night shifts, and a feeling of great camaraderie was generated throughout the music business. In addition, many preconceived barriers between differing branches of the profession were forever removed.

The upshot of everyone's efforts was that the axe did not fall as swiftly as the BBC would have wished. Three orchestras had a stay of execution, after which the musicians were to be offered a contract giving a five-year guarantee of substantial freelance engagements. Other flexible arrangements were agreed upon for the remaining two orchestras, and players who were to be made redundant were offered severance payments. Further details were agreed upon with the Union, but all potentially injured parties decided that the price of reasonable treatment from the BBC would have to be eternal vigilance.

At the end of the strike, a gargantuan shindig was thrown by the somewhat cheered MRO players for the CBSO and friends. The nearest pub to the Beeb was a familiar venue, an upper room was commandeered, alcohol flowed like water and we were eventually thrown out well after midnight. The next morning many bleary-eyed players stumbled into rehearsal at the last minute. Our leader, Felix, earned himself a round of applause as he stalked in on the downbeat, green at the gills, straight as a ramrod and carefully ignoring all around him. It had been a very good party!

12
"Simon Sez" ...!

It should be remembered that Simon Rattle took over excellent raw material in an experienced but somewhat demoralised orchestra. From the outset, he described us as "the best French orchestra outside France" and discovered that he had inherited a woodwind team that had remained the same for eighteen years, forming a solid and dependable core in the orchestra, plenty of experienced string players, along with reliable brass and percussion. For instance, I had to pinch myself to accept the fact that by 1980 I had been around for over twenty years. When we realised that his vision was to scale the heights, it gradually dawned on us that, yes, with his inspirational enthusiasm we *could* do it. Soon after he was appointed, I wrote home to dad saying:

> *Playing for our new conductor, Simon Rattle, is like hearing music with new ears – so refreshing. We took Liverpool by storm on Saturday, really made them sit up! Royal Festival Hall on Friday. It's such a special programme that I'm taking Fiona off school so that she can come with me, and hopefully we can 'do' an art gallery or museum whilst we're there.*

A minimum of a whole day of six hours plus three hours on the concert day is normally allotted for rehearsal time for standard repertoire, but in reality more time is often available, especially for guest conductors or more unusual programmes. Simon always plans his rehearsals meticulously, with time included, if necessary, for working at half-speed to learn lesser-known works more thoroughly, revealing and building a logical construction of the whole picture and enabling everyone to appreciate how a piece should sound throughout the orchestra: familiar jigsaw puzzles clarified and completed. Thankfully, he seemed to have the natural skills necessary to generate a positive working style. As he announced early on in our relationship: "I need to work through very thoroughly in rehearsal. I am a rehearser ... I need to build a runway so that the plane can take off."

Subsequently, well-known pieces were constantly being sold afresh to ever-growing, delighted and eager audiences: marvellous for the morale of the orchestra, and a boon for box-office takings. It was not long before Birmingham audiences and a wide swathe of Midland citizens were aware of our new charismatic conductor. Soon after his appointment, the local TV news featured a fleeting, tiny, gesticulating figure fronting every BBC Midlands broadcast, along with the usual familiar local landmarks. Feelings of expectation grew as Simon was quickly adopted by his new city. We no longer had to spell out the meaning of the letters CBSO; they were recognised by all and sundry. No one stood on ceremony. Everybody referred to 'our Simon' by his first name, from the shoppers he encountered in his local supermarket to schoolchildren and the numerous taxi drivers who ferried him around the city.

From the very outset in 1980, Simon fought for his orchestra. He cared about the fact that we were being paid less than some Birmingham bus drivers, and made no bones about how he felt about that, giving the press plenty to get their teeth into. More women players were welcomed, with the rider that, "They help to cut down the rugby team changing-room attitudes of some of the men"!

Naturally, there was also the 'new broom syndrome' as he shifted players around to what he considered more appropriate positions in the orchestra's pecking order. Some fell by the wayside, whilst others stood their ground and fought back. But he always had his own way, supported fully by his friend, general manager Ed Smith. Compromises were suggested in one or two cases, but there were bitter pills to swallow for some long-standing, sometimes complacent musicians. A long-serving key string player was asked to move back in his section for 'artistic reasons', but this was too humiliating for him. After months of wrangling, and in spite of confirmation of the same salary for less responsibility, the player left, unable to face the perceived ignominy of sitting further back in 'his' section. Other removals were not so public, much to everyone's relief. Feelings were mixed amongst friends and colleagues, but we all knew that this is what generally happens when there is a new man in charge. It was only to be expected, but was nonetheless uncomfortable for all concerned.

We sometimes suspected that Simon found it difficult fully to trust his musicians, some of whom remembered him as a bright-eyed thirteen-year-old in the NYO. At the tender age of nineteen he was already conducting such works as Stravinsky's *Rite of Spring*, Berg's Violin Concerto, Bartók's *Music for Strings, Percussion and Celeste*.

Hyper-talented, Simon has a natural and instinctive knowledge of how to sell modern scores to both orchestra and audiences. His confidence is such that he often is dictatorial – with great charm, but he *has* to have the final word on any subject. If he has formulated specific ideas, woe betide anyone who disagrees with or foolishly attempts to better him. During EMI recordings, however, there were situations when he had to accept decisions from the quietly spoken producer, but we were all aware that he did not like this. Super-confident characters can be very difficult when they do not always get their own way.

We also watched with suppressed amusement as two egos clashed during some innovative educational concerts. The orchestra was paying for the expertise of a renowned animateur, Richard McNichol, who, in collaboration with our newly appointed education manager and a core group of players, was responsible for delivering an exciting, groundbreaking concert to a capacity audience of schoolchildren. Simon had to have his say, however, and it soon became obvious that he was less than pleased at being the 'mere conductor' in the carefully crafted, illustrated mini-concert. Underlying animosity flared to the surface from both men, and it seemed to the players that our principal conductor had great difficulty as he grudgingly came to terms with the fact that on these occasions he was not the one in total control.

I noted in my diary at the time:

He was really childish with Richard and really HATES not being in charge and just HAS to have the very last word every time. The orchestra was really pissed off with the bad atmosphere, someone deserved a smacked bottom!

No doubt he felt that he was being upstaged, but Richard was simply doing the job he had spent hours preparing for and one that he was being paid handsomely to do. We were delighted with his rapport with the children and tried to ignore the sulks and mini-tantrums from the rostrum.

Eventually, as Simon became more relaxed and familiar with the orchestra, there were times when woodwind principals in particular would dare to suggest a change in, say, beats in a certain bar, or perhaps even more enterprising ideas of musical content: phrasing, adjustments of dynamics, or whatever. He would put his head on one side, tip of baton between teeth, and then muse, "Okay, let's give it a go!" To our amazement he would occasionally announce, "I'll buy that! Please mark it in everyone." Smiles all round, and a happy woodwind section. After all, we also care about what we are doing, and it is healthy to have home-grown ideas included in the overall global Rattle picture. Mind you, he could just as well say, "Sorry, guys, it just won't work!", but at least we cared enough to try, communicate and discuss.

Initially his beat was refreshingly clear and reliable, on his best 'new boy' behaviour, but eventually, in later years as we all became familiar with each other, we felt that he was often on another planet in his communication by baton. "Oh, I wish he'd stop painting skirting boards," one of the oboes sighed as she was coming off the platform, having experienced some of Simon's more extravagant low-flying, side-sweeping gestures. "We just can't see from where we sit!" This was conveyed with a grin, however, as we were familiar with every nuance of that mobile face by then: silent mouthing and yelling, gimlet eyes staring, the dreaded 'death rays', gentle smiles, cheeky grins, soppy sentimentality – all life is there with Simon. At one concert, when our chorus sang in Polish, I noted with a certain irritation, "I can't bear watching Simon mouthing *nothings* at them, because he can't possibly know the words", although I now realise that any approach was better than no attempt at face-to-face contact.

Watching with the sound 'turned off', I often thought that it must be possible for onlookers to tell what was being played solely by viewing the uninhibited show from the rostrum. For instance, Simon mirrors Petrushka in much of Stravinsky's score, and we could imagine perfectly his vivid suggestion of the 'sexy swirl of a silk dress' in a particularly voluptuous Ravel phrase. "You're giving me low cut, but what I want is topless – *topless!*" His positive approach during rehearsals gave us the feeling that we were all taking part in a great exploration, discovering aspects of familiar scores that we had not encountered or dreamed of with other conductors.

Some woodwind players have said that they were concerned that Simon did not play a true melody instrument, suspecting that his experiences as a percussionist and pianist were simply not broad enough for the creation of, say, a flowing melodic line sculptured by individual instrumental technique. He knew what he wanted, but sometimes fell short of achieving his goal, as was the case in a Mahler symphony when, try as he might, two bars of a particular string effect eluded him. Fascinated percussionists counted eleven attempts, but eventually he rolled his eyes, announcing, "I just don't know what to do now … we need caffeine!" There was no return to this problematic area after the break, and nothing more was said about it, but I am sure that it remains forever in the minds of all those who were present on that occasion. When consulted or questioned about a particular part of the music for which one is personally responsible, one would imagine that a specialist's input would be of irrefutable value - not necessarily so.

In spite of the fact that Simon had played orchestral percussion in former years, he sometimes failed to appreciate the problems that are peculiar to certain of our instruments. For instance, tubular bells are everyone's nightmare at the back there. One needs at least three eyes for the job: for bells, conductor and music. It is impossible to stand facing square-on to the front, because a normal set of one-and-a-half octaves of chromatic bells hanging on a two-metre tall frame needs to be set at an angle to play. Arms are lifted high and inevitably block sight lines to the conductor and music; neither can a normal music stand be raised to the level of the player's eyes, or placed at a proper angle for the musician to see a far distant baton – a no-win situation if ever there was one; the shortest of all short straws. The player needs all possible aural cues to stay on track from behind that metal wall, but even then there is much head turning and disconnection with the music as one aims for the tops of the narrow lengths of tubing with rawhide hammers.

I was castigated when, in 1984, during a rehearsal for TV of Messiaen's massive *Turangalîla* symphony, I was asked to play the awkward, disjointed tubular-bell part *solo* and 'to the stick'. Without the rest of the orchestra, this was an impossible task, as I needed to hear the shape of the music around me. Dodging about with odd bell notes, keeping track on my difficult-to-read part, and trying to play to a silent, jabbing baton was not my idea of useful rehearsing. Simon became more and more steely calm as I became more flustered and frustrated. He eventually ended with faintly raised eyebrows and a deliberately damning, offhand, "We'd better go on ...", as he realised that my perceived shortcomings were eating into his carefully planned rehearsal schedule.

In the cold light of day, I was saddened to realise that there were times when his fertile imagination could not jump the gap between rostrum and individual player. He had the complete picture on the box lid and was able to see my fragments in context, but I was trying to fit in a few tiny, fiddly pieces to a complex jigsaw, none of which made sense on their own. What is more, at that juncture the end result was still an unfamiliar picture for the most part, some areas being more memorable than others, a massively complicated undertaking that only became recognisable with maximum exposure and frequent performances.

This was me 'for the high jump'. Within a matter of days, I was peremptorily summoned to the conductor's room where Huw Ceredig, my section principal, was in attendance along with manager Ed Smith. Simon was sitting hunched in a chair when, after a quick glance as I entered, he did not meet my eyes once as he told me that he was not happy with my playing, announcing that I was not to be included in *Turangalîla*, either for the TV programme, foreseeable performances or the EMI recording sessions scheduled for later on. There was no discussion apart from confirmation that I understood the charge. I left the room with as much tattered dignity as it was possible to muster, returning home in a state of total shock.

Some days later, Huw came to my house to suggest that I should take lessons to improve my playing (not giving any specific criticism on any aspects of my work), after which he flatly announced that in truth he thought that it would be far better for everyone if I left the orchestra. In other words, 'clear your desk, go, and don't argue'. I had become an embarrassment, as I soon appreciated when it became obvious that not one of my closest colleagues was going to be supportive, sympathetic or even communicative. The only response from the management was the request of, "Don't take it to the Union." I was flabbergasted, devastated, tearful, angry and self-pitying. Now that knives had been drawn, it was expected that I would quietly roll up my carpet and disappear into the sand dunes. Eventually, when my emotions had settled to dull dismay, I took stock, and miserably accepted that over the previous few months many things *had* distracted me from full concentration in the orchestra, causing silly, inexcusable mistakes. 'You are only as good as your last performance.' How true!

For, at that time, numerous domestic trials and tribulations had become a constant worry. My husband had taken early retirement within the past year and was unsettled in what he perceived as a non-status role. We were now dependent on his university pension and my meagre salary. My son, by now at Business College and hating it, was not taking his studying seriously enough and was living inside a cloud of all-pervading resentfulness at home. My daughter was flexing her adolescence with callow youths, a speeding fine landed in my lap, the cat had been run over and our ancient dog had to be put to sleep. I was compensating for domestic unrest by spending far too much time organising WMG chamber concerts, trying to be an ideal mum, driving to Birmingham regularly, and consequently, as it turned out, not caring about my beloved orchestra enough – absently trusting years of experience and my automatic pilot far too much, I suspect. I was at home in disgrace and, as such, felt ashamed and unable to speak of my problems with anyone in the orchestra, however close a friend. The feeling of isolation was stultifying as

I kept my head up and my feelings hidden from everyone, family included.

Eventually I phoned a colleague in another orchestra to discuss the possibility of lessons, an admission that caused much amazement, disbelief and cries of "Nonsense!" from him. At last there was someone to whom I could talk, a friend who would help me to see a wider perspective. Lessons, as such, never happened, but I did hours of technical exercises, silently hammering away at a muted snare drum behind closed doors.

As I was not being included in the orchestra's work, there was no contact from anyone there, but plenty of time for me to brood. I was sick to the heart, but, by the time the dreaded Messiaen was well under everyone else's skin, I had decided to tackle Rattle to find out what it was that he was not happy about concerning my contributions in our orchestra. I could feel a stubborn belligerence building up, and so I arranged to see him in his lair at the London Coliseum where he was conducting the English National Opera, as it was obvious that there would never be any feedback from him unless prompted by me. After much procrastination by the CBSO management, a date and time were arranged. A dear friend came with me as a much-needed support. Ed Smith also arrived in London at the appointed time, determined to be in Rattle's dressing room for the confrontation of my life, but I was adamant that this should not be; consequently, he remained outside the room whilst I bearded the monster alone. Simon was full of a feverish cold, hardly able to speak, red in the eye and not happy to be tracked down by me.

Straight to the jugular I asked, "What is it you don't like about my playing? Am I unrhythmical, insensitive, too loud, too quiet, too fast, too slow, behind the beat, before the beat, unimaginative? Just tell me."

There was a long pause, and then he looked at me somewhat shiftily and replied, "I don't know what to say … you're uncoordinated."

"Hmm, that can mean anything, or nothing!"

"You take too long to get something right."

I was furious and reminded him of the infamous eleven attempts to get two bars of strings to his liking in the aforesaid Mahler. By that time I had got past caring. Standing stiff and upright, I looked him in the eye and then stalked out of the room.

This was a most unsatisfactory outcome, and a further blow to my confidence, but at least I had tried. It seemed to me that no one appreciated the fact that there should be room for manoeuvre, dialogue and debate in such a potentially life-changing event, but no, not in this case. Simon had spoken and that, apparently, was THAT. There was an unbelievable lack of man management in the whole situation. I am also only too aware of the ponderous procedure for getting rid of players, one under which only the most hardened character could possibly give any creditable public performances. Being under unimaginable pressure when trying to keep a sense of proportion whilst performing is a road that no one would be willing to go down, however ('don't take it to the Union'), the outcome being almost inevitable: painful dismissal at the end of an arbitrary professional mauling.

After that, Huw took it upon himself to present me with, among other awkward things, nasty side-drum parts: my least favourite and rarely played instrument. Hands shook and my heart thumped as I took great care to appear calm, but in reality I felt that my whole world was falling apart. I was coolly ostracised by my close colleagues, with only the extra players showing any overt kindness. An occasional whispered, "You're doing fine," was treasure indeed. It was an intolerable situation for anyone to be in. Trying to perform unfamiliar parts in public with any kind of normality was almost impossible. This state of affairs continued for many, many weeks until Simon caught up with me at the Royal Albert Hall one day to tell me that he was very pleased with my efforts and that things, from now on, would be 'back to normal'. How naïve, and how impossible! Whatever were the rights and wrongs, I had lost my trust in several people, and in the many years that I continued to play in the CBSO things were never to be quite the same again. It was of little comfort to realise eventually that numerous others had been given similar treatment in Rattle's quest for perfection. We were merely the tools of his trade.

For instance, in the fullness of time it was discovered that three years of concealed persecution had been meted out to a well-respected, fine player of over twenty years' service: a man of integrity and dignified professionalism who eventually left the orchestra when the stress of the situation became too much to bear, in spite of massive support from his nearest colleagues. When this state of affairs became common knowledge, respect for the maestro slipped a few notches in the minds and hearts of many of his previously amenable workforce. It was little comfort to realise that one was not alone in this kind of situation, but at least players became more willing to discuss their troubles more openly as it became obvious that Rattle was a tough man with a mission, and seemingly had carte blanche to choose other players to fill any gaps in the orchestra once those positions became vacant by whatever means, fair or otherwise.

A mute baton is an ultimate frustration, a conductor's occupational vulnerability. It is inevitable that any conductor is a dictator: that is the nature of the position he holds. The words 'control freak' often spring to mind, however, as we mere players become irritated and thwarted by the constraints of someone else interpreting what, after all, is music close to our hearts too. We also have feelings, although it would not do to be too confrontational, as we constantly learn to be adaptable for whoever is wielding that authoritarian baton. In truth, players are simply a conduit between the dots on the page to the ears of a listener, hopefully inspired by the conductor. For the most part, we doggedly do as we are bid, yet also hope to add our own strands of personal magic when the little white stick comes down on the night.

SIMON RATTLE

13
Roller Coaster Ride

As the momentum grew both with audience and orchestra, it was realised that more events could be incorporated into our annual concert season. Consequently, the Thursday concerts were augmented by a Tuesday Series, with the extra enticement of a healthy discount for early bookings. The main season was extended slightly and, in addition, seven Saturday concerts were designated as Family Concerts with a 7.00pm start, planned to avoid late finishes. A new-look logo and a trumpeting slogan of 'Musically Yours!' set the scene in spanking style.

Simon let it be known that he wished every concert to be 'An Event'. Indeed, his first few programmes were an eclectic mix of works by Sibelius, Tippett, Janácek, Szymanowski and a gargantuan performance in Leeds of Mahler's massive *Resurrection* symphony – the latter conducted without a score.

Simon told us that his intention was not only to explore the symphony orchestra repertoire, but also that he proposed to delve into the world of early music; if possible with authentic-sounding instruments. He owned a pair of old-fashioned deep-bowled copper kettledrums (hand-tuned timpani - nicknamed 'the piss pots' by irreverent players) with calf heads, which were the very devil to keep in tune, but when played with hard felt beaters their gutsy resonances delivered a satisfyingly antique sound. These were duly stored with the rest of our instruments, occasionally seeing the light of day for Early Music ventures.

More sectional rehearsals were introduced, something hardly ever encountered in a symphony orchestra's normal work schedule. There were times when groups of players might get together to sort out thorny problems before a main rehearsal, but only by mutual consent and with a feeling of foreboding in case a full orchestra rehearsal might highlight avoidable shortcomings. A South American conductor came as a guest at one point, bringing with him Ginastera's complex Harp Concerto. This colourful and rarely performed piece features interesting exposed patches of challenging and clever percussion writing. The three of us realised that this could be an embarrassing disaster in front of our colleagues, so we rehearsed together privately until we were all satisfied that we had done our best. When it came

184

to the first full rehearsal, we negotiated our awkward corners with calm aplomb, whereupon the maestro stopped in amazement, saying that he had never heard it played so well even for the recordings he had done with his own orchestra. "Have you played this piece before?" Wide-eyed and innocent, we could truthfully say, "No, never." (Cheers and tapping of music stands from colleagues …) No doubt this added to the legend that British orchestras are the best sight-readers in the world.

All the string players have definite opinions on Simon's ability to determine how the music should be bowed – an accepted part of a conductor's responsibility, with or without the help of leader and string principals. Emotions ran high, and indeed still do, whenever the word 'bowings' was introduced. "Where did you get these Marks & Spencer bowings?"– this from guest conductor, fine violinist and one-time youngest leader of the Vienna Philharmonic Orchestra, Walter Weller. There was much erasing of previous pencilled directions for that guest maestro. It is nigh-on impossible for non-string players to understand the thorny intricacies of bowings, but this is not to say that the rest of us aren't fascinated by what we can see happening at the front during rehearsals. It stands to reason that, as the largest group of instruments in an orchestra, the coherence of the strings is of paramount importance. And, to an innocent onlooker, it would seem that an end result of togetherness is all. But no, this is too simplistic: totally understandable, but deeply uninformed.

This is a specialised, involved and vast subject on which many books have been written, therefore the following is merely a surface skim attempting to explain as clearly but as simply as possible the basic ins and outs of the matter. Or, as one of the fiddles wearily noted with a shrug, "What goes up, must come down." However, the way the notes are grouped in a movement of the bow subtly affects the phrasing and character of the music. It is vital for all those playing the same musical line to be doing the same bowing for several reasons – not least of all for tidiness from the audience's viewpoint. Contemporary scores give plenty of scope for unilateral declarations of independence but, even so, for much of the repertoire the first and second violins play similar lines and the basses frequently chug away in unison with the cellos (but an octave lower), with violas as the middle of the sandwich encountering both upper and lower strings and bowing accordingly, or separately, as the situation dictates. A composer can have noted every detail of the bowings, but his ideas may not coincide with those of the musicians responsible for interpreting his music, especially if he is not a string player.

After all, the players are the true experts in the field.

Particular types of bowing techniques, all part of the legitimate armoury of a knowledgeable composer, are used with greater or lesser effect, such as: *ricochet* (bouncing), *col legno* (tapping with the wood of the bow), *spiccato* (a form of staccato), *saltando* (leaping), and so on – a veritable maze of instructions. Care must also be taken not to run out of bow when slurring one note into the next, or groups of notes in one bow movement.

Watching my colleagues skilfully pleating and weaving their sounds, I like to think of bowings as music's way of breathing, and muse about how differing punctuation in the spoken language can totally change the meaning of a sentence, or how subtle verbal inflection can have a similar effect, altering the meaning of one word (e.g., **contract** – noun; con**tract** – verb) or a whole sentence. Or how difficult it is to convey understated sarcasm or an implied question and suchlike in mere written script. For instance: 'a woman, without her man, is nothing; a woman: without her, man is nothing'.

Sensitive bowings can alter the overall sound of an orchestra. This is a minefield in which a conductor can be creative or conversely where insistence on unnatural bowings can get in the way of the music. Thus, when Simon returned after current music director, Sakari Oramo, a violinist, had been in charge for some time, he admitted that the strings sounded better than when he himself was in the driving seat. As one string player remarked: "We almost took pride in coping with some of Simon's awkward bowings." Then followed with a wry grin by, "They were un-fiddlesticks!"

In Simon's quest to 'find the sound', it was decided to invite Viktor Liberman to come to the orchestra to take string sectionals. As a highly respected violinist and leader of Amsterdam's Concertgebouw Orchestra, Liberman certainly got to grips with technical problems, pencils were sharpened and bowings were duly marked in, with everyone pulling together for that special sound thus created. The only problem was that when Simon returned he gradually altered Liberman's bowings back to ungainly square one, thus negating any work done with and by the internationally acclaimed expert. "He just can't let go!" bleated one of the cellists.

Not only did section principals find that they were also having to take sectional rehearsals, but also other specialists such as violinist Iona Brown were taken on board. Contract in hand as guest director, this expert chamber music leader/director was given time to enable her to get to know the players, refine the string sound and deliver stylish performances of Mozart, Vivaldi, Bach, and suchlike. Phil Head, violinist and assistant librarian, noted that, "she was very eccentric about anyone stealing or using her bowings, and insisted that the music was collected up immediately at the end of the concert so that we could not photocopy any of it for archive purposes". She also caused much angst during her residency because of her unremitting search for perfection at all times. Nothing but the very best would do for this highly respected and totally demanding artist. I learnt to my amazement that conscientious, experienced violinists were secretly taking tranquillisers to offset the nerves they had never previously experienced. Gut-wrenching nervousness creates a phenomenon known in the trade as 'the pearlies'. When bow approaches string, the hand trembles, resulting in a jittery, juddering contact. (Percussionists can also suffer from the same effect when playing a very quiet snare drum or triangle.)

Simon was not the only conductor to bring fresh challenges to us, as I discovered when the City Choir's quiet and unassuming conductor, Christopher Robinson, programmed Messiaen's enormous oratorio *Transfiguration of Our Lord Jesus Christ* for a town hall concert. Three percussion soloists are needed for this very exacting work – vibraphone, marimba and xylophone – but, as Douglas, our principal player, was not a tuned percussion specialist and Annie couldn't face the piece or the work involved, it was left to me, James Strebing (timpanist, but not needed in Messiaen's music) and Jim Jones, one of our extras, to do the honours. I borrowed the orchestra's marimba many months in advance of the performance date and set to work. The part looked almost impossible to read: black with notes, almost every bar with a different time signature, covered with copious instructions to the player in French, and all, of course, totally exposed. Nonetheless, I relished the challenge as I doggedly ploughed on page after page. Messiaen writes fiendishly difficult music: skittering fragments, short, fast scale passages, awkward intervals at speed – but fortunately, with plenty of personal practice, it is all playable. When I realised that we were imitating exotic birds, I went to the library to look them up – all the better to focus on the effect he wanted. (Some years later I was on holiday in the Seychelles when I heard one of Messiaen's birds exactly as he had noted it down for the marimba, and found myself eye to eye with an 'exotic starling' resplendent in black, shot through with deep metallic turquoise - amazing!)

We soloists stood in front of the orchestra feeling somewhat self-conscious, but there was no time to be nervous. Every awkward rhythm had been tamed and every teasing interval conquered, as we had all worked extremely hard for this one-off concert. I wore my prettiest long coloured dress and was thrilled to receive a large bouquet of flowers at the end of our successful performance. This was my one and only venture as a real soloist and I had been determined to make the most of it.

Meanwhile, in September 1983, Simon and Ellie had become proud parents of Sacha: fair of hair and wide of eyes. Those of us who had been through the life-changing phenomenon of a tiny baby totally taking over every minute of the day watched with amused interest as Simon, with dark circles under his eyes, stifled yawns and enthused about his new baby. Ellie soon came into rehearsals to introduce us to 'Baby Rattle' (his father's media nickname when his appointment was announced in 1980), after which he became a regular, and eventually a scampering-around little character; another part of the CBSO scene.

I still smile at the memory of tiny Sacha sitting on Simon's knee at a long refectory table in The Maltings concert hall restaurant in Aldeburgh. Next to Simon was the Japanese composer Toru Takemitsu, with a massive, newly completed score on the table. Both men were totally absorbed in discussing the music, but, with dad absently posting bits of cucumber into Sacha's mouth, the quiet child waiting patiently for the next morsel to materialise for all the world looked like a baby bird on a twig.

As soon as Sacha was walking, Simon brought him to the back of the band to show him our fascinating collection of sounds and sights, where he shyly stood by the largest gong beater (parked upright), which almost matched him in height. I suspected that this was Simon's ploy to have a go at the instruments himself, although we were all very careful not to play anything above *piano*. It was lovely to hear Sacha's bubbling giggle from time to time, although having a lively small child around was also somewhat distracting.

Life was hotting up on the orchestra front too, with everyone soon learning to become rather blasé about the many photographers who constantly littered our rehearsal spaces. Simon was very patient with them as they crawled on the floor, stood on chairs, got in the way and clicked and whirred incessantly. I only recall one occasion when he asked someone to leave: during a BBC recording session. It never seemed to dawn on them that firing off continuous exposures and then noisily changing reels and cartridges was highly irritating for all concerned. Only one had the foresight to attempt to muffle the sound with thick padding over his camera, but even then our sharp ears heard the click of the shutter every time.

At one point during the afternoon of a BBC Prom rehearsal, we were amazed to find out that the TV cameramen were unfamiliar with the names of our instruments; so much so that labels were hung on the front of glockenspiel, vibraphone, xylophone and marimba. I facetiously threatened to add to this by writing 'Hello mum' on my knuckles so that the folks at home would know that I was the one behind the inevitable close-up shot of hands. "What on earth do you mean?" quizzed the producer. We patiently explained that we had noticed over the years that percussionists are rarely, if ever, shown on screen, and that we were only ever represented by so-called artistic shots of hands, sticks, reflections, weird close-ups and odd angles, much to the annoyance and disappointment of the children we work with, colleagues, family and friends. A heated discussion ensued, but ever afterwards there were rare glimpses of real humans giving their all in our department. Bribing the nearest cameraman with mints had not previously done the trick, but now, at last, the message got through. Live broadcasts and television appearances came thick and fast. Rattle and the CBSO were rapidly becoming the exciting new classical flavour of the decade.

Dear Douglas, our amiable percussion principal, found the job more and more demanding as Simon's programmes became increasingly challenging. The endless paperwork and responsibilities for hiring instruments and extra players had become tiresome and time-consuming, and so in July 1982 he retired.

A marvellous advert duly appeared in the national press:

Applications are invited for the position of PRINCIPAL PERCUSSION. The successful candidate will normally sit at no 3 in the FIRST VIOLINS and will be required to lead in the absence of the Leader.

Oops!

Auditions were held and eventually the new incumbent, Huw Ceredig, arrived. Annie and I were soon made to realise that from now on life in the CBSO percussion section would be very different. I discovered that not only did Huw's temper have a very short fuse, but also he instantly became impatient and irritated with my facetious attempts at relaxed friendliness. I was delighted, however, to note that he could also laugh until helpless tears took over. A somewhat stultifying air of serious endeavour pervaded our tiny working group for much of the time, with Huw very much in control and expecting us to play in the way he covertly dictated. I suspect that he was anxious to make a good impression, as his previous position in an orchestra

189

had been that of a timpanist. He had never held a professional percussion position before, but we discovered that he was a highly competent all-rounder and, incidentally, a man with two degrees tucked under his belt.

It is the responsibility of the one in charge to make sure that there are enough players to cover the demands of the score and that the correct instruments are available – whether owned by the orchestra or obtained from the specialist London hire firms. He also has to dole out the parts for the section to play, having spent hours working out who plays what, where and when, bearing in mind which player is most comfortable and competent at playing which instrument. We need to be able to play all percussion instruments, but obviously have our favourites. There are time-honoured pecking orders, however, as the principal is expected to take the most difficult part for himself/herself, and then the rest follow on in a predicted order. For example, the sequence is often tuned percussion (e.g., evil exposed xylophone solos), snare drum (ditto), then cymbals, with the rest following on until all instruments are taken care of. Naturally, much depends on the music, as perversely the principal part could be anything from the ever-audible triangle to a single gong note. All platform arrangements – the positioning of instruments, beaters, music stands, etc. – are carefully thought out by the section, as are physical moves during a piece: **nothing** is left to chance. In complicated set-ups it is very useful for everyone, including platform staff, to have access to a simple hand-drawn map, but even this is not infallible, as we have to be adaptable to the configuration of different stages.

Huw was not the easiest of people to get to know, and Annie and I often found ourselves gloom-ridden by the perceived air of silent disapproval emanating from him. These downward spirals were difficult to come to terms with, bringing out the worst in me in the shape of straight-faced annoyance, as the non-communication got in the way of the music. We realised that it could not have been easy for Huw to find himself landed with two long-serving players, both older than himself, who were having problems adapting to his unique and different ways of organising the way we worked. Gone were the comfortable days with Douglas, and, as far as I was concerned, the deadly earnest approach brought unexpected nerves and unimagined anxieties. Huw was very much a loner, something Annie found very difficult to accept. We **no longer were the perc. gang going around together, getting in the teas and cursing instruments and stands: life became much more intense as we were** constantly being given copious and often superfluous instructions, finding ourselves on yet another steep learning curve.

Television appearances and more touring were on the menu for the CBSO as our confidence as an orchestra gradually developed, but we still had to pinch ourselves as invitations rolled in to play in prestigious festivals both at home and abroad. Our first venture to Berlin followed a one-night stand in Paris in September 1984. Hopping around Europe for the odd concert here and there was perceived by many as bringing us closer to true international status.

A most sumptuous reception was given after the Berlin Festival concert, also attended by many members of the Berlin Philharmonic Orchestra (BPO). During this period they were in the thick of heavy orchestral politics with their conductor Herbert von Karajan, so we all had plenty to talk about as the beer and wine flowed. At one point Simon grabbed me as I manoeuvred by with a full plate towards a parking place with my colleagues. He was sitting at a round table solely occupied by sombrely dressed men to whom he introduced me (with an excruciating mock German accent) as, "Ziss is zee voman vith zee beeg bass drum!", and I realised that they were all BPO players: how embarrassing. I grinned feebly as one of them smiled, commenting, "You're not very tall!" "No," I responded, "but I can pack a punch!", leaving Simon to explain that one in German. I felt very strongly about waving the flag for my country, working hard at becoming adept with small talk, looking smart and remembering to smile. This was all to nought at one point on this occasion, however, as I was approached by an expensively dressed middle-aged woman, who on discovering that I was a 'schlagzeug' player looked in turn startled, then horrified, after which she firmly turned her back on me and walked away without a further word. So much for manners, I thought, stranded in the middle of the room.

The following day we read a splendid review in the *Berliner Zeitung*, a photo of Annie and I playing cymbals and bass drum being much in evidence. We were obviously of great curiosity value. Added to which, much was made of the fact that our orchestra boasted forty women out of ninety-five musicians, a most unusual sight on any concert platform in Berlin, or indeed Germany, at the time.

* * *

Up to the mid-eighties, after his early retirement from the university, my husband was engaged in a self-employed capacity by a Careers Development Service in Birmingham. He also travelled around the country working with private clients, made regular trips to Berlin and visited London frequently as the occupational psychologist on the Civil Service Selection Board, a prestigious position that gave him much job satisfaction. As our children entered their teenage years, the family became increasingly independent and involved with their own lives. Whenever possible, Sunday lunch was still the immovable family meal of the week, but there was a distinct feeling that we were all going our separate ways in spite of still living under the same roof. Over the years, I managed to squeeze in summer holiday trips to Australia and Canada to visit friends, encouraged by Geoff but not joined by him. On these occasions, he was the one who stayed at home, taking care of domestic arrangements and, of course, son and daughter.

Once Alistair had completed his business studies course in Evesham, he found work locally in the Parts Department of a very large, thriving garage, still living at home until he found his feet in the world of work. Fiona gained a place at the Birmingham Polytechnic for a BA Honours course in three-dimensional design, specialising in jewellery and silversmithing, eventually sharing a scruffy, overpriced flat with a bunch of students, financed, of course, by parents. We had always said that the only thing that our young would gain when they left their comfortable nest would be their independence.

Fiona and I had a final fling that summer, as I had saved up for a very special trip to Kenya. A package holiday was never on the cards for this adventure, as we were tied into dates for both the CBSO and the start of autumn term. However, I managed to arrange a safari trip starting from Nairobi, followed by a few days on a tea plantation in high, misty hills, after which we met the child I sponsored (for his schooling), one of several such youngsters I have sponsored since 1975.

I hired a cheerful driver – "I am James, a Kikuyu" – with sturdy minibus to take us to young Kyalo's school. This was situated off the beaten track in arid bush and scrub country 200 miles south-east of Nairobi. We spent a thought-provoking, scorching hot day hearing the school choir, talking to children and teachers and meeting Kyalo's mother, Esther, being acutely aware of the sharp contrast in our lives. We had taken a variety of gifts, from a school glockenspiel and children's simple picture-reference books to coloured pencils, non-sticky (for the hot African climate) sweeties, balloons and non-denominational, gaily coloured, folding-paper decorations, much to everyone's amazement and delight. When I asked the headmaster what they needed most, his answer was plain and simple: "Water!" The last rain had fallen four years previously. After much discussion and questioning, I told him that musicians are very capable of raising money with the skills we have, and so I could definitely guarantee funds for the building of a huge concrete water-collection tank and for him to go ahead with the practicalities. Strategically placed, a tank could catch the run-off from the only building with a corrugated iron roof capable of channelling any rainfall.

This happened in due course, with much generous encouragement from friends and colleagues in the UK. More than enough money was raised, and so we were able to provide funds for concrete floors for the outdoor classrooms and more corrugated roofing to gather the sparse rainfall. The legend, 'Started on 7/3/1986 Builted by orchastre, five brothers constructed', was scratched into the wet concrete of the massive, covered water tank, noting a curious, heart-warming connection between UK musicians and Third World Africa. We ended our journeying with a week in the Seychelles as a precious mother/daughter get-together, after which I had to face the fact that the first of my chicks had left home for good.

During 1987, after many family discussions, it was decided that we would make a major move from Worcester when the family had begun to thin out. Geoff made it clear that he was not happy at the prospect of returning to Birmingham: "I just want to live in the middle of a field with no one around me." I think we both realised that this was the beginning of the parting of the marital waves, but neither was prepared to discuss the matter at that point. Brum was where I wanted to be. I missed the stimulation of the big city and my friends, but most of all I was sick of travelling all those miles to work. However, Geoff was ready for the quiet life: the 14-year gap in our ages was beginning to bite.

In spring, house-hunting began in earnest, unfortunately coinciding with a time of high inflation and daily escalating house prices. I regularly scoured the estate agents' windows, only to find that there were no prices on view as they were constantly changing from day to day. 'Gazumping' became the new word on many lips as, no sooner had a sum been agreed, than many vendors realised that more money could be made by rescinding agreements and waiting for galloping inflation to overtake, thus bumping up spiralling house prices yet again. Mistrust, instability and anxiety created a nightmarish situation.

As I was the one working in the city, I sought out the properties and we looked at everything within our price range, trying to balance ideas for the future. First and foremost, a tiny, modern maisonette was found in Worcester

193

for Alistair; luckily, it was possible to make this comfortable with furniture from home. We hoped that our huge family house would raise sufficient funds to buy two further properties: any necessary mortgages should not be too enormous, so it was all systems go. What did we want – a house in the country with a small flat in town, or a family house in town and small cottage in deepest Shropshire for Geoff?

Disappointments turned to despair until a friend told me of a house for sale near to our old stamping ground in Moseley. I immediately went to check it out, finding not an agent's sign, but a hand-painted 'For Sale' board stuck in the front lawn with a telephone number added. The house was an early-1930s semi but, best of all, it was located at the end of a quiet cul-de-sac. I phoned that evening from the town hall and discovered that there was no estate agent involved and this was to be a private sale. A Methodist minister and family rented the property from a woman minister in Manchester, who needed to sell it as quickly as possible. I certainly could see the potential in the house, as there had been no attempt at modernisation: an ideal situation for us – all the better to put our own stamp on it.

Geoff came to view the house the next morning, after which we returned home and did our sums. The Worcester house had a cash buyer waiting in the wings eager to move in, and so, after a survey and heavy discussions, we made an offer for the white house with the green pantiled roof, which was accepted, much to our astonishment and relief.

As our Worcester buyer needed to be settled in in time for the new school year, things began to move quickly. I went to Japan with the orchestra for two weeks, then off again to Canada in the summer break, and all too soon we found ourselves planning what to take to Birmingham, what to squirrel away and what to sell or give away. It is a well-known fact that moving house can be traumatic, but this had the added edge of the family splitting up for the first time. There seemed to be never-ending packing sessions in spite of Alistair and Fiona being responsible for their remaining belongings. My heart broke to see the big oval table being carried down the path by an eager buyer. Of all our possessions, this was the one item that said 'the Brown family' to me. It had been the centre of so many significant activities: family parties, formal dinners, huge buffet suppers, homework, flower arranging, marking music, sewing sessions, mending bits of cars, art and craft work, games sessions, cooking, the dog hiding underneath it after canine misbehaviour, and so on; that very special table had seen it all, but there was no place for it at the new house.

Our two cats were ensconced in a smart cattery, and then the military operation began in earnest some weeks prior to our move. We were determined to do as much work on the property as was possible while it was empty. Consequently, I stayed nearby with friends so that I could be there for the gang of workmen who descended like locusts to remove walls, block doorways, demolish ugly fireplaces, fit new windows, replace hideous interior frosted glass, rewire throughout, enlarge the bathroom, replaster walls, paint and decorate. We discovered a large loft, ideal for storing family treasures, my space-consuming bass drum and empty tea chests for future use. A floor was duly laid and access improved, with a large drop-down hatch and safety ladder. There seemed to be a continuous parade of builders' skips being filled and removed, much to neighbours' interest and comments. An alarm system and upstairs telephone were installed, as were washbasins in bedrooms, and I insisted on a deep, square Belfast sink for the laundry area, and finally, much to my delight, we discovered original terracotta tiles underneath the unsightly lino in the kitchen.

Two large removal vans trundled up to Birmingham a day prior to our final departure. One load was to be put into store for future reference, and the other went to the new house. Then, on September 10th 1987, we finally left Worcester, after Fiona, a friend and I had spent the morning frantically cleaning the place. Lastly, house plants and final bits and pieces were packed into a small van. I waved goodbye, and then stood at the end of our beautiful Georgian square in tears, waiting for my lift to Birmingham and thence to the airport and Helsinki: the start of yet another tour.

I returned eight days later from Berlin to a strange house, unable to locate anything in the kitchen or indeed anywhere else. Geoff had manfully emptied six tea chests of kitchen goods with the help of a dear friend, the house was incredibly clean and tidy, there were flowers on the hall chest and yet I had never felt so miserable in my life. I was a stranger in my own home. Fortunately, there was a lull in the orchestra schedule for me, so I had four days' grace in which to gather my wits and come to terms with our new situation, determined to look forward and not back.

* * *

Earlier in 1987, the orchestra had begun to have meetings about a possible change in its make-up. Invitations to perform were arriving thick and fast from home and abroad; our concerts output had doubled, recordings were a regular part of our schedules, and hardly a week went by without some kind of appearance on radio or TV. In addition, the programming became increasingly demanding as further twentieth-century music appeared in the folders. With the best will in the world, it was becoming obvious that this particular orchestra and conductor would not be able to sustain this pace for ever. If only we could have more breathing space; if only there were more players to share the burdens of heavy schedules ... These were pipe dreams, but no, with Simon at the vanguard anything seemed possible.

All the regional orchestras were members of the Association of British Orchestras (ABO): comparable salaries and working practices being agreed with the MU. The implementing of new structures in our orchestra meant that we would have to go it alone and cease our membership of the ABO, but we initially put our trust in pledged increased financial backing from the Arts Council and our ever-supportive city council. We were painfully aware of the fact that cities such as Munich valued their orchestras to the tune of more financial support than all of our regional orchestras put together. This cut no ice with our government, however, and in our minority profession we came to the realisation that relying on commercial sponsorship was also a way forward. European orchestras worked differently, with a larger pool of players to call upon. This was seen as the future for us. A carrot of higher salaries and incremental scales based on time served was dangled, with more *release* and on-call days available for everyone – so far, so good.

Much hot air was expended as discussions raged back and forth. Initially, it was feared that there would be an almighty shake-up, with re-auditioning throughout resulting in inevitable redundancies, but this was far from the case. Instead, we were offered substantial pay increases, which were noted in a hefty handout of all the Development Plan proposals that had been sent to every member of the orchestra just prior to the summer holidays. Eleven newly created jobs were up for grabs: nine extra strings, a second principal horn and another timpanist, who had to play percussion when required. Seven other vacancies were also being contested, and consequently over 600 applications were received, including some from members of eminent London orchestras.

Simon made arrangements for every player to meet him to discuss the implications of the master plan. Consequently, small groups were invited to informal tea parties in the conductor's room so that any questions could be answered and worries aired. I was not alone in thinking that there would be an *Orchestra A* and *Orchestra B* situation after the initial novelty wore off.

But no, Simon was adamant that this would not be so. Nevertheless, I suspected that he would be like a kid in a sweet shop, being given full reign to pick and choose which guest player would be invited to replace legally released players, and that no one would dare challenge his decisions. There were numerous unspoken misgivings, although most appreciated that there was merit too in what was being proposed. The planned package lured us with good pay rises, but we also felt that there was a touch of blackmail in the air, as we strongly suspected that Simon would go from here if the overall scheme was not accepted.

After weeks of negotiations between CBSO management, the MU and the Players' Committee, a ballot was held (January 1988) as to whether or not to accept the proposals and the Development Plan. Out of eighty-four people, eighty-three returned voting papers: forty-four for the Plan; thirty-nine against. Little was said after the meeting, for we were immersed in our own thoughts, wondering what Simon would think about his divided orchestra. The January timing was significant as, after the USA tour in April, he would not be around during another sabbatical year, giving us a long period in which to come to terms with our new modus operandi. By the time he returned, the die would be well and truly cast. There would be no turning back.

When I joined in 1959, I gave all my loyalty to the orchestra, to my friends and colleagues, and to the music in our care. After 1988, I felt that there was a blurring at the edges of 100% commitment from everyone, as strangers (one string player commuted from Holland) frequently appeared in key positions whilst the contracted players saved up their release days to play for other orchestras, teach, go on holiday or whatever. Fortunately, I was rarely in the position of someone else being asked to do what I regarded as *my* job. We percussionists were only too familiar with flexible working arrangements – at the whim of the principal, or by personal request. The orchestral manager was only too pleased for Huw to decide which extra players were employed, and to be responsible for sorting out who did what, of course – not so now for the rest of the band. Guest players eventually appeared in all sections, so much so that members of the audience began to ask questions and some of us feared that the CBSO was no longer the orchestra most of us had joined initially.

After many months I felt moved to make my feelings known by writing to the Chairman of the Players' Committee and the two players on the Board of Directors:

Since its inception the CBSO has endeavoured to work as a close-knit team. There is now a replacement player system, using freelance players for key positions, which many colleagues feel is most detrimental to the morale of contracted players and the overall sound of the CBSO.

As one knows of the immense care taken to appoint permanent principal players, this apparently cavalier approach is very disturbing to many players in the orchestra. At one concert 34 non-contracted players were in the orchestra. Inevitably a number of these were bona fide 'extra' players: percussion, keyboards and also a number of trialists, but the majority were replacing CBSO musicians with a full contract.

Audiences are now noticing that our own players are often not to be seen and, more importantly, not heard for concert after concert. They are asking questions, which are increasingly more difficult to answer diplomatically.

A number of non-string players prefer to be working in the orchestra and feel frustrated and demoralised when outside people are brought in to replace them. Situations sometimes occur when the contracted player is not included in a specific concert because the 'Release Day' figures MUST be adhered to in a set period.

Do 'Release Days' have to be compulsory? Would it be possible for a player to choose whether or not to play on an offered 'Release Day'? If the player worked on the day(s) in question, could he/she have the days counted as 'Release Days', thus keeping the books straight?

It has been suggested that the MU would object to players working on allotted 'Release Days' (in their own job, in their own orchestra) because of 'loss of work for freelance players'. Surely the orchestra is creating work for freelance players by having the system and this is a bonus for such musicians when it is implemented.

It is bizarre to know that some players wishing to play (we do like music) are sitting at home when the orchestra is paying out vast sums of money for replacement people to do their rightful jobs. This cannot be conducive to a settled and happy orchestra.

At least I had said my bit instead of constantly fuming, but, needless to say, I was not surprised that there was no response whatsoever from the powers-that-be.

General manager, Mike Buckley, was the one with the responsibility for making it all work. Having been a violinist in the orchestra for many years previously, he now found himself in the unenviable position of smoothing down ruffled feathers, and some bruised egos, whilst new working practices were implemented. This was seen by the players as something of a noughts and crosses game; one that must have given Mike many a migraine.

When the Development Plan finally came to fruition, we were all required to sign new contracts. Huw immediately handed back his contract unsigned, pointing out that he was now expected to be section principal (playing timpani as required) for about an extra £850 per annum (before tax), whereas Annie would be on principal rate with no extra duties and no responsibilities excepting when Huw was absent for any reason. I would be at the bottom of our particular pile, still being expected to play anything and everything (including timpani), but not having attained the status of a principal position. Indeed, all percussionists, including extras, were expected to play any and every part if asked. Part of me couldn't care less about the status thing – after all, who would know? But I was bitter about the unfairness of the situation after all the years in which I had imagined that Annie and I were of an equal standing. All other sub-principal positions, apart from a trumpet and a horn, were shunted up to principal status as the next in line after newly created section principal positions. However, in spite of many, many letters, meetings, discussions and grumbles, my position never changed and I had to swallow my … pride?

I could no longer guarantee that if a programme required only two percussionists then I would be free for that concert. Huw consulted us all for the most part, but our long-standing 'gentleman's agreement' of being personally responsible for being available for programmes with small numbers of players now had to be set in stone in the terms of the Development Plan with the formal 'on-call' situation. Perhaps I was too sensitive about this, but I felt that my personal professionalism was somehow being eroded. No doubt there were many niggles in all sections of the orchestra as we learnt to come to terms with the new system, so I had to remind myself that, come what may, we had to live with each other and should not overreact, and that, when all was said and done, we must remember yet again that the music comes first and that 'the earth is a speck of cosmic dust'.

There were more anomalies and feelings of disquiet, particularly as numerous tutti strings felt that they were putting in many more hours than the front desks, who had far higher salaries and many more on-call and release days. I suspect that the grumblers would soon have something to say, however, if they had to attend bowing meetings and string auditions and, additionally, there would be solo passages to learn and total exposure at the front of the section. A larger pool of strings also had the advantage of players being available should a sudden problem occur. In theory, all musicians were now expected to sit in any seat in their section and to play anything put in front of them should the need arise, as the Company "has the right to include any musical works in any rehearsal, session or performance".

As our numbers grew, the orchestra became too expensive for some of the smaller concert venues. Neither could the minor choral societies afford the CBSO, which in turn meant that we no longer found ourselves shivering in ancient cathedrals in the depths of winter – something that was regarded as a bonus by the majority of the players. We also relinquished our regular summer date at the Three Choirs Festival and instead found ourselves featured more at the Edinburgh International Festival as well as summer festivals abroad.

Naturally, the enlargement of the orchestra took some time to achieve, during which period there were many adverse comments from the London mafia. "Sour grapes!" we quietly thought. Some London critics were reluctant to appear for certain innovative performances but, as Rattle wryly observed, "They have their own system of values – it's a little difficult for them to travel up the motorway, poor dears ..."

14 - Solo Act

It was good to be back in Moseley again. It was 1987 and I had come home at last, but the domestic situation was not a happy one. Geoff and I had grown apart to the extent that eventually we decided to buy a property in the country for him and that I should stay put in Birmingham, as we sadly realised that a Darby and Joan scene was not to be on the cards for us. But, once again, we were bedevilled with a daily escalating property boom. Despair set in as we hunted for that elusive perfect country retreat, our efforts gradually becoming less dedicated as prices rose.

Geoff decided that the ultimate solution was for him to travel around visiting friends here and abroad, returning back to Moseley from time to time until his half of the money ran out. After painful discussions, we both reluctantly agreed that living under the same roof was not ideal any more. Yes, we could all congregate here for family occasions, but essentially this house was to be my personal bolt-hole. Also, I had other plans. My intention was to be included on the theatre accommodation lists, being a landlady to artistic types and earning a little extra cash into the bargain. I enjoy having stimulating people to stay, but not for too long and strictly on my terms: this was to be the perfect answer to offset any feelings of loneliness. I realised that this was an unexpected return to my roots, as my maternal grandfather had been a theatre landlord way back in the 1920s.

Once more the search was on, eventually ending up months later in rural Wales, near Abergavenny. Friends there had spotted potential properties in a lovely area of farmland and hills, with plenty of walking opportunities for the self-imposed hermit life desired by Geoff. Whenever possible, Wednesdays were swallowed up with trekking to Wales and trawling round the estate agents. There were plenty of properties to choose from, and to our great relief we eventually found an elderly vendor who was equally sick of the unstable house market. He was anxious to make a move from a quiet lane and interesting old cottage. Decisions were made and, after firm handshakes all round, it was all systems go once more. In just a few weeks, the builders did their magic: upgrading the tiny kitchen, rejigging the ancient bathroom and other basic essentials. Tea chests were unfurled from storage and there was another great sorting out of possessions. Finally, the removal van was ordered, family treasures were loaded and we were in business. Geoff was in his element busily creating his very own nest, his DIY skills coming to the fore. I tried in vain to make some sense out of the garden, but all too soon I had to return to Birmingham and, thankfully, to the orchestra.

This was a very low patch in my life as I experienced every emotion: intense guilt, self-pity, relief, euphoria, black gloom and total misery. After weeping myself dry a number of times, I eventually rationalised the situation and reverted to my usual reasonably optimistic self. One of Geoff's observations about me was that I lived like a butterfly for the present without much reflection on the past and little enough thought for the future. I did not necessarily agree with this verdict, but recognised some truth there as I determined to look on the bright side and enjoy a somewhat more selfish life from now on.

One of my first decisions was to rent an allotment again in an attempt to grow interesting food, meet different people, wear myself out physically and breathe fresh air. This precious bit of land proved to be my salvation when overwhelmed by nostalgia and regrets, as every visit focused my energies on simple, down-to-earth problems. I slogged away, seeing carefully tended plants grow, weeds overwhelm and crops come to fruition, and giving away surplus produce to friends. I always brought something home, even if it was only a handful of cow parsley from the hedgerows – very pretty in a blue vase – or wild blackberries for mouth-watering bramble jelly.

Our two cats revelled in the safety of the quiet crescent and the excitement of exploring the deep overgrown railway embankment beyond the end of my garden. Small furry gifts often were presented, live or otherwise: terrified into rigid paralysis, neatly dispatched or thoughtfully filleted.

I had to learn to ask for help, although perversely I treasured my new-found independence. I discovered that, yes, I was able to remove hairy spiders, but could not face a half-dead rat in the garden; it was possible to drag a huge bag of compost into the garage single-handed, but not flat-pack bookshelves from Ikea; and light tree pruning was a skill I could learn, but not laying concrete paving slabs for a greenhouse floor, and so on. My friends rallied round and I was duly grateful, returning their kindness with home-grown and home-made goodies.

Special dates in the calendar, such as Bonfire Night, came and went. I watched a city display of fireworks from my bedroom window and tried not to think of past excitements: the children dancing with sparklers, parties, bonfires, visiting friends and neighbours, and eating traditional dishes. Nostalgia overwhelmed me at Easter time, Christmas is always a delicate juggling act, and New Year a non-starter as I faced it with the two cats and midnight television. Life was moving on, but I hated the growing up aspect of it all and having to come to terms with the fact that my young were now independent with lives of their own. To some extent, I followed my old rule of: 'If you are not invited *out*, then *import*.' I refused to sit alone in the house feeling sorry for myself, and so frequently threw little gatherings chez nous and had a good time.

Another positive effort was that of doing a foundation year at the Open College of Arts, a correspondence course coincidentally tied in with the nearby Midlands Art Centre. I had always been interested in the visual arts, and exploring the delights of this mixed bag was just up my street, for one year at least. The tutors and other participants were very generous, as the flexible teaching course was manoeuvred around the CBSO work schedules so that I could attend the various sessions. We had a crack at life drawing, self-portraits, pottery, sculpture, working with fabric, painting and printing. We also read a lot and had interminable discussions over endless cups of coffee. Unfortunately, the final weeks of the course coincided with heavy CBSO commitments, culminating in a foreign tour, but in spite of this I gained a lot, thoroughly enjoying the challenges thrown at me. During rehearsals I sat at the back trying to capture my work environment in pencil sketches, but was never happy with the results. It was fun to try though.

This orchestra certainly experiences many unusual concerts: not for us the 'meat and two veg' programmes. Schoenberg's massive *Gurrelieder* was a piece I had heard of, but I had never met anyone who had played it. Percussionists knew that heavy chains were called for – to be shaken for all they were worth – but had no preconceptions about the music, other than to imagine that, being Schoenberg, it would be mind-bending, twelve-tone, difficult and probably, in many minds, seriously ugly. We rehearsed it in the Great Hall of Birmingham University, a huge, echoey space that could accommodate the vast forces required for the piece: chorus, orchestra of a hundred and forty and soloists. But I was totally taken aback from the very outset as we wallowed in swathes of unforeseen romantic sound, evoking Wagner, Respighi, Elgar, R. Strauss and the like: Schoenberg pre-twelve-tone. Such a huge undertaking could only be performed in a large hall, so we took it to London and the Royal Festival Hall (RFH). I seemed to spend the whole of the first rehearsal wallowing in tears. "That's what I like to hear," said Simon when I confessed this as we came off the platform. Then later, in 1991, we had a fascinating time playing for the latest *Henry V* film sessions:

another novelty. Only part of the orchestra was involved in this, but naturally there was plenty of noble brass and lots of drums.

Once again, diary entries capture the occasion:

March 16 & 17 Wembley Studios
*We were behind glass screens, behind Simon. Huge intimidating red recording lights on the ceiling. Faced a massive screen for the visuals. Kenneth Branagh there (director and King Henry V) and composer, orchestrator and loads of technicians. Everything timed to the second, having to fit on screen. E.g. cymbal crashes on explosions. Simon wearing head-phones – 'cans', being cued to stand by with a click track ... "tick, tick, tick, tick!" then "you're IN". We have **all** of our instruments out and ready for anything, it looks like Agincourt in the percussion dept. Lights lowered as we're shown the scene with sound (no music). Was moved to unashamed tears in King Henry's speech. ITV people in for news coverage, and 'our' photographer. This is composing 'on the hoof', things being changed, doubled, removed etc. The music is done with Simon in contact (cans again), then seconds are shown at the edge of the screen. Some of us were able to sit in the control room to listen to what was being said to the boss. He missed a start cue and apologised: much re-winding of film. Very annoyed with himself. Everything must be correct the first time, so he was visibly irritated when a jubilant call of "Fifteen all!" came from a grinning composer. S. had been giving them a v. hard time over the click track, but he's really in his element with all the balls in the air and such novelties to boot. I found myself very nervously playing snare drum in one of the battle scenes, but after 2 hiccups it sounded great with all the swordplay and shouting. Very exciting! Some of the BBC chorus came in, as soldiers singing after the battle. Music haunting, corny, and very effective. Much lifting of English spirits!*

During these heady days, it seemed that the orchestra featured every week on radio or TV, live or recorded. One pre-recorded TV appearance was at 4.30am to 5.30am; hardly peak-time viewing, but there we were, giving our all. And as Ed Smith, our Chief Executive, put it, "The orchestra could be playing abroad for almost every day in the year as invitations are constantly rolling in from far and wide." EMI recording sessions became a regular part of our schedules as we set in concrete a wide slice of the orchestral repertoire, as well as works by contemporary composers and brand new pieces.

One notable effort was our recording of Nicholas Maw's *Odyssey*, the longest one-movement work in existence, which rejoiced in wall-to-wall percussion that took up half the stage on the platform at the town hall. I resisted purchasing this gem and was thankful that, for me, it was totally unmemorable. Consequently, I did not have the irritation of bits of it becoming, as the Germans put it, 'an ear worm', destined to sneak into the brain to drive one mad for many a long day after the deed was done.

* * *

When I arrived in spring 1959, I learnt that Sir Adrian Boult had actually extracted a promise of a new concert hall from the City Fathers as long ago as 1925, with the chosen site being pointed out to anyone who might be interested. Our current home was in the historic town hall, which, in spite of numerous improvements over the intervening years, left much to be desired. One suspects that Simon Rattle took up the gauntlet in this quest for a new home as soon as he arrived in the Midlands in 1980, and to their eternal credit the City Fathers listened and eventually acted. Local newspapers took up cudgels, many letters were published and endless meetings were held. In the early '60s, bemused citizens observed the beginning of a regeneration of the old industrial Birmingham, with new ring roads, the innovative Bull Ring shopping centre and markets, a University of Central England, Aston University, a massive modern public library, new Repertory Theatre, the National Exhibition Centre and finally, years later, the city centre complex of halls, lecture theatres, exhibition spaces and conference halls, soon to be known as the International Convention Centre (ICC), of which Hall 2 was to become our splendid Symphony Hall. It was a city to be proud of.

I imagine that a certain amount of blackmail was used by Simon to persuade the powers-that-be that not only did we desperately need a decent hall, but also that it had to be primarily for concerts and not an all-purpose space trying to be everything for everyone – and if he didn't get what we needed, then he would go elsewhere, taking his exceptional talents with him.

Broad Street was a run-down area within a tangle of dingy canals, warehouses, and derelict and partly demolished old factories, interwoven with overgrown scruffy no-go areas. A terrace of pretty Georgian buildings, trees, a busy antiques market and favourite old pubs were all sacrificed when the bulldozers arrived. Hoardings with tantalising peepholes were erected and work began. As a city of a thousand trades, Birmingham had no problem in functioning whilst being demolished, as experts in all fields were always on hand. Roads were blocked, re-routed and widened with as little fuss as possible, massively heavy machinery trundled on site and a forest of cranes seemed to erupt overnight.

I became very excited at the prospect of seeing our very own hall grow from a crater in the earth, so much so that I cheekily managed to persuade a site manager to let me video the work in progress bit by bit. I was given a hard hat and shown round the area, wondering the while how on earth anyone could possibly have an overview of what looked to me like a vast red canyon in the ground. It became my habit always to have the camera with me when in the city centre, and my enthusiasm eventually led me to asking permission to go to the top of an empty office block nearby so that I could film from above and from different angles, a move that led to my blatant gate-crashing of the Topping Out ceremony on the highest point of the ICC roof on June 5th 1989. I filmed the formalities after being told to "stick with me" by one of the project managers (neatly avoiding Ed Smith), and kept a very low profile during the somewhat exclusive buffet on site. What a nerve!

Not only was the ICC being built, but everything else needed to service such a massive project was also very much to the fore. Canal-side redevelopment was buzzing with hotels, bars, nightclubs, restaurants, shops, pubs and car parks. Centenary Square in front of the ICC ultimately became the focal point for displays, demonstrations, exhibitions, pop concerts, funfairs, firework displays, civic celebrations, general revelry, and somewhere for all and sundry to enjoy their new, vibrant city.

From the first lines on the drawing board, there was communication with the orchestra; we felt involved in our hall. Players and management were invited to a preliminary meeting with the architects, who mounted a fascinating presentation with artists' impressions of the finished article. Questions were encouraged, the whole experience giving everyone much food for thought. To be there from the very start of such an innovative, customised building was very exciting indeed. We were delighted and somewhat amazed to realise that the primary priority was that of superlative acoustics. A large hall was hired in Birmingham at the time that the stage was being constructed, the designers marking out the various areas for the musicians, after which the orchestra was invited to a seating rehearsal complete with instruments, so that everyone could see the plan for our workspace.

One of our constant complaints in the percs territory is that there is rarely enough depth of platform between player and music stand for comfort of performing, so we were determined to prevent any skimping if given half a chance. Armed with measuring tape, we noted down our needs and presented them to the stage designers. "Oh, that can't be right! It's far too big a stretch," they protested. "Come and look," we invited. "It goes like this: tall stool, player, instrument (the large bass drum is a good guinea pig), music stand, and a slight safety margin at the edge of the staging. And not to forget that the musician needs room in which to actually play, stand back, see the music - and ideally there should be room behind for players to move to other parts of the section, something we frequently have to do in the middle of a piece." Wonder of wonders, they believed us and actually took our measurements on board. For instance, it is now possible to park an unwanted xylophone behind the players, move about our space without getting in each other's way and enjoy playing on the most comfortable platform in the business as far as percussionists are concerned.

Backstage took a little time to settle down, but eventually we found ourselves with a small, cosy Artistes' Bar with hot food when necessary, spacious changing rooms and a massive area immediately behind the stage where instruments can be unfurled, with lots of space for tall double-bass cases, cello coffins, bulky percussion crates and boxes, massive wheeled skips containing miles of velvet curtains used as backdrops for a variety of projects in the hall, stacks of spare chairs, tables on which to dump outdoor clothes during rehearsals and a spot for the orchestra's noticeboard – in fact somewhere to call our own. When the configuration of the platform is that of a flat area, then the redundant platform risers are manipulated through the back wall panels, which swing sideways for their exit. In spite of all the apparent clutter, there is still plenty of room for a crowd of milling musicians to be tuning, talking and generally preparing to troop up those stairs onto the platform, into the bright lights.

After spending all of my professional life with the orchestra in the old town hall, I was half-dreading moving out and into the ultra-modern hall down the road. We arrived on a cold January day in 1991, walked in through the Artists Entrance, up onto the platform, and suddenly realised that we were *home* at last. The lights were on, and we were greeted by the hall staff briefly before finding ourselves gazing in wonderment at this splendid, spanking new hall decked out in coral, chrome, pale wood and marble – not quite a shoebox shape, but more like a cross between the *Queen Mary* and a magnificent opera house. Simon came on stage, grinned and said, "Well, this is *it!*", and then immediately dug into Mahler's Ninth Symphony. After about ten minutes he stopped, put down the baton and declared a wide-eyed, "WOW!" There was an air of breathlessness in the place, smiles and discussions about what we could hear that we hadn't heard before, and so on. However, I noted:

January 13 1991

Cellos not happy with their lot. The back desks can only see the backs of people in front of them as there's a riser to their right for the basses which blocks them off from the rest when the basses are standing to play. Flutes feel dead. But WE have glorious depth, which means that someone can walk behind our chairs without everyone having to move to let them pass. Bliss! Simon seems thrilled with the sound. The place is swarming with acousticians and photographers. Fire alarm tested to see if it could be heard through the music - a ghastly taped message guaranteed to terrify an audience. ('Fire Drill and Evacuation' ... by Takemitsu?) The staff seems very friendly. It's warm, full of dust, carpenters, lots of staff wearing their identity badges, and visitors standing around in groups watching and listening. Every tiny sound can be heard from backstage as there's only black canvas baffles behind the orchestra. (These look deceptively substantial from the audience point of view.) There's also a dull background 'heart beat' and swish from air-conditioning. NOT GOOD. (This problem was soon sorted, so much so that the proverbial pin can now be dropped and heard from the very back row of the upper gallery.) Nowhere to eat, so it's nosebags again.

Simon spent much time playing with the massive bright-yellow remote control on the end of a thick serpentine cable, thus activating the acoustic doors and the canopy over the stage area. When all twenty-two doors are open to the massive floor-to-ceiling resonating chambers behind the organ and chorus seating, the hall takes on a definite cathedral-like echo, the opposite being a very acceptable, more intimate ambience for chamber music or recitals: then the canopy is lowered and adjustable screens are manoeuvred in front of the marble walls, thus taking the edge off the brightness required for a full orchestra. I am told that the default setting is still the one that Simon decided on all those years ago, with just sufficient resonance to give a bloom and depth to the sound, but still retaining clarity.

February 17 & 19th

Symphony Hall sessions. NR (not required) but went in to be a steward. Subscribers are coming in to hear the orchestra in the hall and to wander round to choose their seats for the coming season. They all loved the hall and the place took on the air of a Lewis Carroll party. Peter Donohoe took the orch. through Beethoven and Schumann pno. concs. (piano concerto). Yawning, jetlagged, red-eyed orchestra (recently returned from Far East tour). I took in a stack of cookies from my freezer, much appreciated. Audience comments, "I see now why the orchestra grumbles about the Town Hall!" "Acoustically there doesn't seem to be a bad spot anywhere."

April 14th

*All day rehs in S Hall. Simon worked up a good twitch. He looks as though he hasn't slept for nights. The security staff on stage door getting to know us. New lamps being erected, railings painted, gravel around the huge newly planted trees in the Mall, piles of compost bags at the front of the halls, carpenters' bits in piles everywhere, a black curtain fixed at the bottom of the platform steps (so the audience can't see back stage) fixed with big bulldog clips. Simon fussed with **Daphnis**, the quiet stuff so quiet as to be practically inaudible. Percs have to move more slowly as every sound can be heard. It's difficult to pace our 'picking up' and 'putting down' quietly. Got home feeling like chewed string.*

April 15th

'The BIG day' Opening concerts, Symphony Hall
*Morning reh. He shredded **Firebird** to little bits. Ridiculous! Put every note under a microscope, which seemed to me excessively over the top at this point in time. Lots of photographers and TV news cameras around. Home in aft. Intending to sleep, but cooked, made beds, did washing. I left all my guests with a huge casserole, mashed spuds, treacle tart, bananas and custard ...*
*Parked the car miles away. Very excited crowds. The orch wore yellow carnations. **Firebird** disappointing, although I enjoyed the super BD part as ever. It was 'played out' and uninspired, he'd just done too much meddling so there was no spontaneity. 1st audience noisy with coughs and splutters. They'll have to learn. **Daphnis** audience was better. Orch guests had the front rows of the stalls, so very few of us could see them.*

(Inspired choice of seats by our management!) Champers reception with individual boxes of smoked salmon, chicken-nibbles, sandwiches, fruit tart. We were all given a specially struck medal in a case. Super atmosphere. Home to real champers and more smoked salmon. A splendid evening. Too tired to sleep properly.

June 11th

The city is alive with flags everywhere. There's an air of Alice in Wonderland with men planting shrubs, painting railings, hiding eyesores with painted hoardings and so on. The Queen ought to come every week. Heavy security everywhere, with bunches of large policemen dressed in dark blue overalls, airport X-ray machines, and body scanners at the entrance to ICC. Everyone supplied with clip-on passes, each individually signed for. Eager, busy dogs on leashes. My large cookie basket caused much amusement.

The ICC police were sporting incongruous white carnations. All TV lights on and HOT, just like Kew gardens. Were in Artists' Bar as a band room. Very crowded. Took in tons of eats for the band. Mahler 2. Went out front to listen to 4th Mvt. Simon turned and asked what the balance was like (solo singer) ... ME ... I said that the lower register was being lost, which seemed to confirm what he's suspected. After that he checked twice again! 9 cameras. 2 people spent the whole rehearsal weaving flowers for the Royal Box.

The official opening of the International Convention Centre (of which Symphony Hall was a part) took place on June 12th 1991. This was the one time that Simon made an effort to wear more formal daywear, when the Queen and Prince Philip came to open the ICC. Danny, one of the trombone players, spotted him wearing charcoal grey baggy trousers and matching jacket over an informal rehearsal shirt. Grabbing both lapels and almost lifting him off his feet, we were amused to hear Danny's cheeky query, "Is this *almost* a suit, Simon?" Mahler ground to a halt when the royal party arrived and the jacket was put on, to sotto voce ironic noises from the casually dressed orchestra. We all stood as he hopped down from the platform to go to the back of the hall to meet the VIPs. When he returned after the visitors had left, we naturally demanded to know what had been said. "Oh, well ... the Duke of Edinburgh remarked on how different you all look in ordinary clothes," he replied. This was greeted by laughter. "And the Queen observed that, 'The music was loud and quiet!'" Poor thing. What a job! I noted in my diary:

Up at the crack preparing for tonight's party. Shifting furniture, putting out covered food, plates, glasses, drinks, flowers and 'No Smoking' notices everywhere. As there was no opening night 'do' for the orchestra, I went mad and put an 'Open House' notice on the orch. board. I have no idea who or how many will turn up, but it's the principle of the thing: great thinking on the management front. I think NOT! 'Bricks in a wall' yet again?

During our tacet movement, I went out into the Mall just in time to see HM walking past with a small group of officials. My camera battery decided to pack in at that moment, so I got nothing. I had stomach ache prior to the concert, so downed a brandy – the nerves were for the party, not the concert.

Very glittery audience, but lots of empty seats: official guests not bothering with the music, but just coming for the eats and champers afterwards. Not good enough. I noted that the Princess Royal did not go to sleep. Many of us in tears at the end, not just the women. It's the day we've all been waiting for, but no buttonholes for the orchestra, no programmes for the orchestra, no reception for the orchestra. Bloody rude, I call it.

Got home after packing instruments to find a full house including students, some of the TV crew, dear Barrie Gavin (the producer) and Michael Berkley the programme presenter. All in all a great success. Went to bed at 3 00am.

On June 16th I noted:

*This, for us, is the real opening concert, with our proper audience. In an hour early for extra rehs of Birtwistle's **Triumph of Time** (not for this eve.!) - 10 cases of gongs and cyms for starters. 5 of us took a good hour to set up, then spent the break working out what to eliminate. (At a repeat effort of this during the Aldeburgh Festival a few days later, Huw was heard to sigh and announce to no one in particular, "This sort of stuff just **ruins** the day!") Simon overheard someone moaning about the ghastly piece and said, "It's a **great** piece, so just shut up!" It sounded a mess to us. (Some bright spark created an interesting anagram of the man's*

211

name: "'orrible warts in shit'.) It was very hot in there, and then we had to pack everything away and reset for Mahler 2. Exhausted before we even began the concert.

A drunk got into rehearsal, clapping and cheering from the Grand Tier. Security men eventually despatched him.

SR: "Has he gone?" Trombonist sotto voce: "Yes, he's back in the violas!"

The hall was packed – with music lovers this time. A wonderful audience, very quiet. It was a magnificent performance: one for the book. The choir surpassed themselves. At the end of the second of the big 'Scud Missiles' (massively long hair-raising crescendos), I knocked the top off a knuckle and bled profusely over everything whilst playing. Staunched it with a yellow duster, what a mess! BD is now truly blooded. Cliff was off stage in the acoustic chambers playing a large gong for all he was worth. Glad it wasn't me. Conductor Erich Schmid and his wife Martha were there in the place of honour, still very much part of our orchestra 'family' from the problematical Frémaux days. Lovely to see them. The hall is well and truly opened now, with a standing ovation from a very excited, emotional audience, and more tears from performers.

This was the beginning of a new era, as we showed off our new home base to other orchestras with a certain, dare I say, smug pride, being the envy of every visiting musician. Birmingham is now on the international concert circuit with London, the consensus of opinion being that we have the best hall in the country bar none. Thank you, Simon, for pushing a lot harder, and another huge thank you to Birmingham for having the foresight, bravery and generosity to carry out this ambitious dream so splendidly.

As the orchestra's Development Plan kicked in, huge adverts appeared in the national press, and the everlasting auditions began for all the newly created positions. This caused a great stir in the orchestral world, taking many months to achieve any results. As Huw was one of the candidates for the timpani job, it was left to Annie and myself to weed out the applicants, leaving us with five contenders. Simon appeared for the final auditions, announcing at one point, when confronted by a well-known maverick player, "If he comes, I go!" The advertised salary was £13,000-£16,185 – rather less than that of an experienced teacher. After months of the four hopefuls appearing in Rattle concerts, we all found ourselves in agreement, and there were great sighs of relief when Peter Hill from the Bournemouth Symphony

Orchestra finally accepted the job. Jim Strebing would not now be Rattle's principal timpanist – there was no love lost there – but would have more time off and play more percussion, thus changing the focus and pecking order in our section. The one losing out as far as work was concerned was dear Cliff, our regular extra, who seemed very philosophical about the new, somewhat uncompromising arrangements, or was he simply resigned to his fate? We all had to adjust to new working practice come what may, and this was the way forward. We had been only too happy to accept a substantial pay rise, although a number of us suspected that we were now well on the way to a dictatorship, benign or otherwise.

15
Distractions and the end of an era

I inadvertently became involved with various side interests, which eventually ran their course from the end of the old Town Hall days into our new Symphony Hall era, not least the issue of refreshments for the troops, particularly on heavy recording days. I had never particularly considered myself as a mum figure, but recognise the fact that, for the most part, I enjoy looking after people and trying to make life more pleasant by simple, and what seem to me, obvious practical means. Back to my Yorkshire down-to-earth common sense roots perhaps?

The orchestra was always delighted to play at venues near to coffee and snack bars, but these were few and far between and generally we were lucky if the two platform staff could find either the time or the opportunity to set up the electric water boiler in our own hall. A large, battered, picnic-style basket was kept backstage, in which there were unhygienic odd cracked cups and mugs, a huge metal teapot, a bag of sugar, long-life milk and box of tea bags. Boiling water was poured into the tea-loaded pot at the beginning of the break, and then we were left to our own devices as the men attended to the platform: moving pianos, rearranging chairs, and so on. Fifteen minutes are allotted for the necessities of a break for anything up to a hundred people, and so, as the percussionists were nearest to the action, I frequently found myself pouring tea and chivvying everyone to keep the queue moving. "Bossy Boots" was muttered in the ranks, but I noticed that no one refused the tea.

One day my oboe friend Karen dropped a desperate plea into my lap: "You like cooking don't you, and you're not always in everything, so how about making some biscuits or something for orchestra breaks? We never get anything, and as often as not there's no tea …" I must admit that the lack of a hot drink had irked me more than once, so I thought long and hard about the implications of my next step. Yes, it is true, I do like cooking and recognised that a convivial pause during a tough rehearsal puts everyone in a better mood to tackle the music, so – time for action. This appealed to my entrepreneurial genes.

First of all I had a word with our platform staff, who agreed to be responsible for filling, switching on and eventually emptying the catering-sized electric water boiler, and making sure that the tea basket was always available in and out of town. The new regime began after the disgusting collection of cups had been consigned to the dustbin and I went on a shopping spree for polystyrene throwaways, plastic spoons, sugar, catering tea bags, a large jar of instant coffee, a plastic jug for ease of pouring fresh milk, and ingredients for my first experimental buns and biscuits. In the town hall a cubbyhole, normally used by the hall cleaners, was designated for a trial run, and communication via notices and word of mouth soon had the desired effect. Thus I helped to keep blood sugar levels satisfactorily high during rehearsals, recording sessions and out-of-town venues whenever feasible. I also realised that there was no provision for hot drinks in the green room for conductor, leader or soloists, so it seemed obvious to set up a simple system there. A generous donation from the *Friends of the CBSO* provided a new kettle, filter-coffee machine, decent coffee, a tin of biscuits and other necessities. However, as far as I was concerned the orchestra came first every time, as I reckoned that the upper echelons could more or less fend for themselves.

Tea, home-made buns, cakes and cookies, or bought-in individual chocolate biscuits were priced at a nominal amount – enough to cover the costs, although I did not always arrive with my basketful of delicious, warm-from-the-oven goodies. It would not do for everyone to become complacent and take all of this for granted. They had to remember that my first loyalty was to my percussion colleagues, and that there were times when I had other more pressing commitments during breaks and before rehearsals. I discovered some surprising hidden traits too: selfishness, untidiness, dishonesty, generosity, kindness, gratitude and greed. Nevertheless it was fun to indulge the likes and requests of individuals. "What have we got today, Maggie? Mmm, they're still warm." "Ginger and orange, it's an experiment!" A smile and plea for favourites would fire my imagination. Teasing and nagging, friendships were cemented, but inevitably I also irritated others. For the most part, I kept quiet and observed from my web in the corner, but it was good to hear the animated chatter as we sat on the carpeted floor in the upstairs town hall corridor and blocked the stairs. Verbal communication is impossible during concentrated work time, and I like to think that the second half of rehearsals went with a better swing after we'd had a short, sociable break. These arrangements continued until we eventually moved into Symphony Hall in 1991, with special efforts continuing for gritty recording sessions.

One often worried about the lack of imagination from those at the top, especially when Ed Smith, the chief executive, implied that a tea/coffee (or, heaven forbid, alcohol) bar would be an unnecessary outlay purely for the use of players in Symphony Hall, as it was "perfectly possible to find refreshments in the Mall outside", at unrealistically high prices for resident and visiting orchestras I might add. Likewise, when our own CBSO Centre was at the planning stage, he announced that it would be better for players to "have a proper break, and go outside to nearby cafés for any required snacks", and that an informal, all-inclusive common-room area would not be forthcoming, as space was at a premium and needed for more pressing necessities. Needless to say, everyone took a very dim view on both counts, particularly as there were no cafés nearby. He seemed unable to understand what all the fuss was about, especially as he had magnanimously announced that drinking water fountains would be located on every floor of our new centre. In addition, a private space on the second floor had been designated as our band room. Fierce debates raged, the players' committee battled on, and eventually, after many controversial meetings, he had to accede to our wishes. Consequently, there is now a comfortable backstage bar in Symphony Hall supplying hot food during concert days, and our ground-floor refreshment area is the very heart of the CBSO Centre, being a favourite meeting place for performers and audience alike during chamber concerts, recitals, education projects, orchestra rehearsals, and so on. Our CBSO Friends also filled the necessities gap with gifts for both venues of wall clocks and television sets - with closed-circuit connections to the platforms in addition to the normal broadcasting channels – so essential for coffee-drinking, superfluous musicians hanging about, waiting to play. Soon after its installation, the Symphony Hall band-room clock vanished following a visit by an East European orchestra. Within two days, a group of our Friends were visiting backstage to see the new acquisitions, and so, as I was their go-between orchestra player, I was the one to rush off to Birmingham's jewellery quarter to buy a replacement, which was duly attached to the wall with long, tough screws - a nice little challenge for any future light fingers!

* * *

An ongoing personal obsession had begun decades earlier when, as a young girl, I meticulously wrote down the percussion instrumentation and the number of players used for all the pieces I heard in orchestral concerts. These were eventually listed in an index book, added to year by year by any

216

percussionist with pen and tacet bars available, thus creating an invaluable and highly specialised reference source, which eventually became the *Percussion Work Book*. Every few years, the book fell to bits with use, so was laboriously re-copied by hand into a more sturdy index book, the old copy being handed on to our platform staff for their own use. The orchestra librarian frequently borrowed the good copy, as did the orchestra manager responsible for booking extra players. Word got around as our various extra players came and went, and eventually I realised that if I did not make a decent copy available for others someone else would probably jump the gun and profit from all of my efforts over the decades. John, our platform manager, suggested that the way forward was to put it on the computer and that it should "just be a matter of copying out the information".

Oh, those few little words …! I struggled with the technology to list pieces alphabetically by composer, accurately note in detail every instrument required, numbers of players needed (including timpani requirements when available) and any tips for overcoming specific difficulties within the scores. Much midnight oil was burnt and colleagues were pestered and questioned, helping and encouraging me when I despaired of ever completing the wretched thing. I also haunted Birmingham's splendid Central Music Library, where I was given free access to the stacks behind the public areas.

I checked and rechecked, adjusted page layouts, shed tears of frustration, battled with copyright legalities, and wondered if it was worth all the torment and tearing of hair. However, after about a year I was able to contact the British Library, eventually becoming the bemused recipient of my very own group of ISBNs (International Standard Book Numbers). The next step was to find a printer. This was not to be a book for a shelf; this was for a drum box, stick box, music case, briefcase or library table, to be written in, personalised, added to, customised and USED. I had many hundreds of leaflets printed, explaining as succinctly as possible the merits of this comprehensive breakdown of repertoire for our specialised skills, and was deeply grateful for the use of kind, supportive quotes from Evelyn Glennie and James Blades. There was information on how to purchase the book and it was personalised by a photo of myself with the large orchestral bass drum. Once more I pestered the library for possible contact addresses: university music departments; music colleges; specialist music schools; professional orchestras; amateur and youth orchestras; specialist music shops and suchlike. A local print shop took me under its wing, and between us a working copy was created and at last I could hold in my hand the lurid green, ring-bound, very first book. There are no page numbers as I had problems with working out how to do this, but, as it is in alphabetical order, I reasoned that page numbers were not strictly necessary. I spent endless time meticulously collating what I hoped would be the definitive effort, as I was the only one who could understand what look like hieroglyphics to a non-percussionist, although our weird way of noting down our instruments needs no translation to those in the know – another bonus for sales abroad.

A standard letter was concocted both in English and German, packs of window envelopes, many books of stamps and airmail stickers purchased, and more midnight oil taken on board. I underwent more brain bashing as I struggled to set out letters so that with careful folding the address would appear in the envelope window. Many bundles of slim envelopes were plopped into my local pillar-box, and I sat back and waited.

Personally contacted London colleagues were the first to respond, and I learnt with amusement that some had fingers crossed as they had trusted that I would achieve what I had threatened to do all that time ago. In the fullness of time, I was thrilled to send books off to a great mix of orchestras such as the Suisse Romande, Vienna Philharmonic, Israel Philharmonic, St Louis Symphony USA, and so on. Word spread. I met and am still being contacted by players, conductors, musicologists, students, librarians, orchestra managers and specialist percussion shops, and there have been some wonderful responses. Mistakes were noted and corrected, and eventually I discovered that books had found their way to all corners of the globe: Hong Kong, New Zealand, Brazil, Canada, the USA, Japan, Australia, China, far and wide in remotest Scandinavia, and dotted around in just about every other country in Western Europe.

* * *

I had no sooner got the *Percussion Work Book* up and more or less running than I found myself writing out lists of percussion instruments with simple hand drawings, as reference points for colleagues going into schools. These were photocopied and disappeared like snow in summer as non-specialist class teachers clamoured for help with instruments and as interest in education work grew in the orchestra. More and more colleagues were asking about percussion instruments, and so education manager Ann Tennant set up a lunchtime workshop for anyone who wished to come. I dug out lots of the orchestra's own school instruments, and then we proceeded to have a riotous hour, having a go at everything and laughing a lot. We tried out some hip-swinging Latin American rhythms with the appropriate instruments, and this was when I discovered that there was confusion with instrument names: for example, castanets were muddled with maracas, there was embarrassment when confessions were made about naming the guiro (confusingly pronounced 'wheeero') as a scraper, maracas as shakers and sleigh bells as jingles or little bells. "Don't worry about such things! It doesn't really matter as long as you always use the name you decide on. Remember, "A glockenspiel is *made of steel*, and a xylophone is **always** *wooden* as the actual word means *wooden sound*" ... and so on. We explored the many interesting techniques available for the ubiquitous tambourine, after which I hope that I managed to instil some kind of respect for the humble triangle. I also introduced my own strict house rule when working with a class of excited kids: "When you are not playing, put your instruments *down!*" I had visited one school whose teacher had gone even further with her intolerance levels, as she categorically forbade the use of any tambourines in HER school. What a pity! I do agree that there is nothing more irritating than background jingling, but of course I then took great delight in pointing out what a splendid little instrument it is, and that it is the responsibility of the one in charge to instil basic tambourine discipline into the children.

Library and school music catalogues were searched, but we could find no reference book on school percussion instruments as such, so with a bit of persuasion from Ann I set off on the long road to try to rectify this. My first task was to decide how to categorise the instruments: by style of playing, or by what they were made of, or family groups, or alphabetically? What had initially seemed straightforward became more and more complicated. I drew various instruments, photographed others, or photocopied illustrations from various sources, but I was becoming thoroughly bogged down and downhearted by the whole process. However, it was suggested that I should contact a very well-known publisher of educational material and see if they would show an interest in my ideas. A & C Black are long established publishers and well respected throughout the education world. As someone observed, "They must have some of their books on top of every school piano in the land!" After a lot of head scratching, I penned a careful letter and sent some sample pages off to London. To my surprise, I was invited to meet one of the editors on one of our Royal Festival Hall days.

As we talked through the practicalities and my experiences as a percussionists visiting schools, I realised that the timing for all this was very fortuitous as A & C Black were about to publish two jolly books of simple percussion music for junior schools. It was decided that my *Agogo Bells to Xylophone* would fit rather neatly into their 'Percussion Players' series, which was being specially created to make classroom percussion accessible to everyone. Once more, I was on a roll for new experiences.

A five-page contract was drawn up which I eventually signed – the beginning of yet another new adventure. The first germ of this idea had been born in autumn 1993, but it was not until 1996 that I held my latest 'baby' in my hand. In the parlance of my family, it had been another l.h.s. – a *long hard slog*. I loved the jolly, bright cover, clear and accessible layout, and delightful illustrations by an in-house artist. When the little 'friendly guide to classroom percussion' finally hit the bookshops, I had some cheering feedback from teachers and reviewers. At one point, I was stopped in the city centre by a teacher with whom I had worked, who told me that she always kept it on top of the piano, so that the children could also look at it any time they wished. I liked that. One reviewer had obviously read it pretty thoroughly, ending his comprehensive, generous comments with, "Its realism and candour are as attractive as its tone of generous encouragement", and the *Times Educational Supplement* described it as "a treasury of good ideas". Yes, it was worth all the worry, although now when I visit my local library I wonder about all those millions of words locked inside the book covers – how did all those authors do it? I marvel.

* * *

I frequently give talks about working in a symphony orchestra (entitled 'Orchestral Notes') and take great pains to explain that, although life in the CBSO began long before Sir Simon hove into view, after his arrival orchestral life undoubtedly became even more of an exhilarating, if somewhat exhausting adventure. My favourite party trick on these occasions is to produce the sample work schedule to which I have already referred.

Most people naturally ask about the Rattle days, especially after the Development Plan came into being. We had to pinch ourselves as we realised that our status in the orchestral pecking order had changed, as Hugh Canning from *The Sunday Times* observed: "During eighteen years of outstanding work, Simon had taken a fine municipal orchestra into the international league." When, during a visit to Canada, I gatecrashed a Toronto Symphony rehearsal, and naturally went backstage to meet my opposite numbers. After interrupting their instrument-packing activities, I introduced myself and was confronted with dumb amazement.

There was a puzzled pause and then one of them ventured, "A percussionist from Birmingham … England?"

I grinned, thinking of the Alabama alternative. "Well, yes!"

"But that means you're one of Rattle's babes – oh, lucky you! I wish we could have him just once as a guest."

I was bombarded with questions, after which I went away with much new food for thought, viewing my everyday job from a somewhat readjusted perspective.

We 'Rattle Babes' know that Simon's bright flame of genius is able to singe, or conversely, illuminate with astonishing clarity. Music that had been part of our everyday *raison d'être* for so many years became a new experience when heard through his ears. His players watched and learnt, certain that he had been there before, as it seemed impossible that such a young man had such a wealth of knowledge about the subject nearest to our hearts. One of the negatives for players, however, was the feeling that our jobs no longer solely belonged to us individually. As predicted by some, we had become pawns in Simon's orchestral chess games, being shifted around by what seemed, at times, his whims and fancies. If he decided to invite a guest player for a specific piece, then so be it. Contracted players were being paid to stay at home and sit it out, whether they wanted to play in their own orchestra or not.

We realised that Simon's brilliant, restless brain needed constant stimulation, fresh challenges, and new mountains to climb. However, when other conductors appeared in his absence, the effect could be disturbing. Musicians are forever adapting to the needs of the one on the rostrum, but there were times when we found other conductors' methods to be irritating, frustrating and occasionally deeply depressing. Some complained that there was a danger of our becoming too manicured by Simon, but over the years, as we became more comfortable with his ways of working, we hoped that we would be able to instil something of ourselves in the final offerings for our ecstatic audiences.

Ground-breaking television series such as *From East to West* and *Leaving Home* were slotted into the regular concert schedules. Then, in March 1991, we began a long, innovative journey with Simon with *Towards the Millennium*, presenting a series of programmes that highlighted each decade from 1900. The 1900 to 1910 era began in earnest with works by composers as diverse as Elgar, Schoenberg, Ives, Mahler, Stravinsky and Suk. Every period was fascinating, although we were only too painfully aware of the fact that music from the final decade was yet to be written, and that we, in our department, would be scratching our heads as the selected contemporary composers discovered that they had a free hand to write anything they wished. How right we were, wondering which indeed would be true first performances and which were destined to be their last, at one and the same airing. The concerts were repeated in London with some also appearing in Cardiff. No one could accuse the CBSO of promoting boring concerts: innovation was all.

Accolades and awards, television tributes, prizes, public recognition, honorary fellowships, doctorates, degrees, gold medals, the freedom of the city of Birmingham, and a knighthood (to add to his CBE) in the 1994 Birthday Honours List: they all came Simon's way. Without fail, he always insisted that every compliment was a mark of distinction for all of us, and that we all should share the knighthood, or whatever, as we were a team; forever a team. There was a lot of teasing behind closed doors after the knighthood was announced, but oh, we were so proud of him – and he was not yet forty! The hair was becoming more grey than brown, and he was wearing himself to a frazzle as there were more demands on his time, but we were all on that roller coaster ride together. Tours came and went, we were privileged to work with some truly magical soloists and we were playing what must have been some of the most cutting-edge programmes in Europe.

It is a pity that we could not always have been recognised as the *orchestra in residence* at Symphony Hall, but at the time of opening we were regarded as rivals by a hall management desperately trying to attract foreign orchestras to their International Concert Series. Initially, there was scant mention of the CBSO on any of Symphony Hall's promotional literature, as the two concert series were kept strictly apart. Thankfully, in due course this changed, and now we have a positive presence in the building with CBSO banners much in evidence, splendid advertising space and a promotions desk. I take great delight, when meeting members of other orchestras, in innocently asking what they think of our hall. There is always a gratifying pause and then a rolling of the eyes before a sigh and, "Oh, you're so lucky. It's wonderful!"

Another bright star on our horizon was the fact that we were, at last, going to have a proper base as a home of our very own. An old Victorian lead works in Berkley Street, a mere five-minute walk from Symphony Hall, had been purchased as far back as 1990 and was to be converted into a CBSO Centre.

This generated huge interest and anticipation as we had previously had to rely on trooping around the city to rehearse in churches, university halls, Quaker meeting rooms, schools, a BBC studio, and so on: wandering gypsies in our own city. Thankfully, when the Birmingham Conservatoire's Adrian Boult Hall opened in 1985, we were given top priority to use it as our main rehearsal space; the first step to a true residency in our own city. The orchestra's administration department and orchestra library had also moved to the Conservatoire, so at least we were now all under one roof, albeit not one for our sole use. During the next years, there followed gargantuan efforts to secure the £5 million needed for the exciting Berkley Street project. There was much speculation and great interest as the old factory was eventually demolished (but not the 1920s façade), and we wondered what on earth was going on behind all the tarpaulins and scaffolding as noisy construction began in summer 1996.

As the building reached completion, a time capsule was buried under the wooden floor being laid in the main hall, the 1998 contents ranging from one of Simon's batons to a bottle of Scotch and an Argos catalogue. A current copy of the *Birmingham Post* containing an article about the orchestra was also included, along with one of the two little Coventry crosses carved in 1962 by my dad from offcuts of the bishop's throne in Coventry's new cathedral. A cake in the shape of the new Centre was made and consumed after a small but significant ceremony, and then it was simply a matter of waiting for the finishing touches and the official opening day later that year. It would be marvellous to have our own home at last: somewhere for the Birmingham Contemporary Music Group, for the orchestra and choruses to rehearse, storage and space for education and community projects, large library, practice rooms, small studios, our very own band room, a large instrument store, secure parking space for the orchestra van, a fine display space in the large entrance hall, a small licensed bar and refreshments area and, of course, at the heart of the building, a flexible, custom-built auditorium suitable for rehearsals and many styles of concerts. In spite of reluctance from Ed Smith, who was worried that an in-house chamber music series would "detract from the main concert programmes in Symphony Hall" [*sic*], the players insisted on having their own input with the splendid 'Centre Stage' series of lunchtime concerts. These hugely successful presentations now give players the opportunity to perform favourite chamber music, at times working with soloists from our mainstream Symphony Hall offerings. A coming together with different colleagues to put on chamber concerts is usually impossible to achieve when working full-time in a large orchestra, but here positive thinking created the perfect city-centre treat: music played by enthusiastic performers to the accompaniment of a glass of wine, home-made refreshments, decent coffee and a comfortable seat. This is a true recipe for the enjoyment of everyone present.

In November 1998, a small group of players was invited to perform Judith Weir's specially composed *Overture* for the building's opening ceremony. To my surprise, I was one of the chosen few, as my more senior colleagues were not able to take part. Naturally I accepted, to discover that I was being paid a handsome sum to be there, perform for a few minutes, and then enjoy the rest of the evening with a chosen guest in tow – most acceptable.

After the one and only rehearsal, I happened to ask a colleague if he had received his "posh deckle-edged invitation for next Monday". His response to this was blank puzzlement, and then he and I realised that not all of the players had been invited to the official opening ceremony, due in a few days. This was to be a right royal occasion attended by our patron, Prince Edward, many distinguished guests, members of the Board, the Players' Committee (and guests), representatives of the Chorus and administrative staff, and so on - even to the inclusion of the new CBSO catering staff – but not the full orchestra. Amazing! There was little time to spare, but I blew the whistle loud and hard, as I found it difficult to understand how this could be possible. Our player representatives on the Board made a big fuss, whereupon the next day we discovered a mealy-mouthed letter on our noticeboard stating, "It has come to our notice that, as there are more tickets available than first anticipated, it will now be possible for all members of the orchestra and their guests to attend the opening ceremony of the new CBSO Centre." Underneath this appalling display of mismanagement was a space for names of those who wished to avail themselves of this oh-so-generous offer. Needless to say, most people boycotted the whole affair in disgust. 'Bricks in a wall' yet again?

One wondered if Ed Smith had been aware of this sorry omission, as such domestic details would no doubt have been the responsibility of one of his minions. Ed was a shadowy figure for the most part: deeply private, quiet, thoughtful, hard-working and, as far as we were aware, a fair man. In any dealings with Ed, either as a player or player representative, I always found him to be the perfect gentleman, although one was fully aware that there was steely determination behind the courteous exterior. During meetings with the Players' Committee, the only clue to any tension was when he leaned forward, elbows on desk, and twiddled a pencil between his fingers. The accompanying concentrated eye contact meant that we were in business and communicating. It is only too easy to rail against the one at the top, but for the most part there was respect for Ed. He and Simon were a good duo, although we appreciated that our principal conductor usually ruled the roost.

* * *

One day, in February 1995, Simon arrived for rehearsal as white as a sheet: this was the first time we had seen him since well before Christmas. After wishing the orchestra a belated Happy New Year, he announced that he had something to tell us about himself before rumour and conjecture became rife. He simply said that he and Ellie had separated and that they were getting a divorce. He was very miserable, and wanted us to know that he felt very close and loyal to the orchestra and that he had just signed up for another year until 1998. No one had dared ask about his family for a long time, as there had been no sign of Ellie or mention of the children for ages, and we had suspected that something was wrong. When trapped in a tea queue, for instance, one would vaguely resort to asking how the boys were, but they were all too often "in America with their mother" or "away". It was all the more of a shock when Candace, the new lady-love, appeared on the scene, someone who eventually became the second Lady Rattle. We sympathised, empathised and were saddened for all concerned. The papers had a nine-day-wonder frenzy, and Candace was eventually introduced to individual players when appropriate. Life went on much as before as Simon threw himself into demanding programmes, not only with us, but with, among others, the Los Angeles, Vienna and Berlin orchestras, and opera and early music groups. After we cut our teeth on some of his more adventurous repertoire, we discovered that his other symphony orchestras were going down the same road with the same pieces some time later. I liked that: to me it smacked of good housekeeping and appealed to my practical nature, although some complained that he seemed to be using us to test the water.

Almost exactly a year later, we were asked to stay on stage after the end of rehearsal in Symphony Hall. A deep sense of foreboding pervaded the space as we sat in silence waiting for we knew not what. I needed to nip off the platform for something I had forgotten, but was brought up short when I saw that all the office staff were backstage and were beginning to move into the body of the hall. "What's up?" No one would answer. I thought that someone had died, but then today's get-together had obviously been planned in advance, so I rushed back onto the platform just as Ed Smith came to the front, followed closely by a chalk-white Simon. Putting two and two together, we soon realised what was happening. Simon tried to remain calm and smiling, but then pulled a scruffy bit of paper from his pocket and, after stammering that he didn't want us to learn of this in the press tomorrow, he proceeded to read it in a choked voice.

The essence of his announcement was that he had decided not to renew his contract and, therefore, in just over two years' time he would be leaving the orchestra. He began to give the reasons for his decision, not least his recent and present domestic situation and the fact that his children would probably be 6,000 miles away. The commitment as music director "took all his time and energies", and now, at the ripe old age of 41, he realised that if he carried on at the present pace he would "go pop", which is what I'd said for ages. I have never seen him so upset; it must have been one of the most difficult things he had had to do for years. Anyway, he told us that Candace and he would still be living in the UK and that he had not got another job to go to as yet, but that he needed more freedom from the rigours of the music director position. No one moved a hair; we all just sat there in our orchestra seats looking at him. The shock was profound, but there was nothing else to be said at that point. He gave a little tearful shrug and fled, leaving a silent orchestra to try to come to terms with all the implications of the bombshell he had just delivered.

Some were in tears at his news, the cynics were predicting his next move (Berlin? Vienna? Opera?), many were relieved, but most were shocked. Of course we knew that he would not stay in Birmingham forever, but I had thought that he would have relished seeing in the Millennium with all of us. We wondered with interest whether he would take on another 'hands on' appointment, or whether he had had enough – would he really be able to resist involvement with the everyday nuts and bolts of another orchestra?

The announcement hit the local and national news on TV the next day. The accompanying ghastly photo added unflattering years: he looked old and haggard, standing outside by a rough concrete wall. Headlines screamed, "Rattle Quits CBSO – going for more lucrative engagements". Charming! It would be a trying time until the dust settled. Dismay was our foremost emotion, but no doubt we would get over it.

Once more it dawned on us that we were at the end of an era, and yet another search was on for a replacement conductor – not easy, but hopefully not impossible either.

The CBSO's chairman, Sir Michael Checkland, said later in our in-house CBSO magazine, *Music Stand*:

All of us at the CBSO – orchestra, chorus, staff and board – cannot thank Sir Simon enough for his outstanding and challenging artistic leadership over so many years. It has been his total dedication to the orchestra which has transformed the CBSO into the very fine organisation it is today. We must build on the development he has led and greatly welcome his continuing commitment to work with the CBSO beyond summer 1998.

Ed Smith observed the following (in Nicholas Kenyon's *Simon Rattle, from Birmingham to Berlin*):

When Simon was about to step down as music director I spent a long time, but a very enjoyable time, doing some statistics. Between 1980 and 1998, during his time as music director, he conducted 934 concerts including 16 world premieres: 337 concerts in Birmingham; 339 elsewhere in the UK, including 28 BBC Proms, 46 at the Royal Festival Hall, 39 at the Barbican; and 208 concerts on foreign tours to 25 countries on 4 continents.

The 934 concerts that he did included music by 113 composers, of whom 84 were twentieth century and no fewer than 36 were living when we played their pieces. To accomplish all that, Simon rehearsed the orchestra for a staggering - and I use the word advisedly – 5,098 hours. A total of 69 recordings for EMI were made, taking 978 hours in the studio: if you add TV to all that, well it was altogether something like ten thousand hours – an incredible commitment. Is it any wonder that they could play together as such an incredible team?

It is to be remembered that, as far as the orchestra was concerned, this was work with just one of numerous conductors: all part of our normal job as orchestral musicians. And, during this time, Simon also travelled in the UK and abroad, working with other orchestras and opera companies: part of his job as an internationally renowned conductor.

16
Fresh fields and pastures new …

During the 1990s, I was having problems with my health, as my knees were constantly creaking and painful. I am convinced that this condition had been exacerbated by having to lug armfuls of ironmongery around throughout my long career, although I realise that being somewhat more overweight than desirable cannot have helped the matter either. "Take painkillers," was the advice of my doctor. "You're too young for an operation." When at last I saw the X-rays, I pushed for a more positive approach. There's not a lot else that can be done when all that one can see is bone on bone. Nasty! I remarked that one of these days, in the not too distant future, I hoped to have grandchildren and be able to pick them up and play with them. I also promised to save for a future electric wheelchair, if that was what it would take for me to be allowed to have an operation **now** and therefore to be more active at the present time. Fifteen years is predicted for the life of a new knee – not a long period, but then I didn't want to be too decrepit to appreciate indeterminate improvements much later in life. The wrangles went on, but eventually I was taken into hospital where a toss of a coin decided on the left knee first, after which the deed was done early in 1997 just before my sixtieth birthday. My next appearance in public was to play triangle and plonk out a few celeste notes in a Shostakovitch symphony: sitting down, of course. After that, it was back in harness as usual, although my close colleagues were kind and sensitive enough to let me off any heavy lifting. Therefore I became the 'pencil monitor', doing a grand job sorting out the smaller instruments, music, sticks and beaters. After six weeks, I was driving once more and learning to live with my new knee joint.

This had been a serious, life-changing episode in my life, making me think more about my future. For many years the thought of retiring had filled me with total dismay, but as the time drew nearer I was determined to think positively; after all, I was bound sooner or later to either leave the orchestra or retire. I duly designated three shelves in my bedroom for retirement reading, buying interesting books but being determined not to read them until I had left the orchestra. My collection grew and, after the birthday watershed, I became more and more self-conscious about what I was doing at my age and in front of all those people, trying hard not to imagine how I must appear to strangers at our concerts. Until recently, compulsory retirement had been pegged at 65 years for the men and a choice of 63 years or 65 years for the women, but, after much discussion, especially amongst the older members, it had been decided to set the age at a fairer 63 years for everyone.

Simon's final two years with us passed only too quickly, but of course were crammed with innovative programmes and a hectic four-week tour of the USA and Japan. During his final weeks, he was trailed by a BBC TV crew who became so much part of the furniture that for the most part we forgot they were there – flies on the wall and all that. There were the usual summer outdoor concerts and a final bash at Salzburg with Beethoven's Choral Symphony, Birtwistle's hugely scored *Triumph of Time* and a part-staged performance of Szymanowski's opera, *King Roger*. The ultimate intensity of Mahler 2 rehearsals on home ground was diluted by a great party to which Simon invited everyone. A city-centre Chinese restaurant was the venue and the atmosphere was upbeat. We knew that Simon would return as a familiar guest and were safe in the knowledge that we had secured (by a previously unheard-of 100% vote) our next boss: Sakari Oramo from Finland. I was somewhat daunted to learn that Sakari was not only young, but also younger than my son by a year. The only hurdle in the immediate future, however, was that of Rattle's final concert, which most of us dreaded.

This took place in Symphony Hall on Sunday August 30th 1998 with the second of two performances of Mahler's *Resurrection* symphony. I recorded the event immediately afterwards in my diary:

Simon's Last Stand
We did the same programme last night, but somehow I wasn't as 'touched' as I'd expected to be. Maybe it was the heat, the emotionally charged atmosphere, the packed hall and attentive audience which kept me in check. We haven't done a performance of the Mahler for some time and, as I was sitting at an uncomfortable distance to see the music, counting was well to the fore. Soloist Anne Sofie von Otter was next to me, who in spite of being protected by a large perspex screen must have been very uncomfortable so close to the big bass drum. I had apologised for the volume of sound in the rehearsals; both she and the other soloist (Hillevi Martinpelto) sweetly smiled and shrugged their shoulders. This is one piece where there are no holds barred.
Simon was fully charged and wired up to the ceiling for his penultimate effort with 'his' orchestra. He looked exhausted (as well he might be after

the Beethoven series at home and in Salzburg, plus Szymanowski's opera **King Roger** *and numerous contemporary and complicated works during the past weeks). As ever, the orchestra takes everything in its stride, but tonight I dread. Just keep thinking of the three weeks' holiday starting tomorrow ...*

We are still going in for a one-hour 'patching' session for the recording of Thomas Adès' **Asyla** *(first half of concert, being recorded 'live' for EMI): it wasn't wonderful last night. Everyone is somewhat on edge – it is too hot and sticky and the piece isn't particularly straightforward. We have tons of gear (of course), everything from huge frames of gongs to suspended empty salad-oil tins, knives, forks and a washboard. So, all that lot had to be rearranged on stage before the final nit-picking.*

Tickets for this final concert are like gold dust, and people have travelled from all over the world to be here. Friend Jane has arrived from New Zealand and Lesley May from Scotland; both are staying with me, although I will see precious little of them until after the concert. The players were allocated just two tickets each – **not** *complimentary!*

If I'm being honest, I feel that the emotion of the time is something akin to relief that Simon is moving on. Sakari Oramo is the future now, and we are very much looking forward to working with him as soon as possible. The strings have mixed feelings about a fiddle player taking over, but I reckon that the orchestra is in for another challenging and exciting time. I wonder what he will make of tonight's efforts? What a legacy – what an act to follow!

It is very rare for me to wish my time away, but I will be very relieved when all the tears and cheering are finished with and we can get on with normal life once more. I know that I will never play this piece again, and that makes me sad, but I certainly intend to make the most of this one. I reckon that a young man should be playing my hefty part in the proceedings, but they'll have to put up with a Senior Citizen tonight. The off-stage monster gong will cover any shortcomings I may have by the time the two almighty terrifying 'Scud Missile' crescendo rolls come in the finale.

Deferred Radio 3 relay, TV for Channel 4 (cameras in the way, microphones everywhere), live recording for EMI. (Roll on 10.30pm). EMI 'patching session': midday - 1.30pm. Arrived about 11.15am to put the gear on stage. There are eight of us, so it didn't take too long. Simon was full of praise for last night, thanking us for wonderful playing and ending with "I know that Englishmen aren't supposed to say things like this ... but I love you". And with that shot off the platform in a welter of emotion. Everyone felt weary, hot and drained. Percussionists were thankful that instruments were ready for the evening, giving us time to go home and take a quick breather before the final onslaught.

Arrived about one hour early to sort out tickets and try to get in the mood. A reception was in full swing in our new CBSO Centre and the International Conference Centre foyers were already crowded and humming with anticipation. Every familiar face seemed to be present and it was impossible to go a step without someone calling out a greeting. As far as I was concerned, at that point it was pit-of-the-stomach dread of the unknown.

*We seemed to sit on stage forever until the familiar concert procedures kicked in. One could have heard a pin drop as the 'A' sounded. Peter Thomas (leader) was received with vigorous warmth, but when Simon appeared, the place erupted. We all spontaneously stood for him whilst he took his bow, then he grinned and we played **Asyla**. It went very well as far as I could ascertain; the audience apparently loved it. Adès, the composer, came on stage and took his awkward bows (a gawky 26-yr-old, hair flopping, no tie). One down ... still counting!*

After a long interval we were back again. The leader was already ensconced as usual after an interval, then Simon came on to thunderous applause, cheering and stamping, after which he eventually embarked on one of his famous long silences prior to the start of the Mahler. It seemed to go on forever. I was determined not to let it get to me: that had already happened in a small way during rehearsal as we were all on the edge to some extent. I had spent ages tickling with the bass drum to get both heads just right: as a result it was on its magnificent top form, perfect for this music. It is an amazing instrument: some of the quiet notes are like fat velvet cushions, but it can also roar like a wild beast.

*We all put our hearts and souls into the performance. The audience was wonderful, seeming to breathe with the music, with hardly a murmur from that packed assembly. The TV crew had fussed up to the last minute about how they would see the **rute** ('switch' of twigs - in reality two bunches of thin green garden canes) and one lot of solo bass drum notes, but strangely I was not nervous. Adrenalin was definitely there, but not getting in the way this time.*

Simon conducted without the score ('the paper gets in the way'): scary!

He is utterly reliable, and if he says at rehearsal that he'll do something in a certain way then in performance he always fulfils his promise. The two lovely soloists came on during the third movement and sat immediately next to me at the back of a stage in the centre. Anne Sophie von Otter was wonderful – such sensitive, exquisite phrasing – and the pretty soprano, Hillevi Martinpelto, sang like an angel. I didn't envy their having to climb two steps onto a special rostrum during what seemed like the quietest part of the whole piece, and in long dresses too.

The conductor and I stared at each other during the long pianissimo bass drum transition in the finale. This is the setting for the eerie off-stage brass calls which sound spectacular in this hall: echoes floating out from all directions. 'Keep it even, don't take your eyes off him in case he wants it a whisker louder or softer (only one other person in the room) then die away to nothing'.

The unaccompanied entry of the huge chorus pianissimo was totally heart-stopping: everyone breathed with them. Magic! The hair stood up on the back of my neck at the truly awesome chords from the men who were splendid and thrilling.

Somehow I got as far as the cataclysmic last part without shedding a tear until one bit of timpani writing (just two notes) which is always my undoing, but by this time the worst of the counting was over so it didn't really matter if I couldn't see the part clearly. I just knew what needed to be done, and gave it my all. As I don't actually play at the very end, I was able to put my head down with fingers in ears for the unbelievably loud gong rolls. Cliff doesn't know his own strength on the massive gong, so it's a case of earplugs at the back (including the soloists as I discovered later).

Simon was red in the face and with those maniacal eyes blazing brought the baton down for the very last time. "Mad as a hatter" was my first thought - then, "Thank God it's all over!" He'll be back in February. Needless to say, the audience was upstanding, cheering him to the very rafters. The orchestra grinned and thought of holidays, watching everyone going crazy. There were tears a-plenty, soloists went off to appear at the front clutching lavish bouquets, the audience and chorus stamped and yelled. Then after all the shouting and kisses blown to us from Simon, we started to clear the platform. Backstage was knee-deep with a BBC TV crew trying to get some sense out of anyone, and hoping for moist eyes for the documentary on Simon's last weeks. We were busy

232

*trailing on and off the stage and trying not to get irritated with everyone
in our way. I suspect that we were less than 100% discreet with sotto voce
comments. We see them come, we see them go, but the orchestra carries
on to play another day. "The king is dead - long live the king". Welcome
Sakari!*

*Home for champagne, smoked salmon, telephone calls, and a very late
night. No doubt it'll get to me tomorrow.*

* * *

Sakari took over the reins in September 1998, in time for the new season.
Another knee operation was on the horizon for me; I was on edge and was
playing badly. I am not one for being particularly negative in my outlook on
life, but after some months playing for our lovely new conductor I realised
that I had reached my 'sell-by date'. It was time to go. After much discussion
with the management it was decided that I would be allowed to leave a year
early on full pension starting from my 62nd birthday. As things turned out, I
did my last concert in late February, departing clutching a massive bottle of
champagne and a leaving present of a fat cheque from my friends and
colleagues. This was earmarked for the purchase of Jimmy Blades' little
xylophone. I had such a soft spot for it; after all, it was the instrument that had
travelled all those thousands of miles with me on my very first *proper* job in
the profession I loved.

But first Christopher Morley, the chief music critic from the *Birmingham
Post*, came to the house to do an interview. We chatted, drank tea and ate
home-made goodies for what seemed like hours. Christopher took reams of
notes as we went down memory lane together and then, as it came time for
him to leave, he suddenly became very serious. My alarm bells rang as he
said I had to think carefully about what he was going to ask next, and not to
make an impulsive decision. Out of the blue he asked me if I would like to
join the team of *Birmingham Post* music critics, qualifying this by saying that
I had been using my ears in an orchestra for forty years, that he liked the way
I wrote and that I was not afraid of saying what I thought. I digested this in
silence, took a deep breath and defensively commented that, "Yes, I do say
what I think, but not all the time, and hope that I'm never disparaging without
very good reason." As I can rarely resist a challenge, I questioned the
requirements of such a responsible undertaking and was assured that help
would be forthcoming until I found my feet. There would never be any danger

233

of my being required to review CBSO concerts; indeed he realised that I could also be compromised by the fact that I also knew a lot of players in other UK orchestras. However, after speaking about this proposition to various friends and family, with some apprehension I decided to take up the gauntlet and have a go.

Some of my thoughts on the matter became the bones of an article that ultimately appeared in *Classical Music Magazine*:

It is never easy to know how to pitch a review. Amateurs need to be encouraged, but not patronised, although one reminds oneself that the punters have paid good money for tickets, so a decent standard is expected. Young musicians must be encouraged at all costs, but not to the extent that everything is said to be wonderful. Unfortunately many performers deeply resent anyone having an opinion other than their own, which of course is that they always play marvellously well. Not so, but it does not do to be too acerbic with immature starters in the field.

We all do it – listen I mean, and talk about what we have heard, or what we have played ourselves. "Who was on tonight?" "Oh, I don't know, some idiot. Couldn't get near it! Who teaches these characters? He couldn't conduct a bus, didn't know a crotchet from a crowbar, play a slot machine" ... and so on. Sitting at the back of a professional symphony orchestra for many decades, I know only too well what goes on before, during and after performances. You can bet your sweet life that there will be many opinions flying about in the band room as we play for and listen to the great and the good, the incompetent, or just plain rubbish. Then someone buys a paper to see what the one-who-gets-paid-to-criticise observed, assessed, thought. Often, though, it is a case of wondering whether we were all at the same concert, listening to the same notes. After all, the orchestra is doing a job and by definition has a lopsided viewpoint. We hear everything inside out, back to front, but then to us that is normal, we are used to our angle and for the most part can get a reasonable overview unless we are truly in the thick of it. One's own contribution inevitably colours the final thumbs up, thumbs down – orchestral players are far more ruthless than any newspaper employee. I would have to become used to hearing familiar music from the audience's angle. I know now why the critic sometimes slinks off before the end of a concert. There is a deadline to meet, and a phone call to make, dictating all punctuation as well as spelling out awkward names. Getting one's brain together in 250 words is certainly a challenge too, so this is why one's piece occasionally resembles a shopping list. Everyone wants to have a mention, but this is not always possible. Mind you, don't forget to read between the lines. If a certain piece or performer has not been mentioned, it is possibly because there is nothing worth saying that would not see the newspaper in the libel courts. Draw your own conclusions: after all, a review is only the opinion of one person, and it is not the end of the world if you happen to disagree. And when the chips are down, no one is forcing you to buy, never mind read the newspaper.

Poacher turned gamekeeper? Certainly not! However, my sympathies are invariably with the workers backing the big names: I watch the body language with deep interest and, dare I say, perception. "Oh, you spot things that none of the others mention," observed my boss, Christopher. Or as Clare, another colleague, commented, "Her talent for ladling out terrier-like criticism without even a hint of petulance is wonderful." To my surprise I am sent to every kind of classical event, from Grand to not so grand Opera, vocal and instrumental recitals, chamber music of every persuasion, amateur and professional orchestras, chamber choirs, percussion ensembles, a saxophone choir, wind orchestras, Welsh male voice choirs, in-your-face popular classics, the famous and the unknowns. Every performance is a challenge as I sit there with ears pinned back and pencil at the ready to scribble my odd aides-memoire: hieroglyphics and discreet comments scrawled all over the programme. A guest always accompanies me, we have the best seats in the house and often members of the audience will ask me if I am on duty or 'here for the paper', as they tell me that they read and like my reviews. This is very encouraging. Quite often it is the performance where I suspect that I have bitten off more than I can chew that is a revelation and joy. I am constantly being surprised and charmed by unsuspected aspects of music and people, but, on the other side of the coin, disappointed and dismayed by some of the egos and disregard for the fee-paying public encountered along the way. I look at visiting orchestras with fascination, wondering which musician is my alter ego. There are predictable souls in any bunch of musicians.

One of my very first observations on leaving the band was that I would never have to play in the wretched Royal Albert Hall again; indeed I would never have to go to London unless I chose to do so. Oh, and the bliss of no more Elgar or Vaughan Williams or having to travel by coach or fly anywhere unless I wanted to. But I knew that I would need to make specific plans to carry me forward after the wrench of leave-taking, so I took off to collect the xylophone, visited my daughter in Bristol and then back home to the traumas of having the outside of the house painted..

I also discovered to my delight that I was able to make an impact on my beloved but somewhat neglected garden in the run-up to spring, join an upholstery class once more (skilled at 'hammering and braying' as my dad would have put it), pottery classes at the Art Centre, and read anything I wished without feeling guilty about wasting time. Not having a schedule to stick to took some getting used to however, so I devised quaint methods of reminding myself of specific engagements – notes on the front door, stuck to the hall mirror, in the kitchen, and so on. I missed questions such as: 'What time are we on tomorrow?' 'What's the first piece?' 'When does the coach go?' or 'Is he starting with the first movement?' - the trivial verbal oil that had lubricated the daily round for so many years.

When I ventured further afield, I was apprehensive about being responsible for my own travel arrangements too, missing the company of like souls when I went long haul to visit my cousin in California. However, I enjoyed adventures in my small camper van, such as a visit to friends in the Bergen Philharmonic and chasing the Tall Ships Race around Norway. "Oh, you are very brave!" greeted me on my return from this particular jaunt. "No, I'm just selfish!" I replied. I love the novelty of nesting in my own small space with favourite wine and food on board, plenty of books, decent maps and the knowledge that for a short time no one knows where I am and that the world is my oyster.

As soon as I was on the open market, so to speak, I was invited to coach the percussion and timpani students in the Birmingham Schools Concert Orchestra (BSCO) on Saturday mornings. Theirs is a very different repertoire to the one I am familiar with. I delight in and relish the big band arrangements, the singalong standards, theatre music, sweeping Hollywood scores and numerous tasters of the lighter classics. We are all there in a learning capacity, but also to enjoy ourselves, or else there seems little point in spending precious Saturday mornings in a stuffy school hall working hard.

Not only do I feel that it is important that knowledge, skills and lifelong experiences are handed on if at all possible, but also I really love working with young people. Every September there is a new influx of young teenagers and I take great delight in seeing them flourish, grow up and gain in confidence. Not only do I take pride in my team, but also there are times when I find myself playing alongside when we are short of players. All of my kids are drum-kit players. I am not. This causes much amusement as they try to persuade me to have a go … but no, I am not prepared to take on new tricks at this point in my life, so decline their proposals with good humour. This is great fun and a sharp reminder that I must not allow myself to rust – ever! Falling apart is allowed, but never rusting. Life rarely pans out as expected, as I discovered when I had to eat my words with regard to the RAH after the BSCO was chosen, from the whole of the UK, to take part in a Schools Prom there. This was a great honour, which naturally created a huge amount of excitement. Unfortunately, the day before the event one of my players was suddenly whisked into hospital with suspected appendicitis, and I consequently found myself dusting off my long black and stepping into the breach at the last minute. Tutors are allowed to play in cases of dire emergency, so for the first time in my life I found myself playing timpani in the RAH. I was almost as nervous as the kids, but then I was able to hide my feelings, having had much practice in doing just that throughout my career.

There comes a time when everything has to stop, but it was a long time before I could bear to relinquish visits to junior schools. However, I got tired of lugging all my equipment around and decided, reluctantly, to call it a day. Sad to let go, but life was changing.

A continuous worry is what to do about all my instruments now that I'm not playing any more. After much discussion, my wonderful Leedy xylophone found a good home and lots of playing potential with the Slaithwaite Philharmonic Orchestra: one of the very first orchestras I played in, based in the outskirts of Huddersfield – a satisfying homecoming for my old friend. The well-travelled bass drum is still visiting schools and being played by children, as it is now owned by a young woman who does lots of education work as well as freelance playing. My American Degan vibraphone is doing stalwart work in theatres, owned now by another young player. Various small items, favourite beaters, music and useful odds and ends are finding their way into the percussion cases at the BSCO, or to some of the well-deserving youngsters I meet whilst teaching. I cannot bear waste, so eventually I hope that all of my instruments will find themselves being played again, and dare I say, loved?

All my peripheral activities came to an abrupt halt when I found myself once more in hospital having a second knee replacement in early autumn 1999. Fiona, my darling daughter, had given birth to my first grandchild, Carolyn, in June, and it was time for me to get a grip with the promise to myself of playing with and carrying small children. Another layer in the family is a real thrill. Two days after the operation, I was called to the telephone and a tearful, incoherent Fiona telling me that Alice, my stepmother, had died suddenly and, in his panic, dad had fallen downstairs in the middle of the night and was now in hospital having no idea what had happened. Needless to say, I was helpless, unable to do anything, and beside myself with worry. Geoff came to the rescue, and between them all the funeral was arranged. Dad was taken by wheelchair, transformed from a gritty, outspoken Yorkshireman to a pathetic, confused old man. My heart bled for him as I fumed ineffectually in hospital, unable to attend and be supportive.

Thus began months of trauma for all the family. It was as well that I did not have a job to go to, as I moved dad near to me after all the hospitalisation in the north. He eventually met his tiny great-granddaughter and I have a lovely photograph of our four generations together. Dad loved little ones and delighted in meeting with 'that baby', always asking when she was next coming to visit him. I am truly thankful that his last months were spent wrapped in kindness in a lovely care home round the corner from me. I visited every day and his grandchildren came every week, but all too soon we had to face another funeral – this time for the old man. Life took some time to settle after this ghastly period and now I am truly one of the older generation – a somewhat daunting thought.

As I like people and have a house with four bedrooms, I frequently welcome strangers into my home as lodgers or 'paying guests'. Most are a delight to have around, keeping the house alive and keeping me in touch with the Birmingham arts scene. Quite a number of young CBSO players have stayed here, as the orchestra management knows that I am tried and tested, so to speak, sometimes sending homeless musicians to me at a day's notice. I love to hear music in the house, practice is certainly allowed and I am never happier than when a bunch of erstwhile colleagues use my sitting room as an emergency rehearsal space for chamber music. It's not an ideal venue by any means, but I am always welcoming and the room is always available.

The phone rings. "Is that Miss Cotton? I understand that you give talks and wonder ..." Another Women's' Institute visit calls, or perhaps a ladies' luncheon, or a posh after-dinner do. I have been giving talks on life in the orchestra for years: my name gets passed on as I trot around the countryside going on my little ego trips, drinking lots of tea and meeting plenty of delightful strangers. Some repeated engagements are for the Saga holiday groups, who come to Birmingham for short concert breaks. As regular visitors show up on these occasions, I am on my mettle to change the slant of my observations every time. This is no bad thing as it keeps me on my toes. "Have you ever thought of writing all this down?" I am constantly asked, after giving my all and making my listeners laugh. "Oh, yes, but you'll have to wait a while."

My love of plants has led to another delightful sideline, that of growing unusual things for a local shop. This is an old-fashioned, traditional ironmongers, long established. They sell anything from single nails from little boxes to every kind of hand tool, huge gas bottles and 'loose' paraffin. Glass and timber are cut to order, tools sharpened, keys cut, and garden sundries and more and more plants are sold every year: indeed it is a local, unique treasure house. The personal touch is all, customers are greeted by first names, and Jon, the owner, always seems to have time for pleasantries. As this is a favourite stopping-off place, I always pop in for something, but one day I found myself watering desperate-looking plants, gasping in the long entrance yard whilst the shop was full of customers. This led to helping out with potting on crowded seedlings. As I told Jon, "I've got the time now, and I like messing about with plants." There is an amicable arrangement for huge bags of compost to be dropped off at my house in exchange for trays of neat babies to go back to the shop. I love the fact that there is no pressure except from nature. The radio goes on and I am in seventh heaven as I potter about getting my hands dirty, being strangely creative.

As a working musician I rarely listened to music in my spare time, but now I have returned to Radio 3 with a vengeance, and play the piano more and more. My family could never understand why I was the only one in the house without my own personal music-listening system, so they showed great surprise when I installed a neat CD player/radio in the kitchen after I retired.

I now have a grandson, Joe, who shows an interest in music already - jigging around and grinning whenever anything rhythmical catches his ear. Both children are a delight, and I look forward to the time when I can introduce them to some of my passions.

There's life in the old girl yet!

> "We are the music makers,
> we are the dreamers of dreams."

17
"What's your real job?"

Some years ago, I was nattering to a friend in the kitchen, with Classic FM on quietly in the background. Some orchestra or other was ploughing through Beethoven's *Pastoral Symphony* and I absently observed that it surely wasn't a professional bunch. (It turned out to be a youth orchestra broadcasting from a European music festival.) My non-musical guest immediately took me up on my remark and asked how I could possibly say such a thing without knowing which orchestra was playing.

"Oh, it sounds thin, they're not really together," I replied, and then added, head on one side, a final damning of, "… like a strung-out, good-quality, end-of-pier band."

"But it can't be as simple as that. Aren't you just being a wee bit overcritical? It sounds okay to me," she commented.

This set me thinking. We in the music business are often asked, "What is the difference between an amateur and a professional orchestra?", sometimes with the added comment that the enquirer's local amateur orchestra can put on concerts *every bit as good as* the professional crowd in the big city nearby. This is a corker of a question and one that needs careful consideration.

Of course the big difference is that we on the professional side of the great divide get paid, as playing music is our full-time job. That is why, for instance, we always have very short fingernails, or why it is an unwritten law that no one ever plays anything in our band rooms, except perhaps a game of cards. Should any unweaned extras dare to make a squeak, they are soon made to realise the folly of their ways – kindly, but very firmly. We change out of concert dress and rush out of the building as soon as decently possible after a performance, whereas amateur musicians get together and have a social half-hour or so with friends and family in the nearest pub, usually in full concert fig.

As seasoned professionals, we are paid to play the appropriate notes, however difficult or exposed, in the right place and at the right time. We need to keep eyes and ears open for any subtle changes of balance, tempo, phrasing and dynamics, having to be quick on the uptake and sensitive to what is going on in the rest of the orchestra. Rehearsals are the time for mistakes. We soon discovered that Simon Rattle, for instance, would usually react only at one's second attempt to sort out a knotty bit in the music, after which there would be a slight hiatus from the rostrum and then a quiet, "Is there a problem?" Look him straight in the eye, fingers crossed, do your best.

There is never a hiding place for the percussionists, and from long experience we have learnt not to fully trust conductors. We are not paid to look anxious, as this worries the audience – be nervous, 'fluff' entries, go on ego trips, be unsupportive, mess up difficult passages or indeed let faces slip should disaster occur. We pros are obliged to play everything and anything in the symphonic, light orchestral, operatic, ballet, brain-damaging contemporary repertoires, occasional chamber music and exposed solo work. Because of our non-regular working hours, we need to be told advanced details of our lives, so we work from schedules that cover four-week periods in detail. I have amassed these over the years, and one of my party tricks for any sceptic who reckons that we have an easy time *just playing music for a living* is an invitation to pick out any one schedule and read out the composers covered in that period.

For instance, brain fodder by the following was trotted out for a single week of television recordings, where one had to look as well as sound good: Bartok; Schoenberg; Takemitsu; Carter; Boulez; Stravinsky; Mahler; Ives; Debussy; Knussen; Kurtag; John Adams; Wagner; Webern; Ligeti; Britten; R. Strauss; Weill; and Gershwin – nothing trivial ... and so it goes on.

The goods have to be delivered come what may: day in, day out. Unlike amateur players, we are obliged to turn up to all rehearsals appropriate to our instrument, be they 'sectionals' with a handful of players, or the whole shooting match: orchestra, soloists, off-stage effects, choruses, and so on. The actual notes should already be under the belt, and we should be ready to give our all for whichever maestro is up front. The powers-that-be reluctantly allow us to be ill, but death is really the only truly accepted reason for absence and probably would need a doctor's note. As mentioned in an earlier chapter, in the '60s there was no such thing as maternity leave, and so, after a great deal of thought, I reluctantly tendered my notice to leave the orchestra when I realised that I was expecting a baby. Hugo Rignold no doubt caused a mild sensation when he overrode the manager and asked me to consider coming back on full pay two months after becoming a mum. I declined his offer, however, but was still playing two weeks before the baby was born, smartly dressed in an elegantly discreet black maternity evening dress. My husband reckoned that Alistair was born with his fingers in his ears. As ever, the show must go on.

241

The CBSO plays an average of 130 concerts a year during the orchestra season (late September to May), plus television and sound broadcasts, CD recordings, open-air concerts in the summer, national and international music festivals, foreign tours and education work. Added to all this, time must somehow be found for individual practice. British orchestras are renowned for their sight-reading skills; they have to be, as they are not allotted the amount of rehearsal time that other nationalities regard as their right. Our music grapevine (effective long before the Internet) has many eyebrow-raising tales of foreign colleagues being bored to tears with too much rehearsal time. If only we could have that problem from time to time!

Family life has to take a back seat as we remind ourselves that we are in the entertainment business. It is hard luck that we are in America over Easter, or that our holidays do not coincide with school holidays – we never see the fireworks, the operas or the ballets that we accompany, but the other side of that coin is that we often have a grandstand view during special occasions. For instance, we have enjoyed the magnificent opening ceremony of many a Three Choirs Festival, including one with Prince Charles valiantly trying to keep awake during heat-drowsy afternoon prayers. We touch the hems of world-class musicians and work with real-life composers, fine conductors and soloists, playing glorious music in wonderful venues all over the world.

We never forget, however, that we once were all amateur musicians, when we looked forward to the weekly evening rehearsal in preparation for a handful of concerts every year. One of the pleasures then was also that of meeting like-souls. It is the delight, anticipation, and not a little hard work that make amateur music such a joy, with all the effort culminating in performances for friends and family, and hopefully a bunch of faithful supporters. One has had the time to worry away at awkward passages in the music, and not for amateurs the feeling of terminal doom and gloom if a particular tricky passage does not properly resolve itself. Oh, what the hell, let's enjoy the music; if it comes off, well and good. We'll give it a good go, but it's not the end of the world if something untoward happens. On the professional side of the fence, we agonise and have sleepless nights if anything goes awry during a concert; our reputations are at stake. As I was warned early in my career, "You are only as good as your last performance."

It is very refreshing that amateur orchestras – both adult and student – now have such adventurous programmes. There are some fine rehearsal orchestras around that do a huge amount of standard repertoire, but then if you are lucky you can also join the local symphony orchestra, which will give both you and an audience some interesting challenges. Grab it all with both hands, as it is treasure indeed. There are light orchestras, amateur operatics, brass bands, wind bands, string orchestras and chamber groups: the world is your oyster. Music is a joy at any level of expertise. Not for the amateurs the life and death internal wranglings, the incestuous atmosphere of being incarcerated with the same capricious people day in, day out, trying to craft a sensitive performance with some kind of artistic integrity.

I recall many years ago trying to calm one of our woodwind players after he had done what I had vaguely heard as a mild squawk during a performance. He is a sensitive soul and, by the time we had piled on the coaches to return back to base, he had wound himself up to such a state that I thought that he was going to throw himself onto the sharp end of his instrument for an honourable end. It's gone ... a transient memory. It was a non-perfect *live* performance after all, played by flesh and blood people needing to keep a sense of proportion. Fortunately, amateur music for the most part is a relaxation and pleasure for the participants; no one is forcing you to do it and, if you don't like a particular piece, you can guarantee that it won't rear its head again for some time, if ever. We, on the other hand, have to play everything put in front of us even if we detest the music, and we know that it will certainly reappear, time and time again. This is where the professionalism completely takes over as far as I am concerned. In a way I take extra care with music I cannot bear, even if I do pace up and down and grumble during rehearsals.

"You're not enjoying this, are you?" said Simon Rattle, observing the ill-disguised lack of interest and misery on my face during a particularly trying rehearsal.

"No, I'm hating every minute of it!" I replied across the orchestra, as I recalled a comment from Louis Frémaux some years previously.

After flogging through a rehearsal of works by a composer I particularly dislike he had observed, "You are paid to play this music Maggee!"

"Yes, maybe, but I'm not paid to like it!" was my waspish retort on that occasion.

However, I am acutely aware that it is a musician's job and responsibility to be the conduit from composer to listener, and as such it is not acceptable that personal tastes should interfere with the outcome. I do enjoy a good wallow in favourite pieces, however – positively gloating when anticipating a 'really good play', as my old Yorkshire teacher used to say.

One of the first skills I acquired as a young professional was that of

listening. This is a crucial gift that all instrumentalists need, of course, but often it seems that amateur players incline to the 'head down and plough one's own furrow' orchestral technique. It is, as we all know, very difficult to have ears out on stalks, with total awareness of what makes an homogeneous sound. However, this is one of the essential talents that goes towards creating a fine musician. One becomes totally dismissive of untidy entries, ragged chords, and less than perfect ensemble. I yell across the kitchen to the radio: "**Not together**, try harder! And I don't care *which* orchestra you are." It is disappointing when the offending crowd is well established. Why isn't it spotted by the producer or conductor? And errors do happen. A published recording by a certain orchestra (which shall remain nameless – not the CBSO) of a complex Stravinsky piece contained actual mistakes made by the percussion section (the recording was eventually deleted).

Some conductors have ears like bats and there is no escape. It is so crucial to cultivate a good ear and listen to your neighbour, single out sounds from other quarters, balance and assess. This has its uses outside the orchestra too. For instance, I can go to a party and secretly listen to conversations across a very noisy room – no problem.

It is difficult for some professional musicians to retain their love of music, however, and this is such a pity. I look round at some of my more hard-bitten colleagues and wonder if they would still be playing as amateurs if they hadn't initially got on the bandwagon and been unwittingly trapped in the music profession. This sad fate often befalls the child marked down at an early age as being 'so good on the violin'. So he/she wins prizes and is the star turn at school long before the mini-genius is old enough to have any say in the matter. Many youngsters get swept along and, before they know where they are, they are out of music college clutching a diploma or degree, and wondering, 'What next?' They have a natural ability, but many end up by bitterly regretting their choice of a profession that they should love.

I often comment when embarking on a long run of a particular favourite, "Oh, I hope we don't kill this piece and wear out its welcome. I couldn't bear it." But I am afraid that this is precisely what sometimes happens, and there are former loved pieces that I never wanted to play again.

We pros may be either nostalgic – or disparaging – whichever way you wish to interpret it, when we play 'youth orchestra music'. I can play every percussion part of the Vaughan Williams *Folk Song* suite from memory, along with the timpani part of such gems as the *Ruy Blas* overture (the first orchestral piece I every played, burned into my heart), the *Hebrides* and

Merry Wives of Windsor overtures (in the bad old days done to death sixteen times a week at schools' concerts), Dvořák symphonies and many, many more. Most orchestral musicians could play *Messiah* in their sleep, and at one time the CBSO was famed for exciting performances of the Saint-Saëns *Organ Symphony* – twenty-three in all, during seven seasons of the Frémaux reign. In their wisdom, the CBSO management even managed to book some performances in halls without an organ (e.g., Chatham in deepest Kent), necessitating the hiring of plug-in electric cinema-style monstrosities. It was a good box office, however, and one suspected that for this particular money-spinner artistic standards hardly came into the picture.

The CBSO is very fortunate to play to many and varied audiences, but my favourites are those in the smaller towns. They are so appreciative, to the point of coming to seek us out to say thank you, often ending their nervous prepared speech with an apologetic, "But I'm only an amateur." "Oh ..." I pounce, "There's no such thing as *only* an amateur. You are here because you love music. We are all musicians, and have all been amateurs too. None of us would be here if we hadn't had that pleasure." They look and listen with mild amazement, but it is true, oh yes. Long live the backbone of the music profession, the seed corn, the true, unfettered lovers of music – the amateur musicians.

I have no doubt that some of our listeners have romantic notions about their orchestra as we appear on stage smartly turned out, instruments to the fore, ready to give our all for the music. Hopefully at every concert there is an atmosphere of anticipation and a comfortingly, predictable pattern of events, which happen before the first downbeat. We, of course, are at work, dressed appropriately, ready for the off and seemingly oblivious to any outside influences. In reality, however, this is never the complete picture.

After the final rehearsal before a concert, there is the usual search for sustenance, unless one has thought ahead and brought a nosebag. Many wind players choose to eat after the concert, but we starving percussionists would usually go off in a gaggle to catch up with gossip from our extra players. If the home team was playing, I would sometimes risk being dubbed unsociable by the others, as I ate home-made specialities in peace and quiet backstage, with feet up and an undemanding novel to the fore. One might hear some benighted soul practising gritty bits in the distance, but by that time it was too late for any sensible rescue and all one could think of was an uncharitable, "Oh, go away and play in the next street!"

Woe betide any string player foolish enough to park an instrument case on top of a percussion box, however, as this prompts an immediate reaction from us. We remove the offending item as far away as possible from the scene, and then watch in covert amusement at the end of the rehearsal as the agitated player searches for his empty case. The lesson is usually taken on board and nothing further is done or said. Other little diversions occur from time to time – perhaps gentle nagging produces a queue of guys waiting to have dandruff collars brushed by a beady-eyed female colleague. In the '70s, when scruffy male hairstyles were the norm, there were even hair-trimming sessions by fellow percussionist Annie and me.

British orchestras are less formal in their approach to entering a concert platform than many foreign orchestras. Other orchestras walk on in rank order from the back, strictly regimented and silent. This smacks of our youth orchestra days, so we resist any attempt at this kind of rigid discipline, tending to drift on in a relaxed fashion when the final bell has gone. The orchestra manager has done his shepherd act and, as the last to go, the leader is chatting backstage. Percussionists, if not playing in the first piece, are vaguely assembling but keeping out of the way of the conductor. Flowers for the soloist are, by now, on a chair at the ready backstage, the piano tuner has done his stuff after the rehearsal, the harp is being gently tweaked to perfection as the audience drifts in, woodwind reeds are squawking quietly backstage, strings are finely and finally tuned, bow ties are checked and jackets straightened, accompanied by: "Is my hair all right?" "Can you see my navy socks?" "Who's getting the coffee in the interval?" "Who won Wimbledon?" The orchestra manager looks optimistically at the first in the gaggle, then, "Thank you ladies and gentlemen", and on we troop, or maybe the platform manager is in charge for the evening, urging us to "Come on boys and girls, time to play with your toys."

This is the perfect time for the audience to scrutinise body language on stage. If the one with the white stick ignores the orchestra and takes a lavish bow all to himself without even a glance at the leader, the players then usually look anywhere but directly at him. Friendly communication from the rostrum is nil: this is strictly professional. However, if there is a glimmering of acknowledgement of the hundred or so musicians on stage ready and waiting, then there are usually smiles and eye contact: this is a good sign and a promise of 'we're all making music together'.

* * *

Nowadays, peering up at the stage as a member of the audience when I listen to a visiting crowd, I always wonder 'which one am I?' There are the same characters in all orchestras whether from Tokyo or Moscow, not necessarily playing the same instruments, but they are there to be sure. Evening dress uniform helps to give the impression of anonymity, ritualised formality, artistic integrity and passionate involvement in the scores, but this is not always the case in reality. One can guarantee that in every programme there will be some who are loving every minute of the music, others who are grinding their teeth and just getting on with it, whilst the rest simply go with the flow, having no specific thoughts about what they are playing. Mozart is the rare exception, as he is the composer loved by all, his apparent simplicity being the most difficult to achieve without immense care and attention. A competent conductor should be able to add a spark to this mix, and then, if we are lucky, the magic will happen and an assorted bunch of musicians will meld into a focused whole. One looks around at one's colleagues and wonders how this is possible.

Many musicians are single-minded in their involvement with their art – often single emotionally and socially too, with no husband, wife or children to concern them, any domestic details coming far down their list of priorities. These are the rare ones who dread the thought of holidays away from their orchestra, which is the only close daily 'family' they know. Perhaps there is an ancient parent in the background, or nephews and nieces to spoil at Christmas time, but the orchestra is their mainstay, their life, and this is what they understand. I am convinced that every orchestra has a clown, at least one hypochondriac, a number of introverted misers and, of course, lovers of the demon drink.

From our perch at the back of the orchestra, Annie and I have often observed a curious phenomenon. During rehearsals it is possible to look across the orchestra and see that a prominent colour prevails in everyone's choice of casual clothes. Sometimes there is a mainly blue orchestra out there, and at others it is an earth-colour day: brown, dark greens, soft greys. The startling exceptions are always from the extra players: they stand out apart from the rest, perhaps wearing yellow on blue days, or clashing reds and purples at other times. We have often smiled when there is a Russian programme on the music stand, as that is when many crimsons, maroons and scarlets come out of wardrobes. I wonder if this apparent telepathy happens in other orchestras? And there were many times when, without consultation, Annie and I would turn up to rehearsal dressed like peas in a pod: kilt-style skirts and white polo-necked jumpers – very '70s!

It is well known that certain types are often attracted to specific instruments. As a rule, the brass tribe are a jolly lot, although some can be irritatingly extrovert, crude and laddish; woodwind players are frequently the sensitive flowers; string players intense – all those notes; and percussionists lively and regarded as mad by many. But, as we all know, there are many, many exceptions to these perceived stereotypes.

Once, in Leeds, we watched with a certain amused admiration as the orchestra's Lothario flirted outrageously with a pretty girl in the audience from his place in the trombone section. As this is a platform where the audience can breathe down the necks of the musicians, a cheeky grin, wink and whisper had done the trick between the tuning ritual and leader arriving on stage. Pretty good going, we all agreed, as we overheard the arrangements for meeting in the bar after the concert.

Delusions of grandeur occasionally kick in with certain volatile characters, frequently with disastrous consequences, as in the case of another brass player. As the nursery rhyme says, "When he was good, he was very, very good ...", but help, when he was bad, he was a total nightmare. This particular character's behaviour was such that I saw grown men in tears of fury and frustration on stage at a London concert hall. His close colleagues were physically threatened by his unbalanced, aggressive conduct – screaming abuse and vitriol in sight of the audience. He yelled, "I'll knock your bloody head off", after I had quietly suggested through clenched teeth that in future he might not spend the whole of a very quiet encore vigorously buffing fingermarks from his instrument with a bright yellow duster. The next outburst was a threat to kill the principal horn, who had bravely suggested that it might be a good idea to cool down and go *off* the platform. It took two of the men to physically restrain him, with a member of the management team feebly trying to calm the situation. (Afterwards I reminded the latter of the time that Annie was ticked off for reaching behind for a cymbal bag during applause at the end of a concert - so much for support and consistency.) I crept off the stage in tears and, for the only time in my career, was afraid to go back in the second half of the concert, but of course I had to, and the trombone music had to be played whether adjacent colleagues felt threatened or not. More over-the-top behaviour manifested itself for weeks and weeks, until thankfully we saw no more of him. All had seemed calm on the surface, but the atmosphere was one of gloom and despondency, nervous tension and concealed belligerence. A period followed during which the other brass

248

players had to be totally professional, delivering the music as though nothing was awry. In spite of the whole orchestra being permeated by a feeling of unease and insecurity, the outward presentation was that of unruffled calm.

Thankfully, such unstable behaviour is rare, but passions sporadically boil over in our close-knit, somewhat confined artistic community. Scuffles under the band-room table, someone trying to bend a flute round someone else's head, weird behaviour resulting in a cooling of heels in prison, and more, have happened within the orchestra. Soon after we arrived in a small German city at the start of an arduous tour, our managers found themselves at the local police station standing bail for one of the trumpet players. A few of the guys had gone for a drink, and one had foolishly admired a local lass who turned out to be the girlfriend of a great bruiser of a man. A few punches were thrown (fortunately, no one lost any teeth), but our trumpeter was the one who ended up in gaol.

Nothing better illustrates the strength of such a close-knit community than when serious personal problems arise. Internal tragedies and major conflicts bring out the best in everyone: these are times when players close ranks and pull together, supporting each other and presenting a united front to the outside world. During my time with the CBSO, we have lived through numerous deaths, a couple of suicides, life-threatening illnesses, career-threatening injuries, family tragedies, serious disputes with management, and major clashes with conductors. Yes, in extremis, the MU can help with financial and other difficulties in lieu of close family, but it is more often the case that old friends and colleagues will step in with filial-style duties and care when this is necessary. The 'old pro' network – bonds between the disparate groups in any symphony orchestra – is forever strong.

* * *

Orchestras regularly travel to the continent to play in fine musical centres, such as Berlin, Amsterdam, Leipzig, Paris, Salzburg and Vienna. On these trips, wind and string players are occasionally to be found with intense expressions, maps and sometimes train tickets: quests are taking place. It is often the case that specialist instrument-makers are situated in or near such cities and every musician knows this. For instance, a bassoonist may have had a new instrument on order from *the* maker in Europe and is going to collect it; string players are searching for a perfect bow; the horns need to have a 'matched sound' in the section so the hunt is on for instruments; a harpist may even take a large car for delivery of a new 'baby' and brass players seek unusual sounds in the city flea markets and antique shops. Chamber music enthusiasts are happy to trawl for music in little shops tucked away in dim backstreets, usually found only with help from colleagues and friends in the local orchestras. We percussionists look on with interest.

I doubt if anyone ever gives a passing thought to our instruments: no Strads here, no beautifully crafted rosewood oboes, just all that percussion gear at the back of the orchestra, which few people look at twice. But, hang on a minute, every one of our own personal instruments and also of those belonging to the orchestra has a story to tell, and has been chosen – not just bought from over a shop counter. It all began for me when I joined a youth orchestra way back in the fifties. My personal collection was launched with a gift of pear-wood castanets on a handle, golden honey in colour and very old. They have been into many, many schools, taking an active part in a tale (eerie chattering teeth in a ghost story), which I used to illustrate the wide variety of sounds we have at our disposal. My excellent cymbals came from the same generous source, and a lifelong obsession had begun.

My father found a small pre-war orchestral glockenspiel in a junk shop, which he bore away triumphantly for the bargain price of £15. It turned out to be from a fine pre-war maker, with good-quality steel notes sporting a clear ringing tone. My next problem was to find perfect beaters with which to play it. As dad was a wizard with wood, he suggested that he could turn some knobs for a pair of sticks if I could find the appropriate wood; it had to be very hard and unchippable. So I did no more than go to a huge timber yard and ask for a piece of lignum vitæ, one of the hardest woods available; so much so that it needs to be worked with a special metal-cutting saw and is the only wood to sink in water. A small chunk was found under a bench in the foreign woods section, priced by weight. This was ideal and was duly made into two pairs of very special glockenspiel beaters. Single notes sound lovely with no 'click' from the head of the stick as it strikes the metal note: well-balanced, heavy and slightly waxy, even after all these years. I think of my dad every time I play with them; they are totally unique.

After my year as a student at the Royal Academy of Music, I was told of a xylophone for sale, one that had belonged to a player on the *Queen Elizabeth* liner. I had been given the maker's name and model (just like a car), and then contacted the distinguished James Blades for advice, he being the guru of young percussionists. When he heard the name Leedy – a superlative American maker – he offered me £10 more for it than the asking price, whatever that might be. Ten pounds in those early days represented 80 hours of my cleaning job in the student hostel where I lived, but I realised that I had to have it, come what may. Money was scraped together somehow – begged and borrowed, and I became the proud owner of an outstanding instrument, which eventually resided under a beautiful shawl at home waiting for a blast of Messiaen practice or suchlike.

My small concert bass drum was discovered in the attic of a music shop in Leeds, and if I look carefully at the black-painted shell I can just discern the faint outline of a coat of arms. What tales it could tell as I haul it around schools – a great favourite with children of all ages. The same shop yielded a small, battered, battle-scarred brass kettledrum, which was eventually lovingly restored for me as a twenty-first birthday present. I was told that it was a French military instrument, well over a hundred years old and one of a pair, and which would have been played on horseback. Who captured it, when and where and under what gruesome circumstances? Until it was sold through a London auction house many years ago, it could occasionally be heard on concert platforms in our modern symphony orchestra. As far as I know, it now resides in America – probably in a museum. It was sad to see it go, but there is a limit to how many large instruments one can get into a normal house (not forgetting the crates and bulky cases made to house them), so when I got married some drastic pruning was called for. Now, of course, the orchestra owns all the percussion instruments with the exception of a few personal favourites.

The orchestra's huge concert bass drum was specially made many years ago and is my particular favourite. Some time ago - horror of horrors - I split one of the heads, much to my distress. Luckily, it was not the *playing* head. The smaller of our two other instruments was hastily fetched, and eventually the big drum was sent off to our favourite instrument doctor. A calfskin had to be specially ordered from Ireland (did the animal have an ear tab saying CBSO, I ask myself?), 'lapped' onto a wooden hoop whilst wet, fitted onto the drum, and then sent back to Birmingham in the orchestra's big pantechnicon, still somewhat damp and soggy. Convalescence took place in a room at Symphony Hall, with frequent visits by anxious players, who gently added more tension as the head gradually dried out. Much to my relief, eventually it was welcomed back into the fold, playing to full capacity. It was a very worrying time – so much for *just the stuff at the back of the orchestra*.

Percussion instruments can give a very distinctive sound to an orchestra, and there have been numerous occasions when I have recognised one of our recordings on the radio, purely from the sound of a particular tambourine, our Chinese gong, wood block, etc. One of my triangles came from a cinema organ, along with some lovely silvery sleigh bells and a pair of rosewood castanets. Old instruments of good quality are rare and difficult to come by, but greatly prized by players. The CBSO does not need to hire the set of tuned sleigh bells required for Mozart's charming *Sleigh Ride*, as I managed to acquire velvet-covered leather straps of tuned bells from a redundant circus act – no doubt for the liberty horses with their musical ride. Small instruments are constantly being acquired, as none of us can resist the purchase of something interesting or unusual. Rather than ancient Italy or Germany, we look to the New World, the Far East or the Antipodes for inspiration, although I did find a pair of pleasing dancer's castanets in a shop in Madrid, not the pretty painted variety but the real thing: heavy chestnut (castaña) wood, dark and glossy. I was shown how to put them on middle finger or thumb, tighten the slip knot and then play '*click, click, click*' with the right hand and '*clack*' with the left – the basis of castanet playing. "You see," the man behind the counter informed me, "the right hand is female, and the left male … as you know, the ladies talk more than men!" Toy shops have yielded many novelties, and sports shops usually have a splendid variety of whistles and bird calls. My particular weakness is for small bells collected from all over the world – the search is never-ending. An orchestra trip to Brazil in 1997 yielded two bunches of dry-sounding, rattling goat's toenails, which have proved to be a marvellous ice-breaker in junior schools, accompanied by much face pulling and laughter. I have constantly been on the lookout for just the right upgrade for the piles of instruments in the garage, under the stairs, tucked under the piano, or set up ready to play in the sitting room: maybe there is something just that little bit better round the corner. Now, in retirement, my large, old gong hangs on its stand in the sitting room and I defy anyone to pass it without giving it a little nudge, or even a full-blown stroke with the large felt beater temptingly to hand. One or two of my personal babies have gone to good homes, as I feel strongly that instruments should be played, but I suspect that it will be a long time before I can really let everything go: they are all old friends with tales to tell and memories to savour. Perhaps it is as well that some of them *cannot* speak – they might let too many cats out of too many bags!

* * *

Moving a symphony orchestra from A to B is somewhat akin to a military operation. As with the librarian, the back-room boys have a heavy responsibility: they must shift valuable instruments, music, stands, special stools, extra lighting, a first-aid box, the string box containing hundreds of pounds' worth of spare strings, the conductor's rostrum (in reality a shallow box covered with a bit of red carpet) for the less salubrious out-of-town venues, touring wardrobes for trips beyond the Channel, the conductor's wardrobe and, last but certainly not least, the basket containing a water boiler and tea and coffee-making paraphernalia. Nicknamed 'The Flying Shamrock', our huge pantechnicon was emerald green, emblazoned with the orchestra's logo, and visible for miles. Nowadays, the orchestra sports a more sober affair in discreet silver. Times change.

Years ago, the coaches overtook the van at the side of the road, only to discover that it had broken down on the way to the concert hall in deepest Northamptonshire. When it eventually arrived, it was a case of 'all hands to the pumps!': off with jackets and sleeves rolled up, as a chain of players emptied the van, apart from double basses which were left on board in their coffins. Percussionists scrambled to find instruments from boxes in the darker reaches of the van's cave, but the rest was manhandled up a flight of stairs. Everyone – chorus and orchestra, friends and onlookers – assisted in assembling finger-nipping, folding music stands and arranged chairs, and, to everyone's relief and amazement, we were sitting ready and waiting as the first of the audience was allowed into the hall, somewhat later than anticipated. Lack of rehearsal on this occasion was a bonus as far as we were concerned, and the extra adrenalin certainly gave an edge to the overall performance.

It is inevitable that our relationship with instruments colours our working lives, but it is not only the instruments that cause hassle and grief; percussionists cope with many other practicalities too. If anyone needs a basic tool, say, to tighten up a screw or knock in a protruding nail, we hear a cry of, "Ask a percussionist". We scrabble about in our instrument boxes for the small tool bag and can usually comply.

Uniquely in an orchestra, band, pop group or whatever, the drummers are bedevilled with many and various instrument stands. These can take on a persona of their very own and we all have a love/hate relationship with them, but, then again, they are necessary adjuncts for the realisation of our particular arts. Most come in three separate sections, which need assembling and adjusting for every rehearsal and performance and, needless to say, they have to be substantial enough to carry out the job for which they are intended.

Many years ago, we realised that a recently purchased snare-drum stand had a nasty, spiteful temper and nipped unwary fingers when not treated with due care and attention. The new design was smarter and even heavier than the tried and trusted ones we knew and hated. Learning its little ways only took a short time, but not before every member of the CBSO percussion section had been caught out, resulting in each sporting a unique blood blister on the right index finger, inside the top joint. 'Snap', a pointing digit, quick comparisons, titters of laughter, and there we were, members of a secret society. Our colleagues, covertly noting this weird behaviour, sadly shook their heads, rolled their eyes and swiftly moved on. When we tried to vindicate our behaviour by explaining about the new stand, they hurried away 'tutting' quietly, their worst fears confirmed.

There are wing nuts, metal washers, thick felt washers, special clamps and specifically shaped holders, knurled knobs and odd additions, which come loose and live in drifts at the bottom of the various travelling crates. It must be the odd-sock syndrome, but there are seemingly strange bits of metal in all stand boxes with no homes of their own. Where do they come from, and where do the essential bits go, we ask ourselves? These traits manifest themselves especially when there is a coach to catch and we are in a tearing hurry with tons of gear to pack. Note the word *gear*: not for us mere instruments.

Our hearts sink when we see that numerous gongs have been scored for. These little and large darlings have to be suspended from a suitable device, which comes in the shape of a tall, unwieldy coat-rack-shaped frame. It is well to remember to assemble it *in situ*, as it is not always possible to manoeuvre it through doors or up steps as it twists and bends and other musicians get in the way. If you have ever tried to erect a frame tent, then you know what I mean. The hollow pieces of stand fit inside each other by means of little pips, which spring-fit into their own unique holes. This is another case of, "Ouch … where's the sticking plaster?" Oh, and yes, we must remember to slide the gongs or handbells onto the frame top in the correct order before connecting and ramming down the corners (for safety, you understand, not just in temper). If you are lucky it is custom built, with hooks already attached on which to hang the instruments, in which case the last warning does not apply. Stands for single, large gongs or tam-tams have a life of their own too. However careful one is, when being carried they have a habit of biting into ankles with their nasty, sticking-out tripod bird-feet, added

254

"Sounds Interesting". Maggie and Carol Holt, pianist and tambourine recruit

Fiona's Degree ceremony, Birmingham, February 1989.
Fiona, Geoff, step-mother Alice, Maggie, Arthur, Alistair

Huw Ceredig with the Mahler 6
"crack of doom" and walnut

Maggie with one of the largest
gongs in Europe

Pierre Boulez in Symphony Hall with some
of the "gear" for his Notations I - V

"Go on Simon, have a go!" Simon Rattle visiting a Special School
for Hearing Impaired in Birmingham

Brewing up a storm in an
inner city Junior school

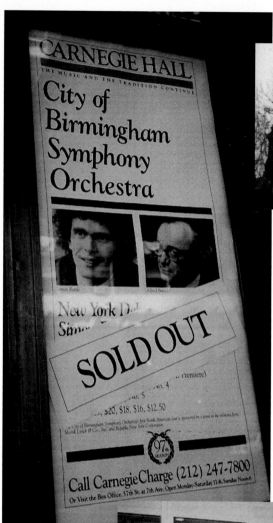

"Chicken ON roll",
David Powell (Cello)

Inspection of Percussion
Work Book, New York,
1991

"Smile please!" Berliner Zeitung front page (1984), Annie Oakley and Maggie

Above: La scala, Milan.
Father and son, Simon
and Sasha

Right: Peter Hill (timpani)
sorting Polish 'shrapnel'.
33,000 Zlotys = £1

The building site

Maggie trying to keep track

"Da-daa! We're IN!"
Maggie and Annie backstage

"WOW" Simon Rattle

Symphony Hall opening concert, April 1991. (Photo: Alan Wood)

to which they exude rust at a continuous rate of knots.

So, this is the scene before a rehearsal. The percussionists present themselves at a prearranged time (long before others' alarm clocks have performed, I suspect) and gloomily survey the accumulated bundles of metal struts, crates, cases and boxes behind the concert platform. If we have a truly huge set-up, then a pattern emerges. First, the percussion boss goes on stage to inspect the space we have to fill (carrying an armful of something or other, of course. As my mum would say, "Never go anywhere empty-handed.") Decisions are being made. Meanwhile, a couple or so home-team players are assembling stands from the opened flight boxes – all numbered so that we know what each contains. However, it is very possible that we don't know, of course, as in the heat of the moment at the end of the last show things may have been crammed in anywhere they would fit, being a case of, "Get IN, you swine!" Our extras grab whatever is at hand and an ant trail of players totters back and forth with stands, instruments and any other paraphernalia we cannot live without. Woe betide any unsuspecting, early-bird colleague who gets in the way; he or she might just be swept along and hung on a bell frame or similar. When all the hardware is in the approximate area of play, everyone gets to work to make some sense out of the mass of individual items as stands are adjusted for height and tightened to within an inch of their lives. At the end of the performance, this results in the inevitable cry of, "Who the hell put this stand up? I can't shift it!" Then the reverse routine happens and eventually all is relatively peaceful once more. When the majority of the orchestra arrives for rehearsal, the percussionists are quietly drinking coffee without an apparent care in the world. There are those who claim that we are clannish, but, with the curious responsibilities we have, I cannot really imagine that we could be any other way, as we are essentially a team in every particular. Work … coffee … and … **then** we have to play!

We envy colleagues who are able to take full responsibility for their own instruments, and who do not have to rely on orchestra staff whose job it is to set up the platforms and take care of the large instruments in transit and at the rehearsal or concert venue.

Nightmare wars of nerves between players and platform staff are wearing and unnecessary. It only needs the platform manager to take matters into his own hands or, worse still, not care, for the rehearsal to begin late, tempers to fray and exhaustion to set in. For many, many years a situation developed and deteriorated, affecting the heavy brigade: harpist, double-bass players, cellists, timpanist and, of course, the percussionists. Negative conduct from the platform manager resulted in his subordinate being intimidated, so little joy in that quarter except when he was working solo on the job, or with outside help when the boss man was off sick (accompanied by sighs of relief from us). Bass players complained, as did we, but blarney from the van-driver-cum-platform-boss translated all our complaints into seemingly childish irritations, and our grievances were ignored by higher management. There were many final straws, however, and eventually a thick dossier from basses and cellos noting damage and uncooperative behaviour was presented to the general manager.

We miserably listed and added our main trouble spots, from valuable timpani bruised and dented from shifting around in the van to the new celeste, costing thousands of pounds, revealing a smashed lid, the case battered and scratched with white wood showing through the black paint, causing Simon to observe that, "the instrument is in a very bad state". The vibraphone was regularly used by the platform staff as a trolley on which to move heavy metal stands, resulting in a warped frame and broken pegs supporting the notes. In spite of many pleas, we observed the big bass drum being bounced down platform steps by one man. This resulted in a non-functioning brake at the front of the frame and eventually a small tear in a drum head where it had been shoved up against angular music stands. Weeks later, after a particular trip to Ireland, the instrument returned, sporting a vastly expensive new calf head, which was duly damaged again before we even had had the opportunity to play it. Mr Nobody was blamed once more. On this occasion, it was repaired by sticking a small, neat patch on the inside with heavy industrial tape and keeping fingers crossed that it would hold. A favoured way of moving a heavy gong was to slide it face down on the staging to where it could be levered over the edge of the platform. Tubular bells fared no better, resulting in a crucial piece being sheared off the foot-pedal mechanism, rendering it useless. And so it went on.

Our grievances resulted in even less cooperation from the platform manager, as more psychological tactics were employed. Instrument boxes were frequently stacked on top of each other facing a wall, requiring players to manhandle them for proper access. There were tiresome games of 'hunt the instruments' in far-flung out-of-town venues, when they were often to be found as far away from the stage as possible. In desperation we would move them closer to the action, only to discover them even further away when the time came to pack up. "Fire department regulations," we were smugly informed, should any of us have the energy or temerity to ask. Usable extra-tall percussion stools were never anywhere to be found when visiting players were in the section. Yes, there were plenty of stools, but promises to mend unsafe legs, loose foot-bars and suchlike were only grudgingly fulfilled after weeks of exhausting nagging. We were the ones who bore the brunt of the conductor's irritation as we stood by our instruments waiting for some crucial item to appear (such as xylophone notes); this after working flat out for over an hour so that everything would be ready on time. Requests, grumbles and dark mutterings all fell on deaf ears. The reply was usually, "Just a minute, Marg. I'll see to it in a minute ...", and other such empty assurances. There he was, arranging chairs, putting out music folders, anything but responding to our urgent needs. Often it was a case of the orchestra manager and percussion players buckling down and getting on with shifting heavy equipment. Verbal appeals added to special requests in writing on the instrument sheets went unheeded. For example, on one occasion the smaller bass drum appeared for a concert instead of the large concert instrument. The principal percussionist was told that the instrument sheets had not materialised early enough and, "anyway the rehearsal hall security people would not cooperate at this late stage ...", whatever that meant. Hired instruments were taken back to the hire firm weeks after we had finished with them, thus costing the orchestra extra fees per day overdue. And so it went on; a catalogue of frustration and non-action.

Eventually another meeting was called with the Chief Executive, attended by bass players, timpanist, percussionists, harpist and a representative from the cello section. A truce of sorts was achieved, but we still felt that we were being let down by the very people whose job it was to help and support us.

Oh to play the piccolo!

18
Trio

Dress Sense

Many moons ago, when I was a schoolgirl, professional musicians had a very different dress code. After symphony concerts I would hang around the back door of my local town hall and gaze enviously at the confident men who would emerge carrying instrument cases and wearing fringed white silk scarves hanging loose around their necks, covering the absence of black bow ties. Long navy, camel hair or black overcoats were de rigueur with warmer weather bringing out a rash of not-so-glamorous mackintoshes, but always with the white scarves. No cloth caps for these guys, but instead trilby hats or even an exotic beret or two, and I was always naively surprised to see how battered the various instrument cases appeared. The few orchestral women looked just the same as my mum, their everyday coats hiding ordinary daywear, but with an additional small case or bag for short evening dress, smart evening shoes and make-up.

When I first became a member of the CBSO in April 1959, I was required to furnish myself with numerous types of uniform black dresses. The 'little black dress' syndrome never touched any Yorkshire ladies in my limited experience, so the search for young-looking black clothes in which I could play and look smart was a challenge to say the least. Indeed, black clothes were still regarded as funeral garb. The orchestra dress code was strict, with no deviation from unrelieved black and no sparkly jewellery, whether cufflinks or earrings. Women had to have three-quarter-length sleeves and discreet necklines (nothing too 'low and behold'), whilst the men were gradually changing from old-fashioned and difficult-to-launder white waistcoats to more practical black cummerbunds.

Concerts, for the most part, were black tie and dinner jackets for the guys, short black for the ladies (no *women* in those days, we were *ladies*). The rare trip to London and smarter concerts brought out white tie and tails and long black dresses, with cathedral concerts requiring sombre lounge suits and daytime short black, as did concerts for schools – whether in the actual schools, or children's concerts in the town hall. My wardrobe slowly filled with black drag, as we put it. I was lucky to have fair hair, as I did not look too bad in this dreary colour, but some looked like death warmed up, and knew it. All the primping and make-up in the world did not improve matters; there is nothing so black as black.

Whereas some have nightmares about flying, falling or whatever, orchestral musicians dream about not having brought the correct dress for concerts. When this happens, it never seems quite so ghastly as in the dream. however, as everyone helps out. There was the occasion when I appeared at a long-dress concert in a colleague's pretty tiered black taffeta petticoat, my newly washed and ironed skirt having been left to air on a hanger in my kitchen. Inappropriate shoes were not a problem for most of the females, as we could walk on with bended knees, and the offending stockinged feet or inappropriate shoes would be hidden under the long dress; not so the men. I can remember being brought up short on more than one occasion when observing one of the chaps slinking onto the platform with black socks *over* non-uniform black shoes. Mild hysteria set in as one was unable to unrivet one's eyes from the self-conscious, ridiculous-looking appendages tucked under a chair.

One year, on arriving in Edinburgh for the International Festival, our principal bassoonist had a phone call from his wife as the orchestra was waiting in the hotel lobby for room keys. Being contacted by a spouse immediately on arrival is a rarity, so everyone pricked up their ears as Andrew was heard to say, "I've got it here, yes, hang on a minute I'll check." His concert dress was supposedly in his gig bag along with the main luggage, but when he opened it a great jumble of clothes, books, shoes and unwanted ornaments spilled out, much to our amazement and mocking amusement. A collection of items destined for the local charity shop had been parked by his front door, and this is what had been carefully lugged all the way to Scotland instead of the identical concert case. After some quick lateral thinking, the evening clothes subsequently came with the CBSO Society Supporters who were travelling north by coach, but not after many suggestions of alternative sartorial styles to the somewhat shell-shocked player.

When the orchestra appeared in my hometown, I was particularly careful to appear the part, as there were usually people out there in the audience whom I knew and might meet in the interval. On one very special occasion, we were playing for the Huddersfield Choral Society at a concert attended by Sir William Walton. As we were hanging up our evening wear, I realised with dismay that I had brought long instead of short black. My contribution to the evening's performance was minimal, so after my patch in the rehearsal I went to the market and bought cheap, navy blue, imitation-leather slippers and a bottle of black shoe dye. Then it was home on the bus for tea, after which my long skirt was pinned up inside with safety pins, and dad dyed the slippers black. I duly arrived at the town hall only to find the place in total silence at 7.10pm, at which point I discovered to my horror that kick-off time was due for 7.15pm and everyone was waiting for the arrival of Sir William in the Mayor's Box. My efforts to insert myself in the percussion section behind the violins were less than auspicious. There I was, edging between the back of the orchestra and the front of the huge choir on the high choral stage, resplendent in pinned-up skirt and dyed slippers, scarlet to the roots: "Sorry, 'scuse me, oops, sorry ...", as I fielded whispered comments such as, "Did you have a nice tea?", "Nice of you to come", and suchlike. Eventually I reached my goal and sat down straight as a ramrod, totally embarrassed by the whole venture. But it wasn't to end there, oh no. Nearby, ears pricked as one of the men in the chorus bent down and said in a quiet conversational tone and rich Yorkshire accent, "Ee, 'ello luv. It's nice to see yer. We 'ad such a good concert last time you were all 'ere ...." I remained still and rigid, giving only a vague hint of acknowledgement. He then rounded off his little homily with, "D'yer remember Fred? He spoke to you. Well, 'eeh, we'd 'ad a **grand** concert. He went 'ome afterwards, walked through his front door ... and ... dropped deead!" This came as a bolt from the blue, but we somehow managed to control our choking hysteria. Sir William arrived, and the evening thereafter continued in its sombre and serious way.

Some years ago, I was one of the two percussionists standing on stepladders and playing large tubular bells behind the stage in Symphony Hall for a concert performance of part of Wagner's *Parsifal*. On repeating it at the Barbican concert hall in London the following Saturday, it was decided at the very end of rehearsal that my offstage contribution was being lost, so please would I play on stage, near the front, behind the cellos and almost in the lap of the audience. As I was not expecting to 'black up', I had not taken any evening clothes for this particular trip and neither were we near any shops - in any case, it was late in the afternoon. Luckily, I was wearing black corduroy velvet trousers and managed to earmark a loan of suitable shoes, but the big problem was that of a suitable top, which would pass close inspection at the edge of the platform. The only possibility of a black top at that late hour was to appeal to our conductor who lived in London. A knock on the green-room door and a plea of, "Please, do you think that you could lend me a black shirt?" was greeted by, "Sure, no problem," from Simon Rattle, grinning at my audacity. In due course, a beautifully laundered, smart, black linen shirt arrived at our band-room door, much to the amusement of my colleagues. I turned back the cuffs, and then collar up at the back, open neck, necklace, earrings and a twirl in front of the mirror. Hmm, not bad.

As Simon came on stage to take his bow, instead of immediately turning to the audience he looked over to where I was standing by my paint-spattered stepladder and huge bells, faintly raised an eyebrow with a twitch of amusement, and then turned to acknowledge the applause as I tried to quell my blushes. Some weeks later, I spotted the shirt on its rightful owner. "Oh, I see you're wearing *our* shirt!" I observed cheekily. "Yes," came the reply, "although I reckon it looks better on you!"

Think of the poor old orchestra when you are snug in winter overcoats in a freezing cathedral in winter. We still need to look as though we are in our special concert attire, but, unbeknown to the punters, we are in double-gusset mode: men in long johns; women in colourful thermal unmentionables. So, no raised eyebrows please when you spot an occasional pair of Dickensian fingerless black mittens. You try playing the oboe (or whatever) in sub-zero temperatures. In the bad old days before cathedrals had any noticeable heating, I often sat waiting to play cuddling a hot water bottle, which was suitably tricked out in a neat black cover.

These days, of course, things have moved on: few professional symphony orchestras play in dinner jackets, and gone are the days when one struggled to cover knees whilst wearing a short black cocktail dress. Cymbal playing, reaching up to play bells, leaning over to pick up beaters – all these and more – brought their very own problems, especially in the days of miniskirts, as it was almost impossible to buy 'decent' short black – that *little black dress* being just that: little! Now, of course, the majority of the women wear evening trousers, which are far more practical, meaning that one can turn up for the evening performance 'semi-professional' or partly clothed in concert black. Or, if in Vienna, with no provision for the female of the species backstage (we share loos out front with the audience, as the Vienna Philharmonic Orchestra is still almost 100% male), we change into evening dress at our nearby hotel and arrive at the hall for last-minute titivating in the general band room with the chaps.

Mishaps can also happen on tours, even when we carry our concert clothes around with us everywhere. For instance, it seemed perfectly normal when a notably absent-minded player packed all his shoes prior to an early start on a snowy foreign tour. The main luggage had been collected at midnight, and a sleepy orchestra was silently stumbling through a 7.00am breakfast when we were suddenly convulsed into a weeping, incoherent menagerie at the sight of our tall, lugubrious colleague standing at the door of the breakfast room, looking pathetic in his socked feet. Typical! we thought. No one was in the least bit sympathetic and another roar went up when he turned to leave and the ones in the lobby spotted his dilemma. However, someone eventually took pity on him and lent him some evening shoes that had missed the main suitcase pack. The problem was temporarily solved in spite of scrunched-up feet for him and endless teasing from the rest of us.

Nowadays, many musical groups have broken with tradition and have moved away from the historic form of dress. White polo necks or coloured shirts? Decisions, decisions. Long coloured dresses for the ladies, but be careful not to clash with your desk partner. This is all very well, but not everyone has good dress sense, and, if the overall effect is that of an end-of-the-pier outfit, it somehow detracts from what we are trying to achieve, and that is a performance of music and not a fashion show. The antiquated uniform always looks smart, especially from a distance, bearing in mind that all shapes and sizes need to be catered for. Now that the men are required to wear cummerbunds rather than old-fashioned waffle-piqué white waistcoats (rarely laundered therefore invariably grubby), there is half a chance that even the beer bellies will not be so noticeable from out front. It is then up to the orchestra manager to 'put the bell round the cat's neck' and, for instance, tell offending cardigan wearers in the distaff side that the aim is to wear *evening* dress.

I feel sorry for the men when the weather is hot. This is where we women win hands down. On our first visit to the Salzburg Festival, I well remember watching as perspiration slowly dripped off a violinist's chin onto his instrument in the heavy humidity and impossible heat during the performance. He came off the platform at the interval and removed a saturated bow tie. After wringing it out, he then had to put it on again for the second half of the performance. Nasty!

Some years ago, an enterprising shirt manufacturer had the bright idea of making formal evening shirts not wholly in white, but with back and sleeves in daft, jolly and sometimes indiscreet or downright rude designs. The audience never suspected the sartorial anarchy hiding under those formal jackets. But when there is a possibility of unspeakable heat, such as at the Henry Wood Proms in the Royal Albert Hall, the men all agree to wear plain white evening shirts, with belts holding up trousers, in the eventuality of a welcome 'jackets off' directive at the start of a long, hot concert. There is some scope for unusual braces too, as we realised when Simon mesmerised the orchestra with piano keyboards on one pair, half-hidden under his tailcoat.

Schoolchildren working with members of the orchestra during a hot summer spell became used to seeing their players in school in informal shorts, tee shirts, sandals, light cottons, and so on, so when they then met up during the interval of the targeted evening concert, they were amazed to see the transformations in spite of having been previously introduced to our outmoded form of dress in their classrooms. This was for real, producing the classic observation from one youngster of, "Doesn't David look different with his clothes on?"

Paper Chase

When I first joined the CBSO, it did not cross my mind to question the practicalities of playing in a professional orchestra. For instance, I took it for granted that music would be in a folder on the music stand for all the rehearsals and concerts. When we percussionists arrived early to organise our instruments, I was only vaguely aware of someone quietly walking around the stage hugging a huge pile of coloured folders, which were being distributed – one for each pair of string players, others for each individual music stand, every folder being named by instrument and individually numbered for additional accuracy.

The full score is on the top of the pile, then comes the leader who plays First Violin, Desk I, and everything else follows in sequence. Harp, percussion and timpani are at the bottom of the pile, the percussion section often having up to four or more folders to contend with, stuffed with music. Storage and distribution are always the same, so we all know where we come in orchestral order and can find our own music quickly in the heap should this be necessary. Spare parts are normally kept in a separate folder at the very bottom of the music boxes, often raided by percussionists for duplicates, particularly when a larger than usual section is spread across a wide area on stage, or split into two levels, one behind the other.

Therefore a crucial hero of the backup team for any orchestra is the orchestral librarian. My first introduction to the mysteries of the library was in the windowless, stuffy, cramped fire trap in the roof space behind the organ in Birmingham Town Hall. It was a mystery to everyone how the librarian managed to produce correct piles of neat folders from the apparent chaos in the miserable area allotted to him. Dusty music was stacked high on shelves, some loosely tied with whiskery parcel string and other sets filed in rows of beige flip-top boxes labelled accordingly. Neat bundles of newly arrived music hired from the various publishing houses were on chairs, on the floor, or spread out on a large table. If any substantial copying was needed, it had to be done by photocopy in a specialist copy shop a few streets away, but this was only officially allowed if duplicated pages were being used solely for rehearsal purposes or for private study. Copyright laws are strict and are policed accordingly, with occasional spot checks by the Performing Rights Society.

Access to recent compositions is only possible through hiring that particular work from the appropriate publisher. An interesting situation then occurs, as each orchestra has individual, pencilled, personal markings on all parts in every section – crucial to sanity. The solution is for publishers to designate a set of parts and full score to be used solely for each individual orchestra. Hopefully, they will then always send out the appropriate stacks of music to the specified destination.

We dread discovering that others have used our parts and sullied them with extraneous markings. Personally, I do not need to know that 'Jack' needs to 'pick up a LARGE bass drum beater', this accompanied by a huge spider-like asterisk untidily scrawled across the page. This is the cue to get out erasers and, with a sense of deep annoyance, scrub the parts clean again. (The most heinous of sins would be to alter or mark any parts in ink.) We know that youth orchestras are the worst culprits, as it would seem that few teachers show their students how to mark music in a way that is both useful yet unobtrusive. Of course there is total consternation if, in their wisdom, the publishers decide to replace the familiar ancient and battered music with virgin, pristine, brand-new copies. If that happens, we have lost our trail of carefully pencilled 'breadcrumbs' and have to rack our brains to remember how we had previously covered that piece – particularly crucial for percussionists, who need to know who plays what, when and where. One of these days we will break all the rules and mark our own individual parts with lurid colour, and then there will be no further discussion on the matter.

An imaginative system of Permanent Loan was created in the early '70s between the CBSO and the publishers Boosey & Hawkes, which eventually extended to other publishing houses. As there is often scant time between the hirings of certain repertoire pieces, it was decided to allow the orchestra to hold on to the bulk of the music, just returning woodwind parts to the publishers (so that there would be no question of cheating and playing from the music without permission). This saves the costs of postage, brown paper and string, and a place is kept on the shelves for stacks of hired parts that are only ever used by the home team. Players can borrow parts for private practice (first signing an appropriate list for each piece) and, when needed, the woodwind parts are sent for and the full fee is then paid. Presumably woodwind players are also able to borrow particular parts by prior arrangement.

Some years ago, Simon Rattle came home from America happily clutching a new score and orchestral parts for a Sibelius symphony. He then spent hours putting in his own detailed markings for perpetuity. However, if the publisher that owned the original parts had discovered that we were going to use what we strongly suspected was *pirated* music from the States, the orchestra would have been in serious trouble. So standard practice had to be followed, much to the orchestra's bemused astonishment. The usual music was hired from the British publishing house, but we rehearsed and eventually performed from Simon's parts. According to the rules of the game, the hired parts had to be on the platform during every performance. So there they were, still in their brown paper wrappings, parked in a neat pile by the rostrum for all to see that needed to. A certain blurring of the total truth maybe, but it was felt that honour was satisfied and everyone was happy.

Nowadays, along with the most up-to-date copier there is the addition of a computer in the librarian's armoury, as well as filing cabinets, a paper guillotine, a long shelf of reference books, and any other paraphernalia useful for the care of sheet music. Presiding over this lot is a full-time librarian, who has an assistant to help out with day-to-day donkey work. Usually a member of the orchestra is the out-of-town assistant, as it is too expensive to take the librarian just to be sure that the correct folders, with the correct contents, get to the correct place on the platform, even for the most prestigious of tours. This chore comes with an extra bit of pocket money, but it is a thankless, often unnoticed, and yet crucial job that few would wish to undertake.

One summer, the orchestra performed a part-staged version of Gershwin's opera *Porgy and Bess* immediately after the main holiday break. As this was in a somewhat shorter form than the original theatre production, many judicious cuts had to be made – a demanding task for the assistant librarian just back from holiday. Each violin part was two-and-a-half inches thick, so there was no time to be lost. Half a ton of paper clips, hundreds of blank bits of paper tailored to the size and shape of each deleted section, miles of adjustable clear sticky tape, and fifty-six hours later the violin parts were sorted. Then it was the turn of the rest of the instruments with no margin for errors. After which came the chore of bowing all the string music for the thirty pairs of players in a standard symphony orchestra. This took a minimum of two hours per part. There is no alternative to writing matched bowings into all the string parts *by hand*. They always have to be in pencil, as they are often changed by the whim or expertise of a conductor or, less often, the leader of the orchestra, and occasionally the fur flies if they disagree. In theory, the principal string players get their heads together before a new programme to discuss particular knotty corners, and then each section sends a carefully bowed master copy to the librarian. The librarian then gets in a supply of midnight oil and the race is on to have all the parts bowed before the downbeat at the first rehearsal. If the pressure is on and many programmes are being prepared, other string players are sometimes recruited to help out. This is pin-money outwork for retired colleagues, who are of course experts in the field. If the conductor of the day disagrees with any of the bowings, time is then wasted in rehearsals readjusting them, scrabbling around for pencils, with often inaudible suggestions from the rostrum being passed back down the line from the front desks: all very time consuming. We lesser mortals sigh and turn again to the crossword puzzle.

I feel that the look of the parts subtly adds to the aura of the piece being played. It would be strange indeed if we worked from identically printed music, and it is interesting to try to sort out unusual scripts. One feels a certain smug triumph when recognising some titles in Russian; however, I confess to being floored by some of the more wordy German directions in Mahler's music, but there is always a tiny frisson of excitement when I see 'Published in Vienna, Austria'. We then muse about which orchestra might have been the first to use this battered set of parts. The old-fashioned continental handwriting suggests that it could have been our Viennese colleagues, or maybe it started life in Leipzig, or Berlin ... certainly not in this country. Who knows? The paper is now somewhat the worse for wear, off-white, dog-eared and scrawled over with sparse pencilled comments in German and English. There are untidy pencilled numbers hastily marking out rows of identical bars: typical percussion music. Our eyes dart to the end of the repeated sections, register the final number, and then it is heads up and gimlet eyes on the conductor. The skill is to rejoin the mêlée and find one's place on the printed page without a hitch.

It is frequently possible to tell who the composer is just by the look of the paper and print. English music of a certain period is often hand-copied on large, very white paper. The same copyists seem to stick to their 'own' composers. For instance, Walton's music always has the same distinctive look, and we can recognise Vaughan Williams from the other side of a room. This applies to many composers up to the present day. Does the job of copying pass down through families I wonder? Shostakovitch favours cramped, handwritten parts, which are never easy to follow, with pinched, narrow spaces between staves. Perhaps this is a case of saving manuscript paper?

'Property of Adrian C. Boult': no prizes for guessing the composer here. Sir Adrian was with the CBO (as it was then) from 1924 to 1930, and when he left to join the BBC he presented a signed score and set of parts of Elgar's *Enigma Variations* to the orchestra. The paper has seen better days, but we still use Sir Adrian's personal gift. When I see the faded, rubber-stamped signature I smile, as I remember the old man standing ramrod straight and bristling - itching to get on with it. The paper is too large for modern music stands, with very old-fashioned printing, and after all these years it is a little floppy, but we manage.

We were ploughing through a piece of English (cowpat) music during a normal rehearsal day not long after I joined the orchestra, when there was a sudden rumpus from the woodwind fraternity. As expected, Tony, the principal flute, was the spokesman: "Sir Adrian - we seem to have two sets of parts on the go, and the rehearsal numbers in one don't tally with the rehearsal letters in the other set. Some seem to have your orchestral parts, but the rest of us have another publisher." This was serious, as communication during rehearsals is of paramount importance. Boult paused, pondered, and then spoke with slow deliberation, letting every word sink in. "Ah, Mr Moroney, then I suppose that you would like me to solve the problem by coming to your house and putting my private parts through your letter box?" I had no idea then why the place erupted as it did, but of course realised in the fullness of time – naughty man!

One particular French publisher favours printing on what we describe as bog-roll paper, creasing and tearing easily, soft in texture and pale buff-coloured. Pencil marks disappear under bright stage lighting and everyone complains. Every corner is wrecked by years of hasty page turns and, given half a chance, the whole lot will slide ignominiously off the music stand when most unexpected and inconvenient. This is a situation that merits a little judicious photocopying, as then the paper will be firm and white, the music will look black and, all in all, it is far clearer than the original. There once was an experiment with printing white notes on black paper for use in orchestra pits, but this novelty was abandoned as being impractical. If we are particularly frustrated by the poor state of the music, we sometimes write sneaky complaints to the publishers - it makes us feel better, but the recipients make no response.

French publishers favour the system of every percussion instrument being written on a separate piece of paper, rather than in short score (written *en bloc* on their own clutch of staves). The advantage of a short score is that we can all see what the rest of the section is up to (or not, as the case may be). With single instrument parts we fly blind, each taking the responsibility for counting our own bars, not knowing what our colleagues are doing, or indeed, the rest of the orchestra. For instance, it can be perfectly feasible for one player to cover sparse triangle, tambourine and gong parts, but easy access to the sounds via the actual printed music is very tricky. It is necessary to keep track of awkward entries, along with something of a juggling act to cover different techniques for the varied instruments we command.

This was often my responsibility, and my heart sank as I took a pencil and, after cleaning off all previous scribblings, marked three pieces of music accordingly, found two or three music stands and prepared for battle. With my own personal clues as familiar guides, I made valiant attempts to clarify the problems of playing bits here and there, with more than one instrument to hand. For instance, after playing the first entry one might continue with a big arrow 'To gong' (on another copy), then to 'V.S. (quickly turn page) tamb.', remembering to whip a page over for a future entry in another part whilst playing on a previous page, dodging from copy to copy, page to page, line to line. No time to think - just DO IT, and stay calm, and all this whilst doggedly counting any bars not being played. Every part looks different, and, if there are any cues from other instruments written in, they are rarely repeated throughout all percussion copies. Yes, and speaking about cues, I would like to get some of the copyists to come and actually listen to the orchestra from where we stand at the back. It is no good writing in a long and complicated low-pitched cor anglais cue buried in a welter of orchestral tutti if the percussionists cannot see, never mind hear, the woodwind department.

The printed music is crucial to every performance, and so, should a part, page or score mysteriously go missing or be forgotten, lost, damaged or otherwise unavailable, then there is a potential emergency that has to be addressed. Creative thinking and action on the part of the librarian are crucial if an insurmountable crisis is to be nipped in the bud. Once, during a rehearsal on a high platform, one of the trombone players dropped his music, which gracefully slid between the wooden boards and disappeared under the staging. This necessitated some part-demolition work and fishing with long poles. Fortunately, the music was eventually retrieved, but this was not the case on a similar occasion. A 'lick and stick job' was the only way to save the day when a woodwind part vanished without trace between rehearsal and show. Our valiant librarian took the full score to the nearest photocopier, returning with fistfuls of separate sheets, scissors, plain paper and paste. Each page had the appropriate instrument filleted from it – snip, snip – and then enormous care was taken to stick the narrow strips in correct sequence onto a clean sheet, thus compiling a part of sorts. Another desperate measure was for a player to read from a conductor's spare score, with an anxious soul sitting alongside being employed simply to turn pages at what seemed like the speed of light. Not a happy situation, but at least the oblivious audience was hearing the music as intended.

In spite of appreciating individuality in the look of our music, it comes as a relief to read from computer-produced parts. These are clear and usually foolproof. Maybe one day we will all be playing music from our own individual computer screens, with automatic page turns and endless possibilities for modifications, bowings, cuts, alterations, etc.

Meanwhile, I constantly try to instil into my students the need for taking care of the copies: a crucial, essential component for delivering a composer's wishes to the ears of our audiences.

Fur, Feathers, Fins

The classical music repertoire is well served with inspirational animals. Various larks trill, hens cluck, swans serenely sail, pigeons and doves coo, cockerels crow triumphantly (golden and otherwise), cuckoos herald spring, nightingales enchant, magpies forever thieve, peacocks preen, scenes with cranes calm and bemuse, and *oiseaux exotiques* descend in great flocks. Luckily, these particular creatures do not find themselves on the same manuscript paper as the bees, wasps, dragonflies, damselflies and butterflies of other compositions - too problematical by half. Fish are represented rather more rarely, but Schubert's trout springs immediately to mind, followed closely by a whole aquarium of fishy friends by courtesy of M. Saint-Saëns in his *Carnival of Animals*. Other creatures encountered include oxen, cats, mice, King Rat, a tiny bat, a red pony, a fox and vixen, three or more bears (tame or otherwise), flocks of sheep, Dan the bulldog, a French elephant, and a prowling wolf possibly sneaking up on a drowsy faun.

You would think that this lot would be enough for any musician, but no, we frequently chance upon the real thing. This causes some amusement, lifting a run-of-the-mill rehearsal or concert to that of a memorable occasion. The possible exception to this is the rare appearance of the Symphony Hall fly in Birmingham's fine concert hall. One can usually predict that he will be awake and buzz around during the most poignant part of a piece, although, to be fair, we are the ones who are disturbing his space. I would be somewhat reluctant to welcome a crowd of 2,000 or so people into my personal domain. He zooms around in huge, lazy arcs, caught in the bright lights and ever persistent. This has been going on for years, so we suspect that he trains his children to follow suit. At one point he foolishly settled on the music of the front desk of cellos during an intense recording session, where he was smartly swiped. A great "Ahhhhh!" went up from the rest of the orchestra as the little corpse fell to the ground – the take was ruined. Nothing changed, however, as one of his family took over aeronautical duties the next day, just like dad, swooping over the orchestra and mesmerising the musicians and yet apparently invisible to members of the audience. The only other creepy-crawly we regularly encountered was the stoical spider who lived inside the deep slit of a wooden log drum, one of a set of three, hired with monotonous regularity for music by a young Composer-in-Residence. This creature always turned up from the London warehouse, no doubt stone deaf and shaken to bits. We tried to release it from what we perceived as a deeply uncomfortable existence, but to no avail. I wondered how it could possibly survive all those miles, all that noise and all those battering vibrations, and what was on its menu, buried as it was so very deep inside a block of wood.

Real birds occasionally feature in the realm of a symphony orchestra too. For years, Worcester Cathedral had a resident robin. This bright-eyed, fearless scrap would land on music stands during rehearsals, glare, and then fly off, no doubt to grumble about our violating his territory. We were delighted, of course. Anything is welcomed to alleviate the tedium encountered when playing for a long-winded local chorus master or organist. And was it Gloucester or Hereford Cathedral cloisters where we were dive-bombed by an occasional bat as light faded in the evening? On one occasion, we were reduced to suppressed giggles during an outdoor performance at one of our regular parks concerts in London. Set by the obligatory lake, the orchestra was ploughing through Berlioz's *Fantastic Symphony* and being eaten alive by the usual clouds of happy mosquitoes when, at the beginning of the slow movement, the offstage cor anglais – soulfully echoing an onstage oboe – was drowned out by furious quacking from park residents. Every time the player began his solo interjections, the ducks joined in with full chorus. Needless to say, the performance was unique but not one of the best, as it is very difficult to play when consumed by mirth. Another programme offered for the open-air fireworks bash invariably concludes with a rip-roaring performance of Tchaikovsky's *1812 Overture*. The sun goes down, maybe rain sets in, but the unwary wildfowl have yet to add their spectacular contributions. This is one part of the performance where the players have a real bird's-eye view. When the cannon eventually roars, the park geese, moorhens, ducks and all their progeny take off in swooping flights, quacking and honking angrily, scared out of their birdbrains by the explosions. Additional peacocks screech up into the lower branches of ancient yews during outdoor spectaculars at Warwick Castle, further cacophony adding to the general feathery mayhem in the moat. I always feel sorry for them, as they must be terrified, especially having finally settled down after resigning themselves to the sound of a mere symphony orchestra and thousands of people in their boudoirs. Poor things – what a ghastly shock!

Another muddy-field occasion yielded a unique creature for the concert platform. We were performing in Wales, and it was seriously WET. Rain had poured forever, so it seemed, but luckily we were in a massive marquee just about holding our own above the racket of teeming water thundering onto the canvas roof. The *Ghost Busters* film music starts with an eerie effect of a struck tubular bell being lowered into a tank of water, so the platform staff were asked if they would supply the water. It duly arrived in an oversized bucket, but, as there was not sufficient drinking water to hand, they had got it from the river. "No problem," we said, and continued with the rehearsal. We played our bit and continued with the piece as the river murk settled. I happened to look into the water, however, and there at the bottom of the bucket, with its fingers in its ears, was a tiny silver fish. The percussion players did not give of their best for the next part of rehearsal, as we spent anxious time catching the shell-shocked tiddler in a teacup. History relates that he soon became lively – but no doubt with a thumping head – and was released back into the river without further ado. Could this be a first for a live fish on a concert platform?

Gone are the days of rats in the Chatham band room, but on our first visit to Japan we encountered wildlife in the shape of cockroaches backstage in one of the most up-to-date halls we play in: the smart Suntory Hall in Tokyo.

And on home ground we accepted that Birmingham Town Hall was bedevilled with mice, the orchestra being asked not to leave any edibles around – difficult when nosebags are the order of the day for some, between rehearsal and concert.

Leeds Town Hall used to have a cat whose favoured snoozing place was inside the grand piano. As the concerto is often the first piece to be rehearsed, the piano is in place long before work starts, and therefore I cannot remember who had the worst shock, the players or the cat, when he fled with streaming flue-brush tail as we began playing. It did not end there, however, as during one concert we of the observer corps spotted a ripple of movement in the cello section. Heads moved as a certain fur person stalked with great dignity through their legs, across the platform and away down the stairs at the back of the stage. Then there was the beautifully behaved Golden Labrador retriever guide dog; an unwitting music critic who frequented concerts with his master in Birmingham Town Hall. We were always pleased to see them sitting in the front row downstairs. When the music swelled to noble proportions, there was a canine accolade of a thumping tail from under the seat, but we were more charmed by the very deliberate stretch and squeaky dog-yawn in the more dreary, quiet passages, as the rest of us drifted off into our own thought-temples. My very favourite animals were the horses used in a splendiferous production of *Carmen* in Birmingham some years ago, when I was employed as orchestra manager for the two-week visit of an international touring opera company. And, yes, they did recognise their music cue. My great delight was to be backstage as the music brewed up to the magnificent Toreador March. Exquisitely costumed ladies were waiting in their lovely antique landau, and the horses would be fizzing to be out there in the spotlights, adrenalin flowing in anticipation of one of opera's highlights. We had a little tacit agreement, the horses and I. Every day I would go backstage to visit my friends (not the thoroughbred black stallion, though, as he was temperamental and prone to nipping strangers), all eight of them. They were in their own cosy stables and always greeted me with excitement, as they knew that I was the bringer of little treats in the shape of apples and carrots. This was not purely altruistic, however, as the resulting products from them were duly returned to me in carefully sealed sacks, eventually doing noble service on my large allotment. Waste not, want not! I was further required to 'fix' orchestras with local freelance players for popular classical concerts in Sheffield and Birmingham. The idea of London freelance players flogging up the motorways, being paid London rates and staying overnight to play standard repertoire concerts was an anathema to me, so the fact that I was able to book local musicians was gratifying and economic, something for which the impresario was no doubt grateful.

Do birds and animals sit quietly in their nests, lairs, dens, etc., listening for the odd drift of music from the two-legged-ones? Perhaps all those exotic birds specially contrived to sing their almost unplayable phrases when they spotted Messiaen hovering nearby with his manuscript notebook? What really puzzles me, though, is the blackbird who regularly tootles the first phrase of Dvořák's *Te Deum* in my garden, always at the same pitch and every note spot on. Did he hear it through an open window and think, 'Hmm, that's an attractive little ditty. I'll have that as my own'? One of these days, I will play the rest of it to him – after all, he gives me such pleasure with his natural musical talent that it seems only fair to share some of my favourites with him. I don't know about the goldfish in my pond though – Water Music for them perhaps?

19
Emperor's New Clothes

Music (-z-), n. Art of combining sounds with a view to beauty of form and expression of emotion; sounds so produced; pleasant sound e.g. song of a bird. Written or printed score of musical composition. (*Concise Oxford Dictionary*)

We were rehearsing Symphony No. 4 by Humphrey Searle (commissioned by Birmingham's Feeney Trust) for the first time.

"You've written a glissando, which can't be played to a note that isn't on the instrument!" yelled an irate trumpet player, standing and waving his trumpet in the air. This was from one of the mildest-tempered people in the whole orchestra, never known to lose his composure, and certainly NEVER known to shout across the orchestra to anyone. At one point in the same piece, one of the bassoons in sheer frustration turned his music upside down and played a whole page from bottom to top - an exercise in lese-majesty, which amazingly drew no comment from the composer-conductor. I found myself muttering that my part was physically impossible, although I suppose that two or more percussionists could have tangled together and played the intermittent xylophone and vibraphone parts between them. This was an obvious case, yet again, of someone writing for such instruments from a piano keyboard with five fingers per hand instead of for one beater per hand, or two in extremis. The only solution seemed to be to scatter notes around like confetti, but to be careful to stop when necessary, hopefully on the correct note. Written in a disjointed twelve-tone style, the theme we were told was a silent bar: "One! Two!" This was announced by the composer with stolid, uncompromising emphasis. Naturally, most of us saw the silly side to all of this and were hard-pressed to remain serious. Consequently, each time the theme appeared there was a faint, ghostly "One! Two!" in the air from the players during rehearsals, and we had the utmost difficulty in remaining silent during the intense presentation of the premiere performance.

At the concert, I felt very self-conscious, as I had been placed alone with my two large instruments opposite to the rest of the percussion gang, beyond the timpani. Luckily, everything went by without any perceivable hitch, but during the interval I was summoned to see the composer. My heart sank as I entered his room; however, I was astonished as he proceeded to give me a bear hug and profusely thank me for my wonderful interpretation of his piece. Oh dear, what a fraud one felt, but then we have all learnt to keep our counsel as we are drawn into such apparent nonsenses. Who played and who heard the previous three symphonies, we wondered, and would our current effort be yet another first/last performance?

Why, oh why, can't some of them learn their craft properly? We get new works written specially for us, and half of the rehearsal time seems to be taken up with trying to sort out basic needlework. In the orchestra, players often comment that, if we performed as badly as some composers wrote for us, we wonder how long we would survive in our overcrowded and exacting trade. Instrumentalists would never dare to disregard professional advice, suggestions and pleadings in the same cavalier way as some of the composers. If only they would ask the players what is workable, that at least would be a step in the right direction. Who teaches these characters? Why are they so supremely confident and adamant/ignorant in their convictions?

And as for writing for percussion instruments ... well! I had a telephone call one day: "Oh, you are one of the percussionists with the CBSO, aren't you? Do you have such a thing as a marimba? You see, I am writing a piece for clarinet and strings and would like to include a marimba." Great, we're getting somewhere at last, one was tempted to think, as I agreed to meet the composer to show her the orchestra's marimba. My boss, Douglas, and I made a special journey into town, and went to a lot of trouble to unearth and assemble the large instrument from the storeroom. It was duly presented to the composer, who looked on with wide eyes and remarked, "Oh, is THAT what it looks like? I liked the name, so I thought that it would go well on the title page"! something-or-other for strings, clarinet and marimba. Never mind what it sounds like, it turned out that she had already written the piece and that this was to be an addition, like icing on a cake. The upshot was that, in spite of telling her to write as if she were playing a piano with two fingers (a beater in each hand – yes?), the finished article was practically unplayable. A marimba is a monster xylophone and can be well over two metres in length, therefore it helps if the player can play it without having to resort to roller skates. I subsequently found myself appearing in the first performance – for a memorial service: a bit of moral blackmail there. Consequently, I didn't have the nerve to ask for a fee for all my time and hard work, not to mention having to transport such a huge instrument in and out of crates, house, car, and eventually back to its nest.

Another composer swept in through the percussion section for the first rehearsal of her magnum opus, clutching the obligatory enormous score, and gushing, "Oh, how **wonderful**! Is all this for me? It looks **just** like a toy shop." Narrow-eyed players chose to ignore this. Another creative genius bumbled through the section and asked about certain items propped against a chair ('anvils', i.e. lengths of scaffolding to be played with heavy hammers) and was amazed when he was informed that "Yes! they **are** for your piece." We know full well that we are regarded as fair game for experimentation, which is fine if there is consultation, however minimal. We wouldn't mind so much if we felt that it was all screaming to be let out, but so much of what the composer George Lloyd called 'squeaky gate music' is so very boring. I can forgive hating it, or finding it difficult to play, and sometimes almost enjoy the challenge, but *boring* – NO. Our eyes glaze over and we think longingly of our next coffee stop.

One of the real difficulties with contemporary creativity is that of trying to remain serious in the concert. The 'lion's roar' effect in some jolly Shostakovitch theatre music is a case in point as diary notes reveal:

> *... it sounds like a giant farting! Of course when it came to it, Pete Hill (timpanist) collapsed in peals of mirth which set us all off. We were weeping whilst enduring Pete's coarse comments as he flapped a handkerchief and held his nose. The conductor (Mark Elder) looked at the hysterical percussion section with incredulity saying, "Let me hear it" ... more gales of laughter. The rest of the orchestra was amazed. I dread tomorrow's performance. Eventually I sort of controlled myself (wiping my eyes on a duster) and we continued with the piece.*

It is okay to laugh discreetly or even uproariously in rehearsals, but it does not do to let the cat out of the bag during performances. However, sometimes this is not humanly possible, and I confess to having problems when tears of laughter blur the scene as we stand there in formal evening dress trying to convince the listeners and ourselves that what we are being asked to do is perfectly normal. There are also times when the most straightforward programme of well-loved music can lie in wait to catch the unwary. The solo part in the 'Cuckoo Polka' sets me off into paroxysms of mirth, as I discovered during the first (and last) time I attempted this novelty part in one of the New Year 'Viennese Nights'. I got incurable giggles at the idiocy of what I was doing, and never actually played a note. It simply is not possible to blow a cuckoo whistle and laugh at the same time, although Annie valiantly managed to answer my spluttering silences with her twittering nightingale. The audience roared delighted approval and the guest conductor very kindly gave me a bow all to myself. But then I had to steel myself to seek him out in the green room and offer my apologies for what had been a serious breach of professional etiquette. Fortunately, many newly minted noises are totally unmemorable – often their only saving grace. At least they don't get into the brain and drive us mad in our own time too.

Composer/conductor: "Do you have another xylophone?" He was very young, this one; confident, though, and not at all intimidated by a large professional orchestra coldly eyeing him from all quarters. "No - sorry," said the player, "this is how they come: 3½ octaves, F to C."

"Well … that's not the E I've written. It has to be an octave higher."

Faintly raised eyebrows from us, as anything higher than the one offered would sound like a strangled wood block.

Have no fear, our brave hero had the solution. "We have a four-octave xylophone at the university. I'll bring it in."

This was acknowledged and the next day he duly arrived, parked illegally and struggled into the city-centre rehearsal hall, piece by awkward piece. Eventually we took pity on him and helped to assemble the monster. What he did not know was that I had sold this instrument to the said university many years previously and had misgivings about the whole venture from the very outset. When it came to *the note*, it was duly played, he smugly smiled and we carried on as if all was well. As he was weaving his way through our section to go, Doug said, "Oh, by the way, you do realise that the E on this instrument is the same pitch as the one on ours, don't you?" This was greeted by disbelief, consternation and deep discussion, and then our own instrument was wheeled over, a tuning fork was produced and the point was conceded; the extra size being covered by the bass end of the immigrant xylophone, not the treble. Doug went away muttering darkly that it wouldn't have been possible to use that big brute on the platform anyway: no space!

Many new works are received with acclamation by critics, the musical elite, the avant-garde et al.; but what about the musicians who have to play them, and the punters who come to listen? Yes, yes, we all know about Beethoven's Ninth, and Stravinsky's *Rite of Spring*: no one loved them in their day either. They were deemed unplayable, as was Tchaikovsky's violin concerto – the list is endless. And yes, we know that we are in the twenty-first century, but some of the stuff we have to play **must** be misplaced jokes, only no one dares to say this. 'Why?' is often mouthed in rehearsals between bemused and despairing musicians after the airing of some particularly crass piece of noise. Perhaps the composers have shares in the publishing houses?

I have to remind myself that orchestral musicians are not obliged to like everything we play, and that we should also feel comfortable enough to admit this. On occasion, I have been cornered by members of the CBSO's sophisticated Birmingham audiences, and have had to field the dreaded question, "Did you enjoy that, then?", often with the emphasis on the word 'you'. One can anticipate such queries after exposure to contemporary music, and we learn to recognise the beady look in the eyes of our predators. However, when pinned down to reply, I initially opt out with a defensive, "Oh, er, it was very challenging/interesting." This is not good enough for most, however. If they have gone to the trouble to speak to a member of the orchestra, you can bet that they would prefer the unvarnished truth from that player. But – be diplomatic, don't let the side down: careful now. So the next step is to mutter something about the piece having enterprising and innovative ideas, pointing out that orchestral players are not really expected to have personal opinions, as we are there solely as a necessary bridge between composer and audience, via the conductor of course.

There are times when we wonder if audiences notice just how bad some performances become when rot sets in, often during the most familiar pieces. I noted one memorable performance of Ravel's *Boléro* in far-flung Exeter as things went from bad to worse, the players becoming more and more twitchy and anxious:

Boléro was a catalogue of events which reduced the orchestra to stifled hysterics. The cathedral clock struck and whirred lengthily at 8.45pm, an audience member exploded (on the beat), something clattered to the floor in the first fiddles, then the final straw was the oboe d'amore which had a key stick, changing the tune to one with much Eastern promise. It was all downhill after that.

Many years ago, I had one of those moments when life takes a divergent turn. A local amateur violinist was bemoaning the fact that her pianist had moved away from the district, so in a mad moment I said that I would enjoy an occasional playing session with her; it would be good for my rusty piano skills. Yes, the Lalo was fun and I settled down to learning the notes. Then it came to Delius. The very first piano chord told me that this was not something I wished to pursue, but I felt honour-bound to persevere. It was no good, however: I could only get to the bottom of the first page before growling with frustration and acknowledging that this was supposed to be of mutual benefit and enjoyment for both pianist and fiddle player. This was the first time in my life that I openly confessed my dislike of much English music, referred to by the more jaundiced as 'cowpat music' or, 'another cow looking over another gate'. "Oh, but its a wonderful piece," my new-found friend protested. "Mmm, sorry, but I just can't bear the sound it makes!" There is nothing wrong with that, and ever afterwards I have tried to be fair and honest, at least to myself, about what I can and cannot tolerate.

We orchestral musicians have few opportunities to have any influence in the choice of programmes. My problem is that my top unfavourites have a nasty habit of haunting the brain and not letting go. I wake in the night with some rat-like phrase running around in the grey matter, grind my teeth, bash the pillow and try to blot it out. One should be allowed *not* to like something, but somehow music seems to be such a difficult area in this respect. Punters observing paintings with screwed-up faces abound in art galleries and negative opinions are seen as totally permissible, so why do we find a similar approach to music less acceptable?

Not only does one join an orchestra and see the world: if you stay there long enough you will get to play everything from 'Hey Nonny Nonny' through to allegorical nonsense. And play it you will, not once or twice, but many, many times.

* * *

Pierre Boulez is very pernickety as to how our many and varied instruments are to be played, the types of sticks used, specific techniques, and so on, so at our first meeting we were ready for anything. "May I 'ear the sound of the motor?" – this to yours truly playing vibraphone: slow, medium, fast speeds designated. We were rehearsing his *Notations 1-1V* in a large BBC studio. Fortunately, I actually had the instrument plugged in and switched on, but as usual the setting was for the medium speed, as 'fast' squeaked and 'slow' was in the seasick zone and far too uncomfortable to live with as it entered one's bones. All four short movements take a total of about nine minutes to complete and are fiendishly tricky to perform. M. Boulez is very serious, and we were all a little nervous of the great man; however, I did no more but grin and play a C major arpeggio slowly, finishing with an ironic flourish. "I asked for the sound of the motorrrrrh, not a chord of C Majorrrrrhh" (not something one finds in his compositions) - the accent rolled out and everyone laughed – a bijou Boulez joke. Amazing! He then wished to time the four tiny pieces but decided, at the last minute, on a different order of play. Unfortunately, some of us at the back had not caught this instruction. Number one: fine. Then I came clattering in with number two, but he had gone on to the last one. Realising my folly, I stopped immediately and grovelled with apologies as the orchestra ground to a halt. We never stop when pieces are being timed and I knew that we would have to go right back to the very beginning. So very unprofessional of me and I was mortified, but somehow the devil took over and I followed my admission of guilt with a cheeky grin and, "But it wasn't in C Major!" Release of tension all round. At the beginning of every rehearsal after that little incident, the maestro looked towards the back and gave me an ironic salute before work began in earnest.

According to Simon Rattle, *Éclat* by Boulez is the only piece the conductor 'plays', giving a variety of specific hand signals to the fifteen players under his nose. Our parts consist of boxed brackets in which everyone has his or her own skittering phrases, which in turn are chosen at random by the conductor, indicated by appropriate numbers of fingers held up in front of his face. We were warned that it goes very fast and sounds like goldfish underwater. Giggles were not far from the surface, never mind fish. After the first rehearsals (six-and-a-quarter hours for an eight-minute piece), we all ended up sitting on the floor in the conductor's room drinking tea. Simon was mother. Fine so far. Until the first performance, Simon spent a lot of time making mistakes (a rare experience for him), apologising and joking about how difficult it was, and that his brain hurt: a favourite justification. So when, on the first play-through, I lashed out at but missed a crucial bell note, accidentally clouting the tall bell frame which was positioned too far behind me for a comfortable visual contact, I yelped a quick, "Oh, sorry Simon!", but was less than happy with his immediate irritated comeback of, "*Sorry* won't do!" With murder in my heart, I silently repositioned the bell frame, and, as I was standing directly in front of the rostrum, players behind me then had to shift around so that they could see properly.

Gloom set in at Cheltenham the following day as we lost about twenty minutes of precious time owing to a fire alarm scare. As the clock crept nearer to six o'clock, it became obvious that a complete final run-through would not be possible without incurring overtime, something the management would not sanction. A hopeful plea for another five minutes from the boss cut no ice with Huw, the principal percussionist, who firmly put down his vibraphone beaters and made a move to the door as the minute hand reached the crucial cut-off time. Simon's "We've lost time because of the fire alarm" and a further request for a few more minutes was met with an uncompromising "That's not my problem. I've got better things to do" from Huw, who promptly left the hall (to be seen later, eating sandwiches in his car). He was technically within his rights, but in the circumstances everyone else was incensed at his unbending attitude. Simon tried the "Well we'll have to cancel the piece as we can't finish a proper run-through" tactic, but to no avail. He was brought to his senses when the orchestral pianist impatiently called out, "Oh, *come on* Simon, stop messing about and just get on with it!" He took a deep breath and then announced, "I'm not here to lose my temper – thank you for staying." The performance went very well in spite of a ghastly atmosphere in our small section. Huw was bouncing about full of self-righteous bravado, Annie was hating him for it, and I was stalking about trying to ignore both of them. The next day I overheard Simon congratulating Huw on his excellent performance the previous evening – a lesson in how to keep crucial communications open with one of his key players.

We were not the only ones twitching about *Éclat* when we played it at the Edinburgh Festival in late August. I noted, with some amazement after mind-numbing Webern that for the Boulez, where the chosen few were right under Simon's nose, "He was nervous – trembling fingers. What a revelation!" It went very well, but afterwards I remarked, "I've not been so nervous for ages … and you were nervous!" It was quite a comfort to get a response of "I was **terrified**!" I replied, "It's the best thing I've seen for ages, **you** shaking."

Gruppen is a rarely performed, gargantuan work by Stockhausen, written for three orchestras which play simultaneously under the direction of three conductors, using between them twelve percussionists, each required to play very many instruments. The practical problems of staging this work are almost insurmountable, but when this Stockhausen experience was mooted we found ourselves at the receiving end of carefully noted maps of the instrumental layouts from the first performance: very handy.

Footnote in percussion parts:

In the score hard and soft are used to denote the mallets for all percussion instruments. As mallets of the same name can give different results in sound (due to the way the material has been prepared) a more exact prescription is dispensed with. Within the categories of hard and soft (leather mallets, heavy iron clappers, vibraphone mallets, mallets with wooden balls, felt, wire brushes, soft rubber, wool, hard rubber, metal rods, etc.) the most varied sorts of mallets should be used, according to the instructions of the conductor.

One particular note eluded me in rehearsal - just a simple treble D# on a vibraphone (at the extreme right-hand end of the instrument). Eventually Simon, *my* conductor, got less than patient, but was unaware that the real problem was that I had to see to many additional things immediately prior to THE note, and that what I really needed was a clear lead from him. Eventually I cracked and had a word with him after rehearsal, requesting a cue for the dreaded note, pointing out to him that at that juncture in the piece I had a) to turn off the vibraphone motor with one hand; b) set the tubular bell pedal with right hand and right foot; c) put down a bell hammer; d) turn two pages of one of the two parts I was following (as a colleague had a desperate dash to that part later on, and it had to be at the correct page); e) pick up a vibraphone beater; and finally, turn my own page – all this without looking directly at what I was doing and trying to keep tabs on the beat, as well as counting bars and ignoring a very strong cue being given to the horns directly in front of me a millisecond before my dreaded note. (It is as well to remember that we get paid for what we *don't do* as much as for what we *do do*.) After that, I got my cue and all went well; but it was still only **one** note. When we eventually listened to the performance, it was impossible to hear it after all, as it was totally obscured by many other instruments.The preferred method of appeasing an eager conductor when different sticks are requested is to make an audible scrabbling noise in the stick box, and then hold up a pair of beaters for the maestro to see, accompanying this with a beatific smile. The usual response from the rostrum is a pleased nod (as if he knows about or can possibly see which sticks are being held out for inspection); we can then carry on as before. The beaters first selected are used throughout, and we just play the dynamics accordingly: simple. This is in the same league as: "Do you have a smaller triangle?" Once more, a fixed smile and weary reply of "Would you like it quieter?" would be proffered (masking the desired reply of "Would you like it stuffed down your throat?") Oh, really!

Many moons ago, when Sir Malcolm Sargent ruled the roost at the BBC Symphony Orchestra, the percussion section had sweet revenge for this type of orchestra game. One of the Viennese overtures features a clock striking eight, played on a tubular bell. Sir Malcolm was less than ecstatic with their first effort, so immediately wove his way through the orchestra to show the percussion section how it *should* sound. Meanwhile there was a search for the scruffiest, most chewed-up leather bell hammer, which was duly presented to the maestro for his egotistical demonstration and lesson on how to strike a uniform eight o'clock. Not one note matched with another as the players stood by calmly listening and trying to hide smug expressions. After returning the instrument and hammer, Sargent wisely returned to his own patch and nothing more was said. One of his more irritating phrases was, "Let me do it for you!", and then he would sing the selected part. Players would mutter, "Any fool can sing it, but just come and play it on the clarinet" (or whatever). On a special BBC anniversary every member of the orchestra was solemnly presented with a pencil and signed photo of Sargent. I am told that, for many months after this event, one of the photos could still be seen in the gents' urinals at Maida Vale Studios, underwritten with the legend, "Let me do it for you!"Clarinets are pitched in various keys depending on the work to be played. Such a choice of instruments led to a notable confession some time after a distinguished clarinettist had broadcast a new concerto, with the composer conducting. The soloist inadvertently managed to spend all rehearsals and the performance playing on the wrong clarinet. This was understandable to a degree, when confronted by squawks, shrieks, squeals and the obligatory unrhythmical twaddle, with nary a tune on the horizon. No one had noticed, including the perpetrator, until much later. It doesn't say much for the composer. *Composer*? One's heart sinks as the word 'aleatory' hangs in the air: on the music, from conductor or composer. ("Latin: *alea*: dice, chance. Aleatoric – a bastard word, to be avoided by those who care for the language. Music which cannot be predicted before the performance.") This is usually indicated on the parts by squiggly lines inside square brackets with seconds or, heaven forbid, minutes and seconds of time required to elapse whilst some hapless musician tries to interpret and improvise freely, at the same time keeping a straight face. To me, this is a total opt-out on the part of the composer. Sometimes we swear that ink is sprayed onto manuscript paper with tails and dots added at a later time. Similarly, brass players in a London orchestra were asked to 'play in a free manner'; "Do what you like at this point" was the instruction from the composer-conductor. So, of course, they got their heads together and when it came to the great moment played '*Happy Birthday*' and '*Colonel Bogey*'. Fury flew from the rostrum: "What on EARTH do you think you're doing?" raged the conductor. "You clearly said that we could play what we liked … this is what we like!" came the reply. Time for the tea break.

On the other side of the coin are, of course, those composers who do stand the test of time. I enjoy music of all periods, and certainly appreciate the stimulation of music from my own century. It is a challenge to be the channel through which new music can be heard, and it is exciting to open a new score and wonder what it will sound like in performance. However, I look forward to the day when orchestral players, and possibly audience members too, no longer feel the urge to mutter the words "Emperor's New Clothes" at airings of some original concoctions.

Our very first Composer-in-Residence was Mark Anthony Turnage. "What a splendid idea!" we agreed after we had all met, chatted, drank coffee and assured Mark that we would be there for him should he wish to hear any of our more unusual instruments or try out any experimental sounds. Other players were equally generous in their hopes and aspirations and all seemed set fair for some interesting creativity. *Three Screaming Popes* was given its first performance in Birmingham, but I was not altogether happy with my lot in the score. One of the instruments I played was a chromatic set of crotales (antique cymbals). These small tuned cymbals come in a specific range: anything higher in pitch would probably sound like a shrill strangled triangle. The problem was that Mark had written a woodwind fragment, followed on by a matching phrase from crotales. These he had unwittingly scored out of their range, so I dropped the whole thing down an octave. This did not work either, as the lower notes 'fell off' the bottom of the range, but as no one, including Simon Rattle, seemed to notice, I continued to split the phrase in this lumpy and unmusical fashion. However, the more I played the piece, the more this irked me, so eventually I confessed to Mark that I couldn't do justice to his piece "because ...". He was very sweet about it and admitted that he hadn't noticed, but still said, "Thank you for telling me!" Sadly, the next time he wrote for crotales a similar thing occurred, so there seemed to be no point in saying anything after that.

There seem to be fashions of instrumental effects, particularly in our department. One such was/is the suspended cymbals game, when many pieces sported not one, or two, but anything up to five suspended cymbals, sizzle or otherwise, or even three hi-hat outfits. I defy anyone to stand blindfold in a concert hall and distinguish between five such instruments (even in immediate juxtaposition with each other), particularly when used in isolation and inside orchestral texture, however veiled. Yes, use a tiny instrument and a large one in the same area, and then perhaps the results might have some discernible merit, but *not* a great splash of all sizes.

However, I am sure that the CBSO players are not unique in finding a solution to this nonsense. We would assemble the requisite number of stands and instruments, but play at the very most only three at the first rehearsal. Then it was a case of removing them gradually, one by one, after the composer had visibly checked our set-up, thus ending up with, and playing no more than, three instruments. No one ever noticed our adaptations and we were happy with less gear to pack away at the end of the sessions. This can also apply to multiple triangles: another fad. Heads in the score, they never realise.

I noted in my diary that the hire fee for percussion equipment in one particular creation by Boulez came to £5,200. Forty-eight boxes arrived for eight players to sort out, taking about an hour to achieve. The four-movement piece took ten minutes to play with over a hundred instruments on stage. I know because I counted them. Fortunately, the orchestra did not have to bear the cost of this, as we were broadcasting a London Prom and the BBC picked up the tab. Somehow this seemed to my Yorkshire soul not only excessive, but also hardly value for money. But who am I to question the creative genius of a flavour-of-the-decade composer? However, I do wonder if future generations of concert-goers will eagerly await performances of some of the stuff we give an airing to – foot tapping, finger snapping – perhaps?

Then there are the composers who have a specific sound in their mind, which they must find at all costs. Another first performance was on the music stand, this time by a very serious, inscrutable Russian, Sofia Gubaidulina. An upward metallic glissando whistle was the effect she desired, so she required three percussionists to supply this, spread out at the back of the orchestra. I was piggy in the middle.

We each had a flexatone, a novelty instrument that at the best of times is awkward to play. A flexible metal tongue is attached to a wire frame with a handle. On each side of the metal sheet is a red wooden knob on a thin springy steel rod. It is shaken, but at the same time the thumb presses the bottom of the plate, thus changing the tension for higher or lower pitch, creating an eerie, weird tremolo as the knobs strike the metal plate. Three large instruments had been hired, but the final straw was that they were required to be played with double-bass bows, stroked on the edge of the metal tongue as the pitch rose. We crept away to practise this bizarre effect in secret, as our colleagues would have gone crazy if they could have heard our pathetic and annoying efforts.

When we came to the significant solo-laden pauses in the new work, Huw, the principal, had the first go, and then it was my turn. We had been told that the composer spoke only Russian and German, but, as she was standing by the rostrum looking at us in a most disconcerting and intense manner, I strove to appear serious on failing to achieve the effect she wanted. There was a pause, and then Simon looked up at me, head inclined, eyebrows raised and a querulous look on his face. I took a deep breath, kept my face straight, and ventured, "I'm sorry, Simon, but the balls got in the way." There was a gasp, followed by a roar of laughter from the troops, whereupon he replied, after a considerable pause for effect, "There's no answer to that!" As quick as a flash, herself took us by surprise as she clawed her way through the orchestra to where we were standing and snapped the balls off all three hired instruments. Huw was incandescent with suppressed rage. Simon was jigging around on the rostrum waving his hands and bleating, "I'll pay for them! I'll pay for them!" Somehow the rehearsal was completed, but as we were packing instruments the composer once more came into our territory, bringing Simon to demonstrate to him (not us) her intentions, but also without any success whatsoever, we were relieved to observe. The premiere did not include any flexatone attempts from us and I often wondered if subsequent performers fared any better than we did with our ignominious efforts, or if other solutions were sought.

* * *

Percussionists sit in the band room gloomily drinking tea and mulling over the latest inspirations from the eager composer who presides over a massive score, agog with the afterglow of hearing his or her masterpiece for the first time. A large symphony orchestra is a splendid beast when given its head and, after all, there is limitless scope for sounds and effects, or so it would seem. Who thinks of these things in the first place?

For instance, was Sir Michael Tippett actually passing a scrapyard when someone unwittingly clouted a rusty brake drum? Did he leap over the fence, cry "Eureka!", shake the man by the hand and award him the honour of creating unique brake-drum sounds for his embryonic *Mask of Time*? Anvils are an alternative we are told. ANVILS? Certainly, anvils have a ring peculiar to themselves. For instance, eighteen are scored for in *Das Rheingold*: six small, six large, six *very* large. Bemused, we go back a few generations and walk past a blacksmith's forge with Wagner.

Yes, Bayreuth has the self-same anvils to this day, but I wonder who supplied them originally? I can imagine the percussionists drinking something somewhat stronger than tea, and shaking their heads over the vagaries of these modern composers, perhaps not appreciating, however, that Praetorius had beaten Wagner to it by a few score years, writing for anvils way back in the early seventeenth century.

Anvils do not appear as if by magic – someone has to locate them. This was most probably the responsibility of the local blacksmith who had inspired Wagner in the first place. They have to be tuned, presumably by the foundry and a tame musician, and then carted off to the opera house. A specific parking place needs to be established, as they are incredibly heavy and awkward to manoeuvre, and one presumes that any designated anvil area would need to have specially reinforced flooring. A catastrophic disappearing act mid-performance would be unacceptable and dangerous. One can imagine the groans of the stage staff when the word *Rheingold* is whispered in the corridors of Bayreuth, even at the present time. We orchestral musicians cheat nowadays, of course, and use chunks of modern scaffolding for unpitched anvils, keeping a beady eye on them in case they roll off the supporting trap tray and clatter onto the floor, thus giving the game away before, say, the 'God of Iron' in Walton's *Belshazzar's Feast*.

Many years ago, I was given the onerous task of finding two car springs. This was before the CBSO hired most of the quaint and curious instruments needed for the more eccentric contemporary works. I dutifully trooped off to a breakers yard and was sold a pair of squiggly, heavy springs. I realise now that the composer (Berio for his *Folk Songs*) probably intended the car springs to be of the leaf variety; they no doubt have a clearer ring to them, but I have yet to work out how one would have suspended them so that they could be played (attacked with a coal hammer) with any degree of accuracy or safety without gyrating wildly.

The musicians alternate between being depressed by the whole idea of supplying weird sounds, to regarding the problems as interesting challenges and a bit of a laugh. Such curiosities invariably lead to contact with the composers of the day – not always a happy experience for either party. There are times when we stand on our dignity and try to keep out of the fray: "I wasn't trained at the Royal Academy (or wherever) to chuck a load of broken glass into a skip. Nor am I going to risk my precious hearing by playing a huge gong so loud that one reaches the bounds of unconsciousness." Surely a line should be drawn somewhere.

There was one occasion when Simon warned the audience at a concert that the noise at the end of a newly hatched piece was so loud as to be dangerous. "Please feel free to put your fingers in your ears!" The ones having to create this row wore gaily coloured industrial ear-protectors at the given moment: very fetching with white tie, tails and long black. Can this be *music* we moan?

Another challenge emerged as we noted with wide-eyed astonishment that another composer desired "an evil, rubbery noise". Various colleagues overheard this gem as we trawled through fresh-from-the-copyist parts backstage. Numerous improper suggestions flowed from all four corners, but reluctantly had to be dismissed for the sake of decency. Inventive lateral thinking was duly brought into play and a bag of multi-coloured balloons purchased, blown up and the jolly bunch tethered not only to our splendid large bass drum, but also another clutch found their way onto the rostrum rail as we were rehearsing on Simon's birthday. I still treasure the memory of a tall, distinguished colleague dressed in formal white tie and tails trying valiantly to hide behind the big drum, clutching a brightly coloured balloon and attempting to squeak it in the required rhythm. Needless to say, the rest of us were helpless with laughter. Tears flowed, balloons burst, and two escaped to float gently over a bemused orchestra whilst the audience looked on with bewilderment as string players were irresistibly drawn to helping the balloons on their airy way with an occasional tap from a well-aimed bow. We do have our moments.

In one particularly inventive season, we hit metal dustbins, did NOT throw broken glass into a large bin (too dangerous), poured water from one container to another (messy), whirled thunder sticks overhead (dangerous), slashed the air with long garden canes to produce a swishing sound (also dangerous), and played knives and forks, tin cans, gongs, a bell lowered in and out of troughs of water, and oil drums (bass clef no less). And one neighbour still proudly shows her guests the battered cake tin that I had borrowed for a first performance requiring "numerous baking tins of differing pitches" [*sic*].

"Do you really want that? It sounds like cornflake packets!" This from Simon to our composer-in-residence during a pre-run of yet another attempt to titillate the ears. 'That' was a set of boo-bams: lengths of large bamboo tubes, each with a drum head and each supposed to produce a pitched sound in a chromatic sequence. Yes, he did want that sound and, yes, the instruments were hired at vast expense, got in the way, were drowned out by the rest of the orchestra and were never played again in my time with the CBSO.

As a student, I had the dubious pleasure of being a guinea-pig percussionist with a summer-school chamber group for some of the young hopefuls who were writing music in the 1950s. At least then it was admissible to say that certain inspirations were impractical, or just downright stupid. "No, I am **not** going to play a long solo triangle trill with a soft timpani stick and I don't care if you do want a visual effect. It's idiotic!" If only we could be so overtly bold now, but as dyed-in-the-wool professionals we cannot do this. Muttering darkly has to suffice.

Anyone going to a symphony concert would not necessarily imagine that water ever has anything to do with the proceedings, but this is not the case. The smallest amounts are, of course, to be found in the little water pots belonging to the oboes and bassoons. These can be seen on hot, dry concert platforms, carefully nursing reeds by appropriate instrumentalists, waiting for their moments of glory. Not so the percussion section. Apart from the minute amounts needed to blurt through bird whistles, we go in for copious quantities of the stuff. This can bring with it certain unique and interesting predicaments.

Most people remember science lessons in junior school, which brought forth some fun experiments with water, milk bottles and teaspoons: "Ping, ping, ping! Ting! Clank!" You know the sort of thing. I like to think that Erik Satie had a great night out with the lads when they started on the empty wine bottles. Then, when he wrote *Parade* in 1917, he included his jolly japes in the shape of a bouteillophone (a chromatic scale of bottles), and for extra effect added a typewriter, water splash and sirens.

It sounds simple, doesn't it? But the problems in preparation and performance are numerous, varied and very time-consuming. First, collect the requisite amount of empty bottles (no great hardship for party-going musicians) and a large, empty coat rack on which to suspend them. Then supply string, scissors, a bucket of water, a jug, a funnel and, last but not least, a tuning fork and marker pen. All this for a single piece. It is fun really, and after mopping up any unintentional puddles we stand back and survey our efforts with amusement and satisfaction. However, it was not until we had to play the same piece in a town many miles away that we realised that our well-laid plans were not infallible. In spite of filling the bottles most carefully to the marked levels, the notes varied enormously. Was it perhaps the different water, or fluctuating temperatures? Consequently, every time we play the piece we must remember to allow plenty of time for retuning.

It would not do to lose one's sense of humour entirely: indeed, as students, we were treated to fun music by Malcolm Arnold, but there are times when limits are reached. We all admire the composers who have something new to declare, so long as what they ask of us is effective. Why don't composers actually *score* for the effects they wish to represent, rather than opting out by landing the hapless percussion section with excessive exotic sound effects and visual nonsense? Oh, to be able to peer into the future. Every age had its rebels, and we realise that we must move forward and embrace the twenty-first century as instruments develop or decline and musicians take on board new ideas. Push out the bounds by all means, but do listen to the ones who actually have to make it all come true. Or, of course, the whiz kids could write some fascinating stuff for the technicians in the radiophonic workshops of the world, but this would naturally reduce the need for real life musicians, and then we would complain that we were being ousted from our jobs.

We came very close to this situation during a live television performance of a new work at the Royal Albert Hall some years ago. The composer had included handbells in his piece, which we duly supplied. Obtained from a specialist percussion hire firm, these brand-new, valuable instruments were carefully removed from their custom-made, velvet-lined cases and hung on large, skeletal, tubular metal frames for ease of playing. The clappers inside the bells are leather-covered, so we played them with cord-wound vibraphone beaters, the result being mellow and gentle but totally inaudible through the rest of the orchestra. The principal percussionist duly sampled the sound on his electronic keyboard, and when it came to our contribution to the new piece he doubled that sound through discreetly placed speakers, playing the part on the keyboard whilst *the performer* was shown playing the actual bells in close-up for the television cameras. No one was any the wiser except, of course, the percussion section and possibly the conductor. I often wonder what happened in later performances of the piece, and if the composer ever realised and appreciated how his music was being delivered to the ears of the listeners. Now it appears that we should all have a basic knowledge of state-of-the-art technology before being employed by a symphony orchestra. Whatever next we wonder?

20
Red Light District

When I was a student at the Royal Academy of Music, the very words 'recording sessions' were regarded with awe. They conjured up a mental picture of smoky studios crammed with microphones, serious men, tension and brilliant playing. Eventually, since joining the CBSO, I had the opportunity to sample the trials and tribulations of recording sessions for myself.

To begin with, there is the studio – a concert or rehearsal hall but rarely a custom-built studio. This needs to be chosen carefully, so that outside noises do not impinge on the angst-ridden hush inside. Sunday is a favoured day, as there is less everyday bustle outside, although on occasions flight paths from Birmingham Airport have been diverted to accommodate CBSO recordings at Warwick University. Large '**EMI No Entry – Recording**' notices guard every door. The world inside is more in keeping with a disaster area as the hall is strewn with newspapers, instruments, cases, coffee cups, mini chess sets, books, knitting and, in the case of our double-bass section, an enormous floor game of snakes and ladders. My best effort was to knit an entire pullover for my daughter during twenty-six hours of interminable sessions for Elgar's *Dream of Gerontius*. One is either bored or scared to death.

Every conductor has his own personal approach to setting the chosen music in concrete for all time, or at least until the disc is deleted. A piece is rarely recorded in the order one would hear it at a concert, because if there is a particularly difficult movement or section this may be left until last, or it may be 'put in the can' at the beginning of the sessions to get it out of the way. We invariably begin with a bitty rehearsal of specific difficulties and then go straight into the first take. The red light is on and we are off. Yes, there really is a red light: near the rostrum, glowing ominously and the size of half an apple. Simon Rattle is well practised in the art, preferring to record in large chunks rather than in bits and pieces. Initially, it is a case of warts and all, and no stopping for anything, although Simon made an exception with what he deemed the 'scud missiles': two massively long crescendos in the finale of Mahler's Symphony No. 2, the *Resurrection* symphony. These are exhausting but exhilarating to play, hair-raising to listen to and end with an unbelievable roar of sound. When the players are fresh, this area of the work is very exciting, but physical exhaustion soon sets in if there are no holds barred and repeats are called for.

Any soloists and chorus usually appear on the scene later in the work schedule, and it is not unknown to add specialist ingredients, such as a large church organ, at a different time altogether. For instance, Westminster Cathedral's splendid instrument became part of our recording of the *Resurrection* symphony (voted 1988 Gramophone Recording of the Year), but we supplied our own organist. During the cutting and splicing of takes in our recording of *Dream of Gerontius*, a single bar of sleigh bells was inadvertently deleted. This omission necessitated the principal percussionist making a special trip to a London studio to record the missing bar for later inclusion. Balance for dynamics can be tweaked by the back-room boys if necessary, but perfection is the player's eventual responsibility, listening through his headphones to match the previously set tempo with spot-on accuracy.

When you listen to the end of our recording of Szymanowski's *Stabat Mater* you will hear two huge bass-drum wallops. Simon had come backstage at the end of some totally unrelated, busy EMI recording sessions and announced that the back-room boys needed these two notes to be re-recorded for the Szymanowski, which we had done ages earlier. Annie had played it originally, but flatly announced, "I'm not doing it, I hurt!", handing the beater to Huw, who then, without really looking at Simon, handed it back to him, saying, "**You** do it!" So ... he did, much to the delight of the orchestra, earning himself a cheer. Our producer had no idea what was going on, and we weren't likely to tell him: just don't tell the Musicians' Union.

It is not easy to give a performance when playing to rows of empty seats in, say, an echoing, empty Watford Town Hall, after a long journey from Birmingham on a wet Sunday. However, our friends in the EMI team know this, so they would amuse themselves by putting a large polystyrene tailor's dummy behind the rostrum. We were solemnly informed that his name was Henry. This gentleman had a painted face, wore a dark blue scarf and was our audience. At Christmas time, the studio may sport additional holly and coloured lights; it all helps to keep things normal. Normal?

David Murray, our producer, always had the final word, his gentle Scottish voice coming with quiet insistence through the microphone from the control room. Simon sometimes found this hard to accept, but he had to, albeit with wry grace. Simon has a particularly colourful way with words, which offsets David's amiable humour, keeping everyone interested and amused. "Lick the sound, don't bite it!", or later, "You are giving me saccharin when what I want is at least honey."

A red telephone, perched near the rostrum, is on hand for communication between producer and conductor, occasionally shocking everyone when it rings during a piece of intense concentration. Sometimes we found ourselves recording small items that we might never have seen before, possibly as fillers for a CD. This is where the British skill of sight-reading comes to the fore. The orchestra rises to the occasion and plays with verve and freshness. Or we may have toured a piece forever and a day, it is all too familiar and we are just about sick of it. The conductor then needs to inject the orchestra with a final spark of interest before shelving it for what we hope will be a very long time.

Sometimes it is the tiny items that create unimaginable endless angst for the participants, such as the occasion when Ellie, Simon's wife, recorded Ravel's atmospheric *Shéhérazade*. This little gem takes all of seven minutes to perform, but perfection was only achieved after two hours and forty-five minutes of serious nagging and nit-picking from the rostrum – certainly not a happy experience for any of us.

Simon works like greased lightning and expects total accuracy, alertness and immediate response from his players. Such is his organisation and awareness of the time allocated that the baton often came down for the concluding chord as the second hand of the clock reached the hour, much to our amazement and amusement. After the final sweep of the fiddle bows we all stay very still, just as in the children's game of 'Statues', after which the spell is broken with a bark of laughter and relief … it is over until the next time. The final effort is for us to record some ambience - the overall sound of the empty hall.

Here are some of my diary extracts:

Thursday December 14th 1989
Watford Town Hall EMI Recording. Mahler 6 AGAIN. Aaaaaargh! I'll be glad to see the back of it.
Cold, prettily decorated with garlands of tinsel and fairy lights in a tent effect from sides to centre, unlit. Clock stopped (ticking can be heard by super-sensitive microphones).
Last movement. Four extra percs booked for off-stage stuff. Came at 2.00pm, not used until 9.00pm which ran into overtime – EMI expense. Tea/coffee on tap all day. Simon said he was doing the last movement,

"As we're all fresh!" Great shout from the players. Hmm – HE might be ... Nice to work with the usual EMI team. They're so good and very friendly. Hammer blows (cracks of doom) done with huge marquee hammer on big hollow box containing microphone, the loose lid having to be held down by one player standing on it. Even so there's a double clatter, but it didn't seem to come through the system onto tape. 9.45pm did offstage 'cows' [strings of large cowbells] with extras. Much silent giggling. Simon conducted from behind door through tiny window, we just saw hands. Extra percs cost about £1000 and they won't be used on the record.

Friday December 15th

10.00am start. Scherzo went remarkably well, didn't have time to get nervous about the xylo solos. Crossword puzzles, books, knitting, newspapers, and clarinettists learning to juggle! (Different). 26 microphones, cables everywhere in coils and snakes. Simon very particular. It's amazing that he can find so much more to do after we've played it so many times. We must be stupid. Finished 4.40pm. 4 of us stayed behind for offstage stuff. All yesterday's efforts therefore apparently redundant?

Saturday December 16th

Later start as we're getting through it well. Played through mvt by mvt. We are all so fed up and switched off. Very dangerous. Cliff has gone home with 'flu. Mark did the hammer blows with Annie and self acting as ballast on either end of the plank holding down the lid of the box. All coffee cups were removed from the area and Simon let the orchestra turn round saying, "Go on, you can have a look at them!"
Christmas lights were on. When Simon announced that they'd have to be turned off there was a great outcry. During 'ambience' I let off a toy cow sound-effect which broke the tension beautifully after the minute's silence. Roar of laughter! Never want to hear the piece again. I gave Simon a tiny cowbell from Switzerland. Seemed amused, then he showed us the photos of the new baby, Eliot. Bonny, and looking like every other baby. HOME.

When Simon's wife was expecting Eliot, Simon was determined to be there at the birth, so, as we were in the thick of recording sessions, another conductor was standing by just in case. The then novelty of a mobile phone had been placed on the conductor's music stand, and the stage was all set for modern communication. We suspected that Simon was not deeply conversant with such technology, and so awaited developments with interest. Nevertheless, when it happened, the ringing of the mobile phone during a take shook everyone to the core. We downed tools and dad took the call.

All ears were twitching, but our end of the conversation was very sparse, consisting of, "Er ...? Yes ... er, no! No, this is a mobile phone ... It's okay. Goodbye."

He switched off and looked up to see a hundred expectant faces eager to know the news: "Well?"

"Wrong number!"

If only the caller had realised what the situation was at our end – what a tale to tell in the pub!

The next day Ellie was safely delivered of Eliot. The proud father was present. John Carewe, our stand-in conductor, did a grand job and everyone was happy.

Another dimension comes into play when a live audience is present for a recording session. In spite of warnings in the programmes, announcements from the platform prior to the performance and a forest of freestanding and hanging microphones in evidence, there is predictably a phantom cougher present; extraneous noises always seeming to occur at the quietest and most difficult parts in the music. One wonders why live recordings are considered to be necessary, but then we all know that they create an indefinable edge that can lift a performance to a higher plane than the safer, manicured studio efforts. Is it raw terror, nerves, or adrenalin? Possibly a mixture of all three.

During 1991, we did many performances of Mahler's Symphony No. 7, culminating in a challenge for EMI in the form of a live recording during the Aldeburgh Festival in July. One of the difficulties for our section was two offstage cowbell passages – referred to by Simon as 'the zoo' – although The Maltings is a perfect venue for this kind of activity, as there is an interior corridor running around the perimeter of the concert hall. Rehearsal went well as the two players tiptoed off to do their stuff, clutching strings of four large bells each, taking care not to clank and give the game away. The clappers had had the Rattle treatment: muted with masking tape, otherwise they were 'too metallic'. This involved much fuss with scissors, tape, walking away to listen, more tape – too thick, too thin – just right! It was all very earnest and none of us dared to laugh. The idea was for the intermittent

Tyrolean sounds to begin close to the stage, and then magically drift away into the mountains. Fine, so far.

After two or three loudish clunks, there was nothing further from outside. Simon's eyes widened, and we firmly faced forward as the scarlet-faced wanderers returned. A little later, they slipped out once more for their next bit of high-altitude scenery. We waited with baited breath as they began again, only to stop soon after they had got into their stride. What was happening? They returned even redder in the face, not daring to look at Simon or the rest of us. It was not until the applause broke after the one-hour-and-twenty-minute performance that they told us that two of the hall stewards had stopped them with much hushing and, "There's a concert going on and you can't do that here"! Two different stewards had done the trick the second time. They must have been pretty dim not to put two and two together. Two people tiptoeing in full evening dress and clutching bells was hardly a normal interruption. Needless to say, after an explanation, the audience was requested to stay put while we re-did those two areas of the music. I suspect that they were rather thrilled to be privy to an unusual inside story.

The most difficult piece I ever had to record took a mere five minutes and twenty-nine seconds to play. I aged ten years and was convinced that my career was on the line. The Australian composer, Percy Grainger, was eccentric and somewhat idiosyncratic with regard to percussion writing. He loved a relaxed approach, gathering together all manner of instruments that could play tunes from bells to the strings inside pianos. His was a mix-and-match approach: the more the merrier. For example, if you don't happen to have a marimba, a xylophone will do. Be inventive. Use vibraphones, bells, glockenspiel, small chimes, metalophone, steel marimba – although we never discovered what the latter was – and make use of any players available.

Grainger's arrangement of Ravel's ravishing *Vallée des Cloches* employs eight percussionists with an array of instruments, and a small handful of string players. Three percussionists spend most of their time grovelling about with heads inside the piano, striking specific strings (carefully labelled with bits of paper) with softish vibraphone beaters and trying to see the music, with another player solely responsible for activating the sustaining pedal in appropriate places. He also vaguely beats time when the interior players dive for cover and lose sight of the official guy with the little white stick. Two players shared the vibraphone and there were two sets of tubular bells, a large gong and, last but not least, an enormous marimba. I had the onerous task of taming the latter, using four beaters and agonising over truly awkward intervals stretched over a wide range and both levels of notes – accidentals and 'white' notes. When listening to the music there does not seem to be a problem, but my part consisted of a pianissimo underlying burble of evenly spaced semiquavers, apparently having nothing whatsoever to do with what anyone else was playing. It sounds to be in groups of four, but on paper it was anything but, crossing bar lines and phrased in an independent manner. From the outset, everything had to be perfect, as it was not possible to cut into the music, there being overlapping sustained chords throughout. I had to look at what I was doing, as the spacing between my notes was such that any tiny misjudgement would wreck the take and we would all have to begin again. The clock was against us, and Simon became more and more 'understanding'. "Oh, don't worry, it's only a little filler. We don't have to do it really." But I knew that it was crucial to get this one right – or else.

Tension was high, but thankfully, with about sixteen minutes to go, I did a clear run, only to discover that one of the bell parts had gone awry and we had to go through the agony again. By this time, I was calm to the point of being paralysed, waiting for that red light and listening with dumb misery to the cue before my first entry. Oh, joy, it went well – teeth unclenched followed by a huge sigh to the point of tears. My reward was a bone-crushing hug and kiss from Simon. "I knew you'd do it ...! Who'd be a percussion player?!" Huw was pleased and I earned a slap on the back from James. I felt that the writing had been well and truly on the wall and, even now, when I hear that particular recording the hairs rise on my arms, my heart thumps and I find that I am holding my breath.

"I can hear a noise," said David, our producer, provoking laughter from everyone, as they thought, 'Yes, that's why we're here!' Simon stood holding the red telephone and pulled a face. "Where?" grinning at us. "It's somewhere in the first fiddles." A gentle whoop greeted this gem, and the violinists sighed and rolled their eyes. The passage was repeated, this time demanding totally focused concentration from the rest of us as we tried to hear the noise. Eventually, after every desk of players had tried out the phrase, it was discovered to be a shoulder rest moving on a dress collar near the front of the section. Those sensitive microphones were also the reason why the bass drum was parked on its own scrap of carpet, and why moving percussionists readily shed footwear. Neither could we indulge in our frequent verbal asides or rustling sweetie papers, as we knew that electronic ears were all around. Therefore, when not required by the music, we would absent ourselves from the scene – it would not do for any extraneous noises to come from redundant percussionists, but we always took the precaution of asking first if we would be needed in the near future. However, our communication with the rostrum was not always foolproof.

Working at Warwick University brought a bonus of a splendid student canteen, and so during some Rachmaninov sessions (Rach. Pag.) we made sure that we would not be needed further during the run up to the tea break. The trouble was that Simon had got his teeth into the piece and, in spite of having shooed us away, he decided to extend the take. The first we knew about it was when the orchestra manager, red-faced and spluttering, discovered us about to pay for trays full of food at the checkout till. "You're ON!" he bawled, but we were too late. As we crept in at the door, we heard from the rostrum, "That's the most unprofessional thing I've ever seen!" – forgetting that we had left the hall at his request. Then came a shuffle of feet from the orchestra, agreeing with this sentiment. ('Shuffling' is the way a bunch of orchestral musicians can indicate approval or disapproval depending on context.) We were personae non gratae with no opportunity to protest. Neither was there any way we could redeem ourselves with our colleagues, who saw us as selfish time-wasters. There were a great many stony glares, the immediate moment passed, but none of us went backstage to attempt an explanation, feeling deeply incensed by the injustice meted out for what we felt was not our crime. In spite of many protestations of our blamelessness, mention of this tiny incident rumbled on for many a long day throughout the orchestra.

* * *

At all times, we are urged to 'go for it', and adrenalin flows. There is little time to spare for nerves, as we work at speed and with 100% intensity, hoping that what we are doing sounds like *a performance* and not just a string of disjointed phrases to be glued together by the back-room boffins at a later date.

See the Appendix for a detailed fly-on-the-wall account of making a short part of a record.

20
Join an Orchestra and See the World

Whenever an orchestra travels anywhere beyond the Channel, be it to Brazil or Belgium, complex planning begins months before departure day. Paperwork takes up much of the orchestra management's time and patience: passports, visas, multiple photographs, work permits, instrument lists for Customs, travel documents for the instruments and orchestra van, and so on. Tours by road to mainland Europe pose interesting logistical problems as, of course, the van has to stick to strict speed limits, often with little time to reach the first destination, be it Helsinki or Athens, added to which special permission is needed for Sunday travel in numerous countries. Some of us still remember the police escort of howling motorbikes on arrival in congested Amsterdam during one tour: destination – the world-famous Concertgebouw.

Prior to all this, there are the inevitable orchestra meetings arranged to discuss the offers on subsistence allowances for the various countries visited. Not a simple matter. For instance, our working day is such that we can sometimes eat only late at night after performances, therefore our daily allowance has to take into account the fact that there are times when it is impossible to find anywhere to eat other than in the expensive hotel restaurants. Our Musicians' Union steward and the Chairman of the Players' Committee negotiate with the orchestra's tour manager, after which subsistence offers are reported back to the orchestra and, if deemed unsatisfactory, back they go for more meetings, more hand waving and more arguing, until eventually some kind of grudging solution is agreed upon. This is always a tediously protracted business. I well recall being in the hot seat as Chairman of the Players' Committee, negotiating for a tour of six countries, during which every single subsistence allowance became a tiresome, time-consuming wrangle. Eventually, after much toing and froing, discussions and brain bashing, I had to accept an ultimatum on behalf of the players, as further debate would have been unproductive.

After the final rehearsal at home, the moment finally arrives when the huge instrument van has to be packed. It matters not if the orchestra is flying to the other side of the world, or hopping off to Paris, the instruments have to be conveyed to the airport, or further, in the orchestra's own pantechnicon. This massive van contains basic cooking facilities and bunk beds, the cargo area temperature being strictly controlled for the instruments. With such an irreplaceable and valuable load on board, it is imperative for someone to be standing by at all times, the only respite being on board ferries. Three drivers are on duty and overnight travel is often the only solution for the longest journeys.

Nowadays, we use large, custom-made, insulated aluminium flight boxes, cosy and padded. Everything has to be listed, every bow counted, all instruments, music boxes and stands noted down. We, in our well-equipped section, start the task with vague interest, which rapidly turns to irritation and cries of, "They're not going to count every beater, surely? Just put *sticks/various*, that'll get 'em jumping at Customs!"

All instrument cases carry a unique number, and everyone receives specially printed stick-on and tie-on labels, many of which never make it as far as the first concert. Everything goes, except for perhaps the celeste, an instrument that we hire or borrow from local orchestras. We check and recheck our instrument lists, as once the orchestra's van is sealed by HM Customs there is no turning back. It is always a strange feeling to see our precious equipment finally disappear into the great maw of the van, but then we are worry-free, unlike our colleagues who constantly fret about their 'babies', although many players take responsibility for their own instruments, as smaller ones can be carried as hand luggage.

Music for each programme is assembled in numbered folders, which stack into custom-made travel boxes, each with a deep flip-up lid for easy access. For one trip to Eastern Europe, along with the concert repertoire, Beethoven's *Eroica* symphony was also included because it contains a funeral march. We had heard that Yugoslavia's President Tito was gravely ill, so … just in case. Three battered metal travelling wardrobes are dusted down for long tours on mainland Europe and wait backstage ready to receive concert dress.

The men always lose out on tours, as they have to take heavy tail suits, black evening shoes, and enough white evening shirts to see them through the trip. Some rely on the laundry services of hotels for the latter, whilst some attempt hand-washing in their rooms; others just don't care and eventually aren't nice to be near. The women are luckier, as we are able to mix and match lightweight evening wear, but, even so, it is convenient to tuck one's uniform into a dress bag and wave goodbye to it until the opening concert.

All journeys begin at predetermined places on the coach routes, be they to Leeds or Los Angeles. However, when the orchestra is off on a trip, there is a special frisson of excitement (never admitted, of course) as the coach draws up. Large luggage is manhandled into the hold, and we note that even the most inveterate car drivers are on board. The coaches are crammed, we wave to our loved ones and from now on we switch over to auto-mode, as we find ourselves standing in long queues of a hundred or more souls at airports, waiting to lug heavy suitcases off the luggage carousels, climbing on and off coaches, and then suffering more congestion as we wait for hotel keys, daily subsistence money and the lifts. 'All we like sheep ...' little snatches of Handel spring readily to the lips. We traipse along hotel corridors, up and down lifts and countless stairs, eventually landing in our own personal space with scarcely time to unpack a toothbrush before we are off again searching for the perfect eating place. Then onward to the concert hall armed with many more queries. We never think for ourselves in our switched-off, neutral mode, driving the orchestra manager crazy with constant pestering.

On one particular trip, every member of the orchestra had to have a number of passport-style photographs for East European visas, so a photographer was booked, time was scheduled after a truncated rehearsal and a long queue of players waited their turn patiently, names being ticked off the list by a vigilant secretary. "Smile please!" There had been a polio scare some weeks prior to our departure date, so everyone was also obliged to have precautionary vaccine jabs. String players fussed mightily about which arm might swell, while others looked on with outward disbelief but secret understanding.

When the orchestra travels further afield, our platform staff sometimes need to go ahead to confirm the finer details of onward travel. In America and the Far East, our chaps are more in a consultative role than in the physical labour team. Unions are strong, therefore our men are not allowed to drive or shift instruments. These rules inevitably lead to less arduous work schedules for our home team, and it is hoped that the local workforce will be extensive and eager to please. For instance, we became very familiar with the sight of a tiny blonde lass hopping down from the cab of the massive articulated truck used to transport everything, when she appeared as the driver on more than one trip to the USA, causing much comment and admiration from the orchestra – especially the lads.

As travel is so much part and parcel of a musician's working life, it is inevitable that most of us have become used to, or possibly immune to, the rigours of new experiences, destinations, customs and deprivations; adapting and coping throughout long or short periods away from the familiarities of home. There is no time to be homesick, as once the initial novelty wears off we know full well that we are not on holiday, and certainly not tourists, regarding our travels from a totally different standpoint.

Over the years, I have fined down my personal requirements for civilised touring. First comes a sturdy suitcase with wheels, one that I can sit on. My golden rule is that I must be able to handle all of my luggage in one go, as it is imperative to check personally to make sure that one's main suitcase goes onto the coach or train, even if this means hanging around in snow or rain. Basic overnightery goes into hand luggage, with a book (essential), iron rations, earplugs, sleep mask, and 'Travel Scrabble' for long, tedious flights.

As far as I am concerned we are *working*, so it is crucial to conserve energy whenever possible, let the management manage, and go with the flow. Thinking for oneself is a thing of the past: we move from place to place, concentrating on the necessities and focusing on our *raison d'être* – concerts. I have lost count of the countries, cities and towns I have played in during many, many tours of Europe, but hope that I have not become blasé about the wide-ranging experiences encountered along the way.

A typical European tour was in late summer 1996 - festival time. This was hard on the heels of two London Proms, stretching the away-from-home situation even further in spite of two free days before leaving the country. As usual, I tried to capture some of the flavour of a tour in diary form at the time:

Music festivals in Switzerland; Denmark; Germany; Belgium; Holland.
Conductor: Simon Rattle Soloist: Alfred Brendel
Our immediate observation on seeing the schedule for the 10 day trip was that we would have to cope with five different currencies during the trip ... roll on the Euro!
Birmingham to Freiburg, Germany.
We flew five times in our very own chartered aircraft, getting to know the crew and having long chats with the pilot, who initially unnerved us somewhat by coming into the cabin to meet everyone, while the plane flew merrily on its way on autopilot. Five flights and many coach journeys clocked up a total of approximately 2,500 miles.
First duty call: Freiburg on the arrival day. A familiar programme. Perhaps as well as we only had a short rehearsal in which to settle down in the brand new Konzerthaus.
Berlioz - Overture, **Le Corsaire***; Ravel - Ballet,* **Mother Goose***; Tippett -* **Fantasia Concertante on a theme of Corelli***; Haydn - Symphony No. 88 in G.*

This was received very warmly by a large audience, a good start to a hectic 10 days. 102 coach-miles later on the following day, we were in Switzerland for two concerts at the Lucerne Festival. A lakeside venue with blue skies, glinting water, and many tourist steamers; a real holiday atmosphere. Here we discovered that the Kunsthaus was due to be demolished to make way for bigger and better things, the CBSO having the dubious honour of playing the final concert there. The first programme was the same as the previous night, apart from Brendel playing Beethoven's Piano Concerto No. 5 instead of the Ravel. This brought in the customers in droves, as expected.

However, not everyone was required for this adapted programme so a number of us found time to enjoy the sights around Lucerne; sunny trips on the lake and novelty cable car and mountain railway jaunts to take in the breathtaking panoramic snow-topped views. Pete, our cor anglais player, went off on his bike, a personal tour treat. He always travels with folding bike and armed with detailed plans, so invariably has a cycling adventure or two to recount to the less active.

The second programme consisted of Messiaen's **Chronochromie** and the massive Bruckner Seventh Symphony. We percussion players were intrigued to find ourselves half hidden in a long curving 'waterfall' of waxy white orchids along the back of the stage; not recommended for hay fever sufferers, but lovely to look at. The serious Swiss audience was less than enthusiastic about Messiaen's **Chronochromie**, but they applauded wildly enough after the Bruckner, now fast becoming a party piece.

Next stop in Denmark's second city, Aarhus, for the Festival there. As one of the string players observed seeing familiar fast-food outlets and well-known shops, "It's just like Middlesborough!" We all enjoyed an informal and enthusiastic reception after the performance, finding ourselves in a unique small marquee complete with bar, dance floor and stained glass windows.

On to Bremen which brought the best remark of the tour – straight from the heart. Our principal bass player was heard to exclaim, "I've died and gone to heaven!" when we eventually reached the next scene of action. He is also an enthusiastic qualified pilot, so was totally taken aback by the completely surrealist experience in store. We found ourselves playing in a **gigantic** aeroplane hangar alongside a colossal A340 Air Bus. The cathedral-like resonances blurred every sound, and pauses were non-existent, but the large audience loved it all. They had had their own adventure too, being ferried across the river to the back of beyond to attend their own Bremen Festival concert, arriving late in a flurry of excitement and chatter. The concert was very well received, the bemused orchestra eventually departing back to reality and the delights of our splendid Bremen hotel, starving hungry and much later than anticipated. Everyone has personal tour highlights; mine was seeing friends on the free day. A forty-five minute pause to change trains on a long journey through the flat lands of northern Germany brought a frantic brief meeting with an ex-au-pair; coffee, talk, family news and photos. Then on to Berlin to stay with other dear friends, more non-stop chatter. The orchestra flew to Berlin the next day, having had the one official free day in Bremen.

The Berlin concert in the Philharmonie (home of the Berlin Philharmonic Orchestra) was splendid with a full house and wonderful warm reception. Messiaen was a triumph and my soloist percussion colleagues were cheered to the rafters along with the woodwind and string soloists. A standing ovation greeted the end of a most thrilling Bruckner 7, after which Simon eventually came back onto the stage to more thunderous applause when most of the orchestra had left. My Berlin friends were duly converted to Bruckner. After the concert it was time for a number of our players to catch up with news and gossip from friends and colleagues in the Berlin orchestra. This is one of the perks of touring, and it is the way that the worldwide orchestra grapevine is kept green and thriving. Wherever we go it seems that someone knows someone in the locality.

Another flight, this time to the Low Countries and another very different but memorable event. Our three large touring coaches were diverted on their way into Brussels and eventually became so entangled in tiny side streets that we thought that they would never be able to extricate themselves. However, we had not reckoned on the ingenuity of the drivers. Out they got and with no more ado uprooted the temporary road signs, then with infinite patience manoeuvred the huge vehicles round impossible corners to the admiring cheers of the occupants.

St Baafs Cathedral in Ghent was our next stop. Not many places to eat, so the wise ones had taken nosebags and everyone struggled to keep warm in the mediaeval splendour. However, we had a lovely audience once more, and the wonderful building with its unique and special ambience more than made up for mere human discomfort.

The long coach trip next day to Amsterdam was a time for catching up on *sleep for many of us. Destination: the now familiar Concertgebouw. This was our final concert in a hall, which as ever came up to expectations (not least the creaky floor and no room to play). The shoebox shape generates a very fine acoustic, strings in particular sounding warm and rich. A fitting finale to our tiring, but most successful mini-tour of Europe.*

No posh hotel after this concert - straight to the airport, and after a long wait for a slot for our charter flight we left the empty airport well after midnight for Birmingham, taxi queues, home and families.

* * *

Naturally, we all have memories of very special occasions during our many journeys. A favourite for me was when we performed in the Alhambra gardens in Granada, which inspired de Falla to write *'Nights in the Gardens of Spain'*. We played outside in a palace courtyard, surrounded by pillared and arched cloister-like walkways, swept by swallows seeking insects during the rehearsal for Beethoven's *Choral Symphony*. After rehearsal, the gardens were closed to the public, so we were privileged to enjoy the filigree Moorish architecture privately, softly golden in the late afternoon sun and reflected in tranquil pools. Gently arching, criss-crossing jets of water were transformed by the sunlight into myriads of iridescent rainbow crystals, and from shady pathways it was possible to overlook the jumble of pantiled terracotta roofs far below in the ancient town. A formally dressed, bejewelled audience gently drifted in for the 10.30pm start, the air was balmy and fragrant, and I had had a wonderful day discovering the most fabulous gardens imaginable. Perfection came with the bats stitching stars to the deep purply-blue sky whilst the sublime music reached out over the perfumed, shadowy gardens. Truly spellbinding.

It is only too easy to forget to arrange a meeting time with one's friends, or to miss everyone in the initial rush to get to the anonymous hotel rooms for a preliminary unpack. However, no one is left to wander strange streets alone, and so, true to form, we percussionists would often take stray players or even conductors under our wing, as was the case on a prestigious visit to Leipzig.

Sunday was free until late afternoon, so a small group had arranged to visit the St Thomas Church in the morning to pay homage to my hero Johann Sebastian. I was happily deadheading a huge trough of pansies outside the hotel when Simon appeared and asked, "What are you guys up to today?"

When I told him, he looked a little wistful and then asked if he could join us. "Yes, sure!" He is really good company 'off the box'.

Off we went, arriving at the large, simple, unadorned Lutheran church just as someone let fly with a gutsy rendering of one of Bach's organ Preludes & Fugues. The five of us plonked down in a pew, listening to what sounded to me like the organist playing solely for himself, no holds barred. After the underlining of the final few phrases with a splendid pedal note, we all let out our breaths as he finished with a very satisfying cadence. I innocently remarked, "Oh, why is it that a pedal note is so gratifying?" Quick as a flash, Simon said, with a grin, "Because it's straight to the crotch!" Such a way with words, but so true!

Leipzig University's museum has a fine collection of ancient instruments, so, nothing ventured, we found ourselves hammering on the door at about midday. The woman curator was less than pleased to see us, announcing in no uncertain terms that the doors would shut in an hour, as she grudgingly led us up the stairs to the small, beautifully kept collection. Simon and Malcolm, the orchestra's pianist, immediately latched on to the fact that some of the instruments did not have protective glass over their keyboards, and therefore correctly assumed that these particular items were in good playing condition and as such were sometimes to be heard at specialist recitals *in situ*. After much hand waving, smiling and fractured German, we managed to persuade Frau Curator to let us to play them. I was thrilled to realise that playing Scarlatti on an original instrument was far simpler than on a larger piano keyboard. So obvious, but something that had never previously occurred to me. Likewise, Simon played the first few bars of Beethoven's *Moonlight Sonata* on a fortepiano, excitedly observing that he now understood why each bar had pedal markings, whereas on a modern instrument with better sustaining powers this could make the music sound blurred and indistinct. I ached to play the glass harmonica and we all loved the little cavalry kettledrums on their bird-feet tripod stands, at the ready to tiptoe across the wooden floor. All too soon we had to leave, however, forcing ourselves to sample the delights of a coffee house (the maestro's treat: he insisted) before returning to the real world again.

A trip to Bratislava on the border between Austria and what was Czechoslovakia gave me much food for thought many years ago when I innocently asked the young interpreter, "What is the difference between your orchestras and ours?" Yes, we were in Eastern Europe, but as we all spoke the same music language I had imagined that we all thought in the same way.

But, no. The immediate response was just two words: "You smile!" Then, after a small pause, looking at some of our laughing fiddle players crammed in a corner, giving gifts of strings and tapes to wide-eyed Czech colleagues, she continued, "And you touch each other." My blood ran cold as she finally added, "I can see the lights of Vienna from my apartment window, but know that I'll never be able to go there." Maybe now she can?

* * *

The Far East. Exotic Japan. When we heard about a proposed visit in 1987, there was every reaction from dumb amazement to deep gloom as none imagined that we would ever go so far afield. We were steadily working our way through all the capital cities of Europe, but Japan was another world. As I usually tried to learn a little of the languages of the countries we visited, I did no more but borrow language tapes from the library and slogged at a number of useful phrases whilst alone in the car. I was determined to make the most of this experience. We eventually visited Japan on four occasions during my time in the orchestra.

The journey was seventeen-and-a-half hours long: exhausting and tedious, our arrival being nine hours ahead of GMT. Our heads were stuffed full of advice, scraps of language and curiosity about what was to come. The top-class Tokyo hotel was staffed by courteous, smiling and bowing English speakers, but I had to have a go. After settling in my luxurious, anonymous room, I took myself to the specially set up CBSO desk and asked in what I hoped was flawless Japanese, "Please do you sell stamps?" After a gasp of surprise and a very deep bow, I was rewarded with, "Your Japanese is *very* good!" I learnt later that I spoke the language with a posh accent, my well-chosen sentences proving to be extremely useful throughout our four Japanese tours.

Later, it was possible to add more vocabulary to my odd collection when asked by a group of Japanese ladies about Simon's rehearsal techniques. I carefully trotted out my usual reply to this question, including the observation that "he has ears like a bat"! This was received with much high-pitched tittering through politely covered mouths, after I managed to mime a bat and its squeaks. "That is, 'Komiri no mimi'" (this and subsequent spellings are phonetic) said one lady. Nothing daunted, I found Simon later to give him the short sentence and the challenge of getting a translation from Jum, our ever-smiling Japanese orchestra manager. Unfortunately, Simon's pronunciation proved to be less than perfect, so I did the honours for Jum. He laughed and, after translating, added, "*We* say, 'Djee jo ku mimi' - ears from hell!" So there: now we know!

Everything was totally strange and I hated feeling so foreign. Schoolchildren often stopped to stare and try out "Hello" with added giggles, watching avidly as we wrote out signatures for them in our, to them, curious script. And we were frequently rescued by kind passers-by as we stood trying to sort out city maps, as it was impossible to hazard a guess at the meaning of any of the street signs. Hall notices (loos, for instance), train directions in the underground, and so on, were total non-starters, but Jum kindly made pictorial notices for us, complete with colourful matchstick people, arrows and flags.

Thankfully, we discovered that indecipherable menus were no problem, as every restaurant and smallest noodle bar had very convincing plastic models of the food on offer in the window. Indeed we were always invited to 'window' with much smiling and waving of hands, whereupon we would stand and discuss the many choices, putting in our orders out there on the pavement. Chopsticks were a skill that we soon got the hang of, although one violinist always insisted on using his own knife and fork wherever we went. I must confess that, in spite of being able to handle two thin xylo beaters in each hand perfectly well, the business of eating slippery noodles with a pair of short, thin plastic or wooden sticks seemed incredibly awkward and plain crazy to me. However, some of us discovered the novelty of eating French fries with chopsticks – somewhat simpler than noodles.

It was possible to buy packed picnic-style meals in neat raffia-tied cardboard boxes, the interior goodies looking like a small art exhibition. Mostly they were pleasing only to the eye, however, and often a big disappointment to the hunger. One would explore the delights, or mysteries, of layers of light batter hiding tiny scraps of indefinable protein, mainly fish – raw or otherwise, or possibly 'sweet and sour cellophane' – in reality very tasty seaweed, thin shreds of fiery pickled ginger, anonymous, brightly coloured, syrupy offerings, and ever-present sticky white rice, which is used as a tool to glue bits of food together to convey it to the mouth; something I never really got the hang of, hating glutinous rice ever after. I secretly longed for and dreamed of home-made brown bread, rather than the polystyrene plastic-wrapped horrors that passed for sandwiches there. Oh for a piece of tasty cheese and peppery watercress … but then the grass is always greener.

Greater Tokyo is an overcrowded, congested concrete nightmare, with a current population of more than 20 million (2004). Highly disciplined pedestrians neatly avoid cyclists weaving in and out along the pavements, and roads are built in layers one above the other, making Birmingham's Spaghetti Junction seem like a country crossroads. Land in Japan's capital city was priced at £9,000 per square inch/2.54cm in 1987.

The first thing one noticed in the hotel rooms was earthquake instructions in many languages: 'Stay in your room, open the door', and there was a significant sturdy hand-torch forever on charge nearby. Japanese cities look messier than their Western counterpoints, as all power cables are looped on poles high in the air alongside the roads. Water, sewerage, gas pipes and suchlike are also above ground. This is serious earthquake territory. We were told that people become used to living with the ever-present threat; one lady saying that once her television set slid off the sideboard into the wall and that water slopped out of the toilet. Seeing steam rising through vents in the roads and a grumbling volcano across a tranquil bay in one of the towns we visited somehow brought the reality even nearer. Little children had fun, however, as they dashed through the warm steam rising through prettily designed iron grids set in the pathways of public gardens.

The beginning of long-distance tours (USA, South America, Japan, Hong Kong) is always the same. We are given two days in which to overcome jet lag, after which the first concert is often a matinee performance or we find ourselves playing for drowsy students in a college or university concert hall. After initial hectic sightseeing, one is convinced that the jet lag demon has been conquered. The first concert says otherwise, however. I always feel totally disembodied, curiously euphoric, incredibly tall and utterly bemused by all the black dots seemingly miles away on the white paper before my eyes. This poses real problems for the conductor too – faced by an unresponding, zonked-out orchestra – especially as tour programmes inevitably contain challenging, difficult pieces. It was only when we boarded the aircraft in America, which was to take us on to Japan for the second part of a very long tour, that I realised that we were into jet lag territory for the second time in one trip. Then, of course, we eventually returned home, having circumnavigated the globe, to encounter yet more jet lag. In fact, I suspect that I never really got to grips with this throughout the whole of that particular trip, after which it took another two weeks before I felt as though I was on terra firma and back to normality once more.

Hospitality is high on the list for visitors to Japan, as we discovered at our first and consequent rehearsals in halls large and small. There was always a wide choice of drinks available, with plastic cups and paper napkins; all very civilised and a godsend in the heat and humidity. Bottled water, fruit juices and large catering-sized flasks of hot or iced tea and coffee were provided without charge. If the halls were lacking in facilities, we discovered that the hotels were required to supply these lifesavers, often adding biscuits, rice crackers or fresh fruit as an extra bonus. Everyone was very impressed and grateful for such thoughtfulness.

A pleasurable aspect of all this travel is when one can meet real people: friends, relatives, sponsors, audience members, colleagues from other orchestras and, as in the case of Tokyo, the percussion tutor from one of the main music colleges.

Annie and I were on our best behaviour, bowing in greeting and smiling with dignity, as befitted our status as visitors with a respected orchestra. So we were somewhat nonplussed when we were asked, "What do you play?" After a slight and puzzled pause, we replied, "Er ... percussion." "Yes, but *what* do you play?" After a replay of question and answer, we confessed that we did not understand what the professor was driving at. Then it dawned on us that he was talking about actual instruments, and proffered our nonchalant confirmation of, "Oh, cymbals, bass drum, snare drum ... well, everything and anything." Shock, horror! The professor then told us that *his* young ladies were only allowed to play tuned percussion and perhaps a little bit of triangle or tambourine. All the rest of the instruments were for the chaps, being far too unfeminine for the likes of well-brought-up and delicate Japanese girls. We then realised why so many fine female marimba players hail from Japan, although even playing this huge instrument could have been at odds with the small stature of many of the dainty women we met. We were told by a young student that any girl growing taller than the tiny average would never be married, as the men only like petite, delicate women.

Everything in Japan is prohibitively expensive, but as we seemed to be swimming in yen we were able to switch on to *toy money mode*. For instance, it did not do to convert the cost of four teas and four bits of cake to familiar currency, on the occasion of meeting two pretty music students in the hotel lobby. Who cares? £40 was a snip; after all, we were in an exorbitantly high-priced five-star hotel. Floral arrangements were lavish and there were very comfortable chairs everywhere: just like home. However, even as a hotel resident, I was relieved of £8.50 for my daily swim in the hotel pools, part of an imaginative swimming complex, and this was in 1987. But allowances are for spending, and I, for one, certainly did not intend to return home with surplus yen, although some always made a point of making a profit on the allowances for any tour, whilst others spent theirs like water and were forever standing at the cash machines with furrowed brows.

Annie was always the treasurer whenever a group of us foraged for food. As soon as the first orders were chosen, she would make columns of the prices for each individual on a scrap of paper. Somehow, in spite of all our vigilance, there would usually be a great argument at the presentation of the bill, something one would never do in any other circumstance when eating out. But we were there to work and not to be fobbed off by imaginative accounting in a restaurant; we *had* to eat. Any surplus coins (shrapnel) were usually left as a tip, much to the waiter's dismay, the paper stuff being saved for the next hunting and gathering effort.

In 1991, the orchestra was once more on track for the Far East, but this time there was a serious problem. Our departure coincided with the start of the Gulf War, and we found ourselves embroiled in meetings to discuss the pros and cons of our safety, and the wisdom or not of leaving the UK. This was a dilemma for the management, who categorically announced that anyone not turning up for the flight would be in breach of contract, and therefore would be given notice. (One positive result from all this angst and wrangling is that it is now possible for a musician to be released from a foreign tour without loss of earnings, on the grounds of conscience, domestic situation or health.) Arguments raged back and forth, but time was of the essence and no compromise was possible. So, of course we set off; after all, it doesn't take a mere WAR to stop a CBSO tour. The flight plan had been changed and we found ourselves flying over Russia, Tibet, Tashkent and Samarkand: all very romantic; a pity it was dark.

Hong Kong first stop, where all I could think about was the long-overdue meeting planned with Barry, my cousin, who I had not seen for over twenty years. As children we were very close, but I had a niggling anxiety that we would perhaps not recognise our older selves. I need not have worried, though, as bone-crushing hugs and kisses said it all. After that we hardly drew breath. An evening's wonderful hospitality for myself and three orchestra friends began what was to be a memorable visit to a most vibrant city, which, in spite of being totally foreign, was full of little clues of British occupation, i.e. double-decker buses, recognisable public telephones, red pillar boxes, driving on the left, a familiar-looking post office and English as the official language.

Overcoming jet lag was a pleasure on this trip as the Hong Kong

Philharmonic Ladies' Committee took us under their wing, looking after everyone right royally. It was all too easy to become used to chauffeured, glossy Jaguar limousines, excursions on the water, picnics and fabulous receptions. And I think that we all loved to rummage around in the noisy markets and overcrowded street stalls. We drooled at designer labels, glittering jewellery, sportswear, and every kind of electronic gadget and device. Buying silk for daughter Fiona was at the top of my list, so I had reason enough to explore every nook and cranny, goggling at birds in cages, bamboo scaffolding on the tallest of skyscrapers, snakes in jars, solemn street musicians, intricate and realistic bamboo grasshoppers, fortune-tellers, rickshaws for tourists, and stalls of totally unrecognisable food everywhere.

The first rehearsal came as a shock to the system, but this was soon tempered for the percussion section as we were welcomed by colleagues from the HK Philharmonic and taken for an unforgettable dim sum feast in a smart restaurant near the concert hall. Tales were told, gossip exchanged and experiences compared, as we tasted our way through what seemed like hundreds of tiny treats, fresh from the kitchen. All too soon, we said goodbye and thought guiltily of how we never offer this kind of hospitality for foreign orchestras visiting Birmingham. This is how worldwide orchestral links are kept alive and kicking. Every time we set foot in a foreign country, there seems to be at least one memorable contact awaiting us, or ex-colleagues eager to pass on the latest news from their neck of the woods.

An exquisite little girl was waiting backstage at the end of the first concert; a diminutive dot dressed in a sugar-pink tutu, swamped by an enormous bouquet of flowers. As soon as the applause began to level out, she was sent on to twinkle through the violins and present her flowers to a delighted Simon. When she smiled shyly, the orchestra was enchanted to see that two front teeth were missing and secretly wondered what the going rate was from tooth fairies in Hong Kong.

Every morning the *South China Times* was pushed under the bedroom door, so for once it was possible to check up on the reviews of our concerts. I noted that the critic thought that our *Daphnis and Chloë* was "positively licentious … full of unalloyed violent sensuality and pre-nuptial tension". Well! This performance was described by the critic as "an ode to copulation". It is perhaps as well that he did not know that earlier on that week Simon had said in the 'Dance Profane' section, "It only works when everyone's completely lost. I don't care *where* you play!"

On the other hand, Messiaen's massive *Turangalîla* was a more difficult

312

piece for some of the audience, who walked out during our efforts. Simon goes to the extreme of pianissimo, so much so that in one place some of the listeners imagined that we had come to a break in the music and began coughing. More observations from the critic: "After delivering a fulsome, complex account of orgiastic *Turangalîla*, the audiences were in little doubt that they had heard one of the loudest orchestras on the planet." I noted in my tour diary that afterwards, "I couldn't face Hitchcock's *Psycho* on TV, *Turangalîla* was quite enough for one night, thank you!"

The final day was free, so Annie, oboist Karen and I went by dusty double-decker bus to the New Territories: what an adventure!

Beyond the outskirts of the city, we ground our way with crashing gears through areas of huge factories by the waterfront, container bases, and monstrous high-rise blocks of flats covered with washing hanging out of hundreds of windows. Everywhere was drab, dirty, untidy and very depressing. Every scrap of open water, whether sea, pond or river, was filthy, thickly polluted and garbage-strewn. One wonders how the earth can sustain this kind of abuse. The winding road was an engineering splendour, however, built on the side of steep hills supported with massive concrete buttresses and affording magnificent views. Our trip was well worth the effort, if only to see this.

The first stop for us was Yuen Long bus station, where we hailed a taxi to take us onward to Lok Ma Chau, the last tiny village before crossing into Communist China. A modest £3 took us for half an hour through narrow country lanes in the hot sun, with tatty banana trees at the side of the road, scummy pools of dark, evil water and broken-down, dusty houses. The whole region is very dry. We were dropped by the small souvenir stalls at a lookout point, where one can stand and gawp at Red China – just down there, over the rice paddies. Old dears in charge of the stalls persisted in trying to sell us something, of course. Annie made the big mistake of vaguely touching things, saying, "Lovely ... Oh, how pretty ... SO unusual", and so on, thus being pounced on at every breath. Karen and I wandered away and left her to beat them off.

Mountains blurred into the distance, fronted by modern industry and a huge bridge leading from the wide trunk road to an obvious border-crossing resplendent with fluttering red flags. Below us was an area of marshland divided into sections, each with a spattering of white ducks being reared for some of the millions of mouths in Hong Kong. Smallholdings under intense cultivation were all around, but one wondered where the ubiquitous fresh broccoli and myriads of salads came from for the big city. We were told that fresh milk was delivered every day from China. Now, there's a thought.

When a little local bus hove into view, we hopped on, much to the driver's consternation. Throughout the whole day, we had seen no other Europeans except at the lookout point, so of course stuck out like sore thumbs. However, a few grins and nods saw us on our way back to Yuen Long, the small town where we stopped to find food, after being waved off by the friendly, smiling driver and passengers. To my shame, I didn't even know how to say 'thank you' in Chinese.

It was then over the road to a huge restaurant full of families and businessmen, as by this time we were starving. We were delighted to receive iced water and a huge pot of tea (China, of course) as soon as we sat at the table. Throughout our travels we keep a tally of disgusting dishes on menus, but this came well out on top with 'Frog boiled in oil'. In spite of some fractured English translations, we had great difficulty in ordering. I ended up by self-consciously miming a chicken, much to everyone's amusement, but could not begin to think how to ask for rice or noodles. New sights and sounds kept us intrigued. For instance, we were very disconcerted to see tiny children wielding chopsticks with great skill, and watched with curiosity as three old dears constantly perambulated around the customers with trolleys stacked high with steamer baskets. As we were waiting for our mysterious order to appear, one of these ladies came by and, with a flourish, swiftly put a dish consisting of deep-fried chicken's feet (minus claws) on our table. These were accepted with total consternation. Annie tried to hide them behind the menu holder, but to no avail. Total removal was not an option, so we had to live with the sight of them, wondering how on earth anyone could possibly eat such things. We learnt later that they are a great delicacy. I am so glad that we managed to keep our faces straight and hope that we did not cause offence by our less than enthusiastic response to the undoubtedly kind gesture. Our meal, when it arrived, was memorable for its excellence: freshly cooked chicken and cashews, king prawns and sweet, succulent walnuts topped with perfect sprigs of steamed broccoli.

Another taxi took us to an impossible-to-find, claustrophobic, tiny walled village where we took photos, and became tourists, eventually landing exhausted back in Hong Kong to hear that our football team had beaten the HK Phil by five goals to three.

The end of our sojourn in this electrifying city was a magnificent meal in a fabulous private house on The Peak. A few randomly chosen players from the orchestra and some of the Ladies' Committee were honoured guests, alongside management and sponsors. This is the life, I thought, as I stood on the patio clutching a glass of champagne and looking with wonder at the breathtaking sight of Victoria Sound twinkling far below. We were above the flight path into the airport, so we were able to see the tiny toy planes taking off and landing. In fact, we realised that tomorrow we would be down there. At our departure for the last ferry, our hostess very kindly gave me a heavy coffee-table cookbook from the HK Philharmonic – food for thought, certainly.

When we arrived in Tokyo, it was to discover that all Americans had pulled out of the hotel, which was next door to the American Embassy, and that the streets were full of riot police waiting silently in armoured vehicles parked in side roads, the Gulf War by this time being in full swing. We were nowhere near restaurants or shops, so had to rely on sustenance from our luxurious base.

This was the only tour on which I felt truly homesick, attempting to counteract this by having an enlarged photograph of a tranquil Scottish loch prominently displayed in my room. Family photos were strictly for private viewing, however, being closely guarded in my capacious black handbag. The chambermaid tidied my personal space every day to such a degree that I became childishly irritated, immediately scattering my belongings around when she had done her duty. I hated to be sucked into the Japanese anonymity of everything being just so, smiling blandness, bowing and scraping. However, I managed to get myself out of this negative way of seeing our hosts as soon as we were presented with waxy white orchids after one concert. Life took on a rosier view when I could see real flowers reflected in the room mirror; a lovely contrast to the endless, hideous concrete, and armed riot troops outside.

Once more we were looked after by dear Jum, who excelled himself at one juncture when the orchestra had to catch the last bullet train to Osaka after the concert. As Tokyo is so overcrowded, it would have taken forever to reach the busy railway station by road, so it was decided to move everyone by the underground system. The train left at 9.00pm, but our early evening concert was due to end only one hour earlier. An enthusiastic audience raved at the end of the scheduled programme, and so Simon did no more but call for an encore. My mind was running like a rat in a cage, wondering how on earth we would pack all the instruments, get out of the building, cross the road to the underground, find the correct stop to disembark and change to the main-line station: panic, panic. To this day, I cannot remember a thing about the encore. All the main luggage had long gone by road, so we *had* to catch that train. At the end of the concert, people rushed off in small groups as we frantically packed all of our equipment and instruments. Oh ye of little faith! Jum was organised to the last man. All we had to do was to follow borrowed hotel staff holding little flags in the air - "This way!" - and everyone was given a pictorial map. We pushed through the smiling crowds at the stage door and found our way to the crowded train without any problems and with time to spare. Trying to board a bullet train with 106 other people in one minute was no picnic, but board it we did, and to everyone's amazement no one was left behind. Boxed meals appeared, delivered by smiling, bowing girls, coffee followed and arrival in Osaka was before midnight, on the dot, as scheduled. What a relief! The final Tokyo concert was so special that I wrote about it in my diary as soon as I had returned to my room:

February 7th 1991Mahler 9 Suntory HallTokyo
Off to Suntory, so nice to be able to dress at the hotel. Near capacity audience.
Just Mahler 9 tonight (who needs more?)
The leader was sent on, then we waited for a good five minutes before Simon appeared. I thought straight away that he looked very odd: wild with an ashen face, hair tight and frizzed as if someone had been at it, seeming to be a wax image of himself. NOT himself as we know him, but in that ghastly manic, frenetic mood with staring, round, pinprick eyes in the back of his head. Terrifying.
Definitely on another planet, he wasn't THERE or seeing us at all, but was with Mahler and somewhere else. Like a crazed demon – agitated, gesturing and mouthing. The whole effect was that of a tight watch spring, such tension and concentration (all from memory of course): it is totally frightening when he gets like that.
After the first mad movement, with the orchestra hanging on with terror, he stood, blinked, and then mopped his face with a white hanky. (At last someone has told him that it doesn't do to wipe his forehead with his coat sleeve like a small child.) He was still tense and white-faced, but very expressive, as always. Oh, I'm so glad I wasn't at the receiving end of some of those grisly death rays!
It's very difficult when he gets carried off like this, as the beat gets very wayward with huge circles and wild swoops. It was the music all the way,

not the players – we just weren't there for him, he was a man possessed. Clare, the first horn, played like an inspired angel. Magical.

The last movement was TOO MUCH. Such raw emotion, he bared his soul, and I for one wouldn't have been surprised if he'd dropped down in a faint or worse. Unbearable. It is not a piece I'm totally crazy about, but I was choked by the time it came to my last entry and I could hardly see him for tears of I know not what ... fear? Scary! I NEVER want to play like that ever again.

He held that stunned audience (they knew) for 27 long seconds of total silence at the end, then the applause broke and he came back to us. My first thoughts were, "Barking mad!" He sent his bouquet up through the orchestra to Clare, much to her embarrassment and consternation.

A human being can take just so much on the knife-edge and I thought that he was pretty close this time. We came off that platform not saying anything, but with eyes speaking volumes. Karen (2nd oboe) caught up with me as we mingled quietly back stage. "What was that all about? What is going on? I was scared!" So it wasn't just me. George and Freda Jonas came back stage and Freda said almost the same thing ... the charged atmosphere was palpable, even out front. I just don't know how Simon can come down to earth after such an experience – how does he talk to anyone? I just wanted to slink away in silence, get drunk, kill myself: something simple!

After the concert Simon attended a reception and I understand from Karen that he behaved perfectly normally (whatever that is). She said that she couldn't cope at all.

Please God, never again

One newspaper commented: "It was highly-wrought, emotionally uncomfortable and an achievement of the highest scale."

* * *

In March 1988. I noted in my diary:

This is the BIG one. After all the anticipation and subdued excitement departure day comes finally, with last minute apprehension and nervous diarrhoea.

317

Our destination was Los Angeles, for the beginning of our very first tour of the States; two more would follow during the next few years. I wrote tour diaries, took scores of photographs, dragged around with a cumbersome video camera and collected mementos right, left and centre, in an attempt to capture every possible impression of these unique, mind-bending journeys. In the fullness of time, highlights come to mind as memories of our many tours inevitably fade, but America was always special.

Neon signs announcing 'Welcome to Simon Rattle and the City of Birmingham Symphony', lofty palm trees and the hottest March day on record greeted us, the sun trying to clear the famous LA traffic pollution haze, exacerbated by hectic multi-lane freeways. As usual, we were granted two days in which to overcome jet lag, as we were now functioning eight hours behind UK time. There had been a lot of preparation for this adventure, with dire warnings ringing in our ears, particularly about the big cities: "Never go anywhere alone, do not walk in quiet streets, do not carry passports or more money than needed, hide cameras or any signs of affluence, watch out for muggers, con men," etc. The Los Angeles Biltmore Hotel was in a rough, mainly Hispanic area, complete with down-and-outs, druggies, mean streets, open-fronted, scruffy shops, and far too many hard-eyed young men aimlessly loafing around. But the hotel itself was a wonder of sumptuous old-world gentility, its panelled walls, ornate ceilings, carved staircases, fountains, palms and ferns often to be seen in Hollywood costume movies.

In spite of the fact that English is spoken everywhere, we soon realised that communication was not as easy as expected. "Hi, how are you today?" elicited blank expressions from us, as did "Have a nice day!" This verbal oil was fine, but the lack of perceived common courtesies such as our 'please' and 'thank you' constantly grated. The ease by which Americans introduce themselves to strangers was a constant source of envy, however, as I learnt to appreciate the differences in our cultures. I found that I became more English as time went on, feeling quaintly sophisticated whenever I spoke. I was constantly being urged to repeat what I'd said in my 'cute accent', but became more reserved and detached, observing with fascination the very different and, to me, brutally frank, offhand, head-on attitudes towards general, everyday living.

Simple requests were easily misunderstood, as I discovered all too soon when in line at a local deli. My timid order of "A chicken roll, please" was received with a bark of "Whadd'ya mean? ... It's ON roll!" I recoiled when shown the thick cylinder of an unidentifiable, pallid sandwich filling, and then nodded and watched in disbelief as twenty-two slices were shaved onto a bare bread roll. "Mayo, pickle, mustard ...?"; the list went on. I smiled feebly and muttered, "No thanks", before handing over the money. It did not take long for us to realise that the massive portions of attractive-looking food served in diners, street cafés, snack bars and many of the smarter restaurants were often totally tasteless. It seemed impossible to buy simple, unadulterated food in small quantities, coming as it did with unasked-for side orders apparently encompassing anything and everything: fries; glops of glutinous mayo; sauerkraut; coleslaw; ketchup; salad dressings containing every conceivable 'erb; pickles; gherkins; sliced, sweet raw onions; whole strawberries; segments of orange; dollops of sour cream; sliced egg – the combinations of flavours were endless. For instance, I discovered that a small tuna sandwich arrived as two slices of brown bread vainly trying to contain a mash of tuna with mayonnaise, a thick layer of shredded lettuce, a slice of rubbery cheese and sliced tomato. One was also totally bemused by the chanted list of coffee on offer, halted only by a smile and firm, very English, "Just an ordinary (US *regular*) coffee with a dash of milk please." On came glasses of chilled water (whereupon Annie immediately removed the mountain of ice cubes) and the knowledge that our cups would be refilled for as long as we sat there.

American hospitality was, as ever, generous and overwhelming, beginning with a delightful welcoming letter for every member of the CBSO from Ernest Fleischmann, the executive director of the Los Angeles Philharmonic. He arrived in person to greet us, handing out brochures, maps, smiles all round and an invitation to party with their orchestra that very first evening. They were all looking forward to meeting us because of the close connection between the LA Phil and Simon Rattle, their principal guest conductor. Dozens of tiny Easter eggs appeared for us in the band room, as well as personal messages from the players – a lovely, generous gesture from our American colleagues, many of whom we were not destined to meet. It was the Easter holidays, after all.

Players from both orchestras arrived at a welcoming fiesta given by philanthropic supporters of the L A Philharmonic on our first evening. A very gracious hostess greeted us, dressed in suitable frills and Mexican hat, and, as the sun went down, we delighted in the extensive candlelit garden, huge swimming pool, Mexican BBQ and Simon's favourite Argentinian musicians, who included much exotic percussion in their evocative entertainment. At one point, one of the American fiddle players distinguished himself on the musical saw, and then everyone was invited to 'have a go' on percussion, our cellists eagerly taking up the offer but the percussionists being notable by their absence. The one exception was Clifton, a whiz on congas. After downing countless tequilas, he joined in, eventually having to be dragged away as he drew blood with his vigorous playing. As he fuzzily remarked later, "I think I peaked a little early!"

Receptions come in all shapes and sizes, providing journeys into the unknown and worrying cliffhangers, as the fare offered could be dainty snacks or a full-blown sit-down affair. Empty bellies after a long journey or a heavy concert do not really appreciate nibbles. What's more, copious amounts of irresistible free alcohol stretch everyone's self-control and physical stamina to the limits. As usual, we arrived after everyone else at one British Embassy welcome party, to be greeted by the ambassador's smiling wife, who confided her relief at seeing women in our orchestra. On a previous concert tour, a well-known, all-male UK symphony orchestra had let the side down badly by running amuck in the ornamental pools, climbing trees in the garden, throwing up and generally being total hooligans. We at least try to be civilised, always attending such events in concert dress, as some of our non-uniform garb is definitely unacceptable for posh flag-waving affairs. We are getting good at social skills, however, adept at mixing with sponsors, civic dignitaries et al.

After the final concert in New York on our first visit, we were all invited to a most memorable dinner. Every table was beautifully set with tall pink candles, beribboned white napkins, solid silver cutlery, three crystal wine glasses per person and a mind-boggling centrepiece of a domed 'dandelion clock' of immaculate white tulips. We all received a gift-wrapped blue Tiffany box containing a silver apple bookmark, engraved with the date and the event, before rounding off the evening with handmade chocolates and champagne. Our hosts were presented with reciprocal gifts of CBSO recordings. As it was by then well past midnight on April 15th, I quietly remarked to my neighbour that the 16th was my birthday, so naturally I was honoured with a rendering of *you-know-what* – a great way to end an unforgettable evening, especially as it was sung reasonably in tune!

A BBC television crew appeared during our first America trip. We were delighted to see old friends running the show, but were nonplussed when an almighty row blew up as our team insisted on using UK sound technicians. Threats to 'pull the plug' thankfully came to nought, so we were introduced to our very own hunky American cameraman, Jan – black shirt open to the waist and chunky gold medallion – and advised him on the cute names he would find in his notes for American *'orchestral bells'*, i.e. glockenspiel, and *'chimes'*, i.e. tubular bells. At one point, we heard our producer tersely mutter to another cameraman, "The violins are the *small* ones!" A run-through of the whole programme for a vision rehearsal was requested. This is when we play 'mouse music'; in other words, everything, however dramatic or heart-stopping, is played ridiculously quietly. The consequences are an orchestra in silly mode, especially as some passages just cannot be played pianissimo, so blare out above the quiet with startling effect. Overt laughter is very much in evidence whilst the TV crew looks on with mild disbelief.

New York was full of surprises, in spite of familiar-from-films yellow cabs everywhere, horns honking, steam coming from street gratings, busy-busy people, bumper-to-bumper traffic, and 'WALK/DON'T WALK' at street intersections. I hadn't realised that the numbered grid system of streets meant that every street was one way: odds ... evens. Nor did I imagine that there would be horses and carriages for tourists, large equestrian statues by the park, smells of cinnamon, hot dogs, pretzels, burgers, coffee, Fifth Avenue perfumes, horse droppings, and so much cacophony – jet planes, sirens, screeching tyres, alarm bells, canned music, shouting – a never-ending challenge for the senses. I loved the street entertainers and meekly obeyed when politely asked not to film by some exceptionally imaginative break-dancers near our hotel. We were definitely tourists for the first two days, as time was rapidly eaten up by museum and art gallery visits, an informative boat trip, whizzing to the top of the Empire State Building, and so on. "Where is it?" we asked, craning upwards from concrete canyons to see a tantalising variety of skyscrapers crammed one aside the other against the glare of the hazy sky: a lesson in perspective.

By the time we were aboard the first ferry to see 'The Lady', we could observe massive queues forming in our wake on shore. Unfortunately, the lifts were out of order, so we either had to forgo our one and only chance to see the Statue of Liberty, or leg it up the equivalent of twenty-two storeys. I had been having serious knee problems for some years, but was not going to miss out on this, so it was a matter of plodding slowly up the crude, twisting wooden staircase, peering into the massive hollow arms, looking with amazement at the cavernous inside-out nostrils, following the guiding rope and eventually reaching the head to gaze out from the pointed windows in the diadem. Chattering schoolchildren clattered by, overtaking us, but we were able to savour the experience in our own time, looking down over the water and picking out famous landmarks. By the time we had staggered back to ground level, the queues were six deep, winding around the statue and sectioned off into waiting time: one, two, three, *four* hours.

Relaxation away from home can be very varied. Some hit Broadway for the shows and others indulged in opera, but a highlight for me was a late evening of jazz, worshipping at the throne of legendary jazz trumpeter, Dizzie Gillespie, in Washington DC – a birthday treat for one of the cellists. The biggest surprise was the wedding of two of our string players, Kathy and Mark. The LA Phil had generously provided a wedding cake, which amply fed everyone at an informal reception. Many went to sports events, and host orchestras joined our lads in friendly football matches. A never-to-be-forgotten ice hockey match was a unique experience for the two Cliffs and me, resulting in a very quiet percussion section the next day, as we had all three lost our voices yelling for the losing home team. Cellist Ian Ludford ran in the Boston Marathon and was cheered to the sky as he arrived over the finishing line, having raised a substantial sum of money for the Birmingham Children's Hospice.

We were somewhat astounded when a New York taxi driver had to ask us the way to Carnegie Hall, and even more so when it dawned on us that he didn't actually speak English. *We* directed **him** to just a few blocks away. Large '*Sold Out*' notices greeted our arrival, where we discovered disgruntled hall staff erecting platform rises for the rehearsal. The majority of American orchestras play 'on the flat', something we hate, so, as these borrowed platforms were not custom-made for this hall, there were problems from the beginning with creaks, holes, splinters, wobbly, ill-fitting sections, and so on. Construction was made all the more challenging as we had our rehearsal in the morning with another orchestra rehearsing in the afternoon, on the flat. All the rises were numbered, so were shifted out after rehearsal and then back in again for our performance in the evening. This made a lot of extra muscle work for us too, as we struck and then reset our instruments, hoping that we had remembered everything and that all was back in its correct place – a big worry.

I had overheard one of the hall staff telling one of our players that on no account was anyone to use a camera of any kind in this hall as it was against Union rules. Needless to say, I regarded this bit of red tape as a challenge, and, as my video camera was being lugged around in an undistinguished tatty old striped canvas bag, it managed to pass gimlet eyes at the stage door. I was determined to record the inside of this lovely old hall, reminiscent of

Edinburgh's Usher Hall, and so I sneaked up to the upper gallery where I managed to video quite a lot of a very relaxed rehearsal. Alfred Brendel, our distinguished soloist, was on stage trying out the piano and, as Simon wished to hear the concerto (Beethoven's 4th) from the audience, Brendel directed it for him from the piano. He is a teddy bear and everyone loved working with him.

There are occasions when a visiting orchestra can galvanise the home team into hearing their own familiar hall with new ears, as was the case when we visited San Francisco's Davis Symphony Hall. This is a relatively new hall, with many acoustic problems. There had been attempts to solve these with see-through perspex acoustic discs floating from the ceiling in a futuristic fashion. Of course, every venue has its little foibles, but Simon had real problems on this occasion. He hopped down from the rostrum once the orchestra had embarked on Ravel's *La Valse* and went into the auditorium to listen. He returned to tell us that the horns sounded louder the further back he went, timpani were too loud, he couldn't hear the woodwind, and so on. More adjustments. At this point of the tour, we felt that we had been playing *La Valse* forever, so we knew it rather well but were fascinated. He moved the horns to one side of the stage, and the percussion section behind the first violins, much to their disgust. This went on for forty-five minutes - repositioning of instruments, careful balancing, listening, adjusting, until the players were almost screaming. Thankfully, after all the torment, *La Valse* took off spectacularly in the evening. The audience erupted at the end, and afterwards we met dewy-eyed local regulars who confessed to never having heard anything like it in their own hall before. The press picked up on this the next day, and we were sure that sighs of relief were heaved as the San Francisco city fathers realised that their hall was not the acoustic disaster that they had previously suspected. Simon is the only conductor we play for who actually listens to the orchestra from the audience's point of view during rehearsals: it makes all the difference.

American audiences sell themselves short in my opinion, as they give screaming, whooping accolades for everything, unless they actually walk out during the music. They often have great difficulty with anything other than what we call 'meat and two veg programmes', so when we play twentieth-century music, even if it is buried in a conventional programme, some will find their way out of the concert hall during the offending piece, come what may, and usually noisily, giving the strong impression of 'I have paid for this ticket and I am NOT going to listen to anything I don't know – so there!' This occurred in New York during a short new work that had been programmed to appear immediately before the interval. Musicians watched with amazement as people crashed out of the hall, barging from the centre of rows, clattering the seats and slamming doors. After the first short movement, Simon took a deep breath, turned to the audience and said, "Ladies and gentlemen, we have spent many hours working on this piece. If others amongst you wish to leave, please would you do so now so that the rest of us can enjoy the music." There was a ghastly hush, a spattering of applause, and then a great rush as dozens more people left the hall. Simon stood very still, and then, after the great exodus, we continued as if nothing had happened. Only in America! It is also perfectly normal to have a standing ovation at the end of every concert, with stamping feet, yelling, cheering and clapping hands above heads, during which time half the audience rushes out of the hall, presumably to reach the car parks before their fellows. We just stand there in amazement, facing a half-empty auditorium. As the orchestra invariably plays one or even two encores, this is when the fleeing audience tries to creep back to hear the extra lollipops. They never seemed to learn.

One of the big bonuses on some of the tours is the possibility of guests joining the party at a very reasonable cost, often resulting in delighted reunions with rarely seen family and friends abroad. Players grow very close by the nature of the job, therefore through the years we naturally meet each other's families. I recognise many colleagues' mums and dads, partners and sweethearts, and have seen children and grandchildren born, grow up and leave the nest. A lot of us go back a long way, are very comfortable with each other and have many shared experiences. Groups of wives would get together on tours, sometimes with teenage offspring, and add another pleasing dimension to the orchestra family. I always enjoyed catching up on family news and seeing how the kids had progressed. It was fun hearing about various jaunts in tourist haunts and trying to spot familiar faces in the audiences.

"Is this the Moseley coach?" "Ha ha! Very funny." The joke wears thin as we pile out of hotels or concert halls, as there are no delineated Birmingham routes on these trips. One of the bonuses on tours, however, is that of meeting colleagues not in one's immediate circle, discovering unexpected fresh topics of conversation and seeing well-known faces with new eyes. I have found myself being informed on such diverse subjects as delphiniums, cricket, black holes, bird migration, computers, sailing, wine making, cycling and magic tricks, and on one long journey a dear friend tried to convince and convert me to religious beliefs. Ever after, this was a banned subject, as we relish and respect our musical friendship far too much to let it founder because of entrenched but nevertheless sincere personal convictions.

As we are cocooned by travel, language and music, every foreign tour takes on the somewhat surreal aspect of living in a different time and place. Home and loved ones can so easily become part of another life as we focus on our superficial, hedonistic existence, so much so that these are the times when long-standing relationships can come to grief, possibly ending in irretrievable breakdown or divorce. Rumour and scandal become the life blood of many a tour, living as we do cheek by jowl, behind private hotel-room doors and often too close for comfort. Gossip is rife as we sympathise with, or castigate, familiar companions. Many find that keeping a fragment of personal space becomes a serious problem too, as we are herded together for work, travel and relaxation. My solution would be to disappear for a long, hot bath, wash my hair, read a book, and then reappear later as a reasonable human being, life's little irritations thus being kept in perspective once more.

* * *

Exotic South America was another whirlwind of impressions, beginning with an interminable flight to Brazil over never-ending rain forest swathed in swirls of mist. My mind boggled to think of the contrast between our modern way of travel and the lives of those living below under that impenetrable dark-green canopy. On terra firma once more, we travelled by coach into São Paulo through squalid slum areas, alongside a wide, garbage-choked, sludgy river. My overriding memory of playing in the Teatro Cultura Artistica was being escorted the short step from the hotel to the stage door by gun-toting guards: 'heavies' supplied by the hotel. Brazil's enormous second city of untold millions stretched to the horizon through layers of industrial haze heavily polluting the stifling air, so it was with great relief that we were able to see and enjoy some of the coastal delights of Rio de Janeiro. Fortunately, we could travel by tram up the steep Corcovado mountain before finally slogging up countless steps to the foot of the awesome Christ the Redeemer statue, arms outstretched, overlooking Sugar Loaf Mountain and the dark volcanic sea. Constantly being pestered by scrounging teenage lads did not enhance our following stroll on the scorching Copacabana beach, however, and I suspect that I was not alone in being relieved to return to base and more familiar activities. When in Brazil ... buy gemstones, which three of us did from a tiny, heavily guarded room in a narrow side street, a somewhat unnerving B-grade movie experience we thought. Weeks later, I took my semi-precious tear-drop-shaped topazes to the Birmingham jewellery quarter, where they were transformed into favourite earrings. Argentina, the next stop, brought more hospitality and enthusiastic audiences. It was hardly surprising that massive beefsteaks were on the menu at one of our receptions, washed down with smooth local red wine. Once more we found ourselves shopping, this time for Latin American percussion instruments in a Buenos Aires tourist area of bright colours, tango dancers and totally tempting open-fronted shops. A privately escorted trip to the city cemetery to see Eva Peron's tomb preceded our final concert in the red and gold splendour of the Teatro Colón. On this occasion, our department had the bonus of a free evening for more wining, dining, and a spin round the postage stamp of a dance floor, thinking the while of colleagues playing their hearts out in interminable Bruckner. For once we were packed and ready for home long before everyone else, another country visited on our 'done it, been there ... tick!' list.

22
I Dreamt I Dwelt in Marble Halls ...

Wandering orchestras trailing round the world, in and out of doors, up and down steps, peering into rooms, asking questions: that's us. We can greet the guardians of the stage doors in many languages; if not, a smile and nod suffice. "Where are the band rooms?" "Is that the way to the platform?" "Where are the instrument boxes?"

Percussionists, basses, cellists and harpist search high and low; the rest will follow. The pattern of arrival is usually the same, with the location of the platform a priority. Then a pause to take it in: "Mmmm - that's okay." Nothing to do with acoustics yet – that is the conductor's domain; ours is the problem of getting everything on stage so that we will actually be able to play. Others rush off to locate watering holes, whilst the heavy brigade start their own version of furniture moving.

We rapidly get to know the pitfalls of the many halls we visit, but initially concentrate on more mundane considerations, mainly to do with our own comfort. Top marks for the halls with available refreshments. Bedworth, near Coventry, is small and concrete, but with an attached chippy-haven selling cholesterol-on-a-plate big enough to satisfy the largest bass player. Cheerful service stimulates a warm inner glow. A good sign for a splendid rehearsal and concert, added to which there is an enthusiastic local audience, making for a pleasing day out. Some UK towns have to make do with dual-purpose venues. Derby staged its symphony concerts in the city's swimming baths for many years, but we never discovered if the water had been drained away under the temporary flooring and spent some time trying to think of appropriate programmes, *The Blue Danube*, *Water Music* and *Vltava* coming at the top of the list. Churches, cathedrals, schools, university halls and marquees, all are pressed into service at some time or other, usually to the detriment of the music they are promoting.

The Barbican Concert Hall and Royal Festival Hall (RFH) have distinctive characteristics. The RFH acoustic is 'dry' and two-dimensional, and we can hear every whisker of sound, including thumping hearts as well as standing and sitting noises, but there often seems to be a curious lack of coherence, as some feel to be out on a limb, hearing only their own contributions and not feeling to be part of the whole. The Barbican is disconcertingly underground (*down* in elevators to the concert platform), with a comprehensive area backstage for meeting friends and having a civilising cuppa. But the stage is claustrophobic, meaning that we free spirits cannot wander on and off at will when not required, as there is no entrance at the back of the platform. Thus, heads down and back to crosswords and reading.

Backstage facilities are very important, and it is helpful to have communication between the platform and behind the scenes, usually in the shape of a monitor and sound system. I well remember a concert in Northampton when my colleague Annie, and I were nattering in one of the tiny dressing rooms after the general exodus onto the stage. It eventually occurred to us that the first half of the concert was proving to be unusually long. On investigation, we discovered that the second half had already started, the orchestra having drunk their cups of interval cheer in the loading bay miles away from the band rooms. We dashed onto the platform to be regaled by the strains of the Elgar symphony we were supposed to be playing in. Luckily, it was possible to stalk on with tattered dignity, and we had not actually missed any of our contributions.

. The Vienna Philharmonic Orchestra has only recently employed female musicians; consequently, on our initial visits, there was no band room for us. (Thank you for the full-length mirrors in the general backstage cattle market – but where do we put on our make-up? Answer: at the front of house in the nearest '*Damen*', alongside somewhat surprised audience ladies.) Their Musikverein, of New Year's Day fame and silky smooth acoustics, is a beautiful old hall, but, since the smallish platform consists of ancient, uneven wooden floorboards, every movement is a calculated nightmare, with the tiniest of sounds being amplified.

The best shape for a concert hall is the 'shoebox', as in the Musikverein, Amsterdam's Concertgebouw and Cheltenham Town Hall. These are invariably older halls and often uncomfortably small for a modern orchestra, but the results are truly wonderful, with a bloom on the sound that is rare and beautiful. Just listen to the richness of Brahms, the exquisite Mozart, and noble Beethoven: a lovely perspective rediscovered. One of the most unusual concert venues we visited was the hall in Santa Barbara, north of San Francisco. I noted in my tour diary:

The place where we play looks like a large Mexican adobe church from outside, but this is nothing compared to inside. Looking out into the auditorium is, for all the world, like looking into a moonlit Mexican

*village square. Roofs, lanterns, balconies, interesting doorways, pretty
casement windows, flowers ... all it needed were a few senoritas in
flounced dresses! The ceiling is black with stars and a single light
hanging down (the moon?), and for a mind-teasing moment we thought
that we were playing outside.*

Other halls stick in the memory too, such as the Shi Ongaku-do hall in
Japan, lined entirely with dark blue, shiny ceramic tiles. One of the
percussion extras looked round with awe and observed, "Just think of all that
grouting!" Someone likened the experience to "playing inside minestrone
soup: lumpy and swishing around". It was a non-starter. Because of the hard
resonances, we were unable to understand spoken directions from the
rostrum, so just gave a general all-purpose performance to the delight,
nevertheless, of the audience. This was the hall with an engraved brass plate
screwed to the pass door between backstage and front-of-house proudly
announcing, 'To the Robby' (translation: 'To the Lobby').

Then my big moment came during a trip to Italy – a chance to sing at La
Scala, Milan. Yorkshire to the core, I could not resist posturing in the centre
of the empty stage and regaling everyone with a solo burst of 'On Ilkley Moor
bah't 'at' as we were waiting to set up, much to the astonishment of the stage
crew and a dinner party tale for many a long year.

It is very often the case that the physical restrictions and characteristics of
a concert hall can create problems with the music; nay, with the conductor
too. Our very first visit to the Salzburg Festival was the feather of all feathers
in Simon Rattle's cap, and one wonders how on earth he managed to bring his
orchestra to this hallowed ground where previously only the Vienna or the
Berlin Philharmonic Orchestras had performed. We discovered that there had
been much controversy in the media about this 'upstart' conductor and his
'unheard-of' orchestra, so it was to be expected that Austria's musical elite
would be at our concerts in force and in superior critical mode.

Our first concert was in the dark, gloomy Grosses Schauspielhaus, and
Simon was understandably anxious during rehearsals for our mould-breaking
concerts: brittle, smiling carefully, working more frenetically against the
clock than usual. We were finishing a rehearsal of the completed version of
Mahler's Tenth Symphony (in Deryck Cooke's performing version), in a
humid and enervating atmosphere, with everyone's patience wearing thin.
My huge bass drum was not happy with the moisture in the air and I had spent
an inordinate amount of time trying to tune it to some kind of decent sound,

but it felt like 'kicking a dead sheep'! I was not best pleased, and even less so when Simon in frustration suddenly let fly with, "Just HIT it ... hit it less in the middle!" I was totally taken aback, mortified and furious to think that he imagined that I was being complacent about the state of the instrument. There was a titter of laughter around the orchestra as the atmosphere lightened somewhat, but, as I looked daggers at him, he repeated the detested words, "Just HIT it!"

During the break I spent more time nursing the instrument to some kind of tension, and then gloomily followed my colleagues to the canteen through deluging rain across an open yard. Everyone else was well into the coffee scene as I waited to be served, when I realised that Simon was queuing behind me with a couple of starry-eyed students clutching Mahler scores. Before I could stop or think, I rounded on him and, through gritted teeth, said in a quasi-teasing way, "I'll KILL you! Don't ever accuse me of HITTING my instruments again, and I for one NEVER play a bass drum in the centre of the head. I've spent *ages* trying to get some sense into that drum, and it's a non-starter until it's settled down after the journey here and until it gets used to the temperature and humidity, but I'm *trying my best*!" Big mistake, but I was still smarting and in unforgiving mood. He was totally startled, held up conciliatory hands and, with mock grovelling, replied, "Sorry ... **sorry!**" However, I knew that he would never forget and that I had very stupidly overstepped the mark. The instrument did eventually come to its senses and the concert was a huge success, but my misdemeanour was noted and, in the fullness of time, this small incident came back to haunt me. I know that I am not alone in crossing swords with Simon, but we were all lulled into a false sense of security, as his normally friendly manner apparently invites one-to-one communication on a 'we're all in this together' basis.

The next day we played in Salzburg's Festspielhaus, another massive concert space in a converted old riding school, sporting two long rows of arched, open-fronted galleries (the old stables) carved into the live rock face at the back of the stage. Over the whole area there is a massive moveable ceiling screen, essential in summer heat, but also necessary for the peculiarities of local weather phenomena: sudden deluging downpours of warm rain funnelling in from the surrounding mountains, creating a heavy, humid atmosphere yet again. As we came into rehearsal, Simon saw me and called out, "Imagine you're hitting me – enjoy yourself!" What can one say?

One of my favourite pieces graced the first half of the concert: Prokofiev's Symphony No. 5, after which sweaty bow ties were literally rung out and copious amounts of water drunk. Then, after the interval, I went to stand at the back of the audience to hear Janácek's *Glagolitic Mass*. During the day I had overheard two men from our CBSO chorus saying how unfriendly the orchestra was, especially as 'we were all here together' and suchlike. I was stung into action at this observation, following them in the street until I could pluck up the courage to remind them that, as we are behind them, we cannot see what they look like, and that they were very wrong in their assumptions. After apologising prettily, we went our separate ways.

That evening I certainly saw and heard the chorus during the Janácek, being totally overwhelmed by their performance and the fact that they sang in Czech without the aid of the music. The audience erupted with an immediate standing ovation and I fled outside (still dressed in long black), trying to repair the ravages of my emotions. As the chorus coaches began to fill, I went into each one to thank them for an unforgettable performance, one that would stay with me for the rest of my life, all the angst with Simon forgotten for the moment. I was told many years later that my comments on that evening were deeply appreciated and long remembered by the surprised singers. I liked that!

More Mahler in Leeds. We were setting up on the difficult, cliff-like platform in Leeds Town Hall for a performance of the Third Symphony when, once again, I unwittingly touched a raw nerve. I was in charge of two bass drums this time, the big concert instrument and a marginally smaller one with a cymbal attached on top for a special effect. There was scant room to play on the steep and unstable staging, and very little space for trumpets to sit in front of me below our heavy artillery. It was imperative to place the instruments for best sighting, but safety was at a premium and I was acutely aware of the fact that the trumpets were in the hot seat: the danger zone. When Simon spotted the deep discussions going on, he clambered up to the back to arbitrate. Realising that there were real problems in this venue, he announced, "Don't worry, I'll give you plenty of cues." As he is totally reliable in such circumstances, I was highly relieved and thankful, but then flippantly observed with a rueful grin, "Oh, thank you, then I'll be fine as long as you don't glare at me!" As quick as a flash, bristling at this unexpected comment, he drew himself up to his full height and snapped, "I don't glare – *you* glare at me!" I was flabbergasted, and came back with a wide-eyed, "Sorry ... but I can't help what the front of my head looks like when I'm concentrating, it's just eye contact." He returned to the rostrum in silent, unaccountable annoyance. I would have to learn to be more careful in future and keep my big mouth shut.

During the following rehearsal we had a little homily from the maestro, which I felt was aimed directly at me. Perhaps he was having a bad day all round. "Two white hunters were stalking savage, ignorant cannibals, but never forget, it's the cannibals who eat the hunters ..." None of us knew why that little gem had come out of the woodwork, but we suspected that there was a lot more in there and that it was just a matter of time.

Needless to say, every cue was spot on. I tried my best to look unglaring, but smiling was out of the question, so he got what he saw: my uncompromising straight face. I noted also that:

> *We had a packed house. Beresford (concert manager) had only reserved the centre bit of the choir seats for chorus and children's choir, so lots of the audience sat on the steps. (Fire hazard.) The little boys behind us were terribly fidgety. Great clumping shoes on wooden staging. I told them off during the performance, it was awful.*

The Royal Albert Hall is another venue to be endured, with many problems highlighted by creaky staging and not enough depth in which to arrange or play many of our larger percussion instruments. Once more I was playing the huge concert drum 'side-saddle', this time for a Henry Wood Promenade concert, live on TV. From the front, the stage area looks big, but it is not until one is in situ that difficulties manifest themselves. It is often impossible to see other percussionists or the timpanist on the different levels of staging through the layers of instruments, players, music stands, cables, cameras, extra lighting, microphone stands, technicians, and so on. Once more, Simon was twitching with anxieties; working within a time slot, and with all the irritations and diversions that such a rehearsal creates. Britten's *Sinfonia da Requiem*, the final piece in rehearsal but first in the concert, begins with solemn, unrelenting beats from unison timpani and bass drum. We were not together, so there was an immediate response from the rostrum to me of, "Don't watch **me**, play to the timps!" I was somewhat startled at this approach and said, "I can't even see him." "Well then MOVE so that you can!" Now, trying to move a huge bass drum on an uneven platform, which is not deep enough to accommodate the instrument with a player standing behind it, is a tall order and one that takes time to accomplish. We were, as usual, taking up sir's precious rehearsal time with what was perceived by everyone else as 'the percs messing about again'. Down came the baton before we were ready, and I was still unable to see the actual contact of timpani sticks to drum head, added to which the triplicate acoustics of the hall were not much help. Rattle was silently fuming, finally shrugging the problem off with, "You'll just have to sort it out. I haven't got time ...." No one had the guts to clarify the problem, and I was left to seethe and worry about how we could possibly be in unison without even trying it first – live television, live radio, thousands of listeners in the hall. These thoughts churned round and round as I tearfully steamed around the Albert Memorial at teatime, avoiding all and sundry. By the time I returned for the beginning of the concert, I was defiant and angry. At that point, I would have willingly handed in my notice, but decided to 'go for it', watch the conductor and give my all. There was no eye contact there, but we were together; no thanks to Rattle, and no support from my colleagues. Once more, an uncomfortable silence reigned. I tried hard not to feel totally inadequate, took deep breaths, pushed my shoulders back and chin in the air, thought of the music, and carried on as well as I was able. I could do no more.

* * *

Our customers are an integral part of the halls we inhabit, of course, but I sometimes wonder if they realise that we take nearly as much interest in them as they do in us. Audiences come in all shapes and sizes, as do the concerts they attend, and as I say to my students, "If you can see the audience, they can see you. They have paid to listen to what you have to offer and they expect to hear and see your best efforts." On the all-too-rare occasions that we get to speak to our listeners, it is obvious that few realise how important a part they play in any concert. There have been many times when I have gently pointed out to starry-eyed concert-goers that without the audience the show would not go on, and musicians such as myself would be out of a job.

"Oh, but I don't understand music, I'm not musical," is a frequent response, to which I reply that, if there are ears on the head that work reasonably well, the *understanding* bit can come later, after more exposures to the music. Just sit there, keep an open mind, listen and give it a go.

After one concert in a cold church full of wide-eyed enthusiasts at the final bash of a summer Music Festival, an elderly couple came up to accessible percussionists, who, as usual, were frantically packing away instruments prior to grabbing decent seats on homeward coaches.

The old lady said, with a dreamy-eyed sigh, "It was that bit when she

333

looked into his eyes … it was so beautiful, I wanted to cry …"

"Come on, Cissy, they haven't got time for your prattle," grumbled the husband self-consciously.

"Not at all. We like it when members of the audience talk to us afterwards. Then we know what you like, and that is important for all of us." (Whatever we say sounds so terribly patronising – you can't win.)

"Well," replied her husband (clearly a man used to having the last word), "she wasn't listening to you properly, she was thinking of that film, *Brief Encounter* … I tell her, she should concentrate on the music."

Who cares? Rachmaninov had moved her to tears, and she had the guts to admit it to a total stranger: that is what matters.

The most difficult aspect of being a member of an audience for me is when a colleague from the orchestra has performed in a solo capacity and one has to go backstage and, in the name of decency, say something. All musicians are critical; indeed most of us are ruthless. Everyone knows the game being played and if given free rein we pull no punches. "What was the fiddle player like?" Answered by a laconic, "Chainsaw massacre … Black and Decker (electric drill), slash and burn." An irritating oboe soloist was dismissed once as sounding like "a cat giving birth to barbed wire". We are the most savage critics of all, especially if the conductor 'couldn't conduct a bus'.

I once attended the 70th birthday celebrations of a regular CBSO supporter, where a small number of colleagues from the orchestra had been invited to entertain the guests at a very posh city-centre hotel. One of these was a double-bass player who was notorious for solo performances on said instrument. Now, as far as I am concerned, a Mozart violin concerto should not be transcribed for a double bass, however skilled or musical the player might be. Nonetheless, we were exposed to a slow movement, beautifully performed I am sure, but not to my mind an entirely ravishing experience. More music of similar ilk was served with supper, and I knew that I would have to say something at rehearsal the following day. The only saving grace of his presentation in my estimation had been a jolly little 'end of pier'-type novelty encore, totally silly but very effective.

As we came face to face in a corridor the next day, there was no escape. I smiled brightly and babbled nervously, "I loved your encore last night … great fun, what a *super* do, lots of people we knew, what a *lovely* idea …." This cut no ice at all. "What about the rest of my programme?" he snappily cut in. He'd been down that road before and wasn't going to be fooled so easily. Not one for telling fibs, or even mincing my words, I was totally caught on the hop, and heard my defensive Yorkshire tones delivering the following bon mot: "Well, quite honestly a double bass isn't really a solo instrument is it? – you can't really take all that stuff seriously, can you?" He turned on his heel and has never spoken another word to me from that day to this!

In a bid to reach more of Brum's vast mixed population, we regularly come out of our splendid Symphony Hall and go into the community - in other words, we play in schools, community centres, old people's homes, day centres, hospitals, reform centres, prisons (the last two for brass players - who else?), a local park, and so on.

I still giggle when I remember overhearing a teacher coming out of the town hall with a bunch of nine-year-olds years ago. "What did you like best?" she asked one of the little lads. In the fruitiest of Birmingham accents came the reply, "Oi loiked the red-'ead with the clan-gers"! The clanging redhead was actually walking alongside the class, resplendent with shopping bag and looking thoroughly mum-like. Gone was the creature in long black dress; down to earth with a bump in daytime disguise.

Much as I like Handel's *Messiah*, there were times in the bad old days when the orchestra regarded this as a bread-and-butter piece as we were sent hither and thither to accompany this or that amateur chorus. So, one Christmas time, I felt very fortunate to be the player who pulled the Huddersfield Choral Society out of the hat, one of eight *Messiah*s around the country that timpanist and percussionists shared out, for the sake of sanity. I was on home ground and thrilled to be playing for the legendary 'Choral'. There were many familiar faces in the audience and I had plenty of time to look around during my many tacet numbers. When we came to 'For Unto Us a Child is Born', I secretly joined in with the soprano part, but then was suddenly struck dumb by the sight of a tiny old woman wildly skipping down the centre aisle towards the stage from the back of the hall. This scruffy 'bag lady', grinning madly, was closely pursued by two uniformed hall attendants who, upon reaching her, scooped her up, one at each elbow, at which point they swiftly turned about without a pause – her legs still pedalling – and rushed her back to the rear doors, whereupon they all disappeared. This happened so quickly that I had to pinch myself to make sure that I hadn't dreamt the whole crazy episode. On further enquiry, I discovered that she was well known and that this was not the first time that she had put in an appearance during town hall concerts. This little episode kept the orchestra bemused for the rest of the show, but I doubt if many in the audience had spotted anything amiss.

Our regular customers at Symphony Hall are, I reckon, the best audiences we ever play for. They are very attentive and will apparently give anything a go. It is very rare for anyone to walk out of our offerings and they are extraordinarily enthusiastic. After a particular riveting performance of Mahler's Seventh Symphony with Simon up front doing another 'memory job', I was tapped on the shoulder by an elderly lady sitting behind us, who said, "I'd never live anywhere else but Birmingham, just for this!" Having said that, they don't blindly accept all on offer, and many times we have had to field such comments as, "Well, that was pretty awful stuff, but our orchestra played it well." Then a pause to ponder, followed by, "You know, we can hear Brahms, Mozart, Beethoven, and so on by any orchestra, but we appreciate that the CBSO does the contemporary stuff very well indeed with Simon, and I suppose we should give it another go."

Such generosity of spirit was not in evidence, however, after the premiere of a Xenakis work in Paris during a posh music festival. As applause broke at the final outpourings, the orchestra watched with delighted astonishment as a man in the balcony leaned over two rows of seats to hit a fellow audience member on the head with a rolled-up programme. Thus abused, the victim turned, climbed up over the intervening rows and set about trying to deliver flailing blows to his aggressor. Nearby, smartly dressed Parisians joined in the mêlée, leaving a grinning orchestra to exit the stage whilst the various factions sorted themselves out. Afterwards, the composer declared himself well pleased to have received some cheers, a few boos and a fist fight. A suggestion that some of the boos came from the orchestra proved impossible to substantiate; however, we all agreed that it was great sport. We might forget the music, but it was certainly a memorable concert.

Italians fidget and whisper to each other, whilst Germans sit quietly in their smart dark suits, and then applaud forever at the end. If the concert has been received well, it may be the case that some of the audience will come down to the front near the stage to cheer, stamp and clap when the only people remaining are percussionists, someone collecting music folders and platform staff. Simon Rattle has had to reappear many times in such circumstances, usually bringing the full score out with him, holding it with two hands above his head.

Enthusiasm comes in a number of guises. In France the shouts of 'Bis, bis!' ('Encore, encore!') sound to our untutored ears rather like booing, and we are further mesmerised by rhythmical, slow handclaps in other parts of Europe, which denote an accolade rather than the opposite. These usually accelerate into general wild clapping and foot stamping, eliciting grins from the stage. The Japanese are totally still until the final chord, at which point they erupt, smiling, cheering, standing on seats, and YELLING. In Tokyo we heard rhythmical chanting at the end of one concert, which we eventually interpreted as, 'Don't go, don't go!' It was also in Japan where every member of the orchestra was given an orchid; the women doing very well out of this as some of the men handed over their flowers with a self-conscious air as we arrived backstage.

Annie and I took great delight in 'audience watching', checking up on the evening outfits out front, secretly spying from the wings. After one particularly exciting concert in Vienna's fine Konzerthaus, I was the tail-end percussionist trailing down the stone stairs backstage with arms full of heavy instrument stands, making my way to the service lift. No glamour here, but wait – an elegant middle-aged woman was also clipping down the steps in high heels, resplendent in understated silk and simple gold jewellery and clutching a programme. She looked a million dollars, and as we acknowledged each other she said in German, "Thank you for a wonderful concert", or words to that effect. I thanked her in my schoolgirl Deutsch, whereupon she replied in English, "We just *love* your *chef* (*d'orchestre*: conductor), and [without a pause] by the way, I'm Mrs von Karajan!" Many words leapt to my mouth, but fortunately an arm came out of the lift and grabbed me just in the nick of time. I gave her a sickly grin and stammered goodnight, thinking, 'Lucky old you, there's no answer to that!' We never know who is going to be in the audience, but it only takes one player to spot a celebrity for the word to get around, after which we are the ones doing the rubbernecking.

After one of our London Prom concerts, I was idly aware of the radio muttering in the background the following morning, when suddenly I realised that my efforts had become the centre of some archbishop or other's 'Thought for the Day' programme. His premise was that even the smallest contributions to life are of value. He had attended a symphony concert where he observed "a young woman sitting quietly at the back of the orchestra, who, when she stood to play, only had one note on a triangle, but this was a significant part of the whole.' Good old Wagner! My first 'ting' in the *Mastersingers* overture represents a shop doorbell, substantiating the joke of a mere triangle player standing up, playing one note, and then sitting down again. Understandably, there was no mention of the dozens of other skills needed for my efforts in the rest of the programme, but I forgave him.

After one Royal Festival Hall concert in the '70s, I was brought down to earth with a bump when I overheard two women conversing on the tube train.

"There are a lot of women in the orchestra, aren't there?" said one. I pricked up my sharp ears, trying my best not to look over to them.

"Oh, yes," the other replied, "but what about the two at the back playing all those percussion instruments? They can't be normal, can they?"

A final observation was delivered after a slight shrug of agreement: "Well, one of them was wearing a wedding ring ... but then that doesn't mean anything these days ...."

I was red with suppressed embarrassment and anger at their assumptions, and as I got up to leave I stalked passed them saying, with as much dignity as possible, "Yes, I do have a wedding ring, also a husband, a son and daughter, and I'm perfectly normal, thank you. Good night!"

Perhaps they were more used to London orchestras who, for the most part, were still wielding their 'keep women out' policies, with the possible exception of harpists and the occasional not-easy-to-ignore fine orchestral player.

I began my career by sometimes being made somewhat self-conscious in my 'man's world' job by unsubtle comments from a minority of colleagues who should have known better, but thankfully not from listeners, at least never to my face. However, in the fullness of time, I was delighted and deeply flattered when rare compliments came my way after performances. It had not dawned on me that our audiences had favourites in their orchestra until one of the Birmingham regulars sought me out to tell me that he always looked out for me at the back there, as he loved to watch me playing. To my utter astonishment, he saw me as "having charisma, and an aura" which "was compelling". I was finally flabbergasted and even more thrown when he said that nowadays, when seeing other orchestras, the all-male percussion sections seem very strange to Birmingham audiences, as they are so used to Annie and I doing our stuff up there at the back. A lovely case of tables turned, I thought, as I often agonise about what I must look like to the public. I dread being perceived as some weird old hag hitting things.

At the other end of the scale are the audiences **not** drawn from the concert-going public. Sports halls in community centres provide one means of reaching different customers: the tickets are cheap, children are admitted free, there is a prize draw, and discounts for selected concerts in Symphony Hall are on offer. The TV era has a lot to answer for, however, as it is obvious that a number of the listeners see no difference between sitting in front of their own television sets and sitting in front of their own symphony orchestra. Children roam around, with a constant stream of little boys trailing out to the loo, and adults talk constantly, paying little heed to their noisy young. But, in spite of this, the overall response is that of animated enthusiasm and bemused, smiling faces. The results are chats with happy customers, and hopefully bigger attendances at our mainstream concerts.

Then, of course, there are the outdoor multitudes ... but they appear elsewhere!

23
Wading in Treacle

There must be a better way to introduce music to children than by throwing great dollops of the stuff at them as we did years ago in the town hall. The orchestra would sit mesmerised as conductors presented our offerings and trotted out such gems as, "Of course, you are all familiar with the monumental works of Beethoven?" or "And now we have a well-known piece by Sibelius". Eyes glazed over, youngsters fidgeted, and we despaired.

Musicians are usually reasonably extrovert by the very nature of their job, but I had never been in the position of having to improvise music or present myself and the instruments to a class full of young schoolchildren. However, my pianist friend, Carol Holt, with whom I had concocted an educational entertainment named 'Sounds Interesting', had many connections in the Worcester area, and we soon found ourselves in demand in private schools, music clubs, some city schools and the Three Choirs Festival in the cathedral cities of Worcester, Gloucester and Hereford. It was the beginning of many years of working with children with varying abilities, something I have always enjoyed.

Within the orchestra there are the more serious chamber groups, but also a small number of people who have the knack of presenting music to children in a vibrant and interesting way. Some of these imaginative offerings were tapped into by our marketing department, who relied on a core of players who felt strongly that doing imaginative education work should also be a relevant part of our musical output. From time to time, the entire percussion section got together to give fun concerts at music festivals, out-of-town venues, the occasional special school and for our own Friends of the CBSO: stalwart supporters all.

We were working on a shoestring with little obvious support from the manager of the orchestra, being told, "It is not our job to teach music in schools." But we did have intermittent input from a keen youngster in the orchestra's general administration staff, who fielded requests from schools and bravely tried to keep us on track and ticking over. Birmingham allotted a substantial amount of money to the CBSO and therefore required its orchestra to deliver music to the city's schoolchildren, primarily via special aforementioned concerts in the town hall. The music adviser from the city's education department liaised with young Sarah in an attempt to meet minimum requirements but, in spite of individual education work being paid *pro rata*, only a tiny handful of players showed any interest, most preferring scheduled non-working days to remain free.

My first exposure to a classroom full of children was in a poor area of the city, where I suspected that I had an easier time than most of my colleagues, as I was using grown-up versions of the familiar instruments that were already in the school. All the pupils were Asian, looking like little flowers in their traditional dress, bright eyes shining when they saw my exciting paraphernalia. They loved the fact that I invited them to have a go and join in with simple sound effects in a story: create a train, soldiers marching, and turbulent weather. We listened with closed eyes to vibrations, pitch, the quietest of bass-drum notes, minuscule bells, and a massive Victorian fire bell. Everything was discussed, as it slowly dawned on me that here was fertile ground for much more ambitious contributions from the orchestra's players.

I discovered that Muslim children were not always present when I visited schools, as music and dance were not normally part of their culture, being frowned upon and discouraged, and that one of the big problems was frequently that of language, as there was often more than one Asian language to contend with. Classroom helpers cheerfully translated, and I sharpened up my acting skills. Eye contact and smiles also worked wonders.

A group of about six stalwarts who dared to venture into schools were encouraged by marketing manager, Julianna Szekely, aided and abetted by secretary Sarah. I suspect that my colleagues thought that what we were trying to do was of no consequence, being seen as a mere drop in the ocean. However, we were determined to make a go of education work, especially when Julianna came up with the innovative idea of an 'Adopt a Player' scheme for Birmingham junior schools. Head teachers were invited to apply for a player to go into school during lesson time, after which six schools were initially chosen to participate, being funded partly by the education department and partly by the orchestra.

Unfortunately, the pilot scheme was soon in serious jeopardy, since it was obvious that our general manager had greater worries to address as the designated education money dwindled to inadequate proportions. Sarah shared her anxieties with us, saying that the letter for a grant application from the Gulbenkian Foundation was at the bottom of the pile on manager Ed's desk, with the closing date fast drawing near. If we missed the deadline, then

341

our onward plans would come to nought. However, Ed was otherwise engaged. "Speak to Simon," was my advice. "Oh, I daren't do that, it wouldn't be right ..." There was far too much at stake for any dithering, so I said that I'd have a word with him. He had often said how committed he was to working within schools and with young people of all ages. This seemed an appropriate time to put his convictions to the test.

The day was Thursday and time was of the essence, so I nervously went to see him in the green room at the Royal Festival Hall. After we'd gone through the coffee-making ritual, those gimlet eyes switched on as I told him the problem, trying very hard not to be negative about Ed's apparent attitude. "What are you saying then? Do you want me to say something to Ed?"

"Er ... yes please. The application has to be sent off before next Tuesday."

A pause ensued and then, "Don't worry, I'll see to it. We're travelling to Liverpool together tomorrow. I'll tell him then."

I was very nervous about the outcome, but would have walked on hot coals to get the message across if necessary. When the Liverpool rehearsal was about to begin, Simon appeared, looked up to find me at the back, gave a great grin accompanied by a thumbs-up, and then mouthed, "Done it!"

Much to our delight and great relief, the CBSO was duly awarded funding from the Gulbenkian Foundation. We began to realise that we were setting the pace for a different style of music education work in schools; therefore we were keen, indeed required, to produce documentation so that others could learn from our experiences.

Primarily, we would always play our instruments and then begin work on a specific piece from a mainstream concert. I found my first few visits as daunting as did the class teacher, as I was not a trained teacher, had no improvisation skills and was often working with a nervous non-music specialist, so it was frequently a case of both of us feeling somewhat vulnerable – but not so the children.

Every class I visited was full of fascinated, enthusiastic youngsters bursting with questions and uninhibited ideas and an eagerness to experiment with the school's percussion instruments. One of the first pieces we used was Holst's *Planets* suite. We never played the recorded music to the children, as first of all we discussed the story, and then the 'ingredients' used by the composer to create that story. Instruments were distributed and the children then split into groups, each with their own relevant topic ... planet? Ideas flowed thick and fast, noise and laughter too, after which we listened to each other's tiny creations, combining them together to make a larger composition. This all took place over many weeks, during which period we discovered that the children often produced additional artwork, dance or poetry based on the music, with their compositions usually being performed for the whole school at the end of our four visits. By this time, there was a great rapport between the schools and musicians so that, by the time the pupils came to part of the CBSO final rehearsal, everyone was totally at ease with one another. Later in the scheme, the final day consisted of a sharing of pieces of music between the participating schools before attending the orchestra's final rehearsal.

Eventually the players themselves were designated to run specific projects, organising a pre-workshop day for teachers and musicians and creating illustrated booklets as a guide for everyone. I always felt like a mother hen when my particular chickens came home to roost, as it was a revelation to hear the children's creations: we were all so proud of them. Every composition was totally unique in spite of being based on the same components, and by this time the teachers were confident and the children were totally starry-eyed. Our work was always based on part of a mainstream concert rather than one aimed specifically at children. Members of the public often commented on how well behaved the youngsters were, and we would assure anxious teachers that if the kids got bored they'd just go to sleep. I loved to see them come into the town hall or Symphony Hall for the first time, as it occurred to me that not every child had been in a very large building before and that this was a real 'Oooh!' and 'Aaah!' experience.

We made great efforts to be especially smart and glamorous for these exceptional evenings. Out came the black velvet and pearls, and on with the make-up and high heels. The effect on our classes was always very gratifying, as we all met up for orange juice in the interval. "Doesn't everybody look different with their clothes on?" confided one little girl. "You are my very favourite player," whispered another. They always behaved impeccably during the music, but afterwards there was much waving and cheering. Days later, a large envelope would flop through my letter box, containing drawings from the children, much to my delight. My fridge made a great display area.

As our work progressed, it was decided, much to our relief, that the best way forward was to appoint a full-time education manager. After much discussion, form-filling, letters and numerous interviews, Ann Tennant was eventually chosen by the players. Here was a woman with a wealth of communication experience behind her, having worked for the BBC amongst other things. She liaised between schools, teachers and players and fired our imaginations, giving us much-needed confidence, and she was always massively supportive and positive with regard to what we were attempting to do. Ann has a dynamic and attractive personality, so much so that it was not long before many other players came on board the education bandwagon as the work developed.

As my instruments are very accessible, I was frequently sent to inner-city schools where the hands-on experience would possibly have a greater impact than in a middle-class school situation. On previous occasions I had also had the pleasure of demonstrating my instruments to pupils at a college for the blind: a fascinating learning experience for all participants. As I became more confident, I suggested that it might be worthwhile for me to concentrate more on special schools as "I enjoy a challenge!", with the idea that perhaps it might be possible for me to do one-off demonstration days rather than participate in the 'Adopt a Player' scheme all the time. However, I was somewhat thrown by the suggestion made for a future school. No, not the Blind College, but a special school for hearing-impaired junior children which had applied for a player, and it had been decided that I was just the one to fit the bill. My colleagues thought that this was the craziest idea they'd ever heard of. "It's like attempting to teach kids who can't walk how to play football!", one of them remarked. "So ... what about wheelchair sports?" I snapped.

My first thought was to talk to a dear friend who has been blind from a very early age. The thought of attempting to introduce classical music to profoundly deaf youngsters was disturbing to say the least, and I needed to get his slant on this. To me it smacked of guinea pig experimentation, opening a Pandora's box, *using* people. But no, my wise friend believed that whatever I did would be a bonus in the lives of those children, but I was still not convinced. We discussed the fact that he could not see or possibly understand what a mountain view, the ocean, colour, or even an orchestra looked like. "It doesn't matter. I read about things and use my imagination in my own way," came the response.

I thought long and hard about all of this, remembering that some months earlier I had walked a blind friend of his through the chairs on stage before a concert, as she had told me that she could not imagine how big an orchestra was. An unexpected bonus of arriving early that evening was that our harpist was tuning prior to the show, so he let her do a gentle glissando over the strings. She was astonished at how huge and heavy this charming instrument is. Words failed her, but I knew that she would enjoy the concerts all the more now that she had a clearer picture in her mind of where everything was

344

placed, and what a large area was covered by a symphony orchestra. But the deaf and 'real' music – not music therapy? I was very dubious about what I could possibly do that would be of any relevance to these ten-year-olds.

David, the head teacher, invited me to visit the school, meet the children and their teacher, and then decide what I wanted to do. My first question was, "Did you ask for a player, or was this in the way of an experiment from the orchestra?" He looked slightly puzzled, and then smiled and replied, "Oh, I definitely asked for a player. You were suggested by Ray, who comes here regularly to work with the children." I was delighted, as trombonist Ray is a family friend of many years. We both have the same daft sense of humour, and I was sure that between us we would be able to achieve something positive in the school.

"I know that the children are profoundly deaf, but what does that mean? Can they feel sound or hear anything?"

"It all depends on what part of the ear is damaged. Some people can hear a specific pitch, but only in a very narrow band. To others, sound is like being underwater with their fingers jammed in their ears. There are very many, varied difficulties, not the least that everyday communication is always a problem. If a child cannot hear, then new words cannot be learnt in the same way that a hearing child takes them on board. We teach BSL (British Sign Language) and lip-reading. New words are also introduced with finger spelling, but to be deaf is not like watching TV with the sound turned off, it's like watching *Russian* TV with the sound turned off. Trying to appreciate the problems our youngsters have is like wading in treacle, so it's good when outsiders come into school because they so often bring with them unusual ideas. We are hell-bent on making sure that the children are equipped to deal with the everyday world as much as possible, but whatever you do will be of benefit for our children, many of whom have additional medical problems to contend with."

In the back of my mind I was remembering the visits, many years ago, of small groups of profoundly deaf toddlers, who were brought into a rehearsal about once a year. Burdened with large hearing aids and each encumbered with a massive microphone box on their chest, they stood in bemused confusion, usually at the back near to our scary instruments. There were tears when the sound was too much, and little if any contact with players and instruments. Our overriding emotion at that time was pity, but there was no further thought of trying to bridge the gap in any practical way as we got on with our work.

My first visit was arranged. I put on my thinking cap, had endless discussions with Ray, and then we both found ourselves in at the deep end. I was met by a smiling secretary and taken to the hall, where I found Ray, complete with trombone, talking to the class teacher, John. We were working with six children and were told, in no uncertain terms, that they would only be able to concentrate for about twenty minutes. It was obvious that John felt that he had better things to do than try to get these youngsters to understand anything about classical music. For once I sympathised and secretly agreed. All speech was duly translated into sign language – a laborious business, setting a slow, tedious pace. I soon learnt to think more simply, getting to the nub of an idea without too much description or use of extraneous language. "Think and speak like a telegram," was another bit of advice I took on board.

To begin with I plonked the snare drum on its stand and then held up a length of wallpaper on which I had written:

MUSIC IS: (listing opposites)

* loud/quiet
* fast/slow
* sad/happy
* exciting/boring
* long/short (and so on)

Eyes kept looking at the drum, but I ignored these, as we needed to do a little groundwork first. The children were sitting on the wooden floor of the hall in the vain hope that somehow some vibrations would seep through into their bodies. Ray began by giving lively trombone demonstrations of loud and quiet, fast and slow, and we all had a laugh.

There were interesting problems with sign language, I discovered, as some of the words I was using did not have a sign. Deaf people are frequently told, "Music is not for you, **you're deaf**." We'll see about that! When I asked the children, "What is music?" one child smiled and signed, "Music is beautiful." There was no going back. "Stand up!", and with appropriate actions, "We're going to do some marching." No translation needed for that idea. The kids had been marvellous, and we discovered that they had been riveted for nearly an hour. Marching to the drum and trombone was pretty shambolic, but we all enjoyed ourselves nevertheless. I had to learn to be less fussy and be more relaxed; the youngsters certainly were.

Our next venture was to go to meet the orchestra. Mozart's *Haffner* Symphony was a gentle introduction to our world, something with which conductor, Iona Brown, was only too happy to cooperate. I had managed to make an announcement at a rehearsal to the effect that the children would love to meet some of the players with their instruments during the break and that, in spite of the fact that the children didn't speak as such, everyone should try to be as expressive as possible and not be nervous about using speech when trying to communicate. Colleagues were bemused by the warning that the youngsters were not always aware of the fact that they were making sounds, in spite of being cautioned to be quiet, so anything vocal could happen.

Three teachers accompanied us and helped to seat the children amongst the musicians, not on chairs but on the wooden staging: better for feeling vibrations. The most sceptical lad was parked between two double basses, placing his hands on the shoulders of the large instruments as they were being played. His eyes nearly popped out of his head at this new experience with organised sound: i.e. music. When asked later what he had 'heard', he thumped his chest, grinned and signed, "There!" After that there were cooperation, a positive attitude and smiles. One of the teachers remarked that she had never before seen the children so animated, explaining that deaf youngsters were not used to expressing themselves with strangers unless constantly encouraged by adults. Their lives consist more of *input* rather than *output*.

After meeting players, being buzzed by the vibrations of a bassoon and watching strings quiver on a cello, they recognised that the bigger instruments had wider vibrations than the smaller ones and excitedly waved their hands accordingly. A visit to the Conservatoire's percussion studio was the final stimulation of the morning. On this occasion, I played a large pair of cymbals behind everyone, but not too loud. The teachers nearly jumped out of their skins, but no one else turned a hair. I was reminded that, whatever I did, the children would never be able to hear. However, we might possibly make them aware of the endless variety of sounds offered by music of all kinds.

Visits by CBSO individuals into schools were very much in their infancy, initially intended for juniors only, but, as our ground-breaking efforts at Longwill Special School had created such interest, it was decided that I would follow the children through to Braidwood, their secondary school, where, to my amazement, I discovered a large music room full of instruments, including a large drum kit, all kinds of percussion from tiny hand drums to school timpani, shelves full of chime bars, tuned percussion (xylophones, glockenspiels, metallophones), bells, a music trolley full of the smaller

347

percussion instruments and, of course, a piano. In spite of all this, my large gong and bass drum caused something of a sensation. Janet, their specialist music teacher, was soon to become a friend and ally.

I was intrigued to realise that 'signing' is a distinctively individual skill. For instance, one teacher's BSL looked jerky and disjointed, whereas Janet created elegant movements, her hands dancing and forming clear, imaginative gestures, which flowed from one piece of information to another. We soon became adept at keeping ideas on the move and I picked up scraps of the language, which I managed to use although with a certain amount of self-consciousness. However, I was never worried about being expressive in other ways, as it was fun to be able to act out thoughts, pull faces, exaggerate and have a laugh. We worked well as a team, and I got on famously with the students. One member of staff remarked that he always knew when his kids had been with me, as he had to 'scrape them off the ceiling'.

Janet was thrilled at the prospect of having a large professional symphony orchestra as an aid to her imaginative teaching, especially when we took a small group to a rehearsal of Beethoven's Ninth Symphony with Simon Rattle. We had been trying to explain about pitch, but as the words 'high' and 'low' are not exclusively for the use of music, this proved to be a difficult concept. This was where the orchestra came in.

I had been promised five minutes at the beginning of rehearsal, so when we arrived the youngsters were introduced to the orchestra and then they stood facing the musicians to watch the proceedings. First, I asked for a high 'A' to be played by all the small instruments, i.e. violins, piccolo, flutes, clarinets and trumpets; then similarly a low note with large instruments, i.e. basses, cellos, bassoons and trombones. There was polite interest from the onlookers, but no overt response, after which everyone played the note in unison. This was greeted with a little more but still slightly puzzled interest: a "What are they doing this for?" type of reaction. The trump card was delivered, however, with a slow downward chromatic scale, starting with piccolo and gradually gathering more instruments on the way, trundling down to the largest five-stringed bass. As the middle range was reached, one of the older boys suddenly yelped, gesticulating madly as he realised what was happening, and began grinning, waving his hands and jigging about. He shook his neighbour, signing frantically, whereupon someone else caught something as the orchestra gathered momentum and, step by step, entered subterranean regions. Eventually there was a great hubbub as they all responded to the lower registers. Our specialised non-vocal communication via that little baton, facial expressions and waving of hands intrigued our onlookers, all part of experiencing Beethoven's music for real: sitting in the orchestra surrounded by a living sound – something that I suspect that none of us would ever forget.

Simon was fascinated with what we were doing, although I found it impossible to formulate a sensible answer when questioned by members of the press. I was still slightly uncomfortable at what I perceived as something of an experiment, especially as it was very difficult to evaluate the worth to the students. However, everyone seemed to be enjoying my visits, especially when pupils joined us from the nearby special school for the physically disabled. It was not long before Simon asked if he could come into school with me and meet everyone. The effect of this request was like that of dropping a large pebble in a pool. Ripples spread far and wide as excitement was generated throughout the whole school and beyond. I promised that there would be no press coverage and made arrangements for the visit.

As the boss has never had time to learn to drive, I found myself anxiously doing the honours as chauffeur. He was nervously apprehensive at the thought of going into the school; more precisely, as he so charmingly put it, "Shit scared!" As for me, the very act of driving 'the great hope for Birmingham music' around in my car gave me much food for thought, my imagination running riot down many 'what if?' roads. On our half-hour journey, a bus driver grinned with recognition, flourishing a hand to let me and my precious cargo into the traffic stream. We stopped briefly and illegally as Simon leapt out to dump an armful of tails suits at the dry cleaners: "They've got my name – I have an account!" Then, with heart thumping, we arrived safely. Simon carried the heavy glock. as we rolled into school to be greeted by a smiling, slightly flustered Janet, the head, numerous support staff and nonchalant kids whom I suspect were rather surprised to see him in jeans and casual shirt, looking far more informal than many other visitors they encountered.

I was in the novel situation of being an observer on this occasion, so found myself sitting out of the way behind the pupils. Janet had prepared a performance of her own arrangement of the main melody from *Rhapsody in Blue* as a party piece. The music (notated by letters for the individual note bars of the tuned instruments) was written on the board in a grid arrangement: blocks of chords to accompany the tune on the piano. One of the boys conducted, pointing in turn to the correct square; the rest watched like hawks, playing at the appropriate place. There was much applause at their sterling efforts, and then Simon asked if he could conduct. Janet was thrilled and

349

handed him a baton - one of his broken ones, which I had begged for earlier and carefully glued. After three chords, he somehow managed to skip a line, whereupon everyone stopped playing and looked at him in a puzzled fashion, eyes rolling: 'Oh, how embarrassing!' Janet grinned and proceeded to teach him his first sign – for 'embarrassing'. This was greeted with delighted hoots of laughter from everyone and the ice was well and truly broken. Consequently, this sign once appeared fleetingly during a CBSO rehearsal, much to my amusement, but no one else realised, of course.

Simon was very natural with everyone, but expecting, and getting, total concentration as he worked on the music. Simple signs were invented for the music's *loud* and *quiet*, with everyone following carefully for slight changes of tempo and shaping of phrases, as their arrangement was transformed into a creative performance. Even so, it was difficult to imagine what the participants got out of their experience musically speaking. Morning break came all too soon, as self-conscious girls served coffee and home-made biscuits for our distinguished guest. He was surrounded by excited pupils as he autographed a CBSO poster for the classroom wall ("for my new friends"), and he then tried to translate what one of the boys was asking: "Is your hair real?" A flustered Janet managed to convey this tactfully, accompanied by shouts of laughter from everyone and "No one in his right mind would do that to his hair if it wasn't real!" from me. This was all taken in good part. A member of staff asked if Simon chose the programmes for the orchestra. "Oh, yes. For instance, some people don't like Elgar, but that's just too bad. They have to play what I like" ... looking hard at me. I cheekily retorted, "... and some people don't like Tchaikovsky, so we never play any with you!" Shock, horror! One shouldn't talk to the boss like that. One of the boys, on discovering that Simon had been a percussionist, handed him a pair of sticks and gestured to the drum kit, and was delighted when his offer was taken up and we had a mini drumming session: loud, rhythmical, eyes closed, no inhibitions.

It was time to teach Simon some signing, so we sat in a circle on the floor and played "My aunt went to market and bought ...", adding on an item of food at every person. As Simon was the last one in the group, he had to remember everything. Needless to say, this was no problem at all. There was much hilarity, especially when 'my aunt' also went on journeys to different countries. But then it was time to go. I had taken lots of photos to remind us of a great morning, there were hugs and kisses for a blushing Janet, whoops of delight from the kids and "See you at the concert" from us.

350

It was decided that the chosen piece was to be Stravinsky's *Firebird* ballet music. I was pretty certain that I would be a huge success with my children, as I was playing, among other things, the very big orchestral bass drum, warning everyone that some of my notes were meant to take everyone by surprise as I represented the entry of a wizard. No one was to talk, the instruction being, "Sit on your hands! If you can see the audience from where you are sitting behind the orchestra, then they can see you."

When I went into school the following day, I was much taken aback to discover that their favourite part of the concert was when they saw me playing tambourine thumb trills. Yes, the bass drum was all right, but the vibrating tambourine jingles were creating a sound that they could see happening and subsequently try for themselves. We fished out tambourines from the percussion trolley and every pupil did a thumb trill (vibrating the skin/jingles by rubbing with a dampened thumb) straight away, without any prompting from me. Janet smiled knowingly, explaining that deaf children have very acute observation skills; another part of their armoury in a hearing world. From what I could gather, everyone seemed to get something out of the experience of attending a concert for the first time.

Clare, a friend of mine who was an IBM systems engineer, suggested a further development in communication. Two specialist computers were on trial in the UK, using 'Speech Viewer', a radical new educational tool aimed at helping those with speech and hearing difficulties. With voice and sound activated through a microphone, the system extracts elements of speech such as pitch, dynamics and duration of sound, displaying the information on screen in a child-friendly form of easy-to-interpret pictures and games.

After seeing a demonstration of this leading-edge technology, members of the orchestra decided to raise money to provide a Speech Viewer package for Braidwood School. IBM generously donated the computer, but we were told that the innovative software could cost anything up to £500. This was no problem for the musicians, however, so it was all systems go. Money began to roll in slowly, but, as soon as Simon got wind of our ongoing efforts, an envelope arrived containing a blank cheque from him; thus it was possible to close the deal quickly, the shortfall being in the region of £350. When I went to thank him for his generous donation, he was very relaxed as he told me that he had recently taken over a concert for an American maestro who'd had to pull out at the last minute. He had been paid thousands more than he had anticipated, so it was a case of "What's money for? It's much better to use it for something worthwhile like this ...." For once, words failed me as I tried to tell him how much his kindness was appreciated. I was subsequently presented with a bill for £1 from IBM for the computer - 'A peppercorn rent'? It is almost worth framing.

Eventually the junior school was also able to purchase a compatible computer with a grant from the National Lottery – all in all, a very satisfactory outcome.

* * *

If some of the orchestra programmes were of a non-percussive nature, I had more time to work, not only in my special school but also taking part in projects in mainstream schools. Visits were spaced out over many weeks; therefore it was perfectly possible to fit them in around my orchestra schedule. I had asked for 'difficult' schools, but there were times when my quest for a challenge was almost my undoing, as I discovered on my first visit to a tough secondary school 120 miles away in deepest Cardiff. The piece chosen for the project was Stravinsky's *Rite of Spring*, and I summed up my first visit to the school in the following notes, written for Ann Tennant, our education manager.

This is a big ugly concrete and glass secondary school in a poor dockland area of Cardiff. My first impression was of drabness: no obvious colour, dark blue school uniforms, long featureless corridors, dreary walls and paintwork. There is an air of scrubbed shabbiness and it is far too quiet.

I was allowed to leave the car by the front door, after surrendering my keys to a pleasant, helpful school secretary who took me what seemed like miles, up to the music room. This was a classroom as far away from the front entrance as possible and on the second floor. Five girls were detailed to help carry the instruments (snare drum, tenor drum, cymbals, various stands, small instruments and two large maps mounted on board). They were not the people I would be working with, but they showed a healthy curiosity as to why I was in school.

The music room has a large blackboard, a minimal drum kit in the corner (looks untouched), a huge padlocked cupboard for school percussion instruments, and a number of tables pushed back to make room for a circle of chairs. NO piano.

As I arrived there was a changeover of classes and 'my' 15 yr olds came in, a slouching silent bunch of boys and girls looking with vague curiosity at the bags of gear dumped on the table. As they arranged themselves in a circle, being chivvied by Liz the music teacher, I busied myself by setting up the instruments, and trying to appear as relaxed and friendly as possible.

Liz is a Canadian of no-nonsense attitude, tending to treat her pupils in a lightly patronising manner, which grated somewhat. Having said that, she can also be very positive and cheerful. I got the impression that music was something to be endured by this group, understandable when Liz introduced them to me saying, "This lot can't do anything else, so they do music." After this appalling statement it seemed to me only natural that there was a strong atmosphere of total switch-off.

I began by asking, "Do you know why I'm here?" Deathly silence. Then my sharp ears picked up a muttered retort from a sullen girl at the back of the group, "To show us up." This comment cut me to the quick, and has haunted me ever since. This is what these kids expect from adults.

First I demonstrated the rope-tensioned tenor drum, then over to the modern snare drum. They were grudgingly interested in the techniques, after which I borrowed the school S.D. from the kit as the snares on mine had decided to fall apart. During the exchange I casually asked who played the kit. No reply. I strongly suspect that no one ever has the opportunity just to 'mess about' or experiment with the instruments, even if a teacher is present. Out came the tambourine with the usual spiel about standing on one leg, all the different sounds it can make, then I got onto thumb rolls. No one was willing to have a go, but eventually, with much bullying from his mates, one gawky lad came forward. He was embarrassed by all the attention, but with maximum encouragement from me (and warning looks to Liz) he was persuaded to keep on trying. After three self-conscious attempts he managed to get a little spurt out of it. Much cheering/jeering sent him back to his seat with a half grin on his face and a casual 'well done' nod from me. One of the girls had a go - no trouble at all, she played a long trill straight away, after which she handed the instrument to Liz. To my secret delight she couldn't get the hang of it. We all had a little laugh at that and she promised to practise before my next visit.

It is always a bit delicate when one goes into another's domain. Liz is obviously the one used to being solely in charge all the time, so I was very aware that I had to be sensitive and adjust my approach accordingly. Not

353

easy in front of fourteen suspicious fifteen-year-olds.
After more laborious efforts with clapping games, I invited questions, but
none were forthcoming. We had run out of time and the class shambled
out for a lunch break. However, the one tiny gleam of hope on the horizon
was when one of the girls smiled and remarked casually as she was
passing, "I like your earrings, miss!"
I'm not sure if I can cope with this challenge, especially as Liz said to the
kids at one point, "Classical music is music for snobs!" I was told at the
pre-project training day that she is "one of the best music teachers in the
city". I despair for the rest.

Ann had her work cut out to persuade me to continue with this uphill task, but joined me as an observer for the second visit. On arrival, we discovered that the group had been divided and was established in two classrooms. This meant that I could work independently without interference from Liz. Meanwhile, Ann met the headmaster, who was amazed to discover that I was in his school, declaring that he had no idea that there had been any contact with the CBSO. Fortunately, he was delighted at the prospect of some of his more difficult teenagers becoming involved with a major symphony orchestra. I was relieved and pleased to discover that work had been done since my first visit, but also realised that my charges were less than happy playing what they regarded as infant-school instruments.

Another long trip down the motorways ensued, this time with a heavily loaded car. I had managed to convince Liz that we would be far more comfortable in the small hall, and so, with this in mind, I had taken my concert xylophone, bass drum, snare drum, glockenspiel, suspended cymbal, pair of cymbals, the orchestra's big gong, and various smaller but still adult instruments. I was duly met by intrigued pupils, who willingly helped cart everything indoors. All the instruments were spaced out around the hall, each with appropriate beaters or sticks nearby, and then we began our session. I explained carefully that these were my own personal instruments, and that I was more than happy for them to be played on condition that the correct beaters were used and that the instruments were not abused in any way. Liz raised an eyebrow at this, protesting vehemently when I insisted on leaving the hall for a coffee during the morning break, the words "I trust you" and "I expect you to be as careful as I would be" hanging in the air as we left. We had taken only two steps down the corridor when a cacophony of sound burst forth. Ignoring Liz's agitation, I dragged her off to the staff room as she muttered about insurance claims, my irresponsible behaviour, her job at stake, and so on.

When we returned, our ears were assailed with the sound of a huge jam session going on: noisy – yes, fun – yes, smiles – yes, and, what is more, a positive willingness to attempt some creative work – YES! By the time I had completed my visits to the school, we had concocted a simple piece of music based on Stravinsky's intervals and rhythms. There had been many excited discussions generated by the music, but a pivotal moment had come when trying to decide how to achieve a dramatic climax for the completed composition. Would we use a loud gong stroke, or a more subtle sudden silence? A vote was taken and, to my delight, the silence was chosen. Liz protested that we should have used the gong note, but no, the youngsters were adamant and their decision won the day.

All the schools taking part shared their pieces prior to the final CBSO rehearsal and, once my group had settled down and controlled their embarrassed giggles, we managed to perform our hard-won creation with a reasonable amount of confidence. I saw them grow with pride as they realised what they had accomplished in a relatively short time. Then it was my turn.

My group sat in the balcony of the concert hall to listen to the orchestra's rehearsal and, when I took a sneaky glance, I saw that they were hardly able to contain their excitement at hearing Stravinsky's hair-raising music for the first time. During the break they rushed backstage to see me, declaring, "You're playing OUR music! He's used OUR ideas!" "Success in the face of all odds", I secretly gloated.

All the school groups were as good as gold throughout the concert, totally riveted by an evening of new experiences. At the end, my bunch erupted with cheers, waving and hand-hurting loud applause. After putting away the instruments, I discovered a knot of youngsters eager to tell me how much they had enjoyed everything. They had been to see Simon for autographs, and one of the boys was so excited that he flung his arms around me and gave me a great big kiss, accompanied by much banter and friendly laughter from the rest – not to mention total astonishment from me! Everyone piled outside to wave to the orchestra coaches as we set off back home to Birmingham, heaving sighs of relief.

The upshot of this project was that that group of pupils requested another visit to the next CBSO concert in Cardiff. They sat through an unprepared concert in their complimentary seats behind the orchestra, much excited and eager to tell me all their news and delighted to see Simon once more in the driving seat. Today's youngsters cope very well with music of their own time, if everyone has an open mind: performers and listeners. I was thrilled that our project had made a tiny impact on their young lives, helping to offset some of the prejudice we encounter all too often.

* * *

Braidwood Special Secondary School certainly adopted me. Everyone knew that I was from the orchestra as I was greeted by all, including the dinner ladies and the caretaker, and was accepted wholeheartedly in the staff room. One difference between this and a mainstream school, however, was that the children did not call out my name when they saw me arrive: I had plenty of cheery waves from the playground, but no shouts of 'Hello Maggie!'

At the beginning of my time there, I was invited to wear hearing aids for a morning. Echoing in the back of my mind was the haunting, thought-provoking statement made by one of the teachers: "If you are blind, you are cut off from things; if you are deaf, you are cut off from people." As I am someone who finds listening to music through headphones a claustrophobic nightmare, wearing hearing aids depressed me more than I could begin to explain, until one of the girls put it in proportion by signing, "Don't worry about us, we're used to it, it's okay!" I was invited to the school Christmas party, we privately visited a Sound Sculpture exhibition at a Birmingham art gallery and during our Holst *Planets* project I joined the group for a special trip to Jodrell Bank Observatory and Astronomy Research Centre, where I was as excited as the kids.

On one school visit, I realised that some everyday sounds that we in the hearing world take for granted were unknown, when I unwittingly shook my jacket to 'see' if the car keys were in a pocket. This little incident spawned much discussion, so much so that I decided to draw a parallel with instrumental and human voices. First, I made large drawings of birds for my group, each with a simple diagram of appropriate birdsong drawn in dots: cuckoo, robin and owl. "What do birds do when they wake up?" Answers varied from "yawn" to "have their breakfast". The two notes of the cuckoo were easy: 'Plink! Plonk!' on the tuned percussion instruments; one high note, one low. I explained that cuckoos all over the world sang that song. We had fun with other birds too, after which one of the younger boys looked very thoughtful, and then carefully signed, "Do butterflies sing?" I pondered cautiously before I replied. "I really don't know, but if they do, I can't hear them as they will sing very quietly." This notion cheered everyone as we continued to explore other aspects of sound: dogs barking, a kettle coming to the boil, bees buzzing, bells ringing, doors slamming, individual footsteps, and so on.

"Time now to explain about individual voices in instruments," I casually announced. Janet looked uncomfortable and wary, as it slowly dawned on us that the pupils would be unlikely to understand the concept of individual human voices, never mind musical instruments. Unless someone reads about differing voices or is told about them, why should they realise? Do blind people know that every single person on the planet has an individual face? This is a difficult fact to absorb, in spite of the evidence before our very eyes and ears. Muttering under the breath – not giving anyone the chance to lip-read – we formulated a plan. Two of us sat in front of our tiny group and each announced a firm, carefully enunciated "Good morning!" followed by an encouraging smile. "Is that the same, or different?" Everyone immediately signed "different" and then qualified their answers by pointing out that Mr Taylor had a beard, I wore a skirt, he had a jacket on, I had fair hair – the comparisons were endless. We tried again and again, but had similar results each time.

Okay … different tactics. I went behind the half-open door and mimed a phone call to Janet who had her back to me at the other side of the room. I said just one word; no name, no clues: "Hello!" Janet's immediate response was, "Oh, it's YOU!" This new game stopped everyone in their tracks, resulting in puzzlement, silence and frowns. We repeated the exercise a few times, until one of the boys slowly began to stroke his throat, signing, "It's there … it's voices …?" "Yes! Well done!" I then went on to explain that we all have our own unique faces, fingerprints, writing and way of walking, and similarly everyone also has a unique, "your very own!" voice. I explained that men's voices are different to women's, and boys' voices change when they become men. This last point was illustrated by one of the more mature Asian lads, who had just begun to grow a faint moustache, his voice had plummeted the depths and he was growing like a weed. We told him that we could hear that he was becoming a man. He was thrilled, leaping about and thumping his friend on the back in triumph. As it dawned on them that all of us could be recognised by the way we speak, the classroom erupted into shouts and words, everyone laughing with excitement.

There was a sobering sequence to this revelation, however, when I visited profoundly deaf Yorkshireman, Paul Whittaker (founder of the charity 'Music and the Deaf') and Mary, his deaf sister, some time later. Paul was intrigued about my various undertakings and always enquired about what we were currently doing in school. I replied casually, "Oh, we're discussing individual voices." Mary looked mystified as she lip-read, so this statement was repeated more carefully, as it became apparent that mature college graduate Mary also had no idea that everyone's voice is unique. When questioned, she told me that she thought that everyone sounded the same.

More visits to rehearsals delved into the intricacies of the insides of a concert grand piano, this with the cheerful help of enthusiastic soloist, Cécile Ousset. There were further introductions to instruments, meeting more players and informal chats with Simon. When I next brought the children into a concert, Simon spotted them behind the orchestra and secretly signed "Hello!" before turning to bow to the main audience. What a star!

Soon after all this easy rapport with the youngsters, Simon turned to me and said with total seriousness, "When are you going to write that book?" I took a deep breath, looked him in the eye and replied, "When people like you promise to come to visit me in jail should I go too far!" There was no further comment.

During summer term, a few physically disabled youngsters joined my group for a visit to Birmingham Town Hall for an afternoon concert. I discovered that one little lad (with hearing, but no speech, and therefore learning to sign) was eleven years old that day. I immediately went to see Simon to give him the signs for *Happy Birthday*. Tim was in a wheelchair on the ground floor in front of the cellos and was at once spotted by grinning, waving players. The deaf children were sitting behind me with other audience members on the choir seating. When Simon appeared to the packed house, he bowed, and then immediately turned to the children and signed *Happy Birthday* to Tim, who nearly fell out of his wheelchair with delight. Then, instead of starting the concert, Simon turned round to the orchestra and called out to me, "Was that right?" I grinned, shrugged and replied, "I don't know, I couldn't see you!" The audience was dumbfounded – musicians do not speak during concerts. He turned back to them and said in a conversational tone, "My friend Tim is eleven today, so we've decided to play for him," and then, looking at the orchestra, he continued, "Can we have this one in the key of G please, and no messing about!" The tradition is that, if a player has a birthday, the rest of the orchestra plays THE tune during the rehearsal. It is always a joke, in every key in the world and a total shambles, accompanied by much laughter. Not this time though. There followed an impeccable and glorious performance of *Happy Birthday*, complete with somewhat moist-eyed cymbal playing me. The audience sang, and there was one very happy little boy wriggling with delight in his wheelchair. Not a dry eye in the house!

After everyone had calmed down, Simon then turned once more to the audience and announced that he had been learning some sign language and asked them to interpret a very special sign invented by one of the boys. Two hands locked at the thumbs, fingers flapping like a bird, immediately followed by one hand slapping the other horizontally, back on back. There were a few attempts at translation: bird, butterfly, aeroplane, and so on, until he turned and asked me, "Was that correct?" I again insisted, "I can't see you ... (laughter) ... why don't you ask Mark?" Handsome Mark was the boy who had invented this musical sign and he happened to be sitting immediately behind me. I had rarely heard him use his voice, but on this occasion he stood in front of all those people, took a deep breath, made the sign and said the one word, "Bat-on!" There was a burst of applause from everyone, including the orchestra. I was so proud of him.

It was soon the end of the school year and the end of the orchestra's season. But there were secrets in the air as Janet and the Braidwood team brought their students to one of our final rehearsals. I was totally in the dark as to what was happening when Ann Tennant announced that everyone was invited to a short performance by the Braidwood group during the lunch break. This was held in a Birmingham Conservatoire small rehearsal hall, with Simon as guest of honour and myself as their adopted player. Many members of the orchestra attended, proving to be an enthusiastic audience for the end product of some very hard work from teachers and pupils. After the imaginative performance, one of the girls presented Simon with flowers, signing, "I'm in love with Simon, but I know that he has lots of girlfriends." Their sign for 'Simon Rattle' was a finger-spelled 'S' – linked little fingers – and a quick mime of shaking a baby rattle in the air. It all made sense. I was given hugs and kisses, flowers and a signed card, but at the time I did not realise that our most exciting project was yet to come.

In 1991, the English composer David Bedford had met Simon and me at the Barbican Centre to discuss the possibility of the CBSO becoming involved in his new work for deaf children and orchestra: *Stories from the Dreamtime*, commissioned by Music and the Deaf. The work is a setting of five aboriginal myths scored for full orchestra, forty deaf children, narrator, sign language interpreter and a further group of hearing children, who surround the audience playing pebbles and wine glasses. Ideally, David wanted Simon and the orchestra to present the first performance, which was being planned for the Huddersfield Contemporary Music Festival in the following year, but unfortunately we were unable to do this as we were involved with a festival of Scandinavian music during that crucial period. However, Simon thought that it would be perfectly possible for me to be released from Birmingham duties and be the professional percussionist involved in leading a group of youngsters invited from Braidwood.

In due course, and after more dialogue with David, the school was asked to provide ten senior students to take part in the big adventure. Forty young deaf people were taking part from all over the country. Each group of ten worked with a professional percussionist; then everyone joined together in Yorkshire to work with the English Northern Philharmonia Orchestra. Our group was marginally more at ease than the others, as they had previously had direct contact with a large symphony orchestra. Everyone was eager to learn, however, as they all came together to work, staying in a residential college prior to the performance.

The colourful legend had been studied most thoroughly by all, as it was essential that the whole story was familiar so that it would be possible to pick up cues before areas of personal responsibility. We took a number of cymbals, and were mainly representing the wind in various guises, although everyone came together with a large variety instruments for specific passages such as violent storms, earthquakes, and so on.

The following is taken from diary entries in November 1992:

Wednesday:
Rehearsals in common room. Too small and stuffy, people were weary from their long journeys. David Bedford deadly serious (lacks humour, nervous?). His daughter (who works in a London Special School) forgot to bring all their percussion instruments. I'm glad it wasn't me! One of my girls very truculent and awkward all afternoon. They're easily distracted and find it boring, not surprising – it is! Depressing and frustrating. All pro. percussionists present, thank goodness. Jenny has a black eye and her neck in a brace from a car crash, Graham has the 'runs'. What a team! Luckily we all know each other. Rehearsed in an upstairs room. All gear had to be lifted via fire escape incl. huge marimba, timps and vibes. Conductor (Elgar/'Garry' Howarth) very difficult for the deaf kids to understand. Finished 8.30pm. Stayed with g'parents. Yorkshire fish and chips.

Thursday:

Early start. Percussionists sorted out cross rhythms in the Hurricane movement. Kids very distracted by everything and I had to nag them to WATCH me. Conductor forever starting before we were ready. Why doesn't he be more sensitive/imaginative? David is worse. Thank goodness Paul Whittaker is around to stop them going on and on. Back down fire escape with gear, then loading into a convoy of 2 big transit vans, 3 estate cars for orchestra rehearsal in Pudsey. Jack, the ENP porter, is a gem, works like a demon.

Ran through the piece, the kids wanted to know if the queen was coming, and if this was where the concert was going to be. The orch parts are lovely in places, some very moving oboe and horn solos. (Mustn't get sentimental, these kids don't miss a thing.) Another great pack-up, then back to Hudds and an adult Indian meal.

Friday - Concert day:

11.30am set-up on high staging in town hall in front of organ. 2.30pm Kids getting bored with the piece. My lot have their backs to the audience; they HAVE to be able to see me. After rehearsing (kids now in Hudds Contemp Festival tee shirts), another re-set for Turnage's **Screaming Popes** *whilst a professional photographer did his stuff with the youngsters.*

(He said later, "the concert was one of the most moving occasions I have ever attended.") It's v. nice not to be working at CBSO pressure on this I must say. I'd forgotten how it could be! After **Popes** *we did our stuff, they were angelic and did very well. I was proud of them. Conductor only got lost once in The Hurricane. Groan. Anyway it was all controlled and v. professional. I was presented with a plant from my group and gave each of them a posh pen. David seemed pleased (his anxious Mona Lisa smile slipping just a little). Loaded the car, home at 1.30am exhausted.*

My favourite part of the weekend was seeing how well everyone got on together. Mealtimes were alive with signing, gestures, laughter and words. Teachers were forever on the lookout for signs of homesickness, but we suspected that there was no time for this, as everyone seemed to be thoroughly enjoying themselves. After a lot of work with individual groups, we joined up with the orchestra for the final rehearsals with pebble and wineglass players from local schools. Huddersfield Town Hall is my old stamping ground, of course, but this lovely Victorian hall came as a surprise to most of the youngsters, especially when they realised how exposed they would be on the high platform. There seemed to be little time in which to instil any kind of stage decorum, but we need not have worried, as everyone behaved impeccably. BBC 3 microphones were everywhere, which made everyone realise that this was, as they say, 'for real'. An added edge of nerves honed everyone's concentration and, to our great relief, the performance was a huge success. When I first started working with hearing-impaired youngsters, I never dreamt that such an event could take place, but there they were, bowing to unreserved applause after broadcasting on the BBC. Everyone was so very impressed with them. Press comments:

'A Dream come true' ... For the children involved, I would guess it was an unforgettable experience - it certainly was for me.' (The Independent)

'Elgar Howarth held it together dramatically. His was no simple task since each group of children, each with its own mammoth set of percussion, had its own conductor, yet every point was brilliantly made. The ENP, of course, are magnificent and in this performance, while they had every musical sympathy with the youngsters, no detail was left unattended, a point which also epitomised the rest of the programme.' (Huddersfield Daily Examiner).

However, as far as I was concerned, the best feedback was from some of the youngsters themselves:
We before wrong all music. This awful because deaf first time with the claves. We concentrate with claves and learn better. All 500 people sit, watch, listen to the music. This was wonderful.

Thank you for your hard work in music. Hearing children use glass in water, like whistling. I feel happy because all children working hard in music. Hearing people say, 'I feel happy'.

The clapping went on for 2 minutes. Did you know that?

The best thing I have done, better than football or any sport.

One teacher observed:

... a profound effect on all the pupils, and indeed the staff. In 20+ years of working with young people, this project has been the highlight for me, with so many unexpected additional experiences and outcomes for the children.

* * *

When I first began working in mainstream schools, I was as apprehensive as the non-musical teachers. There I was, on their patch, and without a shred of teaching experience, but armed with enthusiasm for my subject and a love of children. The more contact I had, the more I enjoyed what I was trying to achieve, although on many an occasion there were more problems with the adults than with the children. The concept of letting the children have their say, use their imaginations, make a noise, 'finger paint with sound', was alien to certain hidebound control freaks in the teaching profession, and I found myself insisting that the end products were to be those of the children, however simple and basic.

At my second visit, one memorable inner-city school delivered 'thump, thump, thump; bash, bash, bash!' from raucous groups of juniors in their overcrowded space. Eyes glazed with resignation, hands on heads if they showed the slightest spark, instruments abused and a continuously shouting teacher did not bode well for any kind of creativity. It was obvious that not one word from me had sunk in at our first session some weeks earlier, so I had to defuse the mayhem tactfully, get the teacher on my side and win over the kids. We ended up doing a sound picture of *Jack and the Beanstalk* – nothing whatsoever to do with the CBSO project, but providing masses of scope for a clumping giant, winding stems, chopping axe, falling beanstalk ... and silences. At last there were sparkling eyes, smiles, sensible discussions and a splendid end product to show to the rest of the school. The teacher purred with pride as the children rose to the occasion, although I doubt if she realised just how much I had manipulated the situation. They all came to the prescribed orchestral concert with the minimum of information tucked under their belts, but, in spite of this, they were angelic and loved the experience.

On another occasion, in an even rougher school in a deprived concrete jungle area, the class teacher was eager to tell me that her children were the only ones in the playground to notice a 'V' formation of geese flying overhead to the local park pond. They had heard them. During my first visit, I had spent a long time trying to settle the disruptive children so that we could listen to some gentle Debussy: *Perfumes of the Night*. I knew that, as I was working with inner-city children, there was no chance of any romanticism about the delights of a summer night. No, here was stark reality. "Me mam shouting at our Kevin", "The TV on loud - nan's deaf!", "The baby yelling", and so on, were their experiences of night sounds (I resisted going down the road of night perfumes!) Recruiting the most disruptive boy as my technical man was a good move. He was responsible for turning on the tape recorder for the three-minute music sample, which he did perfectly well after an over-the-top bragging display for the rest of the class. The harassed, inexperienced and very young teacher was standing behind me, bleakly making lists of *naughty* and *good* children on the blackboard. If any child showed the slightest inclination to answer my quick-fire questions without first putting up a hand, they were in the naughty column, followed rapidly by hands on head and an order of "Silence!" This exhausting attempt at discipline was eventually abandoned as I drew her into what we were trying to do. At last it was possible to play the snippet of music to a quiet, inquisitive bunch of children sitting uncomfortably on the floor. When the sound eventually died away, there was a long pause, and then a small voice whispered, "Can we 'ave it again, miss?"

Later, at coffee time, my young teacher friend remarked that I seemed to 'have a knack' with children. Ah, yes, but then I am the knight in shining armour appearing intermittently with many magical things, whereas she is on duty all the time. Teachers have my total admiration, but teaching was not a career I would have chosen. I love the school experience, but on my terms. We musicians are in the privileged position of delivering 'awe and wonder' and frequently seeing the light of understanding shine from the dullest of children. For me this is an adrenalin buzz, often reaching the point of self-indulgence, that far exceeds many run-of-the-mill symphony concerts. And I suspect that many of us get far more from working in the real world in schools than we would have ever suspected initially. Our imaginations are stretched and our patience is tried, but communication skills are sharpened and the eventual sense of achievement is a constant treasure and delight.

24
The Baton is Silent

"Don't call me maestro!" This was the headline emblazoned across the *New York Times* on the occasion of the first visit to that city by the CBSO. As if we would! This small word is open to many interpretations, and it is rare for a British orchestral musician to use it with the deference expected by some stick-wavers. This is not a case of simple disrespect; it is just the fact that UK orchestras find it very difficult to choke out what we perceive as a fantasy ego-trip title to a mere conductor. After all, we are all there for the purpose of making music and we are the ones who actually create the sounds, thank you very much. Some conductors preen themselves if a player, instead of holding up a hand or instrument for a query, utters "Maestro" instead of the more usual, "Er ... excuse me?" In British orchestras, the word 'maestro' is usually expressed with a barely concealed sense of irony, something that American conductors never seem to realise. To us it is the ubiquitous label of little value constantly trotted out by American musicians. Only on very rare occasions will we utter 'maestro' with sincerity, when perhaps the orchestra is making music with an exceptionally fine guest conductor who speaks little English, because it is a fail-safe way of attracting his attention and, practically speaking, far easier than remembering the guy's name. "Who was carving today?" "No idea, I didn't look." True, all true. Sir Simon Rattle hates to be called maestro, even in jest, as first names were always used both on- and offstage during his long tenure with the CBSO. I occasionally earned myself a twitching eyebrow when barging through the door with, "Oops! Morning maestro!" No reply. Indeed, when Simon returned to the orchestra after his knighthood had been announced in 1994, we discovered a notice on the orchestra noticeboard, which declared: 'Simon Rattle'.

Simon has asked that his new title should only be used in official external publicity (brochures, leaflets, posters, press releases, etc.) The formal title for letter heading, annual report, etc., is Sir Simon Rattle CBE. Internal correspondence, schedules, etc., should continue to refer to him as either music director or Simon Rattle.

This caused much amusement and some initial teasing from us, as I am sure that no one could have spat it out anyway. Soon after the champagne had been drunk and the announcement became public, one of the trombonists was asked by a member of the audience if we had been working with Sir Simon, "No," he replied - "MumMark!" (Try stammering it out loud.)

Legend has it that a large brass band was recruiting new blood and dishing out instruments to the local senior school students. "If you can't read music, take a pair of drumsticks and learn to play the drums," was the condescending instruction when most of the instruments had been chosen. This spawned an immediate response from the percussion tutor: "And if you can't play anything or read music, take just one of those sticks and conduct!"

Many musicians really do seem to become a different breed once they clutch a baton. I have known one particular character since 1954, when we were both members of the National Youth Orchestra; he a precocious red-haired thirteen-year-old, and I an unsophisticated seventeen. He has yet to realise that he does himself no favours when nowadays he announces to all and sundry, in a pseudo self-deprecating fashion, "Just call me maestro!" The sad thing is that we know that he actually relishes this, and thinks that he's made the grade. I'm sorry, but I really cannot take this seriously at all, for all his hard work. He treats the orchestra like a bunch of students, eagerly explaining every Italian term at least twice – a perfect recipe for losing everyone within the first three minutes of standing on the rostrum. Lovely guy *off the box*, as we say, but … oh dear!

It is always the ones with overt personal hopes, fantasies and aspirations who drive the orchestra crazy. Every year the orchestra suffers at Christmas time by being made to rehearse (translation: *play through*) every verse of the audience carols by a chorus master: no chorus, just the orchestra. Is this a lack of imagination, ignorance, fear, or just playing with a big train set? This is when the orchestra joins in by throwing teddies around and being naughty. It brings out many manifestations of childishness, from never looking at him at all to asking crass questions and dropping pencils on the floor – anything to relieve the tedium. I would shut myself off from it all by getting stuck into a monumental rubbishy novel, whereas my immediate colleagues are dab hands at crossword puzzles, all of us occasionally coming up for air to play something. The next one to play does the counting of tacet bars. Working well as a team, we trust each other implicitly. Peace reigns.

The biggest compliment an orchestra can pay to a conductor is to say, "He doesn't get in the way, he lets us play." A sense of humour is at the top of my personal list: it doesn't matter if he speaks the language, is nine or ninety; just keep the angst out of the proceedings, and let us all get on with it. Russian Yuri Temirkanov is an occasional guest conductor, and initially spoke very little English. We did observe, however, that he tried harder to communicate on his very first meeting with the orchestra than on subsequent visits, when he had a very glamorous young interpreter in tow. Language really isn't necessary, as conductors should be able to connect through the music. The majority attempt to sing their ideas, only needing basic vocabulary for the letters of the alphabet and numbers (rehearsal milestones). The words 'before' and 'after', 'yes' and 'no', 'please' and 'thank you' also help. Then we are in business.

There we were, in the middle of a heavy Russian programme, when he stopped, leant back on his high stool and began to address us with much waving of hands and facial expressions. It soon became apparent that he was telling an 'Englishman, Irishman and Scotsman' type of joke – all in Russian, of course. Such are Temirkanov's communication skills that we were riveted. No one understood a single word, but the joke was obviously very comical. When the punchline was reached, the orchestra roared its approval and applauded with much laughter, after which the interpreter translated what he'd been saying and it wasn't funny at all – It's the way they tell 'em!

"Your damned nonsense will I withstand twice or once, but sometimes always, by God, NEVER!": I doubt if Richter had any idea that his anger towards the Hallé Orchestra many decades ago would still echo down the years to the delight of generations of orchestral musicians. Some quick-witted character had scribbled down these bon mots, which swiftly spread through the profession without the aid of the Internet or suchlike. Likewise, Ansermet was obviously irritated beyond endurance when he shouted at an English orchestra, "Don't spoke, don't spoke, if you didn't like it, you went. Just play the notes as they are rotten!" We treasure these gems.

One of the more fastidious fiddle players came off stage for the interval looking decidedly unhappy.

"Anne, whatever's the matter?" I enquired.

"Oh Maggie, we're in the sweat zone … and what's more, he smells!" I remembered seeing great arcs of perspiration flying around over the front desks of strings during rehearsal, so pulled an appropriate face in sympathy.

"There's something to be said about being out of the way at the back," I laughed.

"Well," she replied, "it wasn't so bad this afternoon because Jackie (the leader) had brought in a deodorant spray, so when he turned to direct the cellos she gave a few quick squirts behind his back to clear the air – pssst! pssst! pssst! – and by the time he turned to us again we were playing as normal." Then she added, "But he's not the only one. When some of them get worked up, spittle flies around, or even worse. One particular pianist-cum-conductor … he snorts down his nose and … I just can't bear to say!"

The one of the front-desk violas quietly chipped in with, "Oh yes, talking about spitting, when Sakari (Oramo) got worked up during one of the many climaxes in the scherzo of Mahler 5 a great flob landed on my viola. All I could think about was all those enzymes eating into my 300-year-old varnish!"

I was left with my vivid imagination to think that one through.

It is not advisable to have physical contact with any conductor at the end of any performance, as they are not nice to be near. However, the leader cannot avoid that handshake from the rostrum as the orchestra finally rises to take the applause. As an audience member, I once spotted a swift wiping of the right hand down dress trousers immediately after leader/conductor contact and wondered if it was solely to do with the fact that the maestro was wringing wet or that, according to all the evidence of the body language throughout the performance, they were sworn enemies. I suspect that I was in the minority in noting this, as the rest of the audience was responding to the extravagant antics from the rostrum.

It takes a real pro to apologise to the orchestra, however, if things go awry. Everyone can and does make mistakes, and those in full view on the rostrum are no exception. One gem was when a guest conductor began the last movement of the Brahms Violin Concerto without the soloist. Everything ground to an ignominious halt; then the movement began once more, this time with the violinist. 'Never talk to conductors or management,' was the message hammered home to students when I was at the Royal Academy of Music. One mistake is allowed, but we are not paid to make more: then it becomes an embarrassing "Is there a problem?" Oh dear!

* * *

During our eighteen years with Sir, I never saw him overtly lose his temper during a rehearsal. Here are some of his more colourful observations that I noted over the years:

* When he first arrived as a keen, eager youngster, there was an occasion when he said, "If we play that note a little earlier, then it won't sound so sharp", or was it, "If we play that note a little sharper, then it won't sound so early"? He seemed somewhat taken aback when we responded with an immediate roar of laughter at this overt tact. Yes, yes, the note was late AND sharp. We got the message.

* A favourite instruction to choir and orchestra is: "If you can hear yourself, you're too loud." Guaranteed to scare everyone into nervous twitchings.

* Prokofiev, Symphony No. 5, end of second movement: "Like the edge of a brick coming hard down on your head ... or a sharp knife," and later, "I'm not going to be vindictive ... at least not until tomorrow."

* Stravinsky, *Rite of Spring*:

- Part I: "You're giving me chimpanzees and I want orang-utans," said with appropriate facial expressions - Grrrrrr! (or 'gorillas'). A variation for Slavonic composers is a request for goulash rather than consommé.

- Part 2: "No attack at all - quicksand sound. Tubas from the distance, over the mountains. I don't want 4B pencils ... 2H!" and "Horns: we don't need that industrial sound!"

* Verdi, *Requiem*: To the chorus, "LISTEN ... it's got to sound like broken bones sticking out."

* Copland, *Billy the Kid*: "Grits, sweetcorn, potatoes in goose fat sort of sound. Caramel."

* Mahler 1, at the very beginning: "If you're not sure it's the right note, don't try to find out."

* Mahler 9:

- End of quiet movement: "Don't scratch armpits too soon, keep the suspense."

- Beginning of the final movement: "This is where the paramedics come to cart us off."

* Shostakovitch First Symphony:

- First movement: "It should sound like shoeshine bowing, though it's not, more like a little Scotch terrier scratching someone to bits ... think of a conductor."

- Second movement, to violins: "Any old squeal will do ... whistle!" Demonstrates a piercing whistle with two fingers. "It's a personal vendetta. (Everything running away out of control) Oops! Start again at the beginning. I shouldn't have said I'd take it fast. I'll take it really S-L-O-W. Try and drag Colin back (1st clarinet). This is the EASY piece in the programme." (The rest being *Varèse Ameriques*, Berg's *Three Pieces from Wozzeck* and Gershwin's *American in Paris*.)

- Slow movement: "You'll have guessed what it'll be after the five *ppp* bit … 'pale' … you shouldn't think that you've heard it after the brass."

* Beethoven 9:

- To the chorus: "I want to avoid music with helmets on." (Or "jackboots", depending on his mood.)

- At the first bass-drum entry in the finale, to me: "I want clods of earth falling on a coffin lid." Then, after being joined by cymbals, we were forever referred to as "the married couple".

* Messaien, *Turangalîla* rehearsals: Simon said that he had remembered a certain passage differently. "Another orchestra?" someone ventured. "Berlin Phil?" from elsewhere. Simon: "You must be joking. *Turangalîla* is something they say their Radio Orchestra would play, but not them. They think that a *celeste* is an exotic instrument!"

* Ravel, *Daphnis and Chloë*: "Lick that note, don't bite it." At one point the contra bassoon's contribution was described as "a celestial passing of wind"! Something to do with its 'farting bedpost' nickname perhaps?

* At the end of a particularly trying day taking Weill's *Seven Deadly Sins* to bits, everyone was tired as we struggled with the tricky music and tried to translate the German titles of the movements and detailed instructions in the score. Simon had enacted a graphic 'story time' for the doom and gloom, we had survived the wall of death areas, and he attempted, as he said, to 'go for the jugular', but, in spite of his pleadings, we were not responding, until he suddenly erupted with a yell of "LUST!" Everyone woke, we got the message, and rehearsal finished with far less angst than anticipated at the outset. But the comment that gave us all the giggles was to the clarinets when they were playing exposed upward arpeggios: "Like farting in the bath"! Just so!

Music is not a prudish profession, but there are times when the one on the rostrum oversteps the mark, as in the Bournemouth Symphony Orchestra some years ago. Their conductor said to the first fiddles, "I wouldn't want to make love to any of you as you all come too early." The players walked out and two went home in disgust. By the same token, he called the trombones "a bunch of wankers". Working in a symphony orchestra is not always what it might appear from the comfortable seats in the audience, as there are times when we too have feet of clay. However, for the most part, the one who wields the wand of authority is courteous, usually friendly and strictly professional, both on and off the concert platform. We are thankful that the days are gone when screaming hysteria was expected from the rostrum, and when ego maniacs wept and raged, threw batons, scores, pencils and anything else to hand at the hapless musicians.

* * *

Some conductors have no beat whatsoever, and then we are really on our mettle. We do not need a bandmaster, but an occasional relevant gesture does help to keep things together. "No downbeat deliveries today," we say to ourselves when confronted with an upbeat-only merchant, the baton action coming across as an irritated upwards flick. Communicate, **communicate**! You don't even have to make a noise with that stick for goodness' sake. Guest conductors invariably arrive clutching an interesting bunch of scores; personal party pieces outside the general repertoire. Foreign visitors sometimes struggle to fill in the allotted rehearsal time, as British orchestras work very quickly, so it is good policy to present the players with motivating challenges.

When the Hallé's new maestro came to us as a guest, he began by giving out his rehearsal plan, beginning with a twenty-minute speech on a Takemitsu piece: mind-numbing and beginning with twelve slow beats to each bar. After fifteen minutes of playing, we had reached bar seven and were at screaming point, and then he jumped to the end to fuss with minutiae, by which time he had 'lost' most of us through unalleviated boredom. I noted in my diary: "He has long silky blue-black hair and looks girlish." This, we learnt later, had earned him the nickname of 'Wash and GO' (more familiarly known as the slogan of a shampoo advertised on TV) by our northern colleagues, but we suspected wishful thinking on their part. Prokofiev's Sixth Symphony was a better bet we reckoned – but no. After running through the first two movements without stopping, he then proceeded to *talk* through the whole of the second movement in monumentally tedious detail. Everyone at the back was totally switched off, trumpets were sneakily keeping tabs on sport with a tiny TV, Annie was doing tapestry, and the rest were reading the Sunday papers. To be fair, we did come up for air when he got to our small contributions. He is one of those characters who gets to the end of a piece and then works backwards. I can't stand that. Where does continuity come in? This was the maestro's first and last guest appearance with the CBSO, being airily dismissed by one of the disillusioned workforce as "all froth and no coffee"!

One eager guest was an Italian who loved the sound of his own voice, talking far too much and constantly changing tactics. Initially, most of his comments were directed at the strings: head in score, inaudible to the rest. We were playing a piece that featured three loud off-beat tambourine notes, which always sound late unless the player anticipates the beat. So, of course, one plays them a fraction early to compensate for the sound of the jingles always coming a whisker after the main note. The larger than normal percussion fraternity had decided that we would have a bet as to when he would tell me that the tambourine was *late*. The first rehearsal went by without incident. Money was placed on the end of the xylophone, and the second slot went by peacefully. More cash was added to the pile, but it wasn't until the very final run-through that he spotted his reminder in the score ("tambourine/late"). We are sure that some mark the scores accordingly before they even meet the orchestra. A shrug of the shoulders, a raising of the delicate dark eyebrows, a pitying look towards the back, and then it came: "Oh, tambourino ... (deep sigh) ... I theenk that you are ... (furrowed brow) ... just a leetle ... (sad shrug) ... LATE." Delighted laughter came from the orchestra as every percussionist chorused the word 'late' with the maestro, and scooped-up coins clinked as the section enjoyed the in-joke. It would have been impossible to explain it to him, so the moment passed, but we guess that the blue crayon markings still remain in his full score.

When a new conductor presents himself or herself to the orchestra, I try to imagine what it must feel like to stand up there on the rostrum and face us. Orchestras can be ruthless and swift to judge, but we do give a little leeway to youngsters flexing their musical muscles. Yes, it must be the loneliest place on the planet, but we are all in it together.

Many years ago, a very young visitor from Japan arrived with his carefully prepared programme. Everyone listened intently during the first rehearsal, as it was obvious that he was having trouble with his English, although it wasn't so much the content that concerned us but the pronunciation that distracted and charmed. We discovered that there were 'froots', 'craarrinets' and a 'piccorrro' deep within the woodwind, and 'viorins', 'vioras' and 'cerroes' in the string department, but the biggest mystery was a 'tliangerrr' in our neck of the woods. He was very pleasant to work with and obviously a stranger in our country, so much so that some of us suggested that he might like to join us for a meal before the concert, though our arrangements were met with dismay as we told him the name of our favourite Italian restaurant: La Galleria. He had no chance of getting his tongue round that one. The only solution was a hand-written reminder in case he got lost. I have to report that the meal was a great success; a furthering of Japanese/British relations, followed by an enjoyable and well-received concert.

Nowadays, the CBSO players certainly have a say in who is invited to fill that illustrious position, whether for the long or short term, and to this end we fill in conductor assessment forms from time to time. These are the ultimate thumbs-up or thumbs-down signals for the management responsible for engaging the artists. A principal guest conductor is usually given a three-year contract and a guarantee of a minimum number of concerts with the orchestra. The pros and cons of various contenders are discussed at Artistic Advisory Committee meetings, one of which I was once obliged to attend as Chairman of the Players' Committee, along with the Union steward and the leader of the orchestra. All the big guns were there, including, of course, Simon. We were fully conscious of the fact that he was very keen for a certain conductor to be invited on the payroll, but I was equally aware that the majority of players were not happy with this choice. Chief Executive, Ed Smith, had the pile of assessment forms in front of him and was obviously only too pleased to agree with Simon on the projected appointment. However, the Chairman of the Board must have interpreted a look on my face as he chipped in with, "Can we know what the orchestra thinks about this?" I had fully intended to say something deeply tactful, but instead, in the heat of the moment, I replied, with quiet emphasis, "They think that he is stultifyingly boring!" Simon rounded on me with an amazed "Maggie!", whereupon, heart thumping, I continued with, "Don't shoot the messenger. This is what YOUR orchestra feels about him." Consequently, the conductor in question was not engaged in the principal guest slot, much to my relief and that of the majority of my colleagues.

When the 'one who should be obeyed' is totally useless, we revert to the worrying game of 'follow the leader', sink or swim. So long as he knows the scores thoroughly and we have done good work in rehearsal, we can respect that person and then the earth really can move for him, the audience and us. There are many times when we are asked, "What does the conductor actually DO?" This was neatly answered by a youngster from a special school where I was teaching. He thought for a while and then said, "He encases the speed in the beat." I couldn't have put it better myself.

A happy orchestra is largely due to the good relationship between players and conductor. We find that visiting players, such as orchestral pianists, percussionists, unusual woodwind instrumentalists and such like, are the ones that immediately spot the atmosphere in the various orchestras with which they work. Word gets around that such and such a crowd are unhappy with their lot, but for the most part our perception is that extras enjoy working with the friendly CBSO. We work hard and are generally a reasonably cheerful bunch, thanks largely to excellent direction from the top. The conductor is the captain of the ship, having the chart for guidance and being responsible for the overall preparations for our voyages. Each one constantly encounters challenges that inevitably colour our modus operandi, every journey being unique as we take on board ideas, suggestions, orders and directions. Most captains know the ropes, but the crew are the ones physically sailing the ship. Nevertheless, we all appreciate the fact that, without skilful direction from the helm, the ship could founder, although it is unlikely to go under. After all, we are all in the same boat, sink or swim.

* * *

Now that I am retired, I am frequently asked, "Do you miss the orchestra?", and I truthfully answer, "No, life moves on. I have played every piece I have ever wanted to play and plenty I haven't. I still have lots of friends and many connections within my orchestra, although strangely enough the only time I miss them all is when they are playing on tour, abroad. Somehow the city seems bereft without them." The other query is a solemn, hesitant, "How are you getting on with retirement?" This is rewarded with a wide smile and, "I LOVE it, and I'm having a ball! – I've been to South Africa, Alaska, China, California, art galleries in Spain ...", and then, after noticing the glazing eyes, I keep quiet. As I have tried to put my thoughts down in a coherent manner, I have felt that life has somehow been on hold for two years. I despair when I look at the snowstorm of papers and notes in my nerve centre, knowing that the tale can never be told to the full, but at least I am now in a position in which I can try to give a general account of the life inside a professional orchestra from the players' perspective. At the time of my retirement, I was much gratified to receive one or two lovely letters from members of our audiences, with heart-warming comments. For example, "Your smiling face amongst all the hardware is a memory to cherish and you will be greatly missed." On a visit to one of our Centre Stage concerts, I was shyly presented with two lovely handmade pottery globes containing rattling ceramic 'seeds'. These were from one of the volunteer hall stewards. She told me that she had to make something special for me when she realised that I was no longer going to be playing in the orchestra. As I shook them gently, I wondered how they had been made, because as a very amateur potter I know that if loose bits of fired clay are put inside an unfired, enclosed ball, they will most likely stick to the inside as the clay dries out. These simple-looking, lovely-to-handle balls were truly a labour of love. I was very touched by the thoughtfulness that had inspired this kind gesture. They sit on my hearth, a reminder of the fact that 'if we can see the audience, they can see us' – or is it the other way round?

Life is sweet and I take comfort in Fiona's question, "What are you going to be when you grow up, mum?"

Appendix
Recording Session

Here is a brief blow-by-blow piece of reportage for all those readers who are curious to have an insight into how Simon Rattle works.

In this case we were recording the third movement of *Prokofiev's Scythian Suite* - according to Simon at the time, 'the loudest piece in the repertoire'. As I was not required to play in this particular movement it was possible for me to be a fly on the wall, and scribble down what was taking place as it happened.

'Observations during EMI. rehearsals for recording sessions Jan. 26 1992.

Symphony Hall Birmingham, City of Birmingham Symphony Orchestra.
Conductor: Simon Rattle.
Producer: David Murray

If David Murray is not happy with a particular 'take', we are brought back to reality with a strident, short ring on the red phone: this stops everything.
'------------------' denotes music being rehearsed;
*. . . . . * denotes music being recorded.

Simon Rattle.
'At Figure 37: firsts get out of the way - 38 . . . '------------------'
Hmm, *absolutely* joined: fingerboard! Right - lets try it '------------------'
I think the celeste is a tiny bit ahead of us: at that distance it's hard to tell.
Yes, I'm getting da *da da* da, [telephone] David, is the celeste ahead?'

David Murray
'Yes, it's very slightly ahead.'

S.R.
'Is it possible at 38 for harps to play a little more? A tiny bit faster, everyone else is freer there - once more [to cor anglais]! Third [*bar*] of 44 - clarinets and bassoons...[he sings the rhythm]

Shouldn't be the same tempo as 44. '--------------------'

Something happens two before 45, horns - on second beat - it gets faster there. Please, trombones make more difference between *f* and *ff*. f is far too loud - then we will hear the timps who will come out more. [telephone] David - can you hear fiddles at all at 47?'

To horns: 'do each bar at 47 with *attack*, and AWAY '--------------------' long descent. At [rehearsal number] 48, 3 oboes, 3 clarinets, mf very strung out.

Just try at 49, flutes, bassoons. Play exactly same dynamics, everybody else exactly half-level. You'll need to push these . . . GOOD!' [Orchestra plays, Simon commenting over the music. ' piano... celeste, bass . . . that'll need to be a tiny bit more'].

D.M. [telephone]
'Before you put it down [record it] I'd like to hear a bit at 38 for balance. Two before 38 can't hear the flutes very well.'

S.R. 'Start f, let's not mess around the bar before 38, let's come down. Less clarinet at 37 ... NOW - tempo stays the same.' '--------------------.'

'Too much?'

D.M.
'Slightly, it's E, E, A, E.'

S.R.
'OK. let's do a take... [impatiently].... red light!'   * . . . . *

S.R. [After 'take'].
'Good let's listen, that'll tell us better than anything.'

He runs at a half-trot out of the hall to the room behind the stage set out as a cramped sound studio. Any member of the orchestra can also go back there to listen, and it is usually the case that numerous players litter the place, ears pinned back, anxiously following their music - trying to look relaxed. We squeeze into the small crowded area; avoiding miles of thick cables, lean against the walls or squat on the floor. A gentle smile from David acknowledges our presence, but Simon's eyes dart about assessing who is there. A quick glance to a specific player is all that is needed should anything be not to his liking.

Simon and David come back into the hall worrying about the position of the two harps and their respective microphones. Harps are eventually moved forward alongside first violins. 'Goodbye,' says a harpist to the pianist; this manoeuvre is followed by the celeste being wheeled forward by Simon and the player.

'Well that's got rid of that lot - been working on that for years!' says the orchestral pianist to a percussion player.

[Shuffling of feet and sotto-voce laughter from orchestra.]

[Simon, pointing to the piano] ' Is that staying where it is?'

D.M.
'Try it.'

S.R.
'Do me just 37 will you, we need to diminuendo even more.'

Celeste Player:
'Simon, was there a problem in bars two and three before figure 35?'

S.R.
'Yes - stay in tempo! Could horns start lighter at 45? Fifth horn is fine, first is pretty heavy. Get away more quickly then we'll hear the strings better.'
. . . . .

D.M.
[now backstage and telephoning] 'I can hear your whip-lash page turn.'

S.R.
(instantaneously): 'It WASN'T me, – it was a harp attack!'

[Off he goes again to 'have a listen.' No one else follows, we all switch off.]

S.R.
Back at a trot, talking as he hops onto the rostrum, looking down at the score.

'Balance-wise probably OK - we'll just do two before 45 for ensemble:
'-------------------'

Yeh! - it doesn't need to go any faster than this and if we do we get into trouble before 49. [then to David] Last chord . . . happy?'

D.M.

'Yes. Harps ppp over big spread chords - slightly less as you're nearer. [Delighted teasing from nearby players bemused at the thought of hooligan harps.]

Harpist:
'Both times?'

D.M.
Yes - just the big chords. Let's do another take – I think that'll be good. You might want to be freer with some of the rhythms now that you're a bit closer.'
     *. . . . . *
Simon off again to listen after the take, interest waning from the rest.

S.R.
' I'd like to get a really good one at 45. We had some unilateral declarations of independence.
David, do we have third [bar] of 50?'

D.M.
'No – if everyone could play in fourth bar I just don't know if we're in tune two before 42. The last chord seems to hang on – mebbe it's the hall?'

S.R.
'Can I start from 49?'

D.M.
'Of course'

S.R.
'I think we should play the third bar of 50 pretty full anyway. It's not terribly cuttable. SO . . . let's do 49 to end. I would love to get the cellos, third of 42, *together*. David, can I go two before 41?'

D.M.
'Yep!'

S.R.
'Can you hear the flutes well at 41?'

D.M.

'The repetitions? - yes!' '--------------------'

S.R.

[To violins and harps]: 'CUT! you're not looking. Do it without me once.
'--------------------'

Hmm! It's worse: I'm encouraged. Do it dead on the beat. SO - let's do two before 41 on a take. David, is the trumpet late third [bar] before 41?'

D.M.

'Ye-e-s! Same place. Harp, the scale at 42 seems loud.'

S.R.

'I'll come out [finish] at 43. You want a beginning . . . yes?'

D.M.

'Could we just check bars four and five at the beginning?'

S.R.

'Can the 'A' get a tiny bit higher? [Harp checks tuning.] I know it's an awful thing to say but I think that we should take the piano B [harp tunes top notes. Total silence as everybody listens. Ironic laughter.] It's low [under pitch - sounding flat] isn't it? [Celeste plonks a low B]. That's a *great* help, thank you [deep irony]. Great! OK.... rrright, just a note at a time. Let's do the beginning.' '--------------------' [Silence: stops after 4 bars.]

'I'll beat a VERY clear third bar.' (In other words, 'everyone WATCH!')

And so on, until what seems like a lifetime later, both producer and conductor are satisfied with the outcome.'

* * *

Eventually everyone is happy with the work done, and after thanking us, the producer asks for silence while he records some ambiance to be used before and after the actual music on the CD This always causes much amusement, as we inevitably have an inane desire to giggle as the red light flickers on for the final time, but have to stay totally still since the slightest sounds are picked up by the super-sensitive microphones. (Shades of John Cage's silent 4'33' maybe?) Eventually someone's stomach rumbles and there is a roar of laughter. Sighs of relief all round, at last it is all over and thankfully we can go home.

Index

to do' 280-81.

behind the Iron Curtain, chapter 24; on Simon Rattle, 176-7; 221-293;on writing reviews, 234-5.

Some none-playing activities
Worcester Music Group,160-63; Gives talks: *Sounds Interesting*, 159; *Orchestral Notes*, 220; Open College of Arts course, 203; allotment,202;'catering' for orchestra,214-5; *PercussionWork Book* published, 216-8; *Agogo Bells to Xylophone* published, 219-220; music critic for *The Birmingham Post*, 233; percussion coach for Birmingham Schools Concert Orchestra, 236; takes in lodgers, 238.

Covent Garden Opera orchestra, 67-8.

Davies , Meredith, CBSO assistant conductor, 100.
Davis Symphony Hall, San Francisco. Rattle tames difficult acoustics of, 323
Development Plan, 196-200.
Donohoe, Peter; with Worcester Music Group, 161-62.
Dvorak, *Carneval* Overture, 28;34.

Edwards, Eddie (CBSO manager), initial disapproval of female percussionists, 82.
Edinburgh International Ballet Company, collapse of tour, 70.

Festspielhaus, Salzburg. 330
Frémaux succeeds Rignold as principal conductor, 139.; orchestra flourishes under, 141 6; seeds of conflict, sudden departure and aftermath, 148-53.

"Gear" - percussion ironmongery, 253-55
Grainger, Percy, recording of Ravel's *Vallée des Cloches* arrangement, 296-7.
Gray, Harold, long-serving associate conductor, 90-91; Nielsen's Fifth Symphony, 113; holds the fort after Frémaux's departure, 154; retirement and tributes to, 91.
Ginastera, Alberto, Harp Concerto, 184-5.
Grosses Schauspielhaus, Salzburg, 329.
Grundy, Phyllis, MC's first piano teacher, 16.
Gubaidulina, Sofia, and the flexatone, 285-6

Handel, *Messiah* in Huddersfield, 335.
Head, Phil (violin), plays in Budapest restaurant, 144.
Hill, Peter (timpani), appointed CBSO, 212.
Hoffnung Festivals and Symphony Orchestra, 45-9.
Holst, *Planets* suite, 103.
Huddersfield Choral Society, 335.
Huddersfield Contemporary Music Festival, 360-63.
Huddersfield Youth Orchestra, 1;21.
Hull City Hall, Tchaikovsky *1812*, 128

Instruments, 249-52

Xylophone, purchase of American instrument (Leedy), 250-51; 'retirement' of same, 237.

Yorkshire Symphony Orchestra, 2; 21.

Wrong Sex, Wrong Instrument

REVIEWS:

"Maggie Cotton, who blazed a trail for female percussionists in Britain in a career with the CBSO spanning 40 years, gives us the first player's-eye account of the orchestra's rise from provincial respectability to world renown – but a lot more besides. From a spartan wartime childhood in working-class Yorkshire to discussing the finer technical points of percussion instruments with Pierre Boulez, she takes us on a unique journey through postwar musical and social history, full of illuminating anecdotes which are sometimes hair-raising, sometimes laugh-out-loud hilarious."
- Terry Grimley, The Birmingham Post (Arts Editor)

"Anyone who wants to know what it's really like behind the scenes in the orchestral world could do no better than take an enjoyable romp through Maggie Cotton's eminently readable book. As the first female percussionist of the City of Birmingham Symphony Orchestra she got to work extensively with Simon Rattle 18 years before the mighty Berlin Philharmonic claimed him, and she witnessed at first hand the dramatic revival of a demoralised orchestra. Opening up the classical music scene from the players' perspective, she is witty, to the point, and winningly down to earth - a brilliant read for music lovers."
- Keith Clarke, Classical Music Magazine (Editor)